Finding Your Social Science Project

The most important step in social science research is the first step – finding a topic. Unfortunately, little guidance on this crucial and difficult challenge is available. Methodological studies and courses tend to focus on theory testing rather than theory generation. This book aims to redress that imbalance. The first part of the book offers an overview of the book's central concerns. How do social scientists arrive at ideas for their work? What are the different ways in which a study can contribute to knowledge in a field? The second part of the book offers suggestions about how to think creatively, including general strategies for finding a topic and heuristics for discovery. The third part of the book shows how data exploration may assist in generating theories and hypotheses. The fourth part of the book offers suggestions about how to fashion disparate ideas into a theory.

John Gerring is Professor of Government at the University of Texas at Austin. He is the author of several books, most recently: *The Production of Knowledge: Enhancing Progress in Social Science* (Cambridge University Press, 2020; with Colin Elman & James Mahoney), and *Population and Politics: The Impact of Scale* (Cambridge University Press, 2020; with Wouter Veenendaal), along with numerous articles.

Jason Seawright is Professor of Political Science at Northwestern University. He is the author of *Party-System Collapse: The Roots of Crisis in Peru and Venezuela* (2012), *Multi-Method Social Science: Combining Qualitative and Quantitative Tools* (Cambridge University Press, 2016), and *Billionaires and Stealth Politics* (2019, with Benjamin I. Page and Matthew Lacombe), along with numerous articles.

Strategies for Social Inquiry

Finding Your Social Science Project: The Research Sandbox

Editors

Colin Elman, *Maxwell School of Syracuse University*
John Gerring, *Boston University*
James Mahoney, *Northwestern University*

Editorial Board

Bear Braumoeller, David Collier, Francesco Guala, Peter Hedström, Theodore Hopf, Uskali Maki, Rose McDermott, Charles Ragin, Theda Skocpol, Peter Spiegler, David Waldner, Lisa Wedeen, Christopher Winship

This book series presents texts on a wide range of issues bearing upon the practice of social inquiry. Strategies are construed broadly to embrace the full spectrum of approaches to analysis, as well as relevant issues in philosophy of social science.

Published Titles

John Gerring and Jason Seawright, *Finding Your Social Science Project: The Research Sandbox*

Jennifer Widner, Michael Woolcock and Daniel Ortega Nieto, *The Case for Case Studies: Methods and Applications in International Development*

Colin Elman, John Gerring and James Mahoney, *The Production of Knowledge: Enhancing Progress in Social Science*

John Boswell, Jack Corbett and R. A. W. Rhodes, *The Art and Craft of Comparison*

John Gerring, *Social Science Methodology: A Unified Framework, 2nd edition*

Michael Coppedge, *Democratization and Research Methods*Thad Dunning, *Natural Experiments in the Social Sciences: A Design-Based Approach*

Carsten Q. Schneider and Claudius Wagemann, *Set-Theoretic Methods for the Social Sciences: A Guide to Qualitative Comparative Analysis*

Nicholas Weller and Jeb Barnes, *Finding Pathways: Mixed-Method Research for Studying Causal Mechanisms*

Andrew Bennett and Jeffrey T. Checkel, *Process Tracing: From Metaphor to Analytic Tool*

Diana Kapiszewski, Lauren M. MacLean and Benjamin L. Read, *Field Research in Political Science: Practices and Principles*

Peter Spiegler, *Behind the Model: A Constructive Critique of Economic Modeling*

James Mahoney and Kathleen Thelen, *Advances in Comparative-Historical Analysis*

Jason Seawright, *Multi-Method Social Science: Combining Qualitative and Quantitative Tools*

John Gerring, *Case Study Research: Principles and Practices, 2nd edition*

Finding Your Social Science Project

The Research Sandbox

John Gerring

The University of Texas at Austin

Jason Seawright

Northwestern University

CAMBRIDGE UNIVERSITY PRESS

CAMBRIDGE
UNIVERSITY PRESS

University Printing House, Cambridge CB2 8BS, United Kingdom

One Liberty Plaza, 20th Floor, New York, NY 10006, USA

477 Williamstown Road, Port Melbourne, VIC 3207, Australia

314–321, 3rd Floor, Plot 3, Splendor Forum, Jasola District Centre,
New Delhi – 110025, India

103 Penang Road, #05–06/07, Visioncrest Commercial, Singapore 238467

Cambridge University Press is part of the University of Cambridge.

It furthers the University's mission by disseminating knowledge in the pursuit of
education, learning, and research at the highest international levels of excellence.

www.cambridge.org
Information on this title: www.cambridge.org/9781009100397
DOI: 10.1017/9781009118620

First published 2022

A catalogue record for this publication is available from the British Library.

ISBN 978-1-009-10039-7 Hardback
ISBN 978-1-009-11491-2 Paperback

Contents

Detailed Contents

Figures

Tables

Acknowledgments

This book grew out of several previous projects, from which we draw ideas and material. Chapter 2 draws on Gerring, Seawright, Shen (2020). Chapter 6 draws on Gerring (2017: chapter 5, section 5.1). Chapter 8 draws on Gerring, Christenson (2017: chapter 5). Portions of the book were presented to the research workshop at the Institute of Qualitative and Multimethod Research at Syracuse University, in June 2019.

For feedback on various drafts we owe thanks to Colin Elman, Mike Findley, Laura Garcia, Gary Goertz, Alan Jacobs, Diana Kapiszewski, Markus Kreuzer, Charlie Kurzman, Jennifer Larson, Carsten Schneider, and Steven Wilson. We also benefited from three excellent reviews as part of the formal review by Cambridge University Press, which helped immeasurably in revising the final version of the manuscript.

We are especially grateful to students and faculty who took time out of their busy schedules to share their experiences and their wisdom on the subject of exploratory research. In some cases, this meant filling out a lengthy survey, in other cases, interviews or discussions with the authors. We hope that this book offers some payoff for their efforts.

Glossary

This short lexicon is limited to terms used repeatedly in the book. Other specialized terms are defined in the text, with chapters of special relevance noted in the final column.

		Chap.
CAUSALITY		
Outcome (Y)	The phenomenon to be explained. Synonyms: dependent variable, explanandum.	1
Causal factor (X)	Hypothesized to affect Y. Synonyms: treatment, independent variable.	1
Antecedent cause (A)	Affects X and may serve as an instrument in a two-stage analysis.	1
Common-cause confounder (C)	Affects both X and Y, and thus potentially confounds the relationship.	1
Mechanism (M)	Conduit through which X affects Y. Synonyms: pathway, intermediate variable, mediator.	1
Noise (B)	Cause of Y uncorrelated with X.	1
Moderator (D)	Moderates the relationship between X and Y.	1
Background factor (Z)	A factor of no theoretical interest, e.g., A, C, B, or D.	1
RESEARCH DESIGNS		
Data generating process (DGP)	How the data under investigation was produced.	
Experiment	Where the treatment of theoretical interest is randomized by the researcher across two or more groups.	2
Natural experiment	Where the treatment of theoretical interest is assigned in an as-if random fashion, but not by the researcher. Variants include regression discontinuity and instrumental variables.	2
Observational	Nonexperimental.	2
Case study	One or several cases form the basis for an argument about a larger population.	4
Case selection	Methods of selecting cases for case study research, e.g., extreme, index, deviant, most-similar, diverse.	4

Continued

ARGUMENTS

Theoretical framework	The broadest sort of theory, diffuse to the point of unfalsifiability.	*9*
Theory	Explanation for an outcome or set of outcomes (if causal).	*10*
Hypothesis	Observable, and hence testable, implication of a theory.	*10*

RESEARCH STAGES

Exploratory	Prior to the identification of a research question, theory, and hypothesis. Synonyms: discovery, theory generation.	*11*
Confirmatory	After a research question, theory, and hypothesis have been identified. Synonyms: appraisal, confirmation, falsification, justification, testing, verification.	*11*

1   Introduction

There is no royal road to science, and only those who do not dread the fatiguing climb of its steep paths have a chance of gaining its luminous summits.

Karl Marx, "Preface to the French Edition," *Capital*

If we knew what we were doing, we wouldn't call it research.

Albert Einstein (attributed)

Finding a topic for research should be easy. Presumably, anyone with an interest in social science has a primal urge to explore the world. One has questions, and one wants better answers than can be found in extant work.

Yet, if the researcher follows their curiosity so many potential topics beckon that it may be difficult to settle on just one. Finding a topic is easy. Finding an *optimal* topic is not so easy.

We have all faced this dilemma at some point in our careers. It is the scientific equivalent of writer's block. How does one go about "finding a topic"? Why are some people better at identifying fruitful topics than others? What should one advise someone who is struggling to find a topic for their thesis, article, or book?

Little assistance will be found in the annals of social science methodology. Consigned to metaphor – bells, brainstorms, dreams, flashes, impregnations, light bulbs, showers, sparks, and whatnot – inspiration falls outside the traditional rubric of methodology. Rarely is exploratory research included in courses or textbooks.

One might imagine that insights could be garnered from published work. Surely, the product of our endeavors sheds light on its origins. However, articles and books are generally unrevealing. Scientific journals do not provide space to expatiate on the origins of ideas or their subsequent development. While books offer more room for reflection, authors are rarely forthcoming.

This is a symptom of a deeper malaise. For professional reasons, authors of scientific studies are forced to engage in an elaborate and stylized game of deception. In order to avoid charges of "curve-fitting" or "fishing" they must adopt the Dogma of Immaculate Conception. Accordingly, they narrate their project as if the theory was hatched in complete isolation from the data used to test it.

Published work follows a standard protocol. Typically, the author begins by outlining a topic or research question. Then, they state a general theory, and thence a specific hypothesis and research design. Finally, the evidence is presented and discussed, and concluding thoughts are offered. Scientific studies thus present an appearance of order and predictability, a step-by-step descent down the ladder of abstraction.

This is nothing at all like the progress of most research – which, in our experience, is circuitous and unpredictable.[1] Unfortunately, we learn little about this process as it is not in the author's interest to divulge deviations from scientific orthodoxy. The early stages of the scientific journey therefore remain mysterious. The *search* part of research is not well understood.[2]

To be clear, there is no right or wrong way to begin. All that matters is where one ends up. And yet, where one ends up has a lot to do with where one starts out. Decisions made at the beginning of a research project structure everything that follows, as changing topics midstream is costly. Once one has developed knowledge and expertise in an area it is difficult to retool. And once one has gathered evidence it is difficult, expensive, and sometimes impossible to revisit research sites, that is, archives, field sites, interviewees, or respondents.

The choice of topic serves as a critical juncture. Once that threshold is crossed the research process is highly path-dependent. It follows that the earliest stage of research, where a topic is identified, is the most crucial stage of all. Nothing of scientific interest is likely to arise from research on a topic that is trivial, redundant, or intractable. No matter how well-executed, little can be expected from it.

To set the stage for this book, we begin by laying out our vision of scientific exploration. Later sections of this chapter delve into specific features of the book that distinguish it from other texts on similar subjects. A brief *coda* reviews the relevant literature.

---

[1] See Howitt, Wilson (2014), Medawar (1963), Merton (1967: 4).
[2] See Swedberg (2019), White (2013).

An Eclectic, Holistic View of Scientific Exploration

Where should one look for inspiration when searching for a research topic? Where should one begin?

The immense oeuvre devoted to methodology, philosophy of science, and history of science suggests four general answers to this question, which we summarize under the labels: *abduction, appraisal, relevance,* and *theory.* These labels correspond to four long-standing paradigms of social science research, which we will briefly review.

Abduction. One group of writers adopts an essentially inductive approach to scientific inquiry, where explanations arise from the researcher's encounter with the world. Accordingly, one's job as a social scientist is to be attentive to signals emanating from the subject under study. To put oneself in the path of discovery is to put oneself in direct contact with some empirical reality. The setting might be ethnographic, archival, or statistical. Regardless of setting, one must "soak and poke" until one figures out that most basic of all scientific questions: *What the devil is going on here?*[3]

Appraisal. A second group of writers follows the precept that criteria for strong appraisal should guide the search for topics; only in this fashion will the area of truth be extended. In practical terms, this means that researchers should look for opportunities to exploit strong research designs, where identification is possible without a lot of potentially problematic assumptions about the data generating process. For causal questions, this entails settings where a treatment is randomly assigned (an experiment) or as-if randomly assigned (a natural experiment). To some, this position may recall the adage of the drunk who looks for their missing key under the lamppost (because that's the only area that is lit). In the drunk's defense, one might point out that efforts to discover a key in pitch-black darkness are likely to be unavailing. Efforts to resolve intractable problems without sufficient empirical evidence may not advance the cause of truth. Accordingly, the central question for this group of scholars focuses on appraisal: *Is it falsifiable (testable)?*[4]

Relevance. A third group of writers believes that important research arises out of important questions or problems, relevant to the real world. Ask a question of social significance and good things will follow. This position is

---

[3] See Glaser, Strauss (1967), Locke (2007), Peirce (1929, 1934, 1992), Swedberg (2012).

[4] This approach is implicit in methods texts with an emphasis on research design, e.g., Angrist, Pischke (2009), Dunning (2012), Gerber, Green (2012), Shadish, Cook, Campbell (2002).

often embraced by those who see social science as responding to problems in society. While there is no well-developed methodology attached to this position (indeed, there is some hostility to the apparent tyranny of methods in academe), there is a clear point of departure: *Does it matter?*[5]

Theory. A fourth group maintains that good research begins with a well-formed theory, sometimes couched in mathematical language, that is, formal theory. This approach is associated with the logico-deductive method,[6] though many who favor theory would not identify themselves with that tradition. In any case, those in the theory camp are perturbed by the ways in which data and statistical models seem to drive research agendas. They would also be perturbed by the problem-driven approach, which views social science as wedded to normative concerns. From their perspective, the best point of departure for important research is abstract: *What's your theory?*[7]

Putting the Pieces Together

In our view, there is much to be said for all four points of departure – abduction, appraisal, relevance, and theory. They are all so plausible and so indispensable that we find ourselves unable to dismiss any of them. Each seems eminently useful in particular contexts.

We conclude that there is no Archimedean point of entry to social science research. There are, instead, many possible points of entry. Indeed, finding a topic for research is even more wide-open than the four-part typology introduced above suggests. One might begin with a general topic, a research question, a key concept, a general theory, a specific hypothesis, a compelling anomaly, an event, a research venue (e.g., a site, archive, or dataset), a method of analysis, and so forth. Accordingly, research may be problem-driven, question-driven, theory-driven, method-driven, or data-driven. Typically, it is a mixture of them all.

Moreover, the various traditions of research introduced above should be understood as complements rather than rivals. To be successful, a social science project must be successful along multiple dimensions. This includes the key concept(s), the theory, the research design, the empirical terrain, and the findings. While a single project is likely to innovate on only one or two dimensions, the finished research must satisfice along other dimensions. A fascinating theory is not very convincing without a strong research design. A

[5] See Flyvbjerg (2001), Shapiro (2005), Shapiro, Smith, Masoud (2004), Smith (2002).
[6] See Hempel, Oppenheim (1948), Popper (1968[1934]).
[7] See Clarke, Primo (2012), Eidlin (2011), Mearsheimer, Walt (2013).

new empirical terrain is not much good without a theory to explain it. A new concept is not much good – indeed, is not even understandable – if it is not connected to other elements of research. And so forth.

Consider the apparent dichotomy between theory (deduction) and empirics (induction). Barefoot empiricists must – at some point – consider the contribution of their data peregrinations to theory. After all, there is no such thing as a purely empirical contribution. (What is it a contribution to?) Likewise, those who claim to adhere to an a priori, theoretical approach must be conscious of the data they will use to test their theory. After all, nothing of scientific interest will arise from a question that is empirically intractable, however theoretically compelling the question might be. (Does God exist?) We conclude that exploratory research ought to be informed by theory *and* data, which one might envision (loosely) as a dialectical process. An extant theory suggests *A* while the data suggests *B*, leading to a new synthesis.

In the business of constructing social science everything is connected to everything else. Empirical investigation is contingent on preformed concepts and theories as well as our general notions of the world; and yet, further investigation may alter these notions in unpredictable ways. In so doing, the researcher revises their conception of what they are studying. A change in concepts entails a change in theory entails a change in research design entails a change in concepts . . . The knee bone is connected to the thigh bone.

Because everything is connected, everything is contingent in the early stages of research. Consequently, researchers are obliged to consider all elements of social science methodology before settling on a research topic. The sooner these diverse elements are brought into view the more efficient the exploratory process is likely to be. Without this bird's-eye view one may become so enamored of a theory, a research setting, or a problem of special concern that other desiderata are neglected. In this fashion, a great deal of time may be spent – and perhaps wasted – on a project that does not have strong legs.

What we have said so far suggests an *eclectic* and *holistic* approach to exploration. At the same time, it is important to clarify that this approach applies only to exploratory research. Once one moves to a *confirmatory* style of research it is appropriate to separate theory and testing (insofar as possible) so that the truth of a hypothesis can be properly evaluated (see Chapter 11).

A Sandbox of Options

If scientific exploration is eclectic and holistic, one may doubt the prospect of identifying a standard set of rules or procedures to guide researchers in their search for an optimal research topic. This point is reinforced when one considers the great variety of researchers and research topics.

Some researchers have trouble generating new ideas; others generate lots of ideas but have difficulty choosing among them. Some think deeply about a single problem, to the point of exhaustion; they would probably benefit from diversifying their portfolio. Others flit from subject to subject without building expertise; they could probably benefit from greater focus. Some can't see the forest for the trees; others can't see the trees for the forest. People are different. They have different strengths and weaknesses, and no piece of advice is likely to be applicable to everyone.

Likewise, subject areas are wildly different. Some are amenable to data-driven analysis. For others, there is little data available but many opportunities for gathering evidence "in the field." Some topics are organized around well-established theoretical frameworks. Others float loosely without any theoretical mooring. And so forth.

Under the circumstances, it is difficult to imagine constructing standard guidelines. What is good for Sid might not be good for Nancy. What is good for international relations might not be good for behavioral psychology.

Moreover, the process of finding a topic involves a certain amount of stochastic variability ("serendipity") that cannot be explained by features inherent in researchers or topics. A key finding from our own research is that there are few consistent predictors of research success (Chapter 2).

Accordingly, we embrace a *sandbox* model of exploratory research. We stipulate that there are many ways to search for a topic. Which one will work for you in a given instance we cannot say, for we don't know you, your research area, or the resources at your disposal. Under the circumstances, it would be presumptuous to offer specific advice.

What we can do is to lay out some of the options – approaches and techniques that have proven useful to others and might be useful for you. None of these options is very time-consuming or expensive, and only a few demand advanced methodological skills. So, the cost of exploration is low. Readers are encouraged to try them out to see which ones work – generating plausible ideas for future projects.

This open-ended framework should be helpful for those who feel that they do not know where to start or feel stuck in a rut. Even those who feel confident about how to proceed may find it helpful. Note that although one may already have identified a provisional topic, it is possible that an even better topic awaits. To reach this lodestar it may be necessary to think about new things, or to think about old things in new ways. You should be prepared to step outside your comfort zone.

You should also be prepared to play. The metaphor of a "sandbox" suggests that good ideas arise out of a spirit of playful provocation. So, throw some sand around and see what shapes arise. Show them to your friends, gauge their responses, and your own. Make revisions accordingly. This is the general idea. Take the job seriously, but not too seriously. Coming up with new ideas should be fun.

This Book

This book aims to enhance scholarly productivity by focusing on the task of topic selection. It should be useful for those who are just setting out and for those who (like the authors) have been kicking around for a while. Several features set this book apart from other work on related subjects (reviewed below).

First, we presume a solid background in social science methodology. This book on beginnings should not be confused with a beginner's guide.[8]

Second, we focus narrowly on exploration, which we understand as the period preceding a researcher's commitment to a specific project.[9] After that, it is possible to conduct "confirmatory" research, where a hypothesis is rigorously tested. We do not have much to say about the latter.

Third, we focus on social science, including the disciplines of economics, political science, sociology, psychology, and their various cognates and offshoots.[10] By contrast, most work on our subject is concerned with natural

---

[8] For those in search of introductory guides to social science methodology there are many options, e.g., Gerring (2012b), Gray et al. (2007), Kellstedt, Whitten (2018), King, Keohane, Verba (1994), Shively (2016). Specialized texts focus on causal inference and econometrics (Angrist, Pischke 2009; Morgan, Winship 2015; Wooldridge 2016), experimental and quasi-experimental research design (Dunning 2012; Gerber, Green 2012; Shadish, Cook, Campbell 2002), case study research (Gerring 2017), field research (Kapiszewski, McLean, Read 2015), ethnography (Agar 1996), and multi-method research (Seawright 2016).

[9] This is similar to what Swedberg (2014a: 26) calls a "prestudy."

[10] Although examples and citations may betray our disciplinary home in political science, nothing that we say is bound by the arbitrary walls that separate these overlapping fields. We exclude anthropology from our list of social sciences as most work in that field nowadays leans heavily toward the humanities, eschewing the ideal of a generalizing science of human affairs.

science, technical invention, or other realms of creative endeavor (e.g., art, music). We recognize that the creative process has some generic features, and occasionally we draw anecdotes or lessons from other regions. However, many features are particular to the social sciences, justifying our narrow focus.

Fourth, within the rubric of social science we focus on work that is empirical, rather than purely theoretical or methodological. We also give preference to work that is generalizing – aiming to shed light on a population of cases rather than on one or several cases of special interest (though the latter may serve as an empirical focus).

Fifth, in deference to well-established practice in the social sciences, our focus is primarily on work whose goal is causal explanation. Even so, much of what we say should also be relevant for work that is descriptive or predictive.[11]

Finally, while other studies focus on innovation as a product of genetics, core personality, upbringing, or education, this book focuses on aspects of research that individuals have control over. It is intended as a practical guide – not a muse, a philosophical study, or a social-psychological analysis. We are interested in what researchers can do to enhance their own creativity and productivity.

Special Features

There is no established method for studying exploratory research. Typically, writers opine about their own experiences, supplemented by a reading of the literature and stories drawn from the history of science. We shall do the same, with several additional features. These include (a) surveys of practicing social scientists, (b) copious examples drawn from social science research, and (c) causal diagrams.

Surveys

To gain traction on our subject we conducted a series of surveys and open-ended interviews with graduate students (pre-PhD) and researchers

---

[11] In our view, causal inference is probably overemphasized, and descriptive work de-emphasized, at least within political science (Gerring 2012a). Nonetheless, causality surely deserves a central place in social science and its preeminence seems secure for the time being. Conveniently, causal work lends itself to distinct phases of research, one in which a hypothesis is identified and another in which it is tested – a key premise of this book. These phases are usually more difficult to separate in work of a descriptive nature.

(post-PhD). In this fashion, we attempt to develop a systematic, replicable methodology for the study of exploratory research. The methodology is laid out in Appendix A and some of the key findings are presented in Chapter 2.

However, it should be emphasized that this is not the sole basis for the observations and recommendations contained in subsequent chapters. It is not possible – at least not yet – to empirically test all propositions relevant to exploratory research.

Examples

Throughout the text we offer examples of social science in use. These examples – typically from published work – serve to make general principles concrete and provide readers with a place to go for more details if they wish to pursue a particular approach.

It should be clarified that we are not endorsing the validity of these studies, most of which fall outside our areas of competence. Some of the cited research is old and has doubtless been superseded. Other studies may be flawed, though perhaps in ways that are methodologically informative.

Our purpose in discussing a particular study is to illustrate a particular methodological point, of which the cited study offers a good example. That is all that readers should infer.

Causal Diagrams

In discussing causal relationships, it is important to distinguish the role of various factors. To that end, we make frequent use of causal diagrams. While every diagram is different, the most common elements are illustrated in Figure 1.1.

By convention, X is the causal factor of theoretical interest and Y is the outcome of interest. Additional causes of Y, if uncorrelated with X, are understood as noise (B). A common-cause confounder (C) affects both X and Y. A moderator (D) affects the impact of X on Y. An antecedent cause (A) lies prior to X and may serve as an instrument in an instrumental-variable analysis. Background factors of all sorts, for example, A, B, C, or D, may be referred to generically as Z. A mechanism (M) lies in between X and Y, representing the pathway through which X generates a change in Y.

These terms, and this sort of diagram, will be referenced at various junctures in the book. Several clarifications follow.

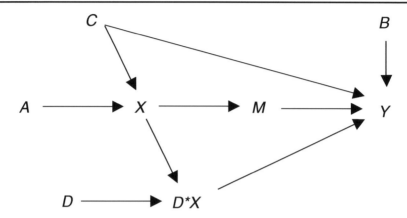

Nodes represent a single variable or a vector. (For emphasis, the latter is often printed in bold.)

A	Antecedent cause, which may serve as an instrument in a two-stage analysis
X	Causal factor of theoretical interest ("treatment")
C	Common-cause confounder
M	Mechanism, aka pathway, intermediate variable, mediator
B	Cause of Y uncorrelated with X ("background noise")
D	Moderator
Z	Any background factor, e.g., A, B, C, or D (not shown)

Figure 1.1   A causal diagram

First, each factor in Figure 1.1 and subsequent figures may refer to a single variable or a vector of variables. In the latter case, we print the variable in bold when used in the text of the book.

Second, any causal diagram depicts *assumptions* about the world. They are true only by assertion. Nonetheless, the diagram plays an important role in clarifying those assumptions.

Third, causal diagrams take shape within the context of a specific piece of research. They are not static, ontological features of the world.

Finally, causal diagrams can serve two, quite different purposes.

If the goal is *theory elaboration*, only factors relevant to the theory (e.g., X, M, and Y) are likely to be included. Here, the causal diagram is a tool for the clarification of an idea.

If the goal is *causal inference*, the causal diagram should represent the entire data generating process (DGP), including the strategy of conditioning that the researcher envisions. In particular, it should represent factors that might serve as confounders.

In methods texts, causal diagrams are generally understood to serve the latter function. Since this book is about exploratory research, including theory development, we must also consider the former function. Hopefully, it will be clear from context which function is in play.

What Lies Ahead

Organizing the refractory subject of exploration is difficult. Accordingly, the chapters that follow offer different "takes" on the subject. Although this involves some redundancy, we believe that each of these dimensions is worthwhile.

The order of presentation is not haphazard. However, later chapters don't depend on earlier chapters in the way they might in a textbook. Accordingly, readers may pick and choose which chapters they find most helpful and may return to sections at different junctures.

The first part of the book offers an overview of our topic.

Chapter 2 surveys *current practices*. How do social scientists arrive at ideas for their work? How does the process of research unfold? How often does research end up in the dustbin ("file drawer")? What different intellectual trajectories are exemplified by the careers of social scientists? Using surveys and interviews, this chapter maps the lay of the land.

Chapter 3 offers an inventory of *contributions to knowledge*. In order to get started it is helpful to understand where one wishes to end up, that is, what the completed study is intended to accomplish. We show that there are many ways to make your mark. Contributions may focus on (a) phenomena, (b) concepts, (c) data and measures, (d) causes, (e) mechanisms and frameworks, (f) research designs, or (g) empirical refinements and extensions.

The second part of the book, entitled *Playing with Ideas*, offers suggestions about how to think creatively.

Chapter 4 discusses general *strategies* for finding a topic. This includes (a) finding your passion, (b) the life of the mind, (c) reading the secondary literature, (d) appraising the state of the world, (e) the familiar and the unfamiliar, (f) specializing and generalizing, and (g) the old and the new.

Chapter 5 offers a variety of *heuristics* for discovery. This includes (a) turning answers into questions, (b) play, (c) skepticism toward words and numbers, (d) error and anomaly, (e) analogies, (f) intellectual arbitrage,

(g) thought experiments, (h) processes and variables, (i) hermeneutics, (j) abstraction, and (k) failure.

The third part of the book, entitled *Playing with Data*, shows how data exploration may assist in generating theories and hypotheses.

One approach is to focus on a particular case or a small number of cases where phenomena can be explored in detail and where connections – possible causal relationships – can be probed in a preliminary fashion. Chapter 6 lays out techniques of *case selection* where the analysis is exploratory rather than confirmatory. These techniques may be categorized as (a) extreme, (b) index, (c) deviant, (d) most-similar, or (e) diverse.

Another approach centers on how data is collected and analyzed. In Chapter 7, we lay out methods for *soaking and poking*, which we categorize broadly as (a) ethnographic, (b) archival, or (c) statistical. (These techniques may be focused on a chosen case, on many cases, or may be enlisted in situations where cases are not well-identified.)

The fourth part of the book, entitled *Playing with Theories*, offers suggestions about how to fashion disparate ideas into a theory.

Chapter 8 lays out a menu of well-traveled *theoretical frameworks*. This includes (a) motivational frameworks (interests, norms, psychology), (b) structural frameworks (material factors, human capital/demography, institutions), and (c) interactive frameworks (adaptation, coordination, diffusion, networks, path dependence).

Chapter 9 introduces the general desiderata of a good theory and trade-offs that flow from this set of oft-conflicting criteria. Next, we discuss various complexities of theorizing – the number of causes and effects embraced by a theory, the specification of mechanisms, and the problem of defining units and levels of analysis.

Chapter 10 offers *tools and tips* for theorizing. We lay out multiple modes of theorizing – spoken word, written word, pictures, key cases, and formal models. Then, we offer some general guidance on the construction of theories.

The fifth and final part of the book, consisting of a single chapter, concludes our study with a close look at the transition from exploration to testing. First, we discuss various steps involved in vetting a research project. This includes a calculation of costs, payoffs, and risks; a consideration of research ethics; and extensive market-testing. In the second section, we discuss when to go public with preliminary ideas and findings. In the third section, we consider what to reveal about the research process. Finally, we discuss the contrast between exploratory and confirmatory research.

Appendix A includes details pertaining to the surveys we conducted and their analysis, as discussed in Chapter 2. Interviews with political scientists are posted on Gerring's website in podcast format.

Coda: Extant Work on Our Subject

The field of methodology has traditionally focused on the problem of appraisal, leaving aside the problem of discovery. Karl Popper (1968[1934]: 32) articulates the common view:

> The question of how it happens that a new idea occurs ... whether it is a musical theme, a dramatic conflict, or a scientific theory – may be of great interest to empirical psychology, but it is irrelevant to the logical analysis of scientific knowledge.

We agree with Popper that once a study has been produced it is probably not so important to know how it originated and developed. Our interest, after all, is in whether the study is true, and significant. However, if we want more studies that are true and significant, we must also concern ourselves with the process of finding and nurturing topics. Some sausage factories are considerably more productive, and more creative, than others. We need to know why.

Unfortunately, studying exploration is difficult, as beginnings are inherently unformulaic. "There is no such thing as a logical method of having new ideas," Popper (1968[1934]: 32) remarks. "Discovery contains 'an irrational element,' or a 'creative intuition.'"[12] It is for this reason, we suppose, that methodologists have left the subject aside. Consequently, work of relevance to this book often emanates from other fields – principally psychology and history/philosophy of science – and from writers of popular books devoted to invention and discovery. There are, in addition, a few renegade social scientists.

This body of work is vast if one considers all that has been written on exploratory research and related subjects over the past century. It would be vain to attempt to review this material in a comprehensive fashion. Nonetheless, it may be helpful to indicate the lay of the land by pointing out several main lines of inquiry. This serves as a point of departure for the

---

[12] Reichenbach (1951: 231) echoes the same point: "The act of discovery escapes logical analysis" (quoted in Swedberg 2012: 4).

book and a point of extension for those who may wish to explore these issues in greater depth.

A Brief Survey

Some authors, many of them schooled in psychology, explore creativity, discovery, and innovation broadly construed, that is, in all realms of life.[13] Often, the focus is on those at the top of their field, "geniuses" of various description.[14] The subject has a long intellectual history, as shown in a bibliography of works that stretches back to the sixteenth century (Rothenberg, Greenberg 1976).

Other studies are focused on the natural sciences.[15] Here, discovery may be understood through the prism of paradigmatic revolutions (Kuhn 1970 [1962]) or scientific progress (Lakatos 1978; Laudan 1977). For some, the entire scientific enterprise is discovery-laden, exploratory (Feyerabend 1993 [1975]). Closely related is a venerable tradition of work in the philosophy and history of science oriented around the problem of induction[16] and the fundamental distinction between the contexts of discovery and justification.[17] A subgenre explores the utility of ignorance, error, and failure in scientific discovery.[18]

Work on organizations, including firms, is also concerned with creativity and innovation, which are viewed as key elements of entrepreneurship.[19]

Discoveries sometimes arise from thought experiments, which involve thinking through an argument or theory by imagining what-if scenarios.

---

[13] See Amabile (1982), Arieti (1980), Boden (2004), Csikszentmihalyi (1997), Dacey, Lennon, Fiore (1998), De Bono (1992), Fauconnier, Turner (2008), Galenson (2006), Gardner (2011), Gholson et al. (1989), Ghiselin (1985), Glaveanu (2019), Grønhaug, Kaufmann (1988), Grosul, Feist (2014), Irvine (2015), Isaksen et al. (1993), John-Steiner (2000), Kaufman, Beghetto (2009), Kaufman, Sternberg (2010), Kirton (1994), Klein (2013), Koestler (1964), Lehrer (2012), Martindale (1990), May (1994), Ogle (2007), Osborn (2013), Paulus, Nijstad (2003), Poole (2016), Root-Bernstein, Root-Bernstein (1999), Rothenberg, Hausman (1976), Runco (1992, 2014), Sawyer (2011), Shavinina (2003), Shenk (2014), Stein (1974), Vosniadou, Ortony (1989), Gruber (1989), Wallas (1926), Ward, Smith, Vaid (1997), Weisberg (1993, 2006), Weisberg, Reeves (2013).
[14] See Briggs (2000), Simonton (2014), Murray (1989), Ochse (1990).
[15] See Ball (2012), Clement (2008), Coleman, Katz, Menzel (1966), Foster, Rzhetsky, Evans (2015), Gertner (2012), Gooding (1990), Gruber (1974), Gruber, Bödeker (2005), Hanson (1958), Holmes (2004), Johnson (2010), Langley et al. (1987), Loehle (1990, 2009), Magnani, Nersessian, Thagard (1999), Meheus, Nickles (2009), Merton, Barber (2006), Nersessian (2010), Oliver (1991), Root-Bernstein (1989), Simonton (2004), Taylor, Barron (1963), Watson (1969).
[16] See Laudan (1981), McLaughlin (1982), Popper (2014), Zahar (1983).
[17] See Popper (1968[1934]), Reichenbach (1938), Schickore, Steinle (2006).
[18] See DeNicola (2017), Firestein (2012, 2015), Gross, McGoey (2015).
[19] See Baumol (2002), Berkun (2010), Ford, Gioia (1995), Von Hippel (2005).

Most studies focus on the natural sciences or philosophy.[20] A few are oriented toward the social sciences, though they are not specifically focused on the problem of discovery.[21]

Closely related to discovery are questions about scholarly productivity and impact, as measured by number of works published, top journal publications, citations, and other indices.[22]

Within the social sciences, a tradition of work examines the histories of specific projects[23] or the lives of social scientists – their biographies,[24] autobiographies,[25] and oral histories.[26]

Some social scientists embrace an inductive approach to learning (Locke 2007). An oft-cited point of departure is the work of Charles Sanders Peirce (1929, 1934, 1992) and his concept of *abduction*.[27] A closely related tradition follows some variant of *grounded theory*, originally proposed by Glaser and Strauss (1967) and subsequently developed by the authors and by others.[28] In this vein, *case-based* research is often regarded as fodder for theory formation.[29] In parallel, a branch of statistics focuses on exploratory data analysis.[30] And several studies offer heuristics for hypothesis generation.[31] Nisbett (1990) offers a humorous treatment of how social science norms inhibit creativity in psychology.

A quite different approach to social science centers on the development of models and theories. Philosophical discussions are legion, though mostly focused on the natural sciences.[32] Within the social sciences, one might follow a formal or rational choice approach;[33] one might focus on

[20] See Brown (1991), Cohen (2008), Frappier, Meynell, Brown (2013), Gendler (2000), Horowitz, Massey (1991), Ierodiakonou, Roux (2011), Sorensen (1992).
[21] See Lebow (2010), Tetlock, Belkin (1996), Tetlock, Lebow, Parker (2006).
[22] See Allison, Stewart (1974), Ballard, Mitchell (1998), Bayer, Smart (1991), Davis, Patterson (2001), Fender, Taylor, Burke (2005), Hill (2020), Hesli, Lee (2011), Levin, Stephan (1991), Maske, Durden, Gaynor (2003).
[23] See Hammond (1967), Jodha (1995), Kohn (1993), Lipset (1964, 1967).
[24] See Backhouse (2007), Blaug (1989), Christenson (1971), Daalder, Allardt (1997), Harcourt (2016), Heilbroner (2011), Vinten-Johansen et al. (2003), Weber (1975).
[25] See Kregel (1988, 1989), Simon (1996), Szenberg (1993, 1998), Szenberg, Ramrattan (2004, 2014).
[26] See Baer, Jewell, Sigelman (2014), Munck, Snyder (2007), Samuelson, Barnett (2009).
[27] See Douven (2011), Fann (1970), Rueschemeyer (2009), Swedberg (2012, 2014a, 2014b, 2016).
[28] See Alvesson, Karreman (2011), Birks, Mills (2015), Charmaz (2006), Hutchison, Johnston, Breckon (2010), Tavory, Timmermans (2014), Timmermans, Tavory (2012).
[29] See Burawoy (2009), Eckstein (1975), Gerring (2017), Ragin (1992), Streb (2010).
[30] See Behrens, Yu (2003), Gelman (2003), Hartwig, Dearing (1979), Martinez, Martinez, Solka (2017), Morgenthaler (2009), Pampel (2004), Tukey (1977).
[31] See McGuire (1973, 1997, 2004), Most (1990), Sandberg, Alvesson (2011).
[32] See e.g., Black (1962), Cartwright (1983), Hesse (1966).
[33] See Clarke, Primo (2012), Coleman (1990), Dixit, Skeath (2015), Hedström (2005), Humphreys (2016), Lave, March (1975), Morton (1999), Varian (2016).

micro-foundations, aka social mechanisms;[34] one might consult work on social theory;[35] or one might explore a smorgasbord of options for theory formation that rest on different assumptions.[36] Some works focus on theory development within particular disciplines, for example, mass communications (Shoemaker, Tankard, Lasorsa 2004) or management (Smith, Hitt 2005).

Several methods texts devote some attention to exploration and theorizing.[37] A few studies focus on the art of finding a topic, though the treatment of this issue is terse in articles[38] and rudimentary (though more lengthy) in books.[39] This question is also addressed briefly in guides to writing research proposals, theses, and other sorts of research,[40] and in advice books focused on how to make it in academia (e.g., Brennan 2020).

Conclusions

As this brief review shows, the intertwined topics of creativity, discovery, exploration, and innovation have been addressed many times and in many contexts. We are by no means starting from scratch. We build on this prodigious literature self-consciously, as demonstrated by numerous citations in the chapters that follow.

Even so, most of the foregoing works are fairly specialized. They focus on one or two aspects relevant to the task of finding a project; often, they are addressed to specialists in psychology, methodology, philosophy of science, or sociology of science. To our knowledge, no one has put all of these pieces together in one place in an easily digestible format. In this respect, our synthetic and practitioner-centered approach is somewhat unique.

---

[34] See Alexander et al. (1987), Blau (1964), Hedström, Swedberg (1998), Little (1998), Raub, Buskens, Van Assen (2011), Schelling (1978).

[35] See Collins (1994), Dubin (1969), Hage (1972), Lemert (2018), Martin (2011, 2015), Merton (1968), Mouzelis (1995), Parsons, Shils (1962), Runciman (1989), Stinchcombe (1968), Swedberg (2014a), Zetterberg (1954), Zhao (1996).

[36] See Alford, Friedland (1985), Elster (2015), Garfinkel (1981), Lichbach, Zuckerman (1997), Little (1991), Parsons (2007).

[37] See Abbott (2004), Becker (1998), Booth et al. (2016), Firebaugh (2008), Geddes (2003), Howard (2017), Kellstedt, Whitten (2018: Ch. 2), Krieger (1991), Luker (2008), Martin (2017), Mills (1959), Shively (2016: Ch. 2), Van Evera (1997), Wildavsky (1993).

[38] See Lei (2009), Merton (1959), Useem (1997).

[39] See Alvesson, Sandberg (2013), Campbell, Daft, Hulin (1982), Stebbins (2001), White (2009).

[40] See Denscombe (2012), Dunleavy (2003), Gerard (2017), Joyner, Rouse, Glatthorn (2018), Roberts (2010), Single (2009).

Part I

Overview

In the first part of the book, we offer an overview of our subject. Chapter 2 reviews current practices, building on surveys and interviews of political scientists. Chapter 3 offers a fairly comprehensive inventory of the ways in which a study can contribute to knowledge in a field – a smorgasbord of options for crafting a research project.

2 Current Practices

The idea of a method that contains firm, unchanging, and absolutely binding principles for conducting the business of science meets considerable difficulty when confronted with the results of historical research. We find, then, that there is not a single rule, however plausible, and however firmly grounded in epistemology, that is not violated at some time or other. It becomes evident that such violations are not accidental events, they are not results of insufficient knowledge or of inattention which might have been avoided. On the contrary, we see that they are necessary for progress. Indeed, one of the most striking features of recent discussions in the history and philosophy of science is the realization that events and developments, such as the invention of atomism in antiquity, the Copernican Revolution, the rise of modem atomism (kinetic theory; dispersion theory; stereochemistry; quantum theory), the gradual emergence of the wave theory of light, occurred only because some thinkers either decided not to be bound by certain "obvious" methodological rules, or because they unwittingly broke them.

Paul Feyerabend (1993[1975]: 14)

The vast library of work on creativity, innovation, and discovery (surveyed synoptically at the end of Chapter 1) is focused primarily – perhaps obsessively – on the right tail of the distribution, that is, on those scholars or works that are deemed especially praiseworthy. Nobel Prize winners are studied; bench scientists are not. Scientific revolutions are studied; normal science is not. Accordingly, we lack a clear sense of how the vast majority of scholars go about their work.

This is important given that most scholarship at any point in time must be normal science; a continual state of revolution will not lead to scientific cumulation. It is also important if we wish to ascertain what distinguishes geniuses, and works of geniuses, from run-of-the-mill authors and publications.

To study the creative process in a systematic fashion we conducted surveys and interviews with political science students and faculty. Since this exercise centers on a single discipline we cannot say with assurance that results are generalizable to other social sciences. However, political science's middling position – in between the more humanistically inclined field of anthropology and the more naturalistically inclined field of economics – suggests that our results may be representative of the social sciences at large. That is how we shall approach the topic.

Surveys were conducted with PhD students (N=84) and holders of PhD degrees (N=556). The PhD students were selected from those attending summer schools in Berlin (sponsored by Humboldt University and WZB), Essex (sponsored by the European Consortium for Political Research), and Syracuse (sponsored by the Institute for Qualitative and Multimethod Research). The PhD holders were chosen from a sampling frame constructed with the *Publish or Perish* software developed by Harzing (2007).

The pre- and post-PhD surveys are similar in most respects. Questions for both surveys generally focus on a particular study. For PhD students this is their dissertation; for PhD holders it is a study randomly chosen from their published oeuvre. This means that both subjects and studies are randomly chosen in the post-PhD survey. (Neither is randomized in the pre-PhD survey.)

Systematic surveys are supplemented by a small number of lengthy interviews with prominent scholars, posted online on John Gerring's homepage. The details of these surveys and interviews – characteristics of the samples, questionnaires, and various analyses of the data – are contained in Appendix A. Here, we present key findings as they pertain to the present subject. Unless otherwise indicated, graphs in this chapter refer to the *post*-PhD sample.

We begin with a discussion of how political scientists identify topics for dissertations and published work. The second section discusses the process and the outcome. The third section reviews work that remains unpublished, in the proverbial "file drawer." In the fourth section, we look at the creative process as it plays out across a researcher's entire career. The final section offers some tentative conclusions.

Identifying a Topic

How do social scientists get ideas for their work – that is, for dissertations, articles, and books? Learning what people have done may not tell us what is best, but it does reveal patterns that have worked in the past. So, this inquiry is of more than abstract interest.

We begin with PhD students. Finding a topic for a dissertation is the first major creative challenge that most scholars face, and often the hardest. Most graduate students start from scratch, as they do not have years of experience and an established research agenda to draw on. Unconstrained by prior work, and less burdened by theoretical and methodological commitments, they are also free to set their course to a greater extent than seasoned professionals. Experience is both a blessing and a burden.

In any case, the first act in an academic career is probably the hardest and the most consequential – as it determines early publications, first jobs, and early grants.

Respondents to our survey are at least one year into their program and most are several years beyond matriculation. (The mean value is around four years.) Nearly all have at least a preliminary dissertation topic, and many say that their topic is already well-developed. Not surprisingly, the process of finding a topic is fairly lengthy, with most respondents reporting that they found their idea between one and three years after beginning postgraduate study. We can assume it was on their mind for some time prior to that.

We asked respondents to estimate how easy it was – relative to other tasks they were/are faced with as graduate students – to come up with a topic. The modal responses, graphed in Figure 2.1, are "difficult" and "somewhat difficult." Only 1 percent reported that it was easy or extremely easy. And for 9 percent, it was "extremely difficult." Bolstering this point, 18 percent reported having examined one other topic, and 57 percent reported having considered several other topics, before settling on their current topic. In thinking about their current dissertation topic, 46 percent reported being "very happy" and 50 percent were "somewhat happy" with their choice. For some, the hard work of searching for a topic seems to have been worthwhile; others are not sure.

In both surveys (pre- and post-PhD), we asked respondents to identify which factor(s) was most critical in identifying the topic for the chosen work. Figure 2.2 shows the results, which are fairly similar across the two samples. Faculty spend more time conversing with colleagues and graduate students spend more time conversing with advisors; otherwise, our two samples are quite similar.

The most common activity is reading broadly in the literature. If we group conversing with advisor along with conversing with colleagues, this is the second most common activity. Next comes news or current events. Other activities follow well behind.

Relatedly, we asked respondents to comment on their point of entrée. What got them interested in the chosen topic? Results are shown in Figure 2.3. The most common points of entrée for both practitioners and

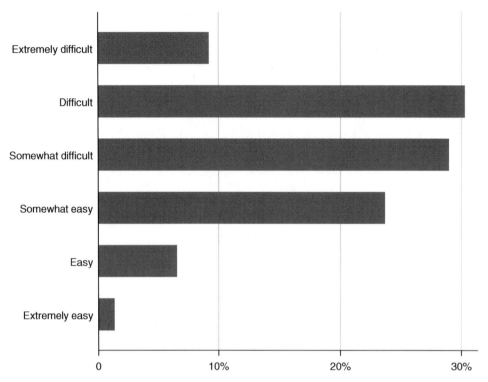

Figure 2.1   Finding a dissertation topic

Question: How easy was/is it to find a topic for your dissertation? (Choose all that pertain) (a) Extremely difficult – harder than any other part of graduate school, (b) Difficult – harder than most other parts of graduate school, (c) Somewhat difficult – harder than a few other parts of graduate school, (d) Somewhat easy – easier than almost all other parts of graduate school, (e) Easy – easier than almost all other parts of graduate school, (f) Extremely easy – easier than any other part of graduate school. *Sample:* pre-PhD.

graduate students are a seminal work in the field, a general topic of interest, or a key concept. "General theory," "compelling anomaly," and "specific hypothesis" are not far behind. Abstracting from these results, one might say that research projects are most often discovered through intellectual engagement with existing scholarly research and less often from knowledge of particular cases, issues, or empirical data.

We are also interested in the extent to which personal characteristics of the researcher may inspire their choice of topics. By this, we mean widely recognized social identities such as sex, sexual identity, race, ethnicity, language, national origin, and family. Results for both samples are depicted in Figure 2.4. To our surprise, nearly 80 percent of practitioners, and nearly

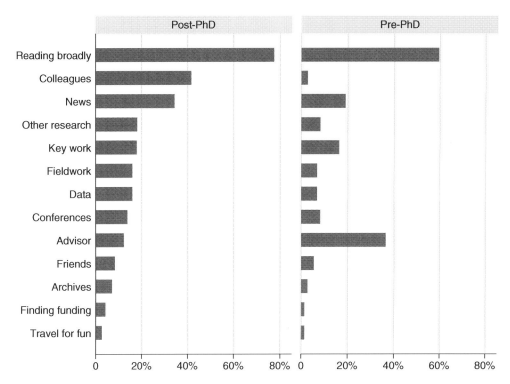

Figure 2.2 Activities
> *Question:* To the best of your recollection, which of the following was most critical to identifying the topic for this project? *Options* (non-exclusive): (a) Reading broadly across related literatures, (b) Conversing with colleagues (post-PhD) or faculty (pre-PhD), (c) Reading news stories or following current events, (d) Engaging in research on other topics, (e) Careful reading and critical thought about a single key publication, (f) Conducting field research, (g) Playing with existing data (exploratory data analysis, scatterplots, simple statistical models, etc.), (h) Attending a conference or workshop, (i) Conversing with faculty advisors or mentors, (j) Conversing with friends outside academia, (k) Other (open field), (l) Conducting archival work, (m) Conversing with students, (n) Available funding, (o) Traveling for fun or personal reasons. *Response options:* No/Yes. *Samples:* post-PhD (left), pre-PhD (right).

50 percent of the graduate students, declared that *none* of these categories inspired the chosen study.

To be sure, nearly 30 percent of the graduate students surveyed said that their natal country influenced their choice of topics – no doubt a product of our sample, of whom 64 percent were born outside the United States. It should also be pointed out that the influence of one's social background and identity may be opaque to the researcher, or if apparent may be suppressed (as unscientific). Likewise, it should be pointed out that we have constructed

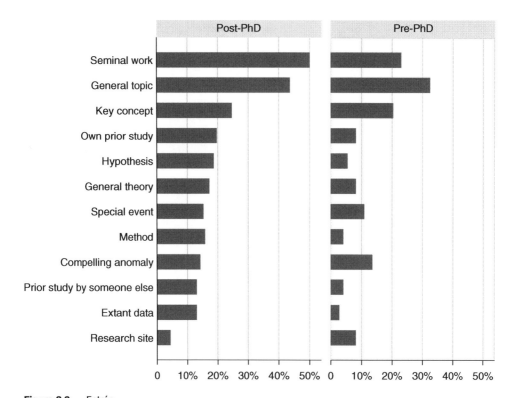

Figure 2.3   Entrée
Question: Which of the following served as your point of entrée to this topic? Where did you begin? *Options* (non-exclusive): (a) A seminal work, (b) A general topic, (c) A key concept, (d) A previous study of your own (Paper from coursework for pre-PhDs), (e) A specific hypothesis, (f) A general theory, (g) An event of special interest, (h) A method of analysis, (i) A compelling anomaly, (j) A previous study of someone else's, (k) A promising (extant) dataset, (l) A research site or archive of special interest. *Response options:* No/Yes. *Samples:* post-PhD (left), pre-PhD (right).

most of these questions to pertain to what might be called (loosely) *minority* characteristics (relative to the general population of political scientists). We can assume that most of our respondents are male, heterosexual, English-speaking from birth, and of an ethnic group that is regarded as part of the majority in the country in which they reside.[1] So, it might seem unsurprising that these characteristics did not inspire their choice of research projects.

Among women practitioners, the number reporting that gender influenced their choice of topics is 16 percent, while among practitioners, for those born outside of the United States the figure reporting that their birth

---

[1] Some of these features are measured in our post-survey questionnaire, shown in Appendix A. Others are inferred.

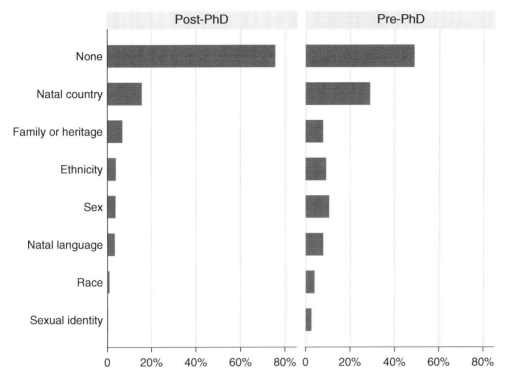

Figure 2.4   Inspiration
Question: Do you see this project as inspired by any of the following personal characteristics? *Options* (non-exclusive): (a) No (none), (b) Your natal country (if not US), (c) Your family or family heritage, (d) Your ethnicity, (e) Your sex (if not male), (f) Your natal language (if not English), (g) Your race (if not white), (h) Your sexual identity (if not heterosexual). *Response options:* No/Yes. *Samples:* post-PhD (left), pre-PhD (right).

country influenced their choice of topics is 31 percent. This is much higher than among the sample at large. Still, it is very far from being a majority of respondents, even within these smaller categories that qualify as "minority." We expect that the same is true for other personal characteristics, though we cannot say for sure as these features (which tend to be sensitive and more difficult to operationalize) are not included in our post-survey questionnaire.

We also asked questions about motivation. How important was it for the project to address a problem in society or politics, to promote social or political justice, and/or to solve an intellectual puzzle? These options were ranked on a four-category scale of importance, with results shown in Figure 2.5. The highest rated option for practitioners is intellectual puzzle-solving, while for graduate students it is understanding a particular social or

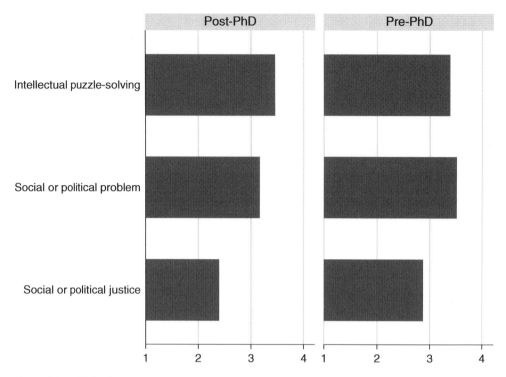

Figure 2.5   Motivation
Question 1: How important was intellectual puzzle-solving to the development of this project? *Question 2*: How important was the promotion of social or political justice to the development of this project? *Question 3*: How important was the prospect of addressing a problem in society or politics (i.e., something that could, through your research, be better understood or ameliorated) to the development of this project? *Response options*: (a) not at all important, (b) not very important, (c) somewhat important, (d) very important. Bars represent sample means. *Samples*: post-PhD (left), pre-PhD (right).

political problem. Much less common – for both samples – are concerns about social or political justice. This reinforces a pattern in which scholars are more responsive to general, theoretical concerns than to concrete engagement with issues or movements.

Process and Outcome

In this section, we interrogate the process and the outcome of research, as viewed through our surveys.

Of considerable interest is the duration of research projects. Accordingly, we asked respondents how much time elapsed from the inception of a project to its eventual acceptance by a journal or press. Within our sample, the mean duration is a little over three years with a standard deviation of almost exactly three years. However, some projects last much longer, accounting for a long right tail (extending up to twenty years).[2]

What occurs during this research process? To shed light on this question we asked practitioners whether there was a "lightbulb" moment for the chosen project, a particular point in time when everything seemed to come together. We also asked about what transpired between the time the project was initially framed and its acceptance for publication, specifically whether any major changes were made to the analysis, the research design, or the theory. Results are displayed in Figure 2.6.

We were somewhat surprised that nearly half of all projects render a moment of inspiration. We were not so surprised to learn that changes to theory, research design, and analysis are fairly common. Note also that these numbers may underestimate the dynamic, exploratory nature of political science research given that some researchers may be disinclined to reveal, or to acknowledge to themselves, these (seemingly undesirable) qualities.

We also asked respondents how often they had a hunch about what they would find once they began researching a subject and how often that hunch was borne out by the empirical portion of their research. Figure 2.7 reveals that nearly all research begins with a hunch (panel a) and that most of these hunches are subsequently confirmed (panel b).

This might mean that political scientists are canny theorists who rarely pursue a misleading intuition. Alternatively, and perhaps more plausibly, it suggests that scholars are resistant to findings that contradict their theoretical starting points. It is also noteworthy that in cases where hunches are not borne out researchers are more likely (by self-report) to change their theory or their research design.

A central concern for scientific progress is innovation. This is not to imply that innovation is the only criterion of progress; indeed, replication of existing studies (which implies the studied absence of innovation on all but perhaps one or two parameters) is essential. Even so, we tend to prize innovative studies over non-innovative studies.

Accordingly, we asked respondents to comment on the innovativeness of their own study. What, to them, is most innovative about the chosen study?

---

[2] A word of caution should be interjected here, as the rate of missingness for this question was much higher than for other questions in our survey, suggesting that the responses might be biased in one direction or another.

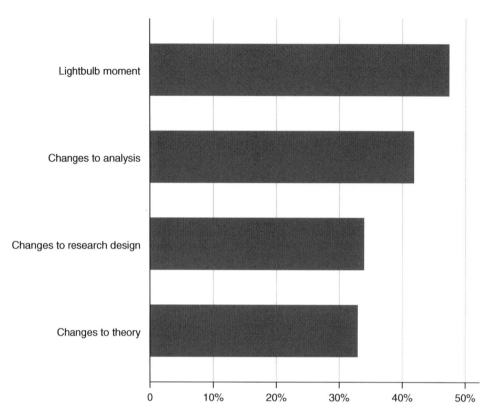

Figure 2.6   Process
Question 1: (a) Was there a "lightbulb" moment (a particular point in time when the idea for the project came together)? *Question 2*: Between the time the project was initially framed (e.g., the first project documents or proposals were produced) and its acceptance for publication, were there any major changes: (b) to the analysis?, (c) to the research design?, (d) to the theory? *Response options*: No/Yes. Bars represent sample means. *Sample*: post-PhD.

Acknowledged, a self-evaluation of innovation has its pitfalls. And yet who, if not the author, is well-positioned to judge the innovativeness of a work? Naturally, authors have different benchmarks for innovativeness, which means that their responses are not entirely comparable. This is not simply a matter of taste or standards, but also of how highly they regard their own work – or how highly they are likely to rate their own work in a survey setting. We must regard these subjective factors as background noise, while being alive to any factors that might influence results in a systematic fashion. Reassuringly, few of the personal characteristics collected in our survey (gender, age, country, etc.) predict responses to our questions on innovation, suggesting that subjective differences may be randomly distributed.

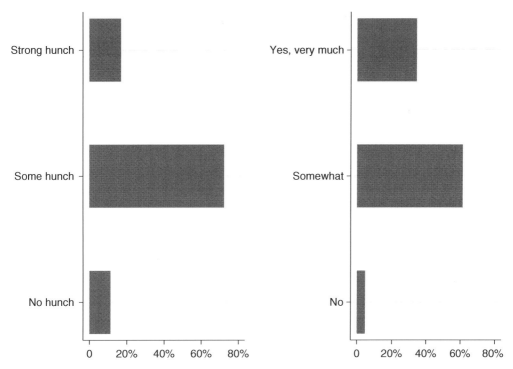

Figure 2.7   Hunches
Question 1: Before the research was conducted, did you have a strong hunch about what you would find? *Question 2*: If you answered "Yes" to the previous question, was your hunch borne out? *Sample*: post-PhD.

With these caveats, let us review the data. Figure 2.8 shows that the most common response (nearly 50%) is a new finding. Somewhat less common are findings that speak to a broader audience of policymakers or lay citizens (37%), apply a new method (32%), or explore a new topic (28%). To our surprise, only 16 percent of the published work in our sample is viewed by the author as contradicting previous work on the subject. Mostly, it seems, researchers see their work as building in a cumulative fashion on an existing intellectual tradition (even if the finding, method, or topic is new).

Unpublished Work

A study that is begun but remains unfinished – or at any rate, unpublished – is widely viewed as a failure. It consumes time and energy, and perhaps also

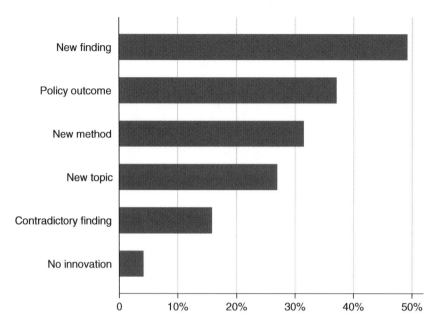

Figure 2.8   Innovation

General question: What, in your view, is most innovative or special about this piece of research? *Areas* (non-exclusive): (a) A new finding that went beyond previous research, (b) A topic that is especially relevant to the concerns of citizens or policymakers, (c) A new method or research design, that is, one that had not been applied to this question, (d) A new topic (previously unexplored), (e) A new finding that contradicted previous research, (f) There is nothing especially innovative. *Response options*: No/ Yes. *Sample*: post-PhD.

money, but brings no acclaim to the author. It is unlikely to attract any citations and cannot be listed under peer-reviewed works on a researcher's CV. Likely as not, the researcher will receive no credit whatsoever for their labors. Next to outright fraud or demonstrated incompetence, this is perhaps the worst possible outcome for anyone concerned with their professional status. Hence, the aphorism: *publish or perish*.

This pit of despair is rarely studied as it is largely invisible. No one wants to talk about their failed projects, and there is no database or website that stores such records. And yet, if we want to better understand the research process we need to delve into the mysterious "file drawer" – project ideas that were abandoned in an unpublished and possibly incomplete form and lie in purgatory, generally out of public view.

Any researcher who has been kicking around for a while has probably accumulated a sizable pile of unpublished projects, and the most fecund researchers presumably have the largest piles. To find out, we asked

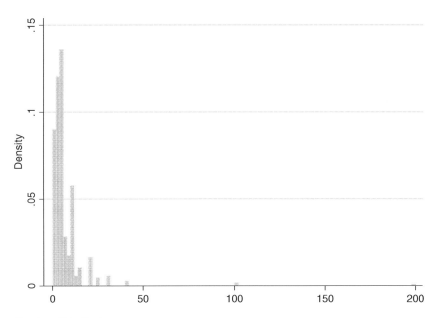

Figure 2.9   The size of the file drawer
How many project ideas lie in your file drawer? Min = 0, Max = 200, Median = 4, Mean = 6, Standard deviation = 12. *Sample:* post-PhD.

respondents to our faculty survey how many of their projects lie dormant. Results, displayed in Figure 2.9, cluster toward the left end of the spectrum, while a long right tail exposes the fate (and the frustration) of a few very fertile minds who are nonetheless unable to bring projects to fruition or are unable to find suitable venues for them.

Next, we asked respondents about the disposition of the last project that ended up in their file drawer. Results, depicted in Figure 2.10, demonstrate that nearly half of these file-drawer projects were never completed, though nearly 30 percent were apparently complete enough to present at a conference. Among those that were completed, many were rejected (once or on multiple occasions) by a journal or press.

What went wrong? To learn more, we asked respondents about the obstacles they encountered. Results are posted in Figure 2.11. To our surprise, 80 percent responded that they had trouble obtaining data. The next most common obstacles were (a) a theory that did not seem sufficiently innovative and (b) insufficient time to complete the project. Other obstacles were less common – though, collectively, they help to account for the fates of many projects.

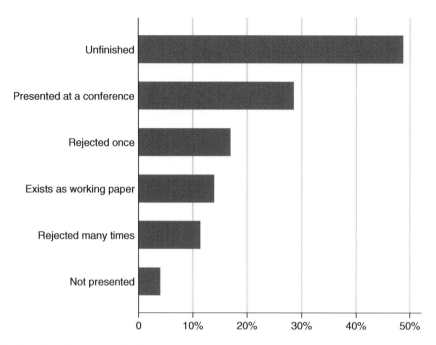

Figure 2.10 The status of projects in the file drawer
What is the current status of the project? (Choose all that pertain) (a) Unfinished, (b) Presented at a conference but not currently available online as a conference/working paper, (c) Rejected by a journal or press, (d) Available online as a conference/working paper but not submitted to a journal or press, (e) Rejected by multiple journals or presses, (f) Completed but not presented at a conference, submitted to a journal, or available online. *Sample*: post-PhD.

When asked whether this particular project should have been published, nearly two-thirds responded in the affirmative. The authors of most of these file-drawer projects think they have merit.

Would researchers have done things differently, knowing what they now know? To our surprise, over 50 percent responded that they would have proceeded as they did, while 15 percent would have changed some things about their approach and 31 percent would have avoided the project entirely. Although researchers are presumably unhappy with the result, most do not regret having made the attempt.

It is difficult to consider these matters without feeling that something important has been lost in the suppression of so much work. Of course, we do not know the quality of these studies, their arguments, or their findings. Nor do we have access to the data and replication files. Perhaps these studies are not highly informative. The point is, we do not know, and by the nature of the situation we will never know.

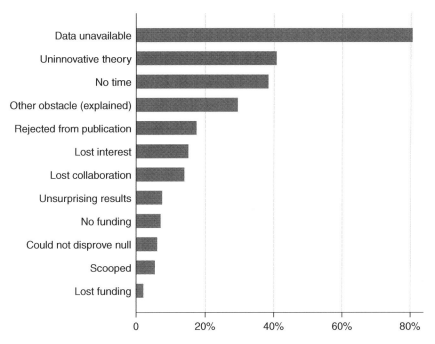

Figure 2.11 Obstacles encountered by projects in the file drawer
What obstacles did you encounter in this project? (Choose all that pertain) (a) Anticipated data turned out to be unavailable, (b) Theory was insufficiently innovative, (c) I/we could not find time to complete the research in a timely manner, (d) Other (please explain), (e) The target publication venue(s) rejected the project, (f) Interest in the topic diminished, (g) Collaboration fell apart, (h) Findings were unsurprising, (i) Funding was not secured, (j) Null hypothesis could not be disproved, (k) We were scooped (other studies were subsequently published that made this one less innovative, or at least appear less innovative), (l) Existing funding ran out. *Sample*: post-PhD.

Studies of publication bias suggest that journals give preference to new and exciting findings (Franco et al. 2014). While this may be a reasonable criterion for a top journal, if all journals follow this precept – or if authors prefer not to be published in less prestigious journals that have more permissive publication standards – then the published record offers a systematically biased sample of all work that has been conducted on a subject. Indeed, the system of academic publication begins to look like journalism, where "man bites dog" stories drive out "dog bites man" stories.

Arguably, any study whose methodology is credible adds something to the sum total of human knowledge, and therefore should reach the light of day via some form of publication. If studies are suppressed, and especially if the pattern of suppression is correlated with their findings, our ability to cumulate knowledge on a subject is seriously impaired.

This survey is the only attempt we are aware of to assess the size and contents of this file drawer. We find that it is nontrivial.

Intellectual Trajectories

In our standardized surveys we treated each project as if it were an independent, self-contained unit, hatched in isolation. And yet, we are well aware that projects are interconnected. Over time, one project leads to another. Taken together, they illustrate a trajectory.

This trajectory is visible in our open-ended interviews, which included scholars at varying points of their careers. Some only recently obtained their PhD; others were nearing retirement. All were asked to reflect upon their research as it transpired over the course of their careers. From their answers, and a perusal of their CVs, it became clear that scholars follow quite different intellectual trajectories.

Some pursue one big question that follows them throughout their career. Some pursue smaller questions in a serial fashion, with one project leading into another. And some experience dramatic changes in focus at various points in their career. These three trajectories are illustrated in a stylized fashion in Figure 2.12.

One Big Question

Some intellectual biographies are unified around a central theme or question. In our interview, Margaret Levi describes her long career:

What really drives me is a set of questions that are pretty much the same set of questions that have followed me since I began thinking about my dissertation.

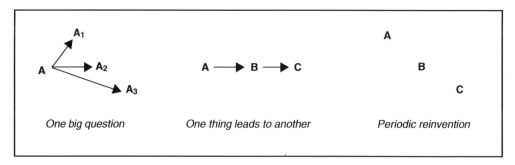

Figure 2.12 Archetypal intellectual biographies

This has to do with the relationship of citizens/subjects and their governments or other organizations that extract resources and seek compliance from their members. This has raised a series of questions about organizational forms and about conditions under which citizens or subjects are more willing to comply voluntarily, or quasi-voluntarily. As each question, or set of questions, reveals itself to me I try to find a way to empirically study it that actually gets some leverage at answering the question, what accounts for the variation and what the mechanisms are. Even though my subjects are quite different from each other – unions, revenue, conscription – all are related in that there is one common theme.

When asked how she came upon this striking theme, she replies that she has been on this trajectory since a young child.

It had to do with the civil rights movement and the conditions under which people expressed dissent from government. My mother took us out to demonstrations when we were little. My father was giving us things to read that were dissident in a whole variety of ways. I got joined the Students for a Democratic Society (SDS) when I was still in high school and was involved in a decision by SDS, later on, to come out against the war in Vietnam. So, those kinds of questions about when citizens will comply and when they will dissent was part of my upbringing, part of what has made me a human.

For Levi, this is a lifelong preoccupation around which virtually all her projects revolve.

Interconnected Questions

Not everyone has such a tightly knit intellectual trajectory. Some researchers pursue lots of projects in a serial fashion, with one project leading to another. Let's call this the John Coltrane paradigm, as Trane's musical biography – despite its evident variety – shows a fairly clear progression from post-bebop to his classic quartet, free jazz, and openly spiritual influences.

In our interview, Kristian Gleditsch recalls,

I have started out with general things that I was interested in – often puzzles. Why do we see these things happening? Eventually, I would try to come up with plausible explanations. Sometimes, it was also related to new data coding projects. So, if you wanted to try to dig into a particular question, what kind of empirical information might be useful in order to adjudicate between competing explanations. Later on, when people have started to develop a research portfolio the research is often more cumulative and incremental. So, once you've started working on a topic there are often natural extensions that suggest themselves.

Periodic Reinvention

Some scholars periodically reinvent themselves, moving to new topics or developing new approaches. Let's call this the Bob Dylan paradigm, after the master of reinvention.

Aaron Wildavsky (1930–1993) began as an expert on policymaking, publishing a landmark book on budgeting which highlighted the role of incrementalism (Wildavsky 1964). Next, he studied the presidency, marked by his theory of the "two presidencies" (1969). While continuing these streams of research, Wildavsky moved on to history and anthropology, collaborating with the anthropologist Mary Douglas on *Risk and Culture* (Douglas, Wildavsky 1982), which inaugurated his exploration of what he later called "cultural theory" (Wildavsky 1987) and included a remarkable biography of Moses, seen through the lens of political leadership (Wildavsky 1984). He also wrote a lively, short treatise on the process of research, from which we have drawn in writing this book (Wildavsky 1993).

Wildavsky was not a polymath but he had an extraordinarily supple mind, and he was able to bring his creative force to bear across a wide range of settings. He was an Americanist, a policy analyst, a comparativist, a theorist, a historian. If he had lived longer – Wildavsky died suddenly at age 63, soon after being diagnosed with cancer – there is no telling to what distant shores his mind may have wandered.[3]

Conclusions

Scholars offer two contrary accounts of where research projects start. At one extreme, we are invited to imagine researchers reading existing research and engaging in acts of theoretical imagination to uncover clever implications of existing theories or gaps that invite conceptual and explanatory innovation. Based on that cogitation, they design and implement a prespecified research project. This is the deductive model of research associated with theory-driven science.

At the opposite pole, we may envision analysts deeply embedded with specific empirical contexts who draw on years of passionate engagement with particular people, places, and things to formulate hard-won hypotheses and tentative explanatory propositions. Research designs then fill the need to

---

[3] Wildavsky, who passed away in 1993, was not interviewed for this book but was an early mentor to one of the authors.

validate and generalize these empirically grounded initial ideas. This is the inductive model of research associated with the moniker "barefoot empiricism."

These descriptions are obviously ideal-types, which researchers approximate to a greater or lesser extent, and which may change from project to project. Nonetheless, it is reasonable to ask which vision better describes actual practice.

The survey and interview data presented in this chapter (and in greater detail in Appendix A) suggests that political scientists generally favor the first vision of research over the second. Scholars formulate projects based on professional and intellectual engagement with an existing scholarly literature and its theoretical tradition. They are less likely to build upon case-specific knowledge, personal experience and social background, and normative commitments. The deductive approach to research is also associated with innovative scholarship.

Naturally, one must be wary of biases in self-report, as this accords with a classical view of the scientific enterprise. Even so, we show (in Appendix A) that this approach to finding a topic is more likely to eventuate in high-impact publications as measured by citation counts.

At the same time, it should be pointed out the evidence gathered in our surveys and interviews is subtle and many responses are not easily classifiable along a deductive-inductive spectrum. There are also many exceptions; not all answers fall into the expected categories. And there is enormous variety.

Likewise, when we look for predictors of innovative work or high-impact work, the vast majority of potential explanatory factors do not reveal clear relationships (Appendix A). Non-findings outnumber findings, and a random forest analysis does not identify any significant interaction effects between background characteristics of researchers and their approaches. If causal heterogeneity exists, it is of the most *recherché* sort.

This suggests that there is no simple recipe for identifying fruitful topics. Different approaches may work for different people, at different times, and in different settings. It seems that there are many roads to discovery. Indeed, this is a central *leitmotif* of our book.

3　Contributions to Knowledge

What color is your parachute?

Richard Bolles (2009)

In the popular imagination, scientific contributions are associated with groundbreaking discoveries like penicillin, the steam engine, and the automobile, or new paradigms of knowledge like the germ theory of disease, the evolutionary model of life, and the theory of relativity. Accordingly, when we think of contributions we think first of these revolutionary discoveries and the celebrated men and women who made them. Hero worship comes naturally, and there is a tendency to trace all manner of innovation back to someone in the recognized canon.

A realistic sociology of knowledge suggests, however, that breakthroughs occur when a field is ripe, not when geniuses arrive on the scene (Johnson 2010: Ch. 1; Kauffman 2000). There are plenty of instances of revolutionary ideas that came too early, before they could be appreciated or implemented. The time was not ripe. When the time *is* ripe for a new idea one often finds that it had been percolating for quite a while before someone managed to formulate it in an explicit fashion. This accounts for the frequency of independent discoveries – where multiple investigators stumble upon the same idea at approximately the same time (Merton 1963; Ogburn, Thomas 1922). The simultaneous discovery of evolution by Charles Darwin and Alfred Russel Wallace offers a classic example. It is not far-fetched to suppose that most fundamental discoveries in science would have occurred at about the same time even if the individual now credited with that discovery had never lived.

A second point concerns the lesser role of fundamental discoveries in the social sciences. Although we have no trouble identifying crucial breakthroughs in the natural sciences it is harder to do so in the social sciences. To be sure, eminent theorists such as Aristotle, Machiavelli, Hobbes, Smith, Malthus, Marx, Durkheim, Weber, Ricardo, Marshall, Freud, Keynes, and Foucault established new ways of thinking about the world, new research questions, and new research programs. We do not wish to gainsay the importance of theorizing from fundamentals or belittle the contributions of our forebearers. Nonetheless, the theories associated with these individuals did not fundamentally transform the work of social science in the way that the theory of relativity transformed physics, or the theory of evolution transformed biology.

In the social sciences, new approaches tend to coexist with, rather than supplant, older ones. Note that theoretical frameworks associated with each of the foregoing figures are ongoing. Today, we can identify Aristotelians, Machiavellians, Hobbesians, Smithians, Malthusians, Marxists, Durkheimians, Weberians, Ricardians, Freudians, Keynesians, Foucaultians, and so forth. Some of these research trajectories are running low and others are running high. But none, we suspect, will ever entirely expire.

Likewise, the arrival of new theories in the social sciences is often difficult to date precisely, or to credit. One is at pains to identify the point in time when "social capital" was invented and the person, or persons, who invented it. The same holds true for many other key social science concepts and theories.

We conclude that progress in this area of science occurs in a gradual, incremental fashion and is the product of many hands and many minds. In contrast to the Great Man/Woman theory of progress – always somewhat mythical, even in the natural sciences – we surmise that myriad scholars work together, over time, to develop understandings in a field.[1] When progress occurs, we can take collective satisfaction, knowing that it is a collective endeavor. It takes a (scientific) village.

We do not want to dampen anyone's theoretical ambition. Setting one's sights on the canon may be an appropriate place to start. If the Founders are wrong, set them right. Be a paradigm-changer. However, we suspect that in the social sciences paradigm changes are more often proclaimed than achieved. There are many departures but few arrivals. Typically, the sort of work that contributes to the growth of knowledge is incremental in nature, falling into the realm of "normal science" rather than "revolutionary science" (Kuhn 1970[1962]).

Within a field, it is common for researchers to play different roles according to their background, expertise, and predilections. Some may focus on identifying new questions and hypotheses; others may be primarily engaged in testing; and still others may focus on theory development and the

[1] See Jacobs (2006), Kuhn (1970[1962]), Merton (1968).

integration of existing studies. Some are subject experts; others bring methodological skills to bear. Some approach a question ethnographically; others explore its history, others its empirical manifestations; and still others devise experiments. When a field is fully integrated, each of these contributions informs the others, paving the way for the growth of knowledge on a subject (Lieberman 2016).

From this perspective, there are many ways to contribute to a scholarly field.[2] At the broadest level, contributions may be classified as *empirical* or *theoretical*. However, these dimensions intermingle and are therefore difficult to distinguish. Any empirical finding reflects on a theory and any theoretical innovation suggests an empirical strategy for testing.

We leave this dichotomy aside in favor of a more detailed inventory of the ways in which empirical research can advance knowledge on a topic. These are sorted into seven categories: (a) phenomena, (b) concepts, (c) data and measures, (d) causes, (e) mechanisms, (f) research designs, and (g) empirical refinements and extensions.[3]

This menu of options should be helpful when facing the head-scratching task of exploratory research. Think about what sort of contribution you would like to make. What is your goal?

Phenomena

Social science addresses outcomes of concern to humans. If approached on a fairly abstract level, these concerns are relatively constant across the millennia. Wealth/poverty, mortality/health, war/peace, democracy/autocracy, and justice/injustice are as topical today as they were in ancient Greece. From this perspective there are no fundamentally new topics in social science. It is the same topics rehashed, again and again.

Yet, when one focuses on more specific phenomena a great deal has changed since Aristotle. This is the sort of novelty in "phenomena" we have in mind.

Even here, we should acknowledge that it is rare for social scientists to be the first observers on the scene. As a rule, journalists and participants offer initial accounts, upon which social science builds. It is entirely appropriate, from this perspective, that social science should follow in the footsteps of

---

[2] See Gutzkow, Lamont, Mallard (2004), NSF (2016).

[3] This typology echoes the careful work of philosophers of science and academics in related fields, e.g., Laudan (1977).

popular understandings. Headlines become history, which are then fodder for social science. Interpretivists and social theorists highlight this kind of contribution by calling attention to social scientists' role in "making visible" or "re-presenting" the experiences and ideas of others.

Social science puzzles over the same questions that citizens puzzle over, though not always in the same ways or with the same conclusions – hence, the value-added. If one were to compare the frequency with which key ordinary language terms are mentioned in the popular media and in social science one would probably discover a fairly close correspondence (Schaffer 2015), with social science lagging behind by several years. This suggests that potential new topics are present everywhere – in the daily news, in Tweets and Google searches, in our communities, and in the lives we lead.

From this perspective, every headline is a potential topic for research – though it may need to be formulated in a more general fashion. Why are some sports (e.g., American football and golf) losing adherents while others (e.g., e-sports) thrive? Has the advent of electronic publishing changed the content of publications? Does knowledge of a sex offender in one's neighborhood change patterns of behavior or social attitudes? Do smartphones inhibit, or facilitate, social contact?

The Present and the Past

Some phenomena, like the Internet, are fundamentally new. While mass communication has been around for centuries, the advent of the worldwide web is different from print media and broadcast media in important ways. This opens new terrain for scholars to explore, for example, the impact of Tweets on politics, the spread of disinformation on the web, attempts by governments to subvert politics in neighboring countries, or the effect of Facebook on happiness (Wilson 2022).

Other phenomena have been around for a while but are new to social science. The distant past – prior, let us say, to the French Revolution – has traditionally been regarded as the province of historians, classicists, and archaeologists. Recently, it has come to the attention of economists (Nunn 2009), political scientists (Knutsen, Møller, Skaaning 2016), and sociologists (Griffin 1995) that there is a lot we can learn from deep history.

Sometimes, this research suggests that the modern world has origins in the distant past. Democracy in the twenty-first century may be grounded in developments within Europe after the fall of the Roman Empire (Stasavage

2016) or, even more distantly, in the geography of natural harbors (Gerring et al. 2022).

Sometimes, this sort of research elucidates fundamental differences between modern and premodern eras. Steven Pinker (2012) argues that levels of violence declined dramatically in the modern era. While that claim is debatable (e.g., Arquilla 2012; Braumoeller 2019; Cirillo, Taleb 2016; Ferguson 2013), attending to long-term trajectories of violence clearly moves the conversation forward.

Discussion

These examples show how scholars have expanded the field of knowledge by drawing scholarly attention to events, patterns, behaviors, and other outcomes that had been relatively neglected. Finding new phenomena to describe, predict, and explain opens conceptual and theoretical opportunities that often go well beyond the ideas of the scholar who introduced the phenomenon to scholarly literature.

Are there unexplored, or under-explored, phenomena in your field?

Concepts

An empirical concept (a concept that performs a referential function) consists of a *term* (label), a *definition* (intension), and a set of *phenomena* identified by the definition (extension). Concept formation is the process of forming new concepts, an important – albeit sometimes neglected – contribution to scholarship.[4]

New concepts are rarely helpful in isolation. Concepts do their work in conjunction with a network of related and opposed ideas. In order to constitute a genuine contribution, a new concept should not only clarify phenomena that were poorly understood but also facilitate a clearer, more systematic understanding of the semantic field (the field of related concepts into which the new or reconceptualized concept falls).

By contrast, unhelpful conceptual innovations steal attributes from neighboring concepts – "playing musical chairs with words," in Sartori's (1975: 9) memorable phrase. Perhaps the easiest way to appear to innovate without

---

[4] For further discussion see Collier, Gerring (2009), Gerring (2012b: Chs. 5–6), Goertz (2012), Sartori (1984), Schaffer (2015).

actually doing so is to invent a new term that mimics an existing term. Innovation must be distinguished from idiosyncrasy.

At the same time, the development of new concepts or the clarification of those that already exist is an important contribution to a field. It is impossible to develop a new theory without developing new concepts, for theories are articulated with concepts. One cannot think in new ways without altering the idea-containers used to express those ideas. Theoretical innovation is inseparable from conceptual innovation. In the following sections we outline three approaches to conceptual innovation: concept clarification and reconstruction, neologism, and typologies.

Clarification and Reconstruction

One sort of conceptual contribution aims to delineate the history of a concept, the range of extant contemporary usages, and a suggested definition suitable for a particular field or subfield.

In this vein, a number of recent studies survey the history of the concept of *corruption*, a term with a very long lineage that resonates in every language we are familiar with.[5] As a general definition, Carl Friedrich (2001: 15) proposes, "Corruption is a kind of behavior which deviates from the norm actually prevalent or believed to prevail in a given context. It is deviant behavior associated with a particular motivation, namely that of private gain at public expense." In the political sphere, Heidenheimer and Johnston (2001: 7–10) distinguish two types of definition, a broad definition centered on behavior that derogates the public interest and a narrower conception centered on deviations from norms appropriate to public office.[6] In recent years, many social science studies adopt an even narrower conception – abuse of public office for private gain. Arguably, the narrowing of corruption's definition over time has contributed to its tractability for social science. At the same time, one must acknowledge that the more specialized term has lost some of its resonance with ordinary speech.

Sometimes, work on a concept involves bringing new life to an old concept. Some years ago, Philippe Schmitter (1974) constructed a detailed intellectual history of the concept of *corporatism*, showing all the ways in which this term had been used from the nineteenth century to the present and suggesting a new definition that purged the concept of its heavily

---

[5] See Friedrich (2001), Génaux (2004), Heidenheimer, Johnston (2001), Philp (1997).

[6] They also identify a "market-centered" definition, but this has not resonated widely and is hard to distinguish from the office-centered definition.

normative overtones and established a more neutral tone suitable for social science inquiry. Accordingly, he proposed,

Corporatism can be defined as a system of interest representation in which the constituent units are organized into a limited number of singular, compulsory, noncompetitive, hierarchically ordered and functionally differentiated categories, recognized or licensed (if not created) by the state and granted a deliberate representational monopoly within their respective categories in exchange for observing certain controls on their selection of leaders and articulation of demands and supports (Schmitter 1974: 93–94).

This article paved the way for a generation of work focused on this rediscovered term. To be sure, it did not entirely settle the semantic field, as scholars continue to argue over how best to define corporatism (Molina, Rhodes 2002). Arguably, a degree of semantic disarray is present along any scientific frontier. Only once the dust settles, is it possible for concepts to congeal.

Every concept has a history (*Begriffsgeschichte*). Charting that history is thus an important contribution to work on that topic. The history of work *on* corruption can be seen in evolving definitions *of* corruption.

Accordingly, conceptual studies have focused on the intellectual history and present-day employment of many widely used concepts in the social science lexicon such as accountability (Schedler 1999) and democracy (Coppedge et al. 2011). These studies, and others like them, play a critical role in research on these subjects and tend to be highly cited.

Neologism

Another sort of conceptual innovation involves the invention of a fundamentally new term.

The study of *genocide* began, one might say, with the term, which combines the Greek word for race with the Latin word for killing. Coined by Raphael Lemkin (1944), this neologism became fodder for the United Nations Genocide Convention, established in 1948. The Convention defined genocide as "acts committed with intent to destroy, in whole or in part, a national, ethnic, racial or religious group."[7]

So defined, genocide is fairly clearly distinguished from neighboring concepts such as mass murder, war, and civil war. Its closest cousin is "ethnic

---

[7] www.un.org/ar/preventgenocide/adviser/pdf/osapg_analysis_framework.pdf.

cleansing," which refers to the expulsion of ethnic groups rather than their destruction. Thus, we may conclude that this neologism is genuinely new, not merely old wine in new labels. No previous term captured the same attributes. Moreover, the term has proven useful, spawning a subfield of work across the social sciences (Bloxham, Moses 2010). Although debate persists over the classification of genocides (which events qualify, and which do not), we can scarcely imagine genocide as an object of study without this newly invented term.

An even more recent example of neologism is *social capital*, a term now ubiquitous in the social sciences. Definitions of social capital usually focus on social networks that extend beyond family and clan. The operating assumption is that the strengths of these networks have positive effects on crime, public health, social trust, governance, and economic productivity. The concept packs a powerful punch, hence its wide appeal. Although the borders of this concept are blurry, it is distinct enough from adjacent concepts – for example, civil society, civic associations, networks, culture, and other forms of capital (physical, human, cultural, political) – to warrant a new concept.

In common with other diffuse concepts, social capital has a complex history (Farr 2004; Woolcock 1998). Ideas now associated with the concept harken back to Alexis de Tocqueville, Jane Jacobs, and John Dewey, among others. The term itself was used in passing by Lyda J. Hanifan, Glenn Loury, Pierre Bourdieu and Jean-Claude Passeron, and was subsequently developed in a more focused manner by James S. Coleman, Ronald Burt, Alejandro Portes, and Robert Putnam in the 1980s and 1990s. Social capital thus offers a good example of the aphorism that important scientific inventions are "already there," rather than invented from scratch. In this case, the idea of social capital seems to have been percolating for centuries.

Typologies

A third species of conceptual innovation involves the formation of a typology. A typology orders a set of concepts such that one superordinate category contains several subordinate concepts that divide up its attribute space into mutually exclusive and exhaustive categories.[8]

Some typologies are simple, for example, a binary contrast of polar types such as democracy and autocracy (Alvarez et al. 1996) or vertical and horizontal accountability (O'Donnell 1998). Other typologies are more

---

[8] See Collier, LaPorte, Seawright (2012), Gerring (2012b: 144–151).

Table 3.1 Illustration of a matrix typology of regime types

		Participation	
		Low	*High*
Contestation	*Low*	"Closed hegemony"	"Inclusive hegemony"
	High	"Competitive oligarchy"	"Polyarchy"

Regime types across two dimensions, drawn from Dahl (1971: 7).

elaborate, involving a large number of categories. Recent work on autocracy identifies different species of nondemocratic rule – for example, military, monarchy, one-party, multiparty, personalist – each of which may have important implications for policies and policy outcomes.[9]

Matrix typologies are formed from the intersection of several categorical concepts. For example, Dahl (1971: 7) perceives two dimensions of democracy, a participation dimension and a contestation dimension. If we imagine these as binary variables, their intersection forms a 2x2 matrix, defining four subtypes of democracy, as illustrated in Table 3.1.

Discussion

Any of these three forms of conceptual research and development – clarification/reconstruction, neologism, and typologies – can open new angles for intellectual progress. As such, they all have the potential to count as important contributions.

At the same time, it is worth emphasizing that the contribution made by conceptual work is not always self-evident. Conceptual progress is most often detectable because it clears the way for new theoretical developments or empirical findings. Research that does conceptual work without demonstrating its value-added may be viewed skeptically. Indeed, most of the examples we have cited are not standalone "conceptual" papers but rather are closely linked to an empirical agenda. Work that is *merely* conceptual is apt to be dismissed.

Moreover, there is a rather limited space for conceptual development. Most conceptual reconstructions, neologisms, and typologies do not stick. They may function in the context of a particular work, but they do not open the way for new research and are not widely adopted. Instead, they fall by the

---

[9] See Geddes, Wright, Frantz (2014), Hadenius, Teorell (2007).

wayside, littering the field with discarded terms and definitions that are no longer used or understood. This is the sort of semantic disarray that Sartori bemoaned when he rediscovered the role of concepts in social science research. We should all think carefully before proposing a novel term or definition, lest it contribute further detritus to the terminological slag heap.

Even so, we can assert with confidence that there are plenty of situations that seem to justify further conceptual work. Are there undeveloped concepts, or concepts with a range of conflicting meanings that might be organized in a more fruitful way, in your area of research?

Data and Measures

Description, analysis, and many normative claims rest upon measurement. Unless one can characterize an entity empirically one cannot gauge its extent or its relationship (causal or noncausal) to other entities. And measurement rests upon data, so the tasks of data gathering and measurement are intertwined. In this section, we review the sort of contributions contained in new data and measures.

Data Collection Projects

Social science revolutions, insofar as they may exist, are often conjoined to revolutions in data collection. Let us consider a few examples.

Prior to the advent of random-sample surveys there was no systematic way to ascertain what mass publics thought about anything. Social scientists might talk to people, read newspapers, listen to popular radio shows, or try to interpret election results and consumer behavior. But these techniques were fairly haphazard, and open to obvious biases (e.g., toward urban and educated citizens). With the development of survey research – at mid-twentieth century in the United States and somewhat later in Europe and other parts of the world – new fields focused on economic behavior, political behavior, and social behavior opened up (Converse 2009; Geer 1996). In the United States, the founding of the National Election Study (NES), the General Social Survey (GSS), and surveys sponsored by the Bureau of Labor Statistics were signal events. Later, the World Values Survey (WVS) and various "barometer" surveys undertaken in regions throughout the world made it possible to gauge opinions across national and linguistic borders. It is fair to say that the social sciences would be unrecognizable without these surveys.

Prior to the development of national accounts, there was no way to measure economic development, that is, no way to say with precision whether one country was richer than another or whether a country was richer today than a decade ago. With the development of "gross domestic (or national) product" (GDP/GNP), in the 1930s and 1940s, along with attendant survey data, economists could make systematic comparisons for the first time (Coyle 2015). As a result, scholars could investigate the possible economic consequences of a change in policy or institution, or the social and political consequences of economic performance. The empirical field of macroeconomics was born.

The study of international relations centers on the occurrence of wars. Yet, prior to the 1960s, there was no systematic measure of interstate conflict through time and across the world. To remedy this, J. David Singer and collaborators founded the Correlates of War (COW) project, which devised an initial definition of war and assayed to measure its occurrence across countries in the modern era (Singer, Small 1972). Since then, the COW dataset has evolved to include a wide variety of indicators of interest to the community of scholars studying international relations. This, in turn, has fostered a branch of empirical research focused on causes and consequences of armed conflict.

The study of comparative politics centers largely on democracy. Prior to the 1970s, there was no systematic cross-national measure of this crucial aspect of political life. The first attempt to do so was the product of a single individual, Raymond Gastil, who completed a survey of "freedom in the world" in 1972, with separate indices for political rights and civil liberties (Gastil 1990). This single-handed effort evolved into an annual survey administered by Freedom House, a nonprofit institution, directed initially by Gastil. Eventually, the Freedom House survey enlisted the services of expert coders around the world, whose coding was harmonized into a seven-point ordinal scale developed by Gastil.

At about the same time, Harry Eckstein and Ted Robert Gurr (1975) advanced a highly abstract framework for understanding authority structures within nation-states. This became the conceptual basis for the Polity survey, which sought to identify patterns of autocracy and democracy throughout the world from 1800 to the present, and which continues today under the directorship of Monte Marshall.[10]

---

[10] See the Polfty website, now housed at the Center for Systemic Peace: www.systemicpeace.org/polity project.html.

More recently, the Varieties of Democracy (V-Dem) project has developed a wide range of indicators, coded by thousands of country experts and aggregated by a latent-variable measurement model, with the goal of measuring various dimensions of democracy for all sizable countries back to 1789 or independence (Coppedge et al. 2020).

These various approaches to measurement have become the foundation of immense scholarly literatures exploring the causes and effects of specific regime types and transitions.

The examples introduced above are massive research projects, testimony to the fact that data collection is often time-consuming, labor-intensive, and thus costly. Most data collection efforts are more modest and may be undertaken by one or several scholars, perhaps with the assistance of student research assistants. These efforts may also yield large rewards, despite minimal funding. In this fashion, binary coding of democracy and autocracy/dictatorship were produced by Adam Przeworski and colleagues (Cheibub, Gandhi, Vreeland 2010) and by Boix, Miller, Rosato (2013). Most of the datasets now associated with COW are the product of individual labors.[11] A small team of scholars generated the Archigos project, a systematic coding of the attributes of top leaders in all sizable countries over the past century and a half (Goemans, Gleditsch, Chiozza 2009). The Global Leadership Project (GLP) codes attributes of political elites for most countries in the current era (Gerring et al. 2019). The Constituency-Level Elections Archive (CLEA) aggregates election data from countries around the world at district levels (Kollman et al. 2018).

In many respects, data collection is becoming easier as time goes on. Many sources are available on the web or can be garnered through email communications. Others are already digitized. Wherever data can be scraped (gathered automatically with a scraping algorithm), it may be possible to collect millions of data points in the virtual blink of an eye (Wilson 2022). Computerized data collection, in conjunction with new statistical methods, has made possible quantitative analysis of the reasons why some Muslim clerics move in a jihadist direction while others remain committed to official state theology (Nielsen 2017), gender dynamics in political science publication (Teele and Thelen 2017), and patterns of public coappearance among politicians (Mahdavi 2019). Each of these topics would have been difficult to study in an unbiased fashion (stemming from selection bias) prior to the emergence of computerized data collection.

---

[11] Interested readers may peruse the COW website: www.correlatesofwar.org/.

The Role of New Data in Theoretical Debates

To show how important data can be to the advance of social science we examine several examples of scholarly controversies that were transformed by the arrival of new data.

Many years ago, Simon Kuznets (1955) proposed that economic growth imposed a curvilinear relationship on the distribution of income, with rising inequality at early stages of development and rising equality at later stages of development. This seemed to fit the data available at the time, composed of historical data for three countries (Germany, the United Kingdom, and the United States) and a smattering of contemporary data for countries elsewhere in the world. The "Kuznets curve" came to refer to any phenomenon, particularly one driven by development, that could be graphed as an upside-down U. However, later research, employing time-series estimates of inequality for a much larger share of countries – and extending several decades into the future (after Kuznets's original publication) – showed little evidence of a curvilinear relationship (Deininger, Squire 1998; Fields 2001).

In the 1970s, Richard Easterlin (1974) discovered a disheartening relationship between economic development and personal happiness, as reported in various surveys taken over several decades in the United States. As the country became richer its citizens apparently did not become happier. This became known as the "Easterlin paradox," as it contradicted the scenario implied by a Panglossian version of modernization theory. The apparent lesson, that money does not buy happiness, also resonated with a generation weary of capitalist triumphalism. Decades later, Betsey Stevenson and Justin Wolfers (2008) returned to this classic question with a much larger sample of data, encompassing myriad surveys of happiness and wellbeing (self-reported) in the United States and around the world over many decades. They find a strong relationship between subjective wellbeing and income – across countries, across individuals, and through time. This constitutes a fairly thorough refutation of the Easterlin paradox – though it should be added that income is measured in a logarithmic form, suggesting that its hedonic benefits are sublinear (evidence of the declining marginal utility of money).

We do not mean to suggest that these lengthy debates have been settled, once and for all. It seems likely that they will continue to evolve, and the resolutions suggested above may yet be overturned. But what seems certain is that these questions rest largely upon the data and measures used to operationalize key concepts. They cannot be resolved in the abstract. Since data gathering is an ongoing process (even for historical topics, new sources are often discovered), the task is never-ending and remains crucial to the evolution of social science.

Discussion

It follows that we should regard data collection as a vital contribution to social science. Data, if made public, is all the more vital because of its downstream effects. Data gathered in the course of one project can be reused by other scholars who may wish to conduct a replication or meta-analysis, or who may have completely different goals in mind. Findings, by contrast, are inert.

Thus, although data collection is laborious, and does not always get the immediate recognition it deserves, the hard-working data collector may make his or her mark. Successful data projects become the basis for other projects and reap citations from those follow-up studies. Monte Marshall is a virtually household name in political science because of his ongoing work on the Polity project. Others may also see a payoff in their Google Scholar citation counts.

Are there opportunities to collect new data in your area of research?

Causes

Another sort of scholarly contribution is the discovery of a new causal factor deemed to be relevant for a well-studied outcome. Commonly, the new cause is an additional factor relevant to Y – represented as B in Figure 1.1 – which coexists with the previously identified cause or vector of causes (X). Sometimes, a new cause, C, displaces or partially displaces a previously identified causal factor. Sometimes, the new factor, A, lies antecedent to the old factor, in which case X becomes a mechanism in the proposed framework. There are many ways in which new causes can contribute to our understanding of Y.

Another Cause of Y

In the world of social science, it is rare that a single cause explains all the variation on an outcome. Monocausal relationships are extremely unusual. Indeed, most outcomes of theoretical interest in social science have innumerable causes. Consider infant mortality, inequality, growth, or regime-type. Presumably, virtually everything going on in a society has some impact on these outcomes. Accordingly, the vector of predictors, X, is essentially infinite. This means that even though these outcomes have been intensively researched for many years it may be possible to identify new causes that affect these outcomes in a nontrivial fashion.

It also means that many causes will not be terribly interesting or important. Consider the question of vote choice in a presidential election. A list of all the reasons why people may have voted as they did in the 2016 US presidential election would inspire many fascinating debates. Potential explanations include sex, race, ethnicity, and religion. No doubt many other worthwhile causes can be added to this short list.

Yet, a truly comprehensive list of causes is likely to contain many uninspiring causes. Did some citizens cast their vote based on candidates' hairstyles, accents, height, and astrological signs? In a very large population, it would be surprising if these factors never mattered. However, it is unlikely that they explain much of the variation in vote choice.

One clue to the space for novelty in the mechanical sense is the fit between X (the established causes) and Y. How much of the variation in Y does X explain – and, by implication, how much is unexplained? If the fit is not so good this suggests that there is more work to be done. In a regression framework, model fit may be measured by "R squared." Naturally, any interpretations one might draw from model-fit statistics are contingent upon the correctness of the model; if it is wrong, all bets are off. But if it is correct, or plausibly so, then one can make inferences about the available space for innovation.

In a qualitative framework, cases that don't fit the general model are referred to as *anomalies* or *deviant cases*. If there are a lot of them, one might infer that there is room for a new causal factor. If there are only one or two deviant cases, it seems less likely that one will be able to offer an important theoretical contribution. So, the same logic applies. The better the extant theory explains the data the less room there appears to be for a new causal explanation.

Let us consider an example. Crime is a well-studied phenomenon. But the crime drop that occurred in the United States in the late twentieth century surprised most experts. In the early 1960s, the United States enjoyed a low homicide rate of 5 murders per 100,000 inhabitants. Over the next two decades, this rate doubled – to 10 per 100,000 inhabitants – peaking in the late 1970s and early 1980s, at which point the United States could claim the highest rate of violent crime of any advanced industrial country. Subsequently, the crime wave began to fall, and it now rests approximately where it was in 1960.[12]

Explanations for this remarkable reversal range widely. One explanation centers on the role of lead, a key ingredient of gasoline prior to environmental regulations in the late 1970s. It is fairly well established that childhood lead exposure can cause aggressive behavior in adults, so it is plausible that the removal of this ingredient from automobile fuel had positive effects on population health for those reaching maturity in the 1980s (Reyes 2007). Another explanation centers on the legalization of abortion after the *Roe* v. *Wade* decision in 1973. According to Donohue and Levitt (2001), this led to a rise in abortion rates among subgroups who were especially prone to violent crime, reducing their prevalence in the general population. Other explanations center on demographic change (a decline in young adults due to the aging of the population), increased incarceration rates (removing violent individuals from the general population), changes in policing strategies, and so forth (Blumstein, Wallman 2006).

It seems unlikely that any single explanation can account for all the variation in US crime rates over the observed period, much less for international patterns in crime, which mirror those in the United States in some respects (Van Dijk, Tseloni, Farrell 2012). Most of these new causal variables open the door for theoretical innovation, as they point toward unexpected kinds of contributions across social domains. As with most social science topics, there is plenty of room – considered both mechanically and theoretically – for new ideas.

Distal Factors

Another sort of explanatory contribution is a cause that is antecedent to the usual explanation (Slater, Simmons 2010). If the conventional understanding is that X causes Y, one might choose to examine the causes of X, represented as A in Figure 1.1.

In the postwar era, when economists grappled with the question of economic growth they tended to focus on investment (Rostow 1956). In subsequent decades, they came to terms with prior factors that presumably affect the rate of foreign and domestic investment such as the quality of political

---

[12] Federal Bureau of Investigation, Uniform Crime Reporting Statistics: www.ucrdatatool.gov/Search/ Crime/State/RunCrimeTrendsInOneVar.cfm.

institutions (Acemoglu, Johnson, Robinson 2005). More recently, they have considered the role of geography as a prime mover in economic development (Olsson 2005). Each factor may be regarded as a step backward (in time and in causal order) from the outcome, representing a more distal causal relationship.

Distal factors often bring advantages relative to their more proximal cousins. They are usually less susceptible to circularity and to common-cause confounders. And they shed light on long-term causal relationships (Pierson 2011). They are, however, usually less amenable to manipulation. One cannot move a geographic feature like a mountain from one region to another. Consequently, distal features are generally more difficult to study experimentally and less useful from a policy perspective. It is also harder to observe a causal path from a distal cause to an outcome occurring years or centuries later. As such, case study modes of research may be unavailing and it may be impossible to measure and test possible mechanisms.

Discussion

For most (general) outcomes – for example, infant mortality, democracy, growth – there are an infinite number of causes. Accordingly, the possibilities for innovation are also infinite. With each additional cause, so long as it is not trivial, we learn more about that outcome.

Are there new causal factors to investigate in your field of research?

Mechanisms

Social science research often begins with a hypothesis about a causal effect ($X \rightarrow Y$) and then proceeds to examine the possible reasons for that effect. Causality implies a set of mechanisms (labeled M in Figure 1.1), understood as factors that connect X to Y.

Where X is a proximal cause, the mechanisms may be fairly straightforward and uninteresting. If consumption of a product increases as price decreases, we do not need to spend a great deal of time discussing the reasons beyond the idea that demand is "elastic."

Where X is a distal cause, there are likely to be a number of plausible mechanisms, some of which may be spelled out in extant work and others of which may remain mysterious. Here, there is genuine puzzling, and considerable controversy.

Why, for example, is per capita GDP positively associated with democracy? Modernization theory suggests a number of possible pathways including income, education, urbanization, class structure, and a change in norms and values (Inglehart, Welzel 2005; Lipset 1959). With respect to class structure, one might credit the rise of the bourgeoisie (Moore 1966) and/or the rise of the working class (Rueschemeyer, Stephens, Stephens 1992).

Why is oil wealth negatively associated with democracy? Michael Ross (2001: 327–328) identifies three possible pathways.

A "rentier effect" ... suggests that resources rich governments use low tax rates and patronage to relieve pressures for greater accountability; a "repression effect" ... argues that resources wealth retards democratization by enabling governments to boost their funding for internal security; and a "modernization effect" ... holds that growth based on the export of oil and minerals fails to bring about the social and cultural changes that tend to produce democratic government.

Why does education reduce fertility rates? Diamond, Newby, and Varle (1999) identify four possible links, which they categorize as: employment/opportunity costs, the nature of marriage, familiarity with bureaucratic institutions, and reference communities.

Discussion

Probing these mechanisms or adding new competitors is a vital task in advancing and refining a causal theory. We want to know why X causes Y, not merely that it does so. This is helpful for ascertaining the scope-conditions of the theory and speculating upon its possible relevance for other contexts (its generalizability). It is also essential for developing policy-relevant interventions.

In some cases, researchers may be successful in reducing the number of potential causes of Y. Perhaps one or two mechanisms can be eliminated. Instead of M_{1-5}, it is M_{1-3}.

In other cases, researchers may find themselves broadening the menu of mechanisms. It is not only M_1 and M_2 – the usual suspects – but also M_3.

Ascertaining mechanisms may also be important in helping to demonstrate that X is actually a cause of Y, especially in situations where experimental designs are impossible to implement. Occasionally, the result of a mechanism-based analysis is at such variance with expectations that it calls into question the theory. In an extensive analysis of democratic transitions in the twentieth century, Haggard and Kaufman (2012) find scant evidence for the existence of distributional conflict, leading them to question theories of regime change premised on assumptions of class conflict (e.g., Acemoglu, Robinson 2005; Boix 2003).

Some mechanisms are so general in import that they qualify as *theoretical frameworks*. They apply not simply to one causal effect ($X \rightarrow Y$) but to a wide range of causal relationships. Examples of this sort of work are discussed in detail in Chapter 8. For now, it is sufficient to note that causal mechanisms may be specific, or general.

Are there important and unresolved questions about mechanisms in your field of research?

Research Designs

In recent years, methodological focus within the social sciences has shifted from econometrics to research design. After all, there is only so much that can be achieved with clever statistical adjustments, given that each adjustment requires a set of assumptions that are generally impossible to verify, and therefore open to objection. If a given causal relationship can be modeled in twenty different ways – for example, with different estimators, specifications, and samples – and if the results of these choices affect the purported relationship between X and Y, it will be difficult to reach any firm conclusions (Seawright 2010).

Accordingly, scholars attempt to design research that is as close as possible to a true experiment in the hopes that assumptions can be minimized and a stronger basis for causal inference can be established. In this fashion, design-based inference displaces statistically-based inference (Dunning 2010; Rubin 2008). We hasten to add that this is not always possible; but where it is feasible, we heartily recommend it.

The most important feature of a research design is probably the assignment to treatment. If this is random and the randomization procedure is controlled by the researcher, we shall call it an *experiment*. If it is random but occurs naturally or by a mechanism the researcher cannot control, we shall refer to it as a *natural experiment*. Among natural experiments we distinguish those that are (a) simple, (b) regression-discontinuity, and (c) instrumental-variable.

Since the technical aspects of experimental and quasi-experimental research have been extensively covered elsewhere (see citations that follow), our emphasis will be on examples, chosen to elucidate the range of options that researchers might find useful. The obstacle to better research designs is not technical but rather circumstantial: scholars must learn to look closely at the world to identify occasions that are amenable to experimental or quasi-experimental designs.

Experiments

In some settings, experiments have revolutionized our understandings of causal relationships.[13] Our understanding of political communication has been profoundly deepened, for example, by generations of experiments on news consumption and framing, with studies now informing us of the kinds of frames that matter, whether and how the source of a message changes its effects, the durability of messages in both homogeneous and heterogeneous communication environments, and so forth. This has left us with a relatively nuanced vision of the general public as conditionally susceptible to political manipulation.

In more specific debates, experiments have opened exciting new windows into questions such as the nature of racism (Sniderman, Carmines 1997). Conversations around racism in the United States and other countries have been ongoing for generations, with scholarship focused on survey data, qualitative interviews, and the interpretation of texts. Experiments have added the opportunity to manipulate social situations in order to introduce race in a variety of subtle ways. Accordingly, they have been able to demonstrate the ongoing importance of racial attitudes in political decision-making and behavior – a key contribution in a domain that is characteristically contentious and politicized. For example, Banks and Hicks (2016) use an experimental framework in which different emotions are induced among treatment groups to show that implicit racial bias is more strongly connected with support for voter ID laws when citizens feel fear than when they feel anger or relaxation. Since experiments on this subject now have a history, they can plausibly capture change over time in causal dynamics related to race. In this vein, Valenzuela and Reny (2021: 452) note that white Americans appear to be *more* affected by explicit racial messages in experiments now than in the relatively recent past, perhaps because "recent trends may have altered the acceptability of racially hostile political rhetoric."

Experimental research has also opened new, more detailed questions about causal relationships in other fields. Experiments have changed the

---

[13] See Druckman et al. (2011), Jackson, Cox (2013), Kagel, Roth (2016).

landscape of debates about the democratic peace hypothesis (Tomz, Weeks 2013), the politics of populism (Busby, Gubler, Hawkins 2019), corruption (Chong et al. 2015), legislative politics (Bergan 2009), and many other domains. While it is possible that some important literatures will prove resistant to experimental methods, recent history suggests that there is often substantial value in devising experimental frameworks to contribute to existing fields heretofore dominated by observational research.

Simple Natural Experiments

In many settings, it is impossible – or unethical – to manipulate a treatment in a way that sheds light on a theoretical question of interest. Nonetheless, there may be naturally occurring experiments that achieve something similar (Dunning 2012). In this section, we explore settings that seem to afford an *as-if random* assignment of treatment.

Mandates. An opportunity arises when a treatment is mandated by some supervisory body, such as a government, a court, a colonial power. For example, a law passed by the Indian government mandated a quota for women in local government, allowing researchers to observe whether women lawmakers behaved differently from men (Chattopadhyay, Duflo 2004). Another example is provided by statutes that impose term limits on lawmakers, allowing scholars to study the impact of tenure in office on their behavior (Dal Bó, Rossi 2011). It is the arbitrariness of the mandate that makes it random (at least with respect to some outcomes), and if it is rigorously enforced one does not have to worry about exceptions to random assignment that might confound the relationship.

Lotteries. Various studies have focused on the impact of lottery winnings – on happiness (Brickman, Coates, Janoff-Bulman 1978), on attitudes toward redistribution (Doherty, Gerber, Green 2006), on ideology (Powdthavee, Oswald 2014), and so forth. Other sorts of lotteries, such as for military service (Angrist 1990) or admission to desirable public schools (Cullen, Jacob, Levitt 2006), are also prime fodder for natural experiments. These studies capitalize on the defining feature of a lottery – its random-ness. To be sure, one must assume the lottery system is not subject to corruption and that winners and losers are truly chosen randomly. But if so, winners and losers should be identical in all other respects.

Borders. Territorial borders may also provide fodder for quasi-experimental comparisons if the placement of the boundary is as-if random. Divisions might occur across electoral districts (Ansolabehere, Snyder, Stewart 2000;

Brady, McNulty 2011) or across countries (McCauley, Posner 2015). If the boundaries are truly random, the people on either side of the border should be similar along a broad set of background conditions. The assumption is that the boundary defines the treatment. Of course, it may also coincide with other factors, which would constitute confounders.

Regression-Discontinuity Designs

Another sort of natural experiment is afforded by discontinuities in a continuous outcome. Here, a threshold condition along a continuous parameter divides those in the treatment group from those in the control group, setting up an opportunity for a regression-discontinuity design (RDD).[14]

For example, welfare benefits may be assigned on the basis of income. So long as the cutoff for eligibility is strict, and subjects are unable to cheat, we may compare subjects who fall just above and below the means-test, who are regarded as comprising the treatment and control groups. This is the as-if random component.

Importantly, the estimate from an RDD pertains most appropriately to subjects who fall near the cutoff and is usually understood as a *local average treatment effect* (LATE). It may or may not have relevance for those falling further away from the cutoff – who may be quite dissimilar on background conditions.

Let us suppose that those with a household income of less than $20,000 are eligible for some benefit. We should be able to compare adults falling just below the threshold (e.g., with household incomes of $19,500–$20,000) with adults falling just above the threshold (e.g., with household incomes of $20,000–$20,500). As in a true experiment, the treatment and control groups should be similar on all background conditions, allowing for an unbiased estimate of any causal effect stemming from welfare benefits.

However, if citizens know about the cutoff point and are able to manipulate their income (e.g., by changing work schedules) the comparison may fail. Likewise, this research design is subverted if factors *other than income* place subjects in the treatment or control groups – if, for example, subjects are able to bribe officials to reclassify them as members of the treatment group.

There are also concerns about noncompliance (subjects who are assigned to the treatment group but for one reason or another do not receive the treatment). However, this situation – known as a "fuzzy" RDD – can usually

---

[14] See Cattaneo, Idrobo, Titiunik (2019), Imbens, Lemieux (2008).

Table 3.2 Occasions for regression discontinuity designs

Continuous outcome	Cutoff	Treatment
Income	Means-test	Welfare benefit ...
Score on a test	Threshold score	Admission to school or job, ...
Votes in an election	Plurality or majority	Holding office, ...
Age	Threshold for eligibility or applicability	Voting, driving a car, passage of law that applies to people of a certain age
Date of birth	Qualification for first year of school	Amount of education (Cascio, Lewis 2006)
Firm size	Threshold for requirement	Anti-bias laws, health insurance, ...
Population	Threshold for requirement	Revenue sharing (Brollo et al. 2013), voting systems (Chamon et al. 2018)

be addressed if the sample is sufficiently large and patterns of noncompliance are not systematic or can be effectively modeled.

To identify RDD opportunities, look for binary treatments (you get it or you don't) where the assignment rests on an arbitrary cutoff along a continuous function. A number of options are listed in Table 3.2. The best RDD designs will involve cutoffs on variables where participants cannot reasonably affect their score (e.g., age, date of birth) or where most or all participants have an across-the-board incentive to score as well as possible on the variable rather than manipulating it in the vicinity of the threshold. This would be true for most exams, where subjects are concerned not only with passing a fixed threshold but also with their score. Outcomes where the threshold offers a known benefit and where participants may have some ability to position themselves strategically create more problematic settings (Caughey, Sekhon 2011).

Instrumental-Variable Designs

If the random element is an antecedent cause (A in Figure 1.1), which affects assignment to treatment for a subset of those in the sample, we shall refer to it as an *instrumental-variable* (IV) design.[15] Importantly, the instrument must affect Y only through X, the variable of theoretical interest. If there are other paths from A to Y these must be conditioned and thereby blocked. Otherwise, confounding will ensue. This is known as the exclusion restriction.

[15] See Angrist, Krueger (2001), Sovey, Green (2011).

One widely used family of instrumental-variable designs involves the Vietnam war draft lottery. In 1969, the United States held a lottery to determine the order by which draft-eligible American men would be conscripted to serve in Vietnam, with the goal of transparently ensuring equity in military service. Because this lottery generated a (reasonably) random assignment of individuals to military service, among the set of people eligible for the draft, it can be used as a natural experiment to study the effect of Vietnam war service on lifetime earnings (Angrist 1990), long-term mortality rates (Conley, Heerwig 2012), attitudes about the war (Bergan 2009), and political attitudes more generally (Erikson, Stoker 2011).

Yet as interesting as it is to learn about the effects of exposure to service in Vietnam on a range of social and political outcomes, such insight is highly context-specific: it teaches us about causal effects for one generation of young men during one historical conflict. The temptation is strong to use this fascinating episode of randomization to discover more general causal inferences. Scholars have thus tried to use the draft lottery as an instrumental variable.

For example, Angrist and Chen (2011) use the draft lottery as an instrument to explore the connection between higher education and annual earnings. Having a low draft lottery increased men's educational attainment in two ways. First, it incentivized them to enroll in college to avoid being drafted. Second, if they were drafted, they qualified for highly subsidized college through the GI Bill. Hence, the draft lottery appears to be a valid, randomized cause of college educational attainment. Angrist and Chen (2011) proceed to calculate an IV estimate of the effect of college attainment on lifetime earnings, concluding that it is very small. This inference requires that military service only affect earnings via the educational pathway; in support of this, Angrist and Chen argue that differences in earnings due to lost work experience during the war should have faded by 2000, the year of census data used in the study. Perhaps there are other pathways by which Vietnam service affects earnings in 2000, but if so, they are excluded by assumption. If the exclusion restriction is valid here, then the conclusion appears to be that the kind of schooling subsidized by the GI Bill mostly had modest effects on the labor market.

Like RDD, IV analyses estimate a local average treatment effect (LATE), which in this case refers to the subjects who were encouraged into the treatment condition of theoretical interest by the instrument. Typically, one knows how weak or strong the instrument is but *not* which subjects it applies to. This makes it challenging to interpret. What portion of the population does the LATE describe?

Discussion

Each of the foregoing approaches is designed to overcome common-cause confounding, as well as the possibility of X/Y endogeneity. Even so, threats to causal inference remain. Some of these threats are post-assignment, for example, interference across groups (contamination) or other varieties of noncompliance. With natural experiments there is the additional problem of ascertaining whether assignment to treatment, which is not under the control of the researcher, is truly random. Typically, this requires some assumptions about the data generating process, which researchers should describe in as much detail as possible, allowing the reader to judge how viable they are. With respect to *all* these designs there are questions about generalizability (Findley, Denly, Kikuta 2022).

In any case, no research design automatically produces a strong causal inference. Each study requires considerable thought and expertise – with respect to the subject under investigation, the technique to be applied to that question, and the interpretation. As with any research, the devil is in the details. There are well-conducted (natural) experiments and poorly conducted (natural) experiments. We do not wish to give the impression that some genres of research are *generically* better than others.

Nonetheless, if properly executed, experimental and quasi-experimental designs usually give a more accurate estimate of a hypothesized causal effect than the analogous observational data analysis (Lalonde 1986). Thus, insofar as researchers can apply these techniques to problems of theoretical interest – and insofar as these studies tell us something we did not already know – we should consider this an important contribution to knowledge, even if experiments never entirely displace observational research.

Are there opportunities for applying experimental or quasi-experimental designs in your area of research?

Empirical Refinements and Extensions

Once a theory has been propounded it must be interrogated by the research community. This entails probing the robustness of the theory and its limits.

We outline several approaches to this task: *sensitivity, functional form, moderators and scope-conditions*, and *replications*.

Sensitivity

An empirical relationship should be robust to alternate tests, so long as these tests are plausible. If the analysis is quantitative, sensitivity tests may involve changes to (a) the specification, (b) indicators used to operationalize key variables, (c) the sample, and (d) the estimator.

If a relationship is found to be robust, that is, estimates for the main relationship are consistent, then one may have greater confidence that the relationship is causal and precisely estimated. One may also be able to specify the *bounds* of a relationship – its largest and smallest magnitude, given different assumptions about the data generating process (Manski 1999). If the relationship shifts dramatically, this may be a cause for concern, or it may lead to new insights about the nature of the relationship. Sometimes, there are good (theoretical) reasons for a test to fail, which become apparent once one is able to examine a diverse range of robustness tests.

Sensitivity tests are time-consuming. However, some portions of this task may be automated. One approach focuses on the specification search, that is, the rejiggering of covariates in a model to gauge the robustness of the result. Specification searches may be assisted by algorithms such as LASSO (discussed in Chapter 7) that systematically test all combinations of covariates identified by the researcher. For example, in arguing that data show little to no relationship between immigration and terrorism, Forrester et al. (2019) worry that their instrumental variables analysis may not have included all relevant controls. Thus, they run a LASSO analysis to find all control variables with a compelling statistical relationship with either immigration or terrorism; repeating the analysis using the selected control variables returns results consistent with their earlier model. Researchers must be careful about drawing conclusions from these analyses if the mix of covariates suggest that there might be problems of collinearity or post-treatment bias.

Functional Form

Estimating a causal effect presumes a functional form – a schedule of changes in X that are alleged to cause changes in Y, a lag structure (if any), a temporal duration, and so forth. Note that in an experiment the functional form is built-in to the research design. However, the theoretical goal is presumably to understand X's relationship to Y, not simply to test one particular functional form. So, experimenters ought to be as interested in functional form as those who work with observational data.

Typically, researchers make simplifying assumptions about functional form, for example, that there is a linear or log-linear relationship, that increases and decreases in X have equivalent effects on Y, and that the relationship is probabilistic. Simplicity may be a reasonable point of departure. But one should also consider the possibility that nature is more complex.

Rein Taagepera (2008), a former physicist, points out that natural scientists employ a great variety of empirical models, while social scientists generally restrict themselves to variations in linearity. He urges us to remove our blinders. Indeed, as "big data" comes to the fore, quantitative scholars can potentially explore classes of nonlinear models in an open-ended way using nonparametric and semiparametric regression models (Yatchew 2003). Qualitative researchers are sometimes more attuned to departures from linearity than quantitative researchers (Pierson 2011), though it should be noted that complexity in this context often refers to patterns that apply to a single case or a small set of cases, and thus are not widely generalizable.

One may cite many examples of scholarly contributions centered on functional form. The "cube law" was devised in the early twentieth century to describe the relationship between votes and seats within single-member district first-past-the-post electoral systems (Kendall, Stuart 1950). Subsequent work has revised and expanded this formula to take account of different electoral rules and to explain outcomes at both district and aggregate levels (Shugart, Taagepera 2017).

Within the democratization literature, an ongoing debate concerns whether modernization (proxied by per capita GDP) affects transitions to democracy (a two-way effect, as argued by Boix, Stokes 2003) or only democratic consolidation (a one-way causal effect, as argued by Przeworski, Limongi 1997).

Within the democratic peace literature, scholars debate whether the presence of a democratic dyad is a sufficient condition for peace (Weart 1998) or a probabilistic feature that increases the likelihood of peace (Ray 1995).

While "complexity" is infinite, and therefore impossible to enumerate in a comprehensive fashion, here is a checklist of possibilities to consider as you look for variations in functional form.

Conjunctures (aka compound cause, configurative cause, combinatorial cause, conjunctive plurality of causes): Where a particular combination of causes act together to produce an effect.

Equifinality (aka multiple causes, multiple causal paths, a disjunctive plurality of causes, redundancy): Where several causes act independently of each other to produce, each on its own, a particular effect.

Monotonicity: Where an increase (decrease) in *X* always causes an increase (decrease) or no change in *Y*.

Linearity/Nonlinearity: If the impact of *X* on *Y* changes across different values of *X* the relationship is nonlinear.

Irreversibility: *X* affects *Y* as *X* increases but not as it decreases, or vice versa.

Asymmetry: A change in *X* affects the movement of Y in one direction but not the other.

Constancy/Delimited: A constant cause operates continually upon an outcome; a delimited cause operates only briefly (though it may have enduring effects).

Proximal/Distal: A proximal cause operates immediately on an outcome; a distal cause has long-term effects.

Sequence: The effect of X_{1-3} on *Y* depends upon the sequence in which X_1, X_2, and X_3 are applied.

Path-dependency (aka critical juncture): A single causal intervention has enduring, and perhaps increasing, effects over time.

Set-theoretic causes: Where *X* is necessary and/or sufficient for *Y*.

A glance at this extensive list is sufficient to demonstrate that the investigation of functional form is an important dimension of social science research. Although some of these terms may sound rather arcane, they are not just fancy terms of art. Whether a relationship is monotonic or non-monotonic, for example, is critical for understanding *X*'s relationship to *Y*. It has important policy repercussions and may also suggest different causal mechanisms.

Moderators and Scope-Conditions

Sometimes, a causal relationship exhibits heterogeneity. *X* has a different impact on *Y* contingent upon some background factor(s), *D*. Occasionally, the sign flips: *X* has a positive effect on *Y* when *D*=0 and a negative effect when *D*=1.

D may be treated as a *moderator*, a factor that changes the relationship between X and Y. Often, this is quite informative and worthy of theorizing and testing. For example, one might hypothesize that there is an interactive relationship between X and D such that $Y = X + D + X^*D$.

D may also be treated as a *scope-condition*, establishing the boundaries of a relationship between X and Y. For example, one might hypothesize that $X {\Rightarrow} Y|D=0$ (X causes Y if D is equal to zero but not – or at least with less certainty – when D is equal to 1).

Sometimes, scope-conditions are stipulated as a matter of theoretical or logical entailment. For example, a theory of electoral systems presumes that there are elections. But even where the scope-conditions seem obvious there is often some ambiguity. For instance, how democratic must those elections be in order for the relationship of interest – centered on electoral systems and some outcome – to manifest itself? A specific boundary condition of this sort is probably not inferable from a theory about how the world works. It may have to be investigated. Accordingly, ascertaining the limits of a theory – where it does and does not pertain – is an important contribution to social science.

Theda Skocpol (1979) claims that her theory of revolutions applies only to countries that had not experienced European colonialism. Others have wondered whether this is a viable scope-condition or an arbitrary domain restriction, intended to keep in cases that fit the predictions of the theory and exclude those that do not. Note that a plausible scope-condition must be theoretically defensible but also have some empirical reality. In this respect, theorizing about scope-conditions is no different from theorizing about causal effects; indeed, one implies the other. For any theory, there are inevitable questions about scope-conditions. How far does the theory extend? What are its boundaries? What is its *population*?

Scope-conditions may refer to territory, units of analysis, types of people, types of organization, time periods – anything that delimits the boundaries of the theory. This is partly a theoretical question and partly an empirical question, as we have emphasized. Ideally, empirical results match up to something that can be theoretically justified.

Sometimes, a theory has no obvious boundaries. In this case, the task of the researcher is to bound the theory. Sometimes, a theory is set forth with very clear scope-conditions, but they are dubious, or they have not yet been proven. Here, the task of the researcher is to test the limits, that is, to examine terrain that falls within the theory to see if it really supports the theory or to examine terrain that falls outside the denoted realm of the theory to see if it might be extended to this new area (perhaps with some added qualifications or a different functional form).

Bear in mind that virtually everything we have just said about scope-conditions pertains to moderators, for they are flip sides of the same coin.

Replications

When a study tests a hypothesis drawn directly from a previous study (that tests the same hypothesis) the result may be described as a *replication*. A replication may be narrowly construed (following the original study closely) or loosely construed (deviating in important respects).

To distinguish types of replications it is helpful to consider two dimensions – the evidence and the strategy of analysis. Evidence may be (a) drawn directly from the original study (reusing the same data), (b) a different sample drawn from the same population, or (c) a sample drawn from a different population. Strategies of analysis, including measurement of key variables, may be (a) the same as the original study or (b) different. The intersection of these two dimensions produces six cells and five different replication types, as illustrated in Table 3.3. (A different analysis of evidence drawn from a different population is not a replication in any sense of the term, which accounts for the empty cell on the bottom right.)

Replication plays an essential role in the cumulation of knowledge (Elman, Gerring, Mahoney 2020). Without it, there is no way of knowing whether extant findings are true. If a finding has never been replicated, or has received only a few replications, a careful follow-up study is especially informative – whether it confirms or disconfirms the original finding. However, one should not view replications as having only a binary outcome – confirm or

Table 3.3 Replication types

		ANALYSIS	
		Same	*Different*
EVIDENCE	*Same data*	1. Verification	2. Sensitivity
	Same population	3. Reproduction	4. Reanalysis
	Different population	5. Extension	

Replication typology, understood as the intersection of evidence types and analysis types. Drawn from Gerring (2020).

disconfirm. Generally, the results are more ambiguous. The original study may involve several hypotheses, some of which are confirmed and others which are not, or only partially so.

Replications that go beyond Type 1 are perhaps best viewed as *extensions* of the original study (in this respect, the term "replication" is misleading). They may offer better data. They may offer a more precise estimate of the main causal effect if the sample is larger, there is less measurement error or less noise (stochastic error). They may offer improvements in research design that promise to overcome threats to inference in the original study. They may probe sensitivity, functional form, mechanisms, moderators, scope-conditions – indeed, all of the topics we have thus far discussed. The topic of replication thus overlaps with previous sections in this chapter. Results from a series of replications may also be combined with the original study in a *meta-analysis*.

Among the many uses of replication is the opportunity for novel insights. In natural science, it is common to begin a new piece of research by replicating an extant piece of research. In this way, novelty builds directly upon what has come before, and replication becomes the precursor to innovation. Note that beginning a new study with a replication assists knowledge cumulation on two levels: it confirms (or disconfirms) the original study, and serves as a benchmark for new discoveries, providing a basis for comparison. Often, it generates new insights. Sometimes, it opens new doors that lead to new avenues of inquiry. For example, Nichter's work on machine parties' incentives to deploy different kinds of clientelist targeting strategies begins from a careful replication of Stokes's earlier, pathbreaking analysis. Finding a more consistent interpretation of Stokes's data, Nichter (2008) was inspired to build a theory explaining why Argentine machine parties seemed to target core supporters rather than swing voters. This theory born from replication extended Stokes's results and motivated a broader and highly influential research trajectory (Gans-Morse, Mazzuca, Nichter 2014; Hidalgo, Nichter 2016).

We encourage researchers to regard replication not as the end of the research road but rather as a way station along the road. In this fashion, confirmatory research becomes a building block for exploratory research.

Conclusions

In this chapter, we have offered an inventory of the various ways in which a study might contribute to a body of scholarship. The breadth of this inventory underlines a major theme of the book, which is that there are many ways to contribute.

Naturally, none of these contributions precludes the others, so the categories are not mutually exclusive. Nonetheless, it is fair to say that most studies are propelled by one or two contributions to knowledge; other dimensions are carried over from previous research and thus lie in the background. Indeed, study that innovated across all dimensions would be truly incomprehensible. Productive research is always a mix of old and new.

True innovation leads the way forward while encompassing the past, rather than simply overturning existing theories. If one differentiates one's work in a radical way from prior work this is likely to render the contribution more difficult to digest, unsettling the field of existing knowledge and impeding cumulation. To be innovative, a new theoretical framework must be superior to existing frameworks on at least one dimension of knowledge; this is what qualifies a research program as progressive (Lakatos 1978). But it must fit with existing frameworks on other dimensions; otherwise, it is undigestible.[16]

---

[16] As an example, let us consider the theoretical apparatus invented by Karl Marx (building on Hegel, Ricardo, and others) and developed by subsequent researchers within the intellectual tradition known as Marxism. There is much we can learn, and have learned, from this venerable research tradition. At the same time, its utility for science is reduced if the concepts and assumptions – the theoretical scaffolding – do not interact with other work in the social sciences. We applaud the efforts of some latter-day researchers to integrate ideas from the Marxist canon into mainstream economics, sociology, and political science (e.g., Acemoglu, Robinson 2005; Roemer 1986; Wright 1997).

Part II

Playing with Ideas

Having offered an overview of our topic, we turn to what might be called the "normative" sections of the book, where we offer advice about how to identify a research project.

This first section is titled "Playing with Ideas" because we want to encourage a playful attitude toward discovery. One cannot plod grimly toward enlightenment; periodically, there must be some diversion.

Chapter 4 sets forth a set of broadly pitched *strategies* for positioning oneself advantageously so that you enhance your probability of success. Chapter 5 offers a set of *heuristics* – ways of thinking about the world that seem likely to generate fruitful ideas for research.

4 Strategies

During my career in science, now nearly a half century in duration, I have grown more and more aware that success in science, paralleling success in most careers, comes not so much to the most gifted, nor the most skillful, nor the most knowledgeable, nor the most affluent of scientists, but rather to the superior strategist and tactician. The individual who is able to maneuver with propriety through the world of science along a course that regularly puts him or her in a position of serendipity is often the one who excels.

Jack Oliver (1991: ix)

Luck is a highly plausible explanation for innovation, featuring prominently in the biographies of many great inventors and researchers.[1] Likewise, our description of exploratory work throughout this book highlights the irregular, disorderly, seemingly chaotic, aspects of scientific discovery. Sometimes, researchers stumble onto great topics. *Presto! Voila! Serendipity!* A research project is born.

Another genre of work on innovation and discovery stresses the role of personality types. Kirton (1994: 10) distinguishes between *Adaptors* and *Innovators*. The Adaptor "challenges rules rarely, cautiously, when assured of strong support," while the Innovator "often challenges rules, has little respect for past custom." The Adaptor "tends to high self-doubt. Reacts to criticism by closer outward conformity. Vulnerable to social pressure and authority; compliant." The Innovator "appears to have low self-doubt when generating ideas, not needing consensus to maintain certitude in face of opposition." The Adaptor "is sensitive to people, maintains group cohesion and co-operation," while the Innovator "appears insensitive to people, often threatens group cohesion and co-operation." And so forth.

While acknowledging the stochastic and personality components of topic selection, we shall emphasize components that researchers have some control over. These, in the end, may be more important than imagined. Successful

---

[1] See Campbell (1960), Merton (1967: 158–162), Merton, Barber (2006).

social scientists, we surmise, are not just lucky or wired for success. They also engage in activities that increase the probability of serendipity.

We categorize these strategic factors under the following headings: (a) work and passion, (b) ambition, (c) scholarly interaction, (d) reading the secondary literature, (e) appraising the state of the world, (f) the familiar and the unfamiliar, (g) specializing and generalizing, and (h) the old and the new.

For every strategy, there are trade-offs – at the very least, opportunity costs. We want readers to understand these trade-offs, so we bring them front-and-center whenever possible. Selecting a canny strategy means understanding the likely benefits, and costs, of that choice.

In discussing these implications, we focus mostly on intellectual issues. Occasionally, we consider professional issues – how you situate yourself within your discipline, relate to colleagues, organize your time, maintain equanimity amid adversity, and manage your career (Loehle 2009). To be effective, researchers must consider both angles – which, regrettably, are not always aligned (Elman, Gerring, Mahoney 2020). One would not want intellectual considerations to overwhelm professional considerations, or the reverse.

Work and Passion

Golf, Jerry Barber observed, is 99 percent luck, and 1 percent hard work. "And the more I practice, the luckier I get."[2] Scholars credited as innovators generally work harder than others. Our surveys and interviews, and our reading of the literature, suggests that inspiration stems from perspiration. We don't wish to imply that greater time-on-task will always result in spectacular insights. But it will surely enhance your chances.

There is, to begin with, an arduous path from novice to expert. Learning a field is required if one is to identify an interesting question or problem. One cannot waltz into a discovery without having learned to waltz. Background knowledge is needed, and this bar is set higher and higher as the social sciences become more specialized, more technical, and more crowded with extant literature. In this respect, proficiency in social science is no different from proficiency in ballet, basketball, or violin. It takes a long time to

---

[2] See: https://quoteinvestigator.com/2010/07/14/luck/. The idea behind this quotation has also been attributed to others including Thomas Jefferson, though no record of it has been identified in Jefferson's writings. On the role of work in creativity and achievement, see Ericsson, Krampe, Tesch-Römer (1993).

develop. Malcolm Gladwell (2008: 40) quotes the neurologist Daniel Levitin, who arrived at the "10,000 hours rule."

Ten thousand hours of practice is required to achieve the level of mastery associated with being a world-class expert – in anything . . . In study after study, of composers, basketball players, fiction writers, ice skaters, concert pianists, chess players, master criminals, and what have you, this number comes up again and again. Of course, this doesn't address why some people get more out of their practice sessions than others do. But no one has yet found a case in which true world-class expertise was accomplished in less time. It seems that it takes the brain this long to assimilate all that it needs to know to achieve true mastery.

There is, second, an extended period of trial and error in which the researcher plays with ideas, tries them out, and – inevitably – encounters failure. This process of discovery also requires a good deal of energy and perseverance.

For most of us, scholarly tasks – reading, writing, calculating, organizing, administering – are tedious if not enlivened by a sense that something important is going on. You need a bee in your bonnet, something that keeps you up at night (and, crucially, during the day). It must be important, at the very least, to *you*.

Granted, this observation applies in a weak form to any type of job and to life in general. But it has special application to academics, where there are no bosses, no regular work hours, no deadlines – no real structure except that which you are able to impose on yourself. Imposing that structure must evolve from your own sense of purpose.

If you don't have this passion, find it. If you can't find it, academic research might not be the best line of work for you. "Without this strange intoxication, ridiculed by every outsider; without this passion . . . you have no calling for science and you should do something else," Max Weber advises.[3]

Our impression is that successful social scientists share a passion to understand the world in a general, theoretical fashion. This sets us apart from the common run of humanity. It makes us boorish company at cocktail parties – unless it is a gathering among members of our tribe, in which case we can happily debate our pet theories into the wee hours. Craig Loehle (2009: 26–27) observes this "inner game."

Professional work is supposed to be an objective, dispassionate business. After all, one is dealing with numbers and facts and schedules, with machines and networks

---

[3] See Weber (1946: 135), quoted in Geddes (2003: 30).

and systems. Sometimes, however, one observes something that is infuriating. This anger is an indication that at some level you recognize that here is a problem that needs resolution. The gut feeling that the other person is wrong, or that there is a better way to do it, or that a product or theory is ugly or klunky, is a good guide to choosing an interesting topic for yourself. Setting out with irrational determination to prove someone wrong provides a drive that can allow you to break out of your preconceptions. Such base emotions can be a strong creative force, causing you to dig deep and work intensely. The effort to refute someone can even lead to evidence supporting them or to a different topic altogether. Intensive rivalries, as in the race to discover DNA, can also provide this essential intensity. Thus whereas the finished product may appear dispassionate, truly creative work is often driven by strong passions.

The first rule of finding a topic is thus quite simple: find something that interests you. Barbara Geddes (2003: 28) writes,

Curiosity, fascination, and indignation should guide the choice of research topic. Emotion has been banned from most of the research enterprise, and properly so. But one place it should remain is in the choosing of research topics. The standard advice on how to choose a topic leaves out the role of such emotions as commitment, irritation, and obsession.

Nurture your obsessions, and follow them (at least, for a while).

Ambition

The topic you choose depends to some considerable extent upon your intellectual ambition. People with modest ambitions are likely to be drawn to topics that are more easily achieved. People with immodest ambitions will be drawn to topics that are harder, less likely to succeed, but more impactful if they do.

This might seem to be a product of personality, ingrained in us – via nature or nurture – by the time we reach adulthood. But it is also a choice. One can choose to be intellectually ambitious. Howard Gruber (1989: 8) points out,

creative people commit themselves to creative tasks. In other words, they hope to make some change in the sum of human knowledge and experience. This is a commitment of some moment, and it is a choice, for it is entirely possible to make the opposite commitment: to live in the hopes of not causing a ripple.

Some observers believe that the deck is stacked against work of great scope and theoretical ambition. Adam Przeworski (quoted in Snyder 2007: 20) states,

The entire structure of incentives of academia ... works against taking big intellectual and political risks. Graduate students and assistant professors learn to package their intellectual ambitions into articles publishable by a few journals and to shy away from anything that might look like a political stance. This professionalism does advance knowledge of narrowly formulated questions, but we do not have forums for spreading our knowledge outside academia.

By the standards of the past century, contemporary social scientists seem like modest scriveners, mere paradigm fillers. Too many graduate students are browbeaten into submission by an over-professionalized discipline, one in which talk about publishing, jobs, and tenure drowns out talk about ideas. "I got one AJPS and two JOP's," says the anxious assistant professor coming up for tenure, neglecting to mention what the articles are *about* (presumably because the substance of the work is not very interesting, to them or their interlocutors).

Excessive attention to social science as a profession can rob the career of its intrinsic interest. There is nothing sadder than a professor who has won tenure in a top department but has lost the desire to conduct research. So, think about your topic not only in professional terms (How will it be received?) but also in scientific terms (What sort of a contribution will it make to your field?).

We are not saying that everyone should aim for the moon. A big project requiring substantial investment of time and money and carrying a high risk of failure must be weighed against smaller projects, usually with lower risk, that might be completed with the same investment.

However, it seems to us that at an exploratory stage it is often advantageous to adopt an ambitious scope. You can always pare things down later on. And since it may not be entirely clear which parts of the project are most feasible, we advise you to begin by Thinking Big.

This requires some fortitude, for there are temptations to adopt small tasks that seem easy to perform and produce another line on one's CV but are unlikely to have lasting impact. Aaron Wildavsky (1993: 6) identifies a "Gresham's law," according to which little projects displace bigger ones. This often occurs in response to an invitation – to contribute to a symposium, to give a talk, to attend a conference, to write a report – and sometimes is accompanied by a modest honorarium or salary.

The temptation is insidious because there is nothing wrong with the requests. Each proposal is desirable in and of itself; the subject is interesting; the research required is worthwhile; and the scholarly purpose is eminently justifiable. The trouble is that these good little projects represent diversions from the main line of scholarly inquiry. It is easy to find one's self committed two years in advance to do one little interesting thing after another, so that the whole is, alas, considerably less than the sum of its parts.

The temptation to accept trivial assignments is akin to another temptation: to chop up a research project into little bits in order to maximize the number of publishable units (Bertamini, Munafo 2012). Accordingly, one big idea can be repackaged in different ways so as to produce many smaller ideas, which are bound to be somewhat redundant. This does a disservice to the production of knowledge, making it harder to track progress and lengthening the stack of studies that future scholars will be obliged to plow through.

Once upon a time, the status of a scholar could be measured by the length of their CV. Nowadays, it is our impression that the quality of publications (judged by the rank of the journal or press), and their impact (measured by citations), matters more than their quantity (Gerring, Karcher, Apfeld 2020). One or two home runs count more than myriad low-quality publications. If so, the payoff to ambitious projects is increasing, reinforcing our admonition to Think Big.

Scholarly Interaction

In the popular mind, innovation is associated with isolation. The slightly mad genius broods pensively, alone with their thoughts, misunderstood by the world. Yet, serious-minded studies of the history and sociology of science usually emphasize its communal character. Ideas are generated in conversation – and sometimes in heated dispute – with others (Dunbar 2001).

In this section, we consider four scholarly activities that may serve as stimuli for finding and developing a topic: pedagogy, professional meetings, informal networking, and collaboration.

Pedagogy

Teaching is what most of us do for a living. It is a contractual obligation associated with faculty jobs and a financial necessity for most PhD students. Relatedly, many of us write textbooks whose goal is pedagogical. One doesn't generally think of pedagogy as conducive to research; indeed, these activities are separated in evaluations for tenure and promotion. But perhaps we should.

Bob Keohane (in open-ended responses to our survey) reports that the bestseller, *Designing Social Inquiry* (King, Keohane, Verba 1994), grew out of a course at Harvard co-taught with Gary King and Sid Verba. The first iteration of the course

was interesting and fun – and the students seemed to learn a lot. We therefore planned to do it again. At that point Gary said, "this time around, we will write a book." So when we taught the course the following year, we met every week for a bag lunch in the Chairman's Office, thrashing out the issues and discussing drafts. Gary devised the template: the systematic methods of quantitative research. The three of us together worked on adapting those methods in an appropriate way for qualitative research. We "road tested" the arguments in the course that year, then wrote up the manuscript.

Teaching a course can help you develop new ideas and figure out ways of articulating them. In effect, you can product-test the book with its intended audience.

Barbara Geddes (interview with the authors) relates that the central ideas behind her analysis of the breakdown of different kinds of authoritarian regimes started in a thoughtful discussion while teaching a graduate seminar. In her case, a routine obligation was transformed into an opportunity for thought and discovery.

Pedagogy also forces one to articulate ideas in a clearer and more specific fashion than one might otherwise. One cannot rely on academic jargon and citations to published work if the audience is oblivious to these references. Gregory Mankiw (1998: 182–183) reports,

Whenever you have to explain something to someone, either in person or on a printed page, you have to think it through more thoroughly than you otherwise would. Preparing a lecture or drafting a textbook chapter reveals holes in your understanding. And, sometimes, as you try to fill these holes, you get ideas for research.

Robert Lucas, another Nobel Prize-winning economist, concurs.

At Chicago, I began teaching graduate macroeconomics regularly for the first time in my career. This was a stimulus for me. My papers "Understanding Business Cycles" and "Problems and Methods in Business Cycle Theory" came out of the experience of organizing my thoughts on the entire field (quoted in Samuelson, Barnett 2009: 63).

Students are another potent source of ideas. Of course, they may not be in a position to judge what a good topic for research is (at least, not without a lot of background reading). But they are in a very good position to ask questions, and they are less burdened by the trepidations usual to those with advanced degrees, who worry they might look silly by asking questions that reveal their ignorance. Sometimes, "obvious" questions are difficult to answer. Or perhaps there is a commonsense answer but no rigorous research on the question. This is a good invitation to further study.

Professional Meetings

The business of academics is old-fashioned in some respects. We still hold live events – conferences, workshops, and seminars – where papers are delivered and discussed. These events are useful in ways that are perhaps hard to appreciate in the electronic age of virtual reality. And they are especially useful for those looking for ideas.

Watching a paper being delivered (live) is a very different experience from reading that same paper. The speaker will need to articulate their ideas afresh, rather than relying on carefully crafted sentences. Audience members will respond, and this will lead to a back-and-forth wherein people and viewpoints jostle for attention and for primacy.

What parts of an argument go down easy? What parts meet resistance? Where do members of the audience disagree? Assuming that members of the audience are at the forefront of their field, this is a glimpse into the frontiers of that field.

Some ideas get people jumping – perhaps with fury, but in any case, with excitement. Other ideas fall flat; they just aren't very stimulating. It is probably not worthwhile investing in a project that doesn't engender interest from others in your field or subfield.

Of course, one must be wary of excessively popular ideas; one is contributing little if one is simply following the multitude. Sometimes, the enthusiasm of a crowd is driven by their ideological approval of a topic or a conclusion. This sort of topic is not likely to be intellectually fecund.

In any case, audience response is illuminating. Academic gatherings are thus an excellent occasion to test the water, and to be exposed to new ideas.

Networking

Creative spaces are often found at the hub of a network – a conference or university where many scholars visit, a café or pub where scholars sit and chat, a hallway or stairwell where people mingle.

Those at the most central nodes of scholarly networks are blessed with more information, more timely information, and more diverse types of information than those who live at the periphery. It seems likely that this enhances their innovation (Burt 2004).

Where is the proverbial watercooler in your field? Where do people congregate? Once you have figured it out, try to attend this informal seminar.

Granted, the electronic communications revolution has to some extent displaced interpersonal contact. You can now converse with other scholars by email, blog, tweet, chatrooms, Skype, Zoom, and in dozens of other venues.

Yet, for purposes of developing new ideas and testing out those ideas, face-to-face communication is still unmatched. Steven Johnson (2010: 61–62) writes,

Even with all the advanced technology of a leading molecular biology lab, the most productive tool for generating good ideas remains a circle of humans at a table, talking shop. The lab meeting creates an environment where new combinations can occur, where information can spill over from one project to another. When you work alone in an office, peering into a microscope, your ideas can get trapped in place, stuck in your own initial biases. The social flow of the group conversation turns that private solid state into a liquid network.

In the act of communicating – and listening to others communicate, in a live, unfiltered environment – one is prompted to think about things in new ways and to make connections that otherwise might be missed.

Collaboration

An academic collaboration is a regular pattern of interaction among two academics or a small circle that culminates (at least, occasionally) in published research. The occasions for such partnerships are many and varied. Collaboration may be stimulated by a shared interest in a particular question, a friendship or romance, spatial proximity (e.g., in the same workplace or residential neighborhood), or a shared hobby. Sometimes, lifelong partnerships are the product of chance events such as sitting together on an airplane.

Sometimes, intellectual communities are assembled in a more purposeful manner, for example, in a laboratory, a fellowship program, or a workshop. Many factors serve to throw our lots together.[4] The question is what we make of these opportunities.

If innovation comes from combining things that don't normally go together, it stands to reason that a single individual is unlikely to possess them. Finding the *yin* to go with your *yang* may require reaching out to others who have different knowledge sets, methodological skills, or ways of thinking. Putting these people together in a room or on a Skype call is an occasion for a creative fusion. Or a destructive explosion. Like all things novel, you can't know for sure until you try.

Successful collaborations usually bring together researchers with different mindsets, skill sets, or knowledge sets. Consider Charles Darwin, the naturalist, and Charles Lyell, a geologist. Their correspondence and conversations over the years, which brought together two disparate fields of knowledge, contributed to the development of the theory of evolution. James Watson, a biologist, and Francis Crick, a physicist, worked closely together to discover the double helix model of DNA (Watson 1969). Daniel Kahneman and Amos Tversky, who laid the groundwork for prospect theory, although both psychologists, were very different personalities (Lewis 2016). In each of these renowned collaborations, members of the team brought diverse ingredients to the table, which seem to have been essential to the scientific advances they are credited with.[5]

There are also sociological factors to consider. Coming up with new ideas is risky. Without a working team composed of close colleagues you can confide in you may be tempted to keep these – potentially embarrassing – ideas to yourself until fully hatched. This is an inefficient mode of knowledge production. Usually, we benefit from conversations with others, and the early conversations are the most essential of all – when an idea is truly a brainstorm, extremely rough around the edges and with low probability of success. Feedback at this early stage can save countless hours of navelgazing, data mining, and literature reviewing.

At any stage of a project, working with others is often the best way to get detailed – and honest – feedback. Friends and professional colleagues have little motivation to think hard about the details of your work, or to offer

[4] See Day, Eodice (2001), Fox, Faver (1984), Melin (2000).
[5] On the importance of working in pairs, see Shenk (2014).

critical comments. However, if they have a stake in the product – as collaborators – they must engage on a deeper level and they must be honest in their responses, for their own time and reputation is on the line. If you really want someone's input, make them a coauthor.

In choosing collaborators, personal "chemistry" is important. One study reports,

The individuals quite simply have to like each other and get along well. They say that there have to be differences in their way of thinking, but also similarities; thus, they will inspire one another and open up new perspectives. They want their minds to think differently but still work along the same lines in order to understand each other. Showing and receiving respect is just another side of this coin (Melin 2000: 36).

Research should be fun. And being part of a team contributes to the fun. A little bit of competitiveness among team members is fine so long as it is tempered by generosity and goodwill. You are all in it together.

Of course, working with others can be trying. Inevitably, there will be disagreements. Inevitably, there will be moments when one member of the team does not appear to be carrying their fair share of the burden. In this vein, Nelson Polsby once remarked, "Co-authorship is when both authors do 60% of the work." One must choose one's partners carefully.

If members are aware of each other's strengths and weaknesses, they can often be of assistance; that is, after all, one of the purposes of collaboration. Some people have trouble getting down to work; a pestering colleague, or an internal deadline, may be the push they need. Some people are more engaged in person than via email. Idiosyncrasies must be attended to. In the best collaborations, the individuals in a team compensate for each other's virtues and vices.

If the team is large, and members do not know each other well, it may be advisable to plan out each individual's responsibilities – and their timeline for completion – in a detailed fashion, so there are no misunderstandings. However, most of the time these details are left unspoken, and are worked out as the project evolves. After all, the incentives of the collaborators are aligned – everyone wants the partnership to succeed, and definitions of success (centered on publication) are widely shared.

If one team member ends up carrying most of the burden, they may be granted first-author status, or a clarification of responsibilities may be added to the acknowledgments. In a research stream with multiple projects different individuals can take lead roles on different projects. Free riding on one project might be followed by extra burdens in another. There are many ways to even out the workload over the long haul if authors are involved in an ongoing collaboration.

A final payoff for working collaboratively is that you can share the pleasure of success, as well as the occasional pain of failure. Research is a lonely enterprise, with long periods of study preceding the eventual publication of results. It is enjoyable to have colleagues to celebrate with and comforting to have people to commiserate with. In these respects, being a member of a team can improve one's morale and one's productivity.

As it happens, there is a fairly strong association between collaboration and scholarly productivity (as judged by publications) and impact (as judged by citations). Nobel Prize winners collaborate at a higher rate than the rest of us, for example (Zuckerman 1967). Whether this association is causal or not is difficult to determine, as researcher behavior is not randomly assigned. However, regression-adjusted analyses as well as instrumental-variable estimates suggest that there are returns to coauthoring.[6] As the complexities of research increase, as well as the investments necessary for a pathbreaking project, it is not surprising that academic partnerships have become increasingly common (Wuchty, Jones, Uzzi 2007).

The Literature

New work on any subject evolves out of a tradition of work that already exists, colloquially referred to as "the literature." This is not a subjective prior. It is established by a field of scholars working on a topic over many years, and it should be apparent in the published work that they have produced. Even a novel topic has some sort of intellectual history. Familiarizing yourself with that history is often a useful jumping-off place.

No one has happened upon a really interesting research topic simply by reading a review of the extant literature. However, it is an efficient method of determining where the state of a field lies, from which one may intuit where the holes are and where the field might be headed.

Unmet Demand

One way to define a good topic is by identifying *unmet demand*: a topic that many people are interested in, but little has been written about. This is known colloquially as a "hole" in the literature.

---

[6] See Ductor (2015), Lee, Bozeman (2005), Parish, Boyack, Ioannidis (2018).

In our interview, Kristian Gleditsch recalls how he found his dissertation topic.

> There was a common understanding that events were influenced by diffusion, or dependence between cases. [At the same time], there was an almost complete absence of empirical work – whether this was democratization, conflict, or mobilization. That led me to think about how one might integrate diffusion into these areas of research.

Gleditsch identified a disjuncture between theoretical expectations and empirical studies – a research hole. And he dived in.

One may look for such holes in an informal fashion by searching the literature for topics that seem important and seeing what has been published on them. This is time-consuming, evidently, and judgments of "importance" remain subjective. What you regard as important might not be regarded as important to others.

Conceivably, this sort of search might be facilitated by online databases in the not-too-distant future. Two measures of demand suggest themselves. Google searches could be viewed as a signal of demand among lay publics. Google Scholar (GS) searches could be viewed as a signal of scholarly demand. In either case, search terms would receive a score corresponding to their popularity. Commonly used search terms suggest high demand.

As a measure of supply, one could use the average "fit" scores assigned to the top-10 results of a GS search. Note that the GS search algorithm, so far as we know, involves popularity (widely cited papers get a higher score than less cited papers) and fit (relative to the subject). Only the latter is relevant for current purposes.

With this information, one could match demand scores and supply scores to find those search terms that score high on the first and low on the second. These would be regarded, prima facie, as potentially fruitful topics for research as there appears to be considerable unmet demand.

Of course, artificial intelligence is not always intelligent. We can anticipate plenty of errors, especially in the early stages of this new widget. More important, unmet demand is not the only issue of relevance to choosing a topic. Lots of people would probably like to know if God exists but it is unclear whether social science has anything useful to say about this question.

Nonetheless, supply and demand are relevant components when one is searching for a topic. It is something we consider even without the assistance of massive databases and fancy algorithms. So, the idea of streamlining this search seems plausible, at the very least.

Knowledge Frontiers

What are the frontiers of knowledge? What do we – collectively, as a discipline – know, and what don't we know? What lies just beyond our grasp?

Nowadays, the trail of published research is fairly easy to follow through search engines. Google Scholar is especially useful for this purpose as it integrates both published and unpublished work – though the latter is included in a scattershot fashion and may appear further down in the search results. Be aware that there may be multiple ways of articulating your topic, so you will need to try different configurations of search terms. Once you have located a paper or book that is on target you can follow the trail of citations, that is, which studies are cited in that study, and which subsequent studies cite that study.

Sometimes, typically in the conclusion of an article or book, scholars will opine upon the future direction of research. This can be useful, though it is likely to reflect the writer's own current research, so by the time you read it these suggestions may no longer be very fresh.

Most journals will send an email alert when a new issue is published, so make sure to sign up for journals in your field. (You do not need a subscription in order to request an email alert.) However, the most recent work on a subject is usually found in conference papers, working papers, blogs, or perhaps simply as a paper title on a CV. Social media is also becoming a principal mode of communication about research in progress. So, consider whose Twitter feed to follow and whom to "friend" on Facebook.

Even so, not every work in progress is visible on the Internet. Some scholars work in isolation and are shy about sharing their ideas until fully formed. To find out who is doing what you may need to reach out to people in the field who are well-networked. Send emails, buttonhole experts at conferences, make a nuisance of yourself until you discover the lay of the land.

Importantly, the knowledge frontier is continually moving. This means that it may be quite different when you have completed your research. So, try to extrapolate from current trends. What will the cutting edge look like ten years from now?

Attitudes toward the Forebearers

In exposing oneself to the literature on a topic one must guard against two common responses. The first is to worship those that have gone before; the second is to summarily dismiss them.

Respect the tradition – don't flagellate the forefathers. There is nothing so juvenile as a reversal of hierarchies ("They're wrong and I'm right"). This cannot foster long-term cumulation. Instead, it treats social science like articles of clothing: visions must be overturned every year to satisfy a thirst for something new.

But don't be awed by the tradition either. Sometimes, tradition can pose a barrier to progress. Loehle (1990: 124–125) recalls,

Because Aristotle was so comprehensive, logical, and brilliant, his writings became the ultimate standard of truth. Galen's works provided a similar barrier in anatomy and medicine. Incremental improvements to such a subject are difficult to incorporate into the mainstream of thought, because people keep returning to the original. New facts become like little pieces of clay stuck onto a large statue: they tend to fall off or not show.

In this vein, a recent study demonstrates that when a major scientific figure dies prematurely, this as-if random event "provides an opportunity for fields to evolve in novel directions that advance the scientific frontier" (Azoulay, Fons-Rosen, Zivin 2019: 2890). As Max Planck (1968) suggested, science advances one funeral at a time.

Rather than waiting for nature to take its course, do your best to counter the impulse to venerate the stars of our time. Try stepping outside the categories that are conventionally used to describe and explain a subject. By this we mean not simply arguing against the common wisdom, but also thinking up new questions, new issues, that have not been sufficiently addressed.

Intellectual History

To deal maturely with "the tradition" it helps to know more about its history – not merely what people think now but how the subject was perceived generations ago, and how it evolved. When did writers start to ponder this question? What did they have to say? How did theories, methods, and findings evolve?

Richard Snyder (2005) reports on Philippe Schmitter's venture to a used bookstore in Rio de Janeiro. There, "Schmitter found an obscure book written in the 1930s that triggered his insight that the system of interest representation in Brazil could be conceptualized as 'corporatist.'" In similar fashion, Snyder (2005) relates,

Theda Skocpol discovered an old, forgotten book on social insurance in the United States in the early 1900s, which argued that Civil War pensions were a major social policy that would soon lead the United States to surpass Europe in the public provision of social benefits. According to Skocpol, "When I read this, it made me curious, because the mere empirical assertion that, in 1913, there was a lot of government social spending going on that amounted to *de facto* old age pensions cut against the grain of the whole literature that saw the United States as a laggard in social provision. I was skeptical at first … but I decided to look into the matter, because I had a hunch it might lead to something."

Indeed, it did – to the landmark publication, *Protecting Soldiers and Mothers* (Skocpol 1995).

At some point, you should delve into the "classics" – the founding texts of a field or subfield (Snyder 2007). This will give one a deeper feel for a subject, and it may prompt one to think about a seemingly familiar subject in new ways. Classic works tend to be evocative, and thus raise questions. A different vocabulary is often employed, and perhaps a different reference point.

Every subject has an intellectual history and it is worthwhile familiarizing yourself with this history, not merely to find a pithy epigraph but also to inform your understanding of a problem. As C. Wright Mills began his study of elites he consulted the works of Marx, Michels, Mosca, Pareto, Schumpeter, Veblen, and Weber. In commenting upon this experience, Mills (1959: 202) reports,

I find that they offer three types of statement: (a) from some, you learn directly by restating systematically what the man says on given points or as a whole; (b) some you accept or refute, giving reasons and arguments; (c) others you use as a source of suggestions for your own elaborations and projects. This involves grasping a point and then asking: How can I put this into testable shape, and how can I test it? How can I use this as a center from which to elaborate – as a perspective from which descriptive details emerge as relevant?

Not every topic is blessed with such a rich heritage; but some are, and there it is worth pausing to read, and to think.

Knowledge, one might argue, evolves from an ongoing conversation between the living with the dead. This is especially true in fields with long intellectual histories such as international relations, where contemporary debates often stretch back to Lao Zi (Laozi), Thucydides, Machiavelli, Hobbes, Kant, von Clausewitz, and other long-deceased writers. Lebow, Schouten and Suganami (2016: 2) explain,

Contemporary debates on international politics are thoroughly rooted in and shaped by the thought of many bygone minds, ancient and modern. The commitment to knowledge in international relations is that of the fox, rather than the hedgehog, to speak with Isaiah Berlin and Archilochus before him. In lieu of any kind of unified, authoritative truths, the real voice of International Relations theory is a web of conversations and unresolved debates that span centuries and continents.

To make this dialogue explicit, the authors tasked contributors to an edited volume with imagining a dialogue with a great thinker of the past in order to develop a theory or explanation of more recent events. This is a useful device for scholars seeking to think fresh on a subject. What would Scholar *X* say about Topic *Y*?

Reading Selectively

There is, of course, a danger in spending too much time with the literature on a subject. The collected works devoted to some subjects are so extensive that one can easily spend years reading and digesting. Francis Bacon opines, "Some books are to be tasted, others to be swallowed, and some few to be chewed and digested: that is, some books are to be read only in parts, others to be read, but not curiously, and some few to be read wholly, and with diligence and attention" (*Essays* [1625], "Of Studies").

You need to sift through the literature for new ideas, for new questions, for old questions that are poorly or incompletely answered. In doing so, you must read *selectively*. Wildavsky (1993: 31) explains,

One examines titles or abstracts, alighting on those that appear intriguing without necessarily being able to say why. Trust your intuition. Read the opening lines, the ending lines, a summary if provided, titles of tables, a paragraph here and there. If a spark strikes, read further; if not, go on.

Scanning is a skill with many names, for example, "skimming," "jumping around," "tasting," "probing," "following a scent," and so forth. You get the gist. Use the texts as a heuristic device to let your mind wander, to explore unfamiliar territory. See what's there, take some notes, daydream.

As you ponder the literature be conscious of what excites you and what bothers you. Which issues are under-explored, or badly understood? Where do you suspect the authorities in a field are on weak ground? What questions have they left unanswered? What questions do you find yourself asking when you finish a study? What is *wrong* with the state of the literature on a topic?

The State of the World

Karl Marx, the quintessential scholar-activist, enjoined us to change the world, not simply interpret it (*Theses On Feuerbach:* Thesis 11 [1845]). For those who practice the dismal sciences this impulse is natural. We are all failed revolutionaries. So, we teach, write, and argue, exercising our urge to right wrongs and fight injustice.

The desire to change the world helps to keep social science relevant to the concerns of lay citizens. We begin as ("normal") people with everyday ("lay") concerns. Over time, we usually attain some distance from our subject, qua scholars. In this fashion, the roles of citizen and scholar engage with one another.[7]

What real-life problem bothers you? And what does it take to make this normative quest a productive, scholarly engagement?

Translating Outrage into Science

Studies show that most social scientists have strong partisan or ideological identities, in addition to our professional identities. We tend to lean to the left relative to the societies in which we live, though there are also those who occupy conservative or libertarian positions. It seems plausible that these political orientations influence our choice of subjects and our perspectives on those subjects, perhaps in ways that we are scarcely aware of (Gross 2013). And there is nothing whatsoever wrong with that, even if it could be avoided.

Naturally, at the end of a project one must have something to say about a topic that goes beyond assertions of right and excoriations of wrong. The topic must be made tractable for scientific inquiry; otherwise, there is no point in approaching it scientifically. If one feels that a topic is too close to one's heart to reflect upon dispassionately then it is probably not a good topic for research.

As a probe, ask yourself whether you would be prepared to publish the results of a study in which your main hypothesis is proven wrong. If you hesitate to answer this question because of normative pre-commitments, you should probably choose another subject. Knowledge is not advanced if scholars ignore or suppress contrary evidence.

---

[7] Gerring and Yesnowitz (2006), Shapiro (2005), Smith (2003).

The world is full of surprises. Unexpected, counterintuitive relationships are emphasized by the "Freakonomics" series of books and radio broadcasts (Levitt, Dubner 2005, 2009, 2015). Well-intentioned policies such as foreign assistance programs to alleviate poverty in the developing world may have unintended consequences (Easterly 2006). And even the most horrific phenomena may bring some positive returns. Chris Blattman (2009) finds that citizens abducted by the Lord's Resistance Army in Uganda had higher rates of political participation than those who escaped molestation by this terrorist group, which he theorizes is a product of the awful violence they witnessed. In a similar vein, European colonialism has been credited with stimulating long-term economic development (Easterly, Levine 2016) and promoting democracy (Olsson 2009).

Discordant findings such as these may be difficult to stomach. However, they are highly informative because they tell us things we wouldn't otherwise have assumed. If social science is an adjunct to common sense, scholars must be willing to speak out when common sense is wrong. If the truth is to set us free, we must remain alive to its nuances no matter how uncomfortable.

In summary, one is well-advised to undertake questions that one feels are important, but not projects in which one has especially strong moral or psychological predilections for accepting or rejecting the null hypothesis (Firebaugh 2008: Ch. 1). Thus, one might be motivated to study the role of school vouchers because one is concerned about the quality of education. But one probably should not undertake a study of vouchers in order to prove what one already knows in one's heart, for example, that they are good or bad.[8]

If you find yourself burdened with a strong normative commitment that cannot – and perhaps should not – be stifled, consider writing an editorial, or a book whose perspective is rhetorical rather than scientific. Many academics maintain two intellectual lives. Einstein wrote many pieces for the popular press that had nothing to do with physics but instead focused on politics, philosophy, and maintaining one's sanity in an age of holocausts and potential nuclear wars (Einstein 1995). When not revolutionizing linguistics, Noam Chomsky was an activist and a prolific writer on the Left (Barsky 1998). For social scientists, maintaining separate identities – academic and

---

[8] In this example, the author's pre-commitment is to the general subject of education. Of course, one may question this pre-commitment as well. Perhaps education isn't an unvarnished good (Caplan 2018). In principle, scholarly activity should be philosophically unconstrained. But this level of meta-exploration is probably not feasible, or at any rate is not an efficient division of labor. Social science does not begin by inquiring about the nature of truth, justice, and reality. We take lots of things for granted.

popular – is more challenging, as the themes tend to intertwine. Nonetheless, it is possible to distinguish Paul Krugman's work in economics (published in economics journals and academic presses) and his political tracts (published in newspapers and popular presses). One mode of thinking does not seem to inhibit – and may fruitfully inform – the other.

The Times

In addition to the urge to reform the world, social scientists often find themselves reacting to events in the world around them.

Robert Heilbroner's (2011) classic study of economic history demonstrates that the great thinkers – from Adam Smith to Joseph Schumpeter – were "worldly." That is, they were intensely engaged in the times in which they lived. This embeddedness shaped their work, even if that work took a highly abstract form.

The same may be said for scholars in other fields. The failure of democracy in the interwar period inspired a generation of political scientists to study democratic survival (Robert Dahl in Munck and Snyder 2007: 137). Threats to democracy at the present time have given rise to a spate of studies on "backsliding" and populism (e.g., Levitsky, Ziblatt 2018). Wars have stimulated scholars of international relations. Scholars of the Soviet Union in the 1990s could scarcely avoid studying the fall of this iconic communist regime.

We live in interesting times, observed Mao. Perhaps all eras are interesting, at least in some respects. This state of affairs inspires and instructs. We want to understand what is going on, its causes, and its probable future course. The invitation, and the burden, of social science is to explain history as it is happening. So, read the newspaper regularly, and think about each headline as a potential topic. How would you reframe a *New York Times* article as a research question?

Of course, one must be wary about projects oriented entirely around current events. The scholar must bring something new to the table other than that which is already provided by popular venues. There is no sense in repeating well-worn verities. Since there is already a large contingent of popular writers, journalists, bloggers, and commentators at work on topics that are topical, social scientists must work hard to add value. Sometimes, this means looking at the more abstruse aspects of a big problem or putting an event into a larger context.

There is also a danger of overinterpreting stochastic events and too-quickly proclaiming the existence of long-term trends. After every

American election someone has the bright idea to proclaim it a "realigning" election. Generally, these prognostications do not bear out (Mayhew 2008). The terrorist attack on the United States on September 11, 2001, spawned a generation of work on terrorist threats, even though the incidence of actual terrorism in the West remained very low (Cordesman 2017). It was, in some sense, a red herring. These are the hazards of following current events.

To be clear, we do not discourage scholars from addressing issues of concern to policymakers and publics. Academics play a vital role in bringing social science to bear on matters of general interest (Lynd 1964[1939]). But, as with any venture, it needs to be carefully thought out. Just because there is a pressing desire to understand some phenomenon of great import does not mean that you will be able to satisfy that demand. Step carefully into the breach.

The Familiar and the Unfamiliar

With questions of method, Charles Sanders Peirce points out, "There is only one place from which we ever can start, . . . and that is from where we are."[9] The easiest and most intuitive way to undertake a new topic is to build upon what one knows and who one is. This includes one's skills (languages, technical skills), connections, life experiences, and interests. After all, there is only so much we can do to alter ourselves, and nothing we can do to alter our past.

C. Wright Mills (1959: 196) tells us,

You must learn to use your life experience in your intellectual work: continually to examine and interpret it. In this sense craftsmanship is the center of yourself and you are personally involved in every intellectual product upon which you may work. To say that you can "have experience," means, for one thing, that your past plays into and affects your present, and that it defines your capacity for future experience. As a social scientist, you have to control this rather elaborate interplay, to capture what you experience and sort it out; only in this way can you hope to use it to guide and test your reflection, and in the process shape yourself as an intellectual craftsman.

Sometimes, personal life experiences have direct ramifications for research. Hal Varian (2016: 82) reports that one day several decades ago he decided to purchase a television set.

---

[9] Kaplan (1964: 86), paraphrasing Charles Sanders Peirce. See also Finlay, Gough (2003), Krieger (1991), Mills (1959), Snyder (2007).

I followed the ads in the newspaper to get an idea of how much it would cost. I noticed that the prices fluctuated quite a bit from week to week. It occurred to me that the challenge to economics was not why the prices were sometimes low (i.e., during sales) but why they were ever high. Who would be so foolish as to buy when the price was high since everyone knew that the item would be on sale in a few weeks? But there must be such people, otherwise the stores would never find it profitable to charge a high price. Armed with this insight, I was able to generate a model of sales. In my model there were two kinds of consumers: informed consumers who read the ads and uninformed consumers who didn't read the ads. The stores had sales in order to price discriminate between the informed and uninformed consumers. Once I developed the model I had a research assistant go through a couple of years' worth of the Ann Arbor News searching for the prices of color TVs. Much to my delight the general pattern of pricing was similar to that predicted by the model.

Notice that Varian is experiencing life through a particular prism, that of the academic economist.

It is the peculiar virtue – and vice – of social science that we often experience the very things we study. By contrast, physicists, chemists, and astronomers cannot conduct research by participant observation. Paying attention to one's personal experience – as a consumer, a citizen, a family member, a friend – can open up potential avenues of inquiry. So, think creatively while you live your life. Where do you see strange patterns of behavior (e.g., wildly varying prices for the same product)? What anomalies does everyday life throw up? Why are things the way they are?

Because the business of social science is to investigate the activities of people, any personal connections we have to those people may serve as useful points of leverage. The hermeneutic act is eased if one can establish some personal connection – however distant or imaginative – with the group in question (Chapter 5).

Hopefully, a chosen topic resonates with your life in some fashion. This is often a source of inspiration and insight, as well as the source from which sustained commitment may be nourished and replenished over the life of a project.

Foreign Turf

Even so, it is also vital for scholars to stray from what is safe, comfortable, and familiar – to move from their home turf to foreign turf.

Note that the academy is emphatically *not* a representative cross-section of humanity. At present, the denizens of social science are disproportionately white, Anglo-European, male, middle class, and left-liberal in political orientation. If members of these disciplines restrict themselves to topics drawn from their personal experience and predilections little attention will be paid to topics relevant to excluded groups.

Even if (as we hope) diversity in race, sex, and national origin is enhanced in future years, other biases – that is, those stemming from social class and ideology – are likely to remain. At the very least, academics will be much better educated than nonacademics, and this is likely to color their viewpoints.

No amount of diversity will ever integrate all of the elements of society that we want to understand. Criminals, mentally disabled persons, illiterates, artists, and elites of any sort (e.g., political leaders, multimillionaires, entertainment figures), are unlikely to pursue an academic career, and might not be welcome if they did. Likewise, we cannot recruit individuals from previous historical eras to study historical topics. The living must study the dead.

It follows that social science cannot restrict itself to topics that social scientists are personally acquainted with. If we did, large tracts of humanity would be left unexplored.

Moreover, "foreign-ness" is not always a handicap. Recall that the contribution of social science is not to reiterate standard ways of viewing a subject. We have popular venues – journalism, television, conversation – for that. Social science, to the extent that it adds value, ought to explore new angles on a subject. For this purpose, being an outsider is sometimes helpful. Those who grow up in a particular milieu, or with a particular identity, are likely to view familiar topics in familiar ways. Those who come from outside may view things differently. Indeed, advances in knowledge often come from outsiders – precisely because they see things differently or bring new tools to bear.

A good ethnography, it is sometimes said, renders the exotic familiar *or* the familiar exotic. Try to think like a stranger when approaching a topic that seems obvious (from your "home turf"). Likewise, do not be afraid to export categories from your home turf into foreign territory – not willfully, and disregarding all evidence to the contrary, but as an operating hypothesis. Sometimes, the foreign-made shoe fits.

The concept of *corporatism* arose initially in the context of Catholic social theory as an alternative to state socialism. It was later adopted by fascist regimes as a way of legitimating their control over important economic and social actors. More recently, it has been seen as a key to explaining the divergent trajectories of welfare states across the OECD (Schmitter 1974), and for explaining the persistence and resilience of authoritarian rule in the developing world (Collier 1995). There are endless ways of adapting old theories to new contexts. Sometimes these transplantations are fruitful, other times, not so much.

In summary, exploratory research may be understood through the lens of what is *familiar* ("home turf") or *unfamiliar* ("foreign turf"). Both perspectives have been successfully pursued. Yet, they involve important trade-offs.

Specializing and Generalizing

Closely related to the familiar and the unfamiliar is the contrast between specializing and generalizing.

Nowadays, the virtues of specialization are widely appreciated. Scholars who make fundamental contributions to an area often spend their professional lives investigating a specific question or problem. This is sometimes necessary, as the increasingly technical techniques and vocabulary developed within each subfield makes it difficult to master more than one area of study.

And yet, specializing in a narrow field can also make it more difficult to see things in new ways. Loehle (1990: 126) comments:

All graduate students are taught that it is essential to become an expert. As a short-term goal it is, of course, valid ... As a lifestyle, however, becoming an expert can inhibit creativity. Why is this? ... The problem revolves around our mental constructs. In learning a subject, we create a network of facts, assumptions, and models. Once we think we understand something, it is linked up to an explanation and supporting ideas. This construct may not be true, but it comes to seem real nevertheless. As one becomes more of an expert, a larger and more complex network of facts and explanations accumulates and solidifies, making it difficult to entertain radical alternative ideas or to recognize new problems.

Cultivating a narrow expertise is apt to lead to work that is theoretically circumscribed or mundane. Loehle (1990: 126) labels this "the small cage habit," after zoo animals who, when moved to a larger cage, restrict their movements to a space roughly equivalent to their old cage. He concludes,

The danger in becoming an expert is that one tends to build one's own cage out of the certainties and facts which one gradually comes to know. Dogmatism builds cages in which the dogmatic then live and expect everyone else to live also.

Indeed, many of the works that we regard today as pathbreaking were the product of exotic encounters across fields and subfields. Consider the career of Gary Becker. He is known for applying economic models to areas of human action that lie far from the traditional topics of economics. In one notable study, Becker (1960) applies cost-benefit analysis to fertility, the home turf of demography. Although this is not the first thing that comes to mind when contemplating the act of reproduction, it has provided a foundation for contemporary theorizing about population growth and decline.

We should recognize that although most of us are compelled to pursue our careers within established departments, this division of academic labor does not always line up with important research questions, methods, and theoretical frameworks. Loehle (1990: 125–126) remarks that "The current system seeks to fill all the square holes with square pegs. The biology department wants one geneticist, one physiologist, and one ecologist, but they don't want three generalists who work in all three areas." Noting that few of the leading lights of science in the eighteenth and nineteenth centuries – including Darwin, Newton, and Fisher – would find a comfortable niche in today's academy, Loehle concludes, "The current rigid departmental system is confining to the truly creative person and discourages the vitally important cross-fertilization of models, data, techniques, and concepts between disciplines."

There is not much we, as individuals, can do about the way the academic world is carved up into disciplines and subdisciplines. But it is important to bear in mind that these divisions impose arbitrary boundaries around our academic lives – in most cases the residue of a very long history, which may or may not have relevance for contemporary research. So, try hard to reach outside your area of training. Talk to people in distant fields. It takes effort, but it may pay off.

To be sure, there is a trade-off between specialization and generalization. Scholars can ill-afford to become mere generalists if they are to contribute to social science problems that are ever more complex. General knowledge usually means introductory knowledge.

To combine the virtues of specialization and cross-field generalization we advise researchers to establish partnerships with those who have specialized skills or special access to areas that it would be costly – perhaps even impossible – for them to cultivate on their own. You need not be an expert on all aspects of your work if you can find collaborators with complementary assets, an issue discussed earlier in this chapter.

Something Old or Something New

One of the most basic questions a researcher must ask is whether to devote themself to a well-trodden field in the hopes of offering some new insight or to strike out in a new direction, exploring an area that has received little attention. While there is no simple answer to this question, here again, we find important trade-offs to ponder.

Something Old

A well-trodden field will offer a research question that is well-framed, a set of established hypotheses to explore, an approach or set of approaches that have been used to explore these questions, and a set of established findings, which serve as a foil for new research.

Even if the topic seems rather mundane and predictable at the outset, it may be worth a venture. Researching the obvious sometimes reveals unforeseen nuances and complications. Sometimes, truisms turn out to be false. Even if the expected answer to a question is confirmed, your research will make a valuable contribution if it reduces our level of uncertainty about this point, that is, if the new evidence is stronger than, or in important ways complementary to, previous evidence. Alternatively, you may be able to extend knowledge of a topic into a new – previously un-researched area – thus expanding the scope of a research paradigm.

Established research trajectories attract new research because someone perceives a gap that is worth filling. And there is a readily identifiable constituency for that work. After all, many researchers care about this topic and if you are able to make a contribution to a crowded field your work is likely to garner attention and attract many citations.

From a professional perspective, it may be helpful to occupy an easily recognized niche – as someone who does "X" – especially if there are journals, book series, conferences, jobs, fellowships, and grants associated with that niche. Joining a cadre of scholars devoted to a subject is akin to finding one's tribe, giving meaning and companionship to the otherwise lonely experience of academic research.

The easiest cadre to join is that which a key advisor or mentor belongs to. They can provide entry into the scholarship on this subject and the group of people who work on it. As a "student of X" you are likely to be granted membership into this network, which can be immensely useful.

Even so, a number of cautionary points must be borne in mind.

First, making a contribution to a crowded field is likely to be difficult. It may seem easy, at first glance. But one must bear in mind that smart people have been banging their heads against this problem for a long time. It is unlikely – though not impossible – that they have missed something important, and feasible.

Second, researchers are notoriously defensive about their turf. If a new piece of work contradicts their earlier finding, or in some way surpasses or encompasses it, they may put up resistance. (This is especially problematic if you are perceived as an outsider, a newbie, without proper credentials.) If established scholars do not respond favorably to your work, it may be difficult to get it published. Even if published, your work may not be widely cited, or positively cited. There are ways, of course, to frame one's contributions that flatter extant studies, rather than ruffling feathers. But, sometimes, it is essential to ruffle feathers. Journals and presses with strong editorial boards should be in a good position to recognize important work even if it threatens established scholars in that field. We do not advocate timidity. The point is simply that these professional minefields must be navigated carefully, and consequences anticipated.

Even if you are successful in getting your paper published and it is accepted by those who do research on the topic it may be hard to establish yourself as an insider – an "expert" – in an area already overflowing with experts. Crowded fields are highly competitive. Usually, the top slots are reserved for those with senior status.

Something New

The alternative is to go for a topic that is relatively unplumbed. Here, the path is easier insofar as there is much that is patently new to be said. You don't have to work hard to differentiate your work from the literature simply because there is very little extant literature relevant to the topic. When reviewed, your work is likely to score high on innovation, and you won't have to worry as much about stepping one someone's toes. A final plus is that you will vault to the top of this small field, becoming a "world expert in X."

But here, too, there are countervailing factors that need to be carefully considered.

First, you will not have a recognized academic niche to fall into or a community of scholars to relate to. The area may be poorly funded and out of synch with teaching and hiring needs. It may be difficult to convince editors and reviewers that this is a subject worth paying attention to.

Alternatively, puzzled editors may be sympathetic but uncertain about whom is an appropriate reviewer for work that falls outside their zone of expertise. Consequently, reviews of your work may be uneven and uninformed. These are the perils of sailing in uncharted waters.

Of course, all this may change. You may uncover a new field that inspires a future generation of scholars. (Every crowded field was once a lonely frontier.) This is evidently the best possible outcome. But is hard to anticipate.

Something Very Old and Therefore New

A third sort of topic is so old that it is passé, and hence new – in the sense of ripe for rediscovery. In this vein, Jared Diamond (1992) rediscovered the role of geography in human institutions, a topic that had lain dormant for decades. Gerring and Veenendaal (2020) rediscovered the role of population in politics, a topic that had not been dealt with in a comprehensive fashion since Robert Dahl and Edward Tufte's classic, *Size and Democracy* (1973). In *Rethink*, Stephen Poole (2016) offers a long compendium of old ideas – technologies, scientific theories, and the like – that were rediscovered and occasionally repurposed to fuel theoretical innovation decades or centuries later. In his words, "Old is the new new" (Poole 2016: Ch. 1).

This sort of work may be difficult for colleagues to classify, as it is both novel and retro. The point is, mining classic literature from the past can be a fruitful point of departure for future work. This is especially the case in social science, where the outcomes of interest are moving targets (the phenomena of interest may have change) and where data is generally more available in the present than in the past (if for no other reason than the fact that it has been accumulating for a longer period of time). Methods also advance, and these may shed new light on old topics even if the data itself has not changed.

Conclusions

This chapter has traversed a broad range of topics – work and passion, ambition, scholarly interaction, the secondary literature, the state of the world, the familiar and the unfamiliar, specializing and generalizing, old and new. Throughout, we have urged researchers to think strategically. What attitudes, activities, and approaches are most likely to culminate in the identification of a fruitful topic? How can you maximize your chances of serendipity?

We are reminded of the old joke about a hapless bloke who asks God's help in winning the lottery.

John, who was in financial difficulty, walked into a church and started to pray. "Listen God," John said. "I know I haven't been perfect but I really need to win the lottery. I don't have a lot of money. Please help me out." He left the church, a week went by, and he hadn't won the lottery, so he walked into a synagogue. "Come on, God," he said. "I really need this money. My mom needs surgery and I have bills to pay. Please let me win the lottery." He left the synagogue, a week went by, and he didn't win the lottery. So, he went to a mosque and started to pray again. "You're starting to disappoint me, God," he said. "I've prayed and prayed. If you just let me win the lottery, I'll be a better person. I don't have to win the jackpot, just enough to get me out of debt. I'll give some to charity, even. Just let me win the lottery." John thought this did it, so he got up and walked outside. The clouds opened up and a booming voice said, "John, buy a ticket!"[10]

Following the "lotto" analogy, *buy a ticket!* In practical terms, this means: Do things that are likely to maximize the probability that you will get lucky and develop your personal strengths so that traits associated with innovation are enhanced.

---

[10] See Comedy Central's website: http://jokes.cc.com/funny-god/1gkcpp/the-lottery-ticket.

5 Heuristics

The long "search for the key" phase of research may appear frustrating and daunting to outsiders, but I find it exciting. Why? Because for me, it is the mental equivalent of free-climbing a new rock face, using only hands and feet for the ascent, or even free-climbing solo, without any ropes, pitons, or harnesses to protect one if one falls. When one starts on a research project, one has only the vaguest notion of the best route, or of whether there is a feasible route at all. One has to discover as one goes along where, or even whether, the next hold or ledge can be found. One spends a lot of time feeling one's way, or even hanging by one's fingertips. There is the constant risk of failure. It takes all of one's concentration and focus over a long stretch of time. But the breathtaking view from the top is worth all of that, and over time one finds even the process of climbing beautiful and exhilarating in its own way.

Avinash Dixit (2014: 119–120)

To be a producer of science is quite different from being a consumer of science.

A consumer is interested in knowing what science has to say about Y (the subject of interest). If this is an important question about which much has been published, they may consult a review of the literature, a textbook, or perhaps delve into the body of published work on their own. If it is a new topic, or less studied, they may interrogate those whose work falls closest to the domain of interest, who can provide an educated guess or perhaps are aware of preliminary results from works currently in progress. Figuring out "what science has to say" can be quite challenging, especially if there are opposing views on a topic and the evidence itself is murky. However, it is not as challenging as the task faced by a producer of science.

A producer is interested in *adding* to the sum total of human knowledge. This contribution may take many forms, as discussed in Chapter 3. But it must be, in some respect, innovative – even if this innovation consists primarily of narrowing or broadening the confidence bounds around an existing finding.

This is a tall order. And requires a different perspective on knowledge and ignorance.

For the consumer of knowledge, ignorance is a problem. They want to know about *Y*, and, if science cannot provide a satisfactory answer, they are bound to feel frustrated.

For the producer of knowledge, ignorance is an opportunity. So, when ignorance is encountered the canny researcher shouts with joy. And the more ignorance there is about a subject, the louder the shout – all other things being equal. ("The present state of knowledge about *Y* is zero. *Hooray!*") In this spirit, James Clerk Maxwell, a celebrated physicist, once commented, "Thoroughly conscious ignorance is the prelude to every real advance in science."[1] Elaborating further, James Firestein (2012: 15), points out that "science traffics in ignorance, cultivates it, and is driven by it."

In this chapter, we consider various heuristics for identifying areas of ignorance. We hope that you will find this inquiry into the unknown exhilarating rather than discouraging.

Note that in order to make an important contribution to scholarship it is often necessary to think about things in a new way. For most of us, this requires some effort. Our natural inclination, drummed into us from decades of formal education, is to reiterate conventional truths.

Note also that exploration is not a logical, rulebound process. Einstein (1951: 683) comments,

The external conditions which are set for [the scientist] by the facts of experience do not permit him to let himself be too much restricted, in the construction of his conceptual world, by the adherence to an epistemological system. He, therefore, must appear to the systematic epistemologist as a type of unscrupulous opportunist.

Accordingly, the suggestions for fostering discovery offered in this chapter are often vague, provocative, or even directly contradictory. One must begin by shaking things up.

In this vein, we begin the chapter with a paean to thinking. Next, we offer a number of tricks for thinking in new ways. This includes (a) turning answers into questions, (b) play, (c) skepticism toward words and numbers, (d) error and anomaly, (e) analogies, (f) intellectual arbitrage, (g) thought experiments, (h) causal pathways and causal effects, (i) cases and populations, (j) hermeneutics, (k) abstraction, and (l) failure.

---

[1] The quote from Maxwell is drawn from Firestein (2012: 7), who has a great deal to say about the contribution of ignorance to science. See also Gross, McGoey (2015).

Evidently, these are not rigid categories and there is a good deal of overlap among them. There are many ways to think about thinking.

Thinking

Once upon a time, life in the academy was extolled as a *vita contemplativa*. Nowadays, it seems that there is a great deal of publishing but relatively little sustained cogitation.

Graduate students are under enormous pressure to complete their MA or PhD programs in a timely fashion. The allowed time frame for doctoral programs has shortened in most disciplines, as has the strictness with which deadlines are enforced. Considerable time may be spent learning methods, which is probably a good investment but is not immediately helpful in identifying a substantive area of research.

For everyone, administrative demands have grown. One might track this growth in the number of requirements attached to grant proposals, IRB protocols, and grant administration. One might also track the amount of faculty time spent in university administration. Such an analysis would reveal a horrific accumulation of "red tape," which presumably deters scholars from investing time in the apparently unproductive task of cogitation.

Most of our time is devoted to administration, implementation, and dissemination. We secure funding, oversee staffs, construct surveys, design experiments, peruse evidence, write up results, give talks, participate in conferences, sit on committees, blog in online forums, review others work, travel the world, all the while maintaining a frenetic email correspondence. Doing overshadows thinking.

Against the current of the times this book is designed to promote thinking. By this, we mean thinking in truly open-ended ways, ways that might lead to new insights. Rather than jumping at the first project idea that comes along we advise researchers to develop a variety of options and to consider the matter carefully before making a final decision. Every piece of research, even the most modest, is time-consuming. One should contemplate that investment carefully. A little thinking up front may save countless hours on the back end and may therefore enhance your overall efficiency.

By the same token, the essence of exploratory research is its preliminary nature. It is an oxymoron to say that one is conducting in-depth exploratory research. Doing anything in-depth requires time, and this investment should be reserved for a later stage, that is, for confirmatory (theory-testing) research. So, although we encourage researchers to think hard before choosing a topic, we do not want to encourage endless navel-gazing.

Time to Think

Prior to the communications revolution, it was easy to find space to meditate on the big questions. One had merely to enter a room and close the door. Nowadays, the ubiquity of information technology makes it a challenge to find solitude. Opportunities to connect must be willfully subverted – by shutting off one's computer and mobile phone, going for a walk (without electronic devices), entering remote territories without cellphone service, and so forth.

Even more threatening than communication with others is *routine*. Most of us are creatures of habit and these habits have a tendency to take over our conscious life, preventing us from thinking deeply. Loehle (1990: 129) is convinced that modern academic rituals and requirements are straitjackets that need to be shed.

The path of creativity is strewn with the bones of those consumed by the vultures of mediocrity, accountability, and responsibility. One cannot schedule creative breakthroughs, budget for them, or prove them in advance to a review panel. An entirely different, flexible approach to science is necessary to encourage creativity. The concept that time is too valuable for staring out the window or reading for pleasure is equivalent to doing lab work while standing on one's head. Free and undirected thought and research are essential. Scientists of the world, throw off your chains!

Take advantage of opportunities to switch off and disconnect. Try to put yourself out of reach every once in a while – especially if you are pondering directions for new research.

There are numerous stories of discoveries that occurred in the interstices of life – while waiting for a bus or commuter rail, stuck at an airport or in a traffic jam, or jetlagged in a hotel. It is telling that so many of these occasions arise while traveling, as this is one of the few situations where we are jolted out of our quotidian lives, bereft of things to do and left alone with our thoughts.

Thinking along Multiple Tracks

Rather than working single-mindedly toward One Big Idea, consider the benefits of working simultaneously along several tracks. Develop lots of (big) ideas. The more you have, the easier it will be to develop others. Like anything else, ideation becomes easier with practice.

Likewise, the best way to make a good choice about a research topic is to have multiple options before you. Comparing them to each other will help you identify their strengths and weaknesses. And with multiple options you are less likely to become overly committed to a single one. In this vein, Linus Pauling advises us to "have lots of ideas and throw away the bad ones."[2]

For this to work, you need to maintain a record of your thoughts as you go along. Take a look at this idea-diary every so often and see which projects you find yourself coming back to, obsessing about, inquiring about. The objective should be to keep your mind as open as possible for as long as possible (given the practicalities of life and scholarly deadlines). "Let your mind become a moving prism catching light from as many angles as possible," advises Mills (1959: 214).

Thinking Softly

Research on creativity is virtually united in recognizing the role of unconscious thought in discovery (Wallas 1926). In order to let the unconscious do its work, you need to give it a question to work on. So, once you have a question, let it percolate (Sio, Ormerod 2009). We call this *thinking softly*.

Some recent experiments suggest that sleep enhances problem-solving (Sanders et al. 2019; Sio, Monaghan, Ormerod 2013). You may try bringing a problem to mind at night so that it is implanted in your subconscious once you nod off. Sleep on it, and then revisit the question the next day.

Most problems will not be solved overnight. So, think about your question or problem now and again, without beating your head against the wall. Read about it (if there is a literature). Scribble notes to yourself. Chat with friends. Imagine dialogues with the living and the dead. Devote your spare time (waiting for the bus, walking, intermissions) to it.

If you are immersing yourself in a problem, then your mind is prepared to make connections to that problem based on seemingly unrelated intellectual or cultural activities. We will subsequently discuss how Wedeen's reading of a work of literary history opened insights into the role of humor in authoritarianism. Other scholars routinely report having similar moments, based on a conversation they had in a shop, a film they saw, or a seemingly unrelated scholarly article they read.

---

[2] Quoted in Root-Bernstein (1989: 409).

Keep a diary of your thoughts and periodically look back at it to see if you can elaborate them further, connecting features that may have once seemed disconnected – or discarding features that don't seem to fit. You may find that looking back at an idea or question after several months – or even several years – provides new insights and new directions. Perhaps your angle on the subject has changed, or you have learned some new things, or you notice a problem or possibility that was not apparent to you previously.

Asking Questions

Social scientists are trained to answer questions. That is the traditional focus of education at any level – elementary, secondary, or tertiary. We are taught to take a question and crank on it. Those who get the right answers are pronounced the winners. They are likely to advance quickly through the educational system, ending up in graduate programs and in line for academic positions.

Unfortunately, this traditional metric of intelligence does not ensure that the bearer will make important contributions to science. Once one finishes coursework and advances to candidacy there are no further exams, assignments, or deadlines. There is little oversight, period. Each researcher is their own boss. At this stage, they must chart their own path.

The most influential social scientists are not renowned for their ability to answer pre-defined questions, that is, for their knowledge of the world or their methodological chops. They are renowned because they have managed to identify interesting and fruitful questions. Einstein and Infeld (1938: 83) remark, "The formulation of a problem is often more essential than its solution . . .. To raise new questions, new possibilities, to regard old problems from a new angle, requires imagination and marks real advance in science." The art of asking good questions, not the comparatively mechanical skill of answering questions, is what differentiates path-breakers from path-followers (Runco 2014: 16–19).

Loehle (1990: 125) points out that "when Darwin wrote his book on the origin of coral reefs . . ., other scientists did not even recognize that there was a problem to be solved. When Darwin found earthworms interesting enough to write a book about them . . ., the world of science was quite surprised." Although any comparisons with Darwin are bound to be deflating, the same observations have been made about intellectual heroes in other fields.

"Why does Bob Dahl stand out so much as a scholar?" Charles Lindblom asked David Mayhew. Answer: "Because he asks such good questions." To illustrate the point, Mayhew (2015) draws out the key questions animating each of Dahl's key works.

What are the conditions under which numerous individuals can maximize the attainment of their goals through the use of social mechanisms? – *Politics, Economics and Welfare* (Dahl, Lindblom 1976: xlv).

How does popular sovereignty function in America? – *A Preface to Democratic Theory* (Dahl 1956).

In a political system where nearly every adult may vote but where knowledge, wealth, social position, access to officials, and other resources are unequally distributed, who actually governs? – *Who Governs?* (Dahl 1961: 1).

Given a regime in which the opponents of the government cannot openly and legally organize into political parties in order to oppose the government in free and fair elections, what conditions favor or impede a transformation into a regime in which they can? – *Polyarchy* (Dahl 1971: 1).

[I]s "democracy" related in any way to "size"? How large should a political system be in order to facilitate rational control by its citizens? – *Size and Democracy* (Dahl, Tufte 1973: 1).

Dahl is surely one of the most influential political scientists of the twentieth century. Although he had no particular advantage in the methodological arena, he had an uncanny ability to ask good questions. This, we believe, is what propelled his career.

So, consider how you might turn answers into questions. It is like playing Jeopardy, except that the answers and questions are considerably more abstract. And by no means easy. Robert Merton observes, "it is often more difficult to find and to formulate a problem than to solve it."[3] The *explanandum* is more recalcitrant than the *explanans*.

Play

Discovery stems from curiosity (Ball 2012; Benedict 2002). As such, curiosity must be considered a critical component in the personality of a successful social scientist. Foucault (1996: 305) notes,

[3] Merton (1959: ix), quoted in Swedberg (2014a: 38).

Curiosity is a vice that has been stigmatized in turn by Christianity, by philosophy, and even by a certain conception of science. Curiosity, futility. The word, however, pleases me. To me it suggests something altogether different: it evokes "concern"; it evokes the care one takes for what exists and could exist; a readiness to find strange and singular what surrounds us; a certain readiness to break up our familiarities and to regard otherwise the same things; a fervor to grasp what is happening and what passes; a casualness in regard to the traditional hierarchies of the important and the essential.

Curiosity, Foucault suggests, stems from the need to understand, an openness to novelty, and a willingness to transgress. This is not necessarily associated with a high IQ, an ability to memorize facts, or performance on achievement tests. The literature on invention and discovery – penned by science writers, philosophers of science, and by inventors themselves – is in consensus on this point. Root-Bernstein (1989: 408) is emphatic:

Famous scientists aren't any more intelligent than those who aren't famous. I'm convinced that successful ones aren't right any more often than their colleagues, either. I believe that the architects of science are simply more curious, more iconoclastic, more persistent, readier to make detours, and more willing to tackle bigger and more fundamental problems. Most important, they possess intellectual courage, daring. They work at the edge of their competence; their reach exceeds their grasp ... Thus, they not only succeed more often and out of all proportion; they also fail more often and on the same scale. Even their failures, however, better define the limits of science than the successes of more conventional and safe scientists, and thus the pioneers better serve science.

The key question is, "How can one best survive on the edge of ignorance?" (Root-Bernstein 1989: 408).

One way of answering this question is suggested by Richard Hofstadter (1963: 30), who describes intellectual life as a counterpoint of *piety* and *playfulness*. The first refers to the somber and dogged search for truth. The second, which saves the enterprise from dogmatism, is the intellectual's capacity to play.

Ideally, the pursuit of truth is ... at the heart of the intellectual's business, but this credits his business too much and not quite enough. As with the pursuit of happiness, the pursuit of truth is itself gratifying whereas the consummation often turns out to be elusive. Truth captured loses its glamor; truths long known and widely believed have a way of turning false with time; easy truths are a bore, and too many of them become half-truths. Whatever the intellectual is too certain of, if he is healthily playful, he begins to find unsatisfactory. The meaning of his intellectual life lies not in the possession of truth but in the quest for new uncertainties.

Echoing Hofstadter, one might say that there are two distinct moments in any research project. The first is open-ended, playful; here, a wide variety of different ideas are generated and given a trial run. The second is filled with zeal and piety; here, one grips tightly to a single idea in the quest to develop it into a full-blown theory and test it against some empirical reality. This conforms to the distinction between exploration and appraisal that underpins this book. Whatever the shortcomings of this dichotomy, there is no question that the academic endeavor requires a crucial shift of attitude at some point in the enterprise. Since we are concerned here with the initial phase, we dwell on techniques of playfulness.

What frame of mind does this require? How does one think outside the box of established thought?

Step one in this venture is to free oneself from whatever preoccupations currently occupy one's mind. Richard Schmalensee (1998: 246) testifies, "Ideas for new research projects come to me mainly when I am not concentrating on my current agenda but am rather contemplating economic issues and ideas in a relaxed, open state of mind. To most people this looks like goofing off, but it involves sustained mental effort."

Step two is to "relinquish conscious controls," to block out the academic superego that inhibits new thoughts by punishing transgressions against the tradition (Koestler 1964: 169). Koestler (1964: 210) continues,

Just as in the dream the codes of logical reasoning are suspended, so "thinking aside" is a temporary liberation from the tyranny of over-precise verbal concepts, of the axioms and prejudices engrained in the very texture of specialized ways of thought. It allows the mind to discard the strait-jacket of habit, to shrug off apparent contradictions, to un-learn and forget – and to acquire, in exchange, a greater fluidity, versatility, and gullibility. This rebellion against constraints which are necessary to maintain the order and discipline of conventional thought, but an impediment to the creative leap, is symptomatic both of the genius and the crank; what distinguishes them is the intuitive guidance which only the former enjoys.

It might be added that what also distinguishes the genius and the crank, is that the former has mastered the tradition of work on a subject. Their liminal moments are creative because they take place on a foundation of knowledge. In order to forget, and thence recombine features of a problem, one must first know.

The analogy of discovery with a dreamlike trance, although it borders on silliness, may not be far off. Koestler (1964: 210) writes:

The dreamer constantly bisociates – innocently as it were – frames of reference which are regarded as incompatible in the waking state; he drifts effortlessly from matrix to matrix, without being aware of it; in his inner landscape, the bisociative techniques of humour and discovery are reflected upside down, like trees in a pond. The most fertile region seems to be the marshy shore, the borderland between sleep and full awakening – where the matrices of disciplined thought are already operating but have not yet sufficiently hardened to obstruct the dreamlike fluidity of imagination.

Skepticism toward Words and Numbers

One can't think without words, but sometimes one can't think well with them either (Wicker 1985). Ordinary language often serves to constrain thought-patterns, reifying phenomena that are scarcely present. When we define, Edmund Burke commented, "we seem in danger of circumscribing nature within the bounds of our own notions."[4]

Language suggests, for example, that where a referential term exists a coherent class of entities also exists, and where two referential terms exist there are two empirically differentiable classes of entities. Sometimes this is true, and sometimes not. Just because we have a word for "social movement" does not mean that there are phenomena out there that fit this description – being similar to each other and differentiable from other phenomena. Ditto for "social capital," "interest group," "ethnicity," "state," "firm," and every other key concept in the social science lexicon. Words do not always carve nature at its joints. Sometimes, they are highly arbitrary.

The reader might respond that concepts are defined the way they are because they are useful for some purposes. Quite so. However, it follows that these same concepts may not be useful for *other* purposes. And since one's objective at an early stage of research is to think unconventionally, it is important to call into question conventional usages. Revolutions in thinking are also conceptual revolutions (Thagard 1992). Concepts must be brought under scrutiny.

For heuristic purposes, try assuming a nominalist perspective. Words are arbitrary lexical containers. So, put brackets around your key terms (e.g., "social capital"). Try out different cognates and near-synonyms of that word (e.g., civil society, civic association, voluntary association, participation,

---

[4] Quoted in Robinson (1954: 6).

trust) to see if that changes your perspective or offers a better fit. Another technique for thinking anew about a subject is to consider analogous terms from foreign lexicons or ancient lexicons (e.g., Latin or Greek). Often, they will have different connotations or suggest different distinctions among phenomena.

Equal skepticism must be extended to *numbers,* which also naturalize phenomena that may, or may not, go together in the suggested fashion. Here, the claim is more complicated. First, the use of a numeric measure is explicitly linked to a concept – for example, temperature, GDP, auto accidents – that is thought to be relevant in some way. Second, the imposition of a numerical scale presupposes a particular type of relationship between phenomena with different scores on that variable – nominal, ordinal, interval, or ratio, according to the type of scale. Ask yourself, does this relationship really exist? More broadly, is this the dimension that matters for understanding the topic in question? Are there other dimensions, perhaps less readily quantified, that provide more accurate or insightful information?

With respect to words and numbers – not to mention full-blown theories – it is important to maintain a skeptical attitude. Perhaps they are true and useful, perhaps only partially so, or only for certain purposes. In order to test their utility, adopt a Socratic guise of complete ignorance. Once having assumed this pose, you are then free to pose naive questions of sources, of experts, and of informants. It is a canny strategy and can be extraordinarily revealing – particularly when "obvious" questions cannot be readily answered or are answered in unexpected ways.

Ironically, much of the conceptual and theoretical language we inherit as social scientists is itself the product of creative acts of conceptual and theoretical skepticism. Contemporary studies of regime change, for example, make strong distinctions between military, party-based, and personalistic authoritarian regimes, and between democracy and electoral authoritarianism. These relatively new categories are the result of scholars' critical revision of past ideas. Linz (2000), Geddes (1999), and others asked in incisive ways whether all "dictatorships" are interchangeable. Levitsky and coauthors (Collier, Levitsky 1997; Levitsky, Way 2010) created a new conceptual paradigm by asking whether there might be a simple distinction at the core of a messy array of terminology surrounding quasi-democratic countries. One way to honor these past innovations is to follow their example by picking *their* concepts apart and reassembling them in new ways.

Error and Anomaly

F. Scott Fitzgerald (2009: 59) declared, "The test of a first-rate intelligence is the ability to hold two opposed ideas in mind at the same time and still retain the ability to function." His concerns were far from science. But there is something in this much-repeated quotation that speaks to the task of innovation. Research in psychology suggests that people are more creative when forced to confront conflicting ideas (Kaufmann 1988: 118–119) – sometimes referred to as *Janusian thinking* (Rothenberg 1976).

In science, order is desirable as an end-product but it can be constraining when one is looking for new ideas. Consider a well-constructed textbook. Topics are logically organized and presented; each fits in its place; there are no loose ends or errors. It is coherent and complete. While this might be useful as a point of entrée it is unlikely to stimulate innovation, for everything is thoroughly digested, tied down, settled, completed.

Innovation thrives in a slightly (but not completely) disordered environment, where chaos threatens the order provided by extant theories (Langton 1992). When it comes to thinking new thoughts, error is your friend. It scarcely matters whether the error is someone else's or your own. Johnson (2010: 142) notes,

Good ideas are more likely to emerge in environments that contain a certain amount of noise and error. You would think that innovation would be more strongly correlated with the values of accuracy, clarity, and focus. A good idea has to be *correct* on some basic level, and we value good ideas because they tend to have a high signal-to-noise ratio. But that doesn't mean you want to cultivate those ideas in noise-free environments, because noise-free environments end up being too sterile and predictable in their output. The best innovation labs are always a little contaminated.

If a good theory brings order to chaos, then theorizing – by definition – starts in a state of chaos. Your job, at the initial stages of research, is to find that chaos. In some fields, chaos is not hard to find; everyone disagrees with everyone. In others, it is carefully hidden behind a wall of apparent consensus.

In these situations, keep a close eye for *anomalies* – features of the world that don't fit comfortably with existing theories or common sense.[5] If these

---

[5] See Kuhn (1970[1962]), Lakatos (1978), Laudan (1977), Lightman, Gingerich (1992), Star, Gerson (1987).

paradoxes can be solved the frontiers of knowledge are pushed forward. Perhaps, a new theory or even a new paradigm of knowledge will emerge.

Some anomalies arise out of theoretical puzzles. A forthright example is provided by Adam Przeworski, who discusses the origins of his early work (Przeworski 1985; Przeworski, Sprague 1986) in an interview (recorded in Munck, Snyder 2007: 463).

I was a Marxist, and I was trying to make political sense of social democracy. My question was, "Why was there no revolution in the West?" Marxism offered a theory that I thought was generally reasonable, which said that in industrialized countries there should be a revolution supported, if not led, by an organized working class. Yet the obvious observation was that there was no revolution and there probably would not be one. I was trying to figure out why not.

Marxism is a fairly loose theory, especially when one considers all the adaptations and adumbrations of subsequent Marxist theorizing. This leads to the rather general question that motivated Przeworski.

Not all anomalies are grand. Many point to particular empirical nuances that are not quite as they should be, or as they are expected to be.

Why was Botswana the fastest growing economy in the world for many decades, despite possessing characteristics that would seem to serve as serious impediments to growth (low levels of education, diffuse population settlement, a landlocked geography, high exposure to HIV/AIDS, and diamonds (a presumed resource curse)?[6] Why is Papua New Guinea democratic, despite having characteristics – low levels of education and economic development, high diversity – that would seem to predict autocratic outcomes?[7]

Sometimes, empirical anomalies are the product of error in measurement or estimation. Sometimes, these errors are stochastic; other times, they are the result of deliberate bias. China's growth rates may be genuinely exceptional, or they may be partly fabricated to meet political incentives – a possibility that has spurred an interesting intellectual debate (Klein, Ozmucur 2003).

Even if the case(s) is well measured and estimated, it may be dismissed by those holding fast to existing models and preconceptions. A key element of "normal science" – not to mention common sense – is the way it normalizes phenomena, domesticating them for consumption by existing theories. Sometimes, anomalies go unrecognized until a new theoretical framework

---

[6] See Acemoglu, Johnson, Robinson (2003).   [7] See Reilly (2001).

reveals them, and also explains them (Lightman, Gingerich 1992). Apparent anomalies may be explained in an ad hoc fashion or viewed as "exceptions that prove the rule." Initial resistance is a key element of Kuhnian and Lakatosian models of scientific progress (Kuhn 1970[1962]; Lakatos 1978).

This resistance may be well-grounded, given the considerable costs involved in theoretical reformulation. The bigger the reformulation, the bigger the cost and the more carefully this step should be considered. Yet, some anomalies deserve to be taken seriously. Arguably, this is especially true in the social sciences, where there is rarely a strong theoretical framework that might unify existing knowledge of a subject, and where resistance to novelty is accordingly weaker.

In our interview, Kristian Gleditsch talks about a puzzle he encountered.

I had always been interested in inequality. It was striking that even though we had all these theories indicating that inequality was an important motivator there was not much evidence to indicate any empirical connection to conflict.

Perhaps, Gleditsch reasoned, inequality matters only when one considers it as a group-level (rather than individual-level) characteristic. This perception led to a research agenda centered on ethnicity and inequality (e.g., Buhaug, Cederman, Gleditsch 2014).

If background data on a problem is readily available, anomalies can be identified by depicting the data in a graph or scatterplot. If the relationship is causal, anomalies are "outliers" (high-residual cases) that do not fit existing causal models very well. They fall far from the regression line (if the model is regression-based). This is the underlying logic behind the "deviant-case" strategy of case-selection (Chapter 6).

To be sure, the investigation of anomalies is less productive if the resulting explanation is ad hoc, focusing on the peculiarities of a specific case. One hopes that a close investigation of peculiar cases leads to generalizations that are theoretically fruitful in the sense of explaining a large number of cases. In any case, explaining a particular case offers a point of departure for a more nomothetic style of inquiry.

Analogies

William Landes (1998: 156) remarks that the trick of discovery is "to see what is right in front of one's nose." In this vein, Arthur Koestler (1964: 119–120) emphasizes that discoveries are usually "already there," in the sense of being present in some body of work – though perhaps not the body of work that it had heretofore been associated with. To discover is, therefore, to connect things that had previously been considered separate.

This leads to the paradox that the more original a discovery the more obvious it seems afterwards. The creative act is not an act of creation in the sense of the Old Testament. It does not create something out of nothing; it uncovers, selects, reshuffles, combines, synthesizes already existing facts, ideas, faculties, skills. The more familiar the parts, the more striking the new whole. Man's knowledge of the changes of the tides and the phases of the moon is as old as his observation that apples fall to earth in the ripeness of time. Yet the combination of these and other equally familiar data in Newton's theory of gravity changed mankind's outlook on the world (Koestler 1964: 119–120).

Putting old things together in new ways is sometimes called analogical thinking (Clement 2008; Vosniadou, Ortony 1989). Here, the researcher inquires, what is X like? What other things does X resemble? The genius of Isaac Newton, remarks Loehle (1990: 125), "was in recognizing that a ball thrown in the air and a planet circling the sun are 'the same' with respect to gravity." Thinking analogically means juxtaposing things that don't seem to fit together naturally.

What do boy scouts, criminal syndicates, revolutionary movements, interest groups, and nation-states have in common? Among other things, they all have governance structures.

What do schools, prisons, and mental hospitals have in common? David Rothman (1971) argues that they are all institutional mechanisms for dealing with perceived threats to the social order.

What do bodily fluids and social categories such as race, gender, and age have in common? Mary Douglas (1966) argues that they are all efforts to segregate categories and thereby avoid ritual pollution.

What does everyday life and stage acting have in common? Erving Goffman (1959) argues that they are both attempts to craft a presentation of self that meets with general approval.

What do colonialism, federalism, and corporatism have in common? Gerring et al. (2011) argue that they are all systems of indirect rule.

Another way of analogizing is to start with a particular case and ask what it is a case of. What is the general phenomenon that X illustrates? Charles Ragin (1992) refers to this as *casing*. You are likely to find that a single phenomenon can be differently interpreted – as an example (case) of A, B, or C. That is why case-based learning is so fundamental to innovation: it helps us to think in novel ways.

Another technique for thinking analogically is through *metaphor*, which in this context means enlisting a word from a different language region and applying it to the topic at hand. Shoemaker, Tankard, and Lasorsa (2004: 159) offer an inventory or terms that have been enlisted from other language regions to help understand the communications process. This list includes:

- Advocacy role
- Agenda setting
- Attitude
- Boomerang effect
- Broadcasting (comes from throwing out seeds)
- Bullet theory
- Cafeteria line
- Canalizing
- Channel
- Cultivation theory
- Decoding
- Encoding
- Enlightenment
- Flow (of news, of information)
- Frames and framing
- Gap (knowledge)
- Gatekeeping
- Home page
- Hypodermic needle
- Inoculation
- Invasion (cultural)
- J-curve of diffusion
- Mainstreaming
- Nervous system
- Page (on the WWW)
- Placement
- Position
- Positioning
- Projection
- Psychological warfare
- Receiver

- S-curve of diffusion
- Site (on the WWW)
- Sleeper effect
- Snowball sampling
- Spin
- Spiral of silence
- Stalagmite
- Surveillance
- Target (group or population)
- Town crier
- Traffic
- Transmission belt
- Transmitter
- Watchdog
- Watches the horizon for danger
- Watchman
- Watchman on the hill.

Each of these familiar terms had (and continues to have) a "home territory" and an original meaning. Subsequently, the term was appropriated for use in explaining how mass communications processes work in the modern era. In some cases, the latter usage has come to overshadow the original usage.

This extensive itinerary forces us to recognize the crucial role that metaphor plays in thinking, and in theorizing. One is tempted to say that there is no such thing as a new theory without some use of metaphor.

Consider the key terms in your neck of the academic woods. How many of these were originally drawn from other language regions? Why did they resonate? How did they prompt researchers to think about new things, or about old things in new ways?

Intellectual Arbitrage

One way to probe a theory is to extend its purview, considering its application in a very different context. This might mean scaling up from micro- to macro-levels or scaling down from macro- to micro-levels. It might mean transporting an idea to a different realm. It might mean exploring new implications of the theory: "If X causes Y, then X must also affect Z."

A lot of social science involves borrowing methods or theoretical frameworks from one setting and applying it – perhaps with some modifications – to another setting. One can think of this as a form of intellectual arbitrage.

Game theory was born in mathematics and from thence imported into economics and other social science fields. Randomized experimental methods grew out of work on crop yields, from whence it spread across the natural sciences and eventually became a mainstay of social science. Ethnography grew out of anthropology, spreading from there to urban sociology, comparative politics, and other subfields. Techniques for automated text mining and analysis migrated from computer science and linguistics into other fields.

These are major imports. Smaller imports happen all the time – so much so that we are scarcely aware of them. Keith Poole and Howard Rosenthal employed a method of scaling common in psychometrics to roll-call votes in the US Congress (Poole, Rosenthal 2000).

In this vein, Alex Debs (in responses to our open-ended survey questions) advises researchers to think about "market inefficiencies" in the production of knowledge.

Are there conversations that are not taking place because the set of scholars studying a particular question employ different methodologies and do not engage each other's work. Could it be possible to bridge the gap between methodological approaches or intellectual traditions?

Think about how your skills and knowledge match up to new areas. What can you bring to the table that others might not know or be able to implement? Likewise, think about what others might bring to your corner of the world. Note that to be successful in intellectual arbitrage you need to know about what is going on in fields outside your own, an issue discussed in the previous chapter.

Thought Experiments

Thought experiments have many uses, which vary by context.[8]

In philosophy, thought experiments help to elucidate features of morality (what is right or commendable) or ontology (what exists). For example, brain-in-a-vat scenarios allow us to envision the possibility that we do not have a corporeal existence but are, instead, brains in a vat stimulated by

---

[8] See Frappier, Meynell, Brown (2013), Gendler (2000), Hawthorn (1991), Ierodiakonou, Roux (2011), Sorensen (1992).

electrical impulses from a computer that is programmed to simulate life as we (think we) experience it. Since the possibility cannot be discarded out of hand, this thought experiment is sometimes regarded as evidence in favor of thoroughgoing skepticism (Weiss 2000).

In natural science, thought experiments help to provide insight into settings where actual experimentation would be difficult, perhaps even impossible.[9] The classic instance is Galileo's (1974: 66 f.) demonstration that all bodies fall at the same speed. Brown (1991: 1–2) relates,

[Galileo] begins by noting Aristotle's view that heavier bodies fall faster than light ones (H > L). We are then asked to imagine that a heavy cannon ball is attached to a light musket ball. What would happen if they were released together? Reasoning in the Aristotelian manner leads to an absurd conclusion. First, the light ball will slow up the heavy one (acting as a kind of drag), so the speed of the combined system would be slower than the speed of the heavy ball falling alone (H > H+L). On the other hand, the combined system is heavier than the heavy ball alone, so it should fall faster (H+L > H). We now have the absurd consequence that the heavy ball is both faster and slower than the even heavier combined system. Thus, the Aristotelian theory of falling bodies is destroyed. But the question remains, "Which falls fastest?" The right answer is now plain as day. The paradox is resolved by making them equal; they all fall at the same speed (H=L=H+L).

In history and social science, thought experiments serve a similar function, usually centered on a causal proposition. That is, the researcher imagines the counterfactual condition in situations where it cannot easily be manipulated and hence subjected to an actual experiment. If $X=1$ in the observed condition, the counterfactual thought experiment involves imagining the likely outcome when $X=0$.[10]

Such scenarios are eminently useful – arguably, they are essential – when contemplating specific cases. Note for a unit-level causal relationship it is impossible to observe the counterfactual, as a single unit can manifest only one condition (Holland 1986). As such, thought experiments are widely regarded as a key tool of case study analysis (Gerring 2017) or of any theory that attempts to explain a single case or event such as a critical juncture/path dependent sequence.[11]

In constructing a counterfactual thought experiment one identifies a key event or condition in the past and asks whether history would have played

---

[9] See Brown (1991), Cohen (2008), Horowitz, Massey (1991).
[10] See Bunzl (2004), Ferguson (2008), Fogel (1966), Lebow (2010), Tetlock, Belkin (1996), Tetlock, Lebow, Parker (2006).
[11] See Capoccia, Keleman (2007), Mahoney (2000).

out differently if this element had been different.[12] Keohane (2009: 4) offers several examples:

- If Charles I had not been executed in 1649, would Great Britain have a different political system now?
- If nuclear weapons had not been invented, would the United States and the Soviet Union have fought World War III?
- If Hillary Rodham Clinton had planned beyond Super Tuesday, February 5, would she have won the Democratic nomination for president?
- If the United States and Great Britain had occupied Iraq with twice as many troops, would the insurgency have been prevented?

Rather than accepting history as deterministic – something that had to be the way it was – thought experiments help us to recognize the contingency of history, overcoming hindsight bias. In particular, they help us distinguish elements of the past that were more or less determined (path-dependent) from those that might have gone differently (contingencies). These turning points, or critical junctures, rightly attract attention.

Thought experiments of this sort are informative to the extent that the envisioned counterfactual is *realistic*. It does little violence to the actual course of events. Otherwise stated, things could have gone differently. Ideally, the counterfactual embodies a condition that, a priori, was just as likely to occur as the factual. It is as-if random, and in this respect embodies the logic of a natural experiment (Dunning 2012). If the counterfactual is far-fetched – if it involves a great many assumptions or massive departures from the way the world generally works – it is not very informative.

The foregoing thought experiments focus on a single case. But thought experiments are also useful when pondering causal relationships across a population of cases. This is because most observational data involve potential confounders, which means that the observed covariation between X and Y may be spurious. In this situation, our intuitions – our attempt to replay history in our heads – may provide valuable clues about the viability of a proposition. A few examples will provide the gist of this way of thinking.

- Would Indian states ruled in a direct fashion within the British Empire have undergone greater human and economic development if they had been ruled in an indirect fashion (Iyer 2010)?

---

[12] For further examples, see Cowley (2000, 2003), Roberts (2004), Tetlock, Lebow, Parker (2006).

- Would regions of the developing world colonized by France, Portugal, and Spain have been more democratic, post-independence, if they had been colonized by Britain (Olsson 2009)?
- Would American economic growth in the late nineteenth century have occurred at the same pace without the construction of railroads (Fogel 1964)?

Thought experiments help us to play out these scenarios in our heads in situations where it is impossible – or at any rate costly, time-consuming, or ethically problematic – to conduct real experiments. Assuming we know enough about the specifics of the research setting we ought to have some intuition about how likely these scenarios are, and hence how viable the hypotheses are. Where our intuition seems to contradict published work, or where an area is unexplored, this is a sign that the topic may merit further research.

So, try to convert your ideas into thought experiments. Probe various counterfactuals, which can be played out against the way things actually occurred in an arena. These should be as specific as possible so that the scenarios can be thought through in a realistic fashion. Otherwise, they are unlikely to be very informative.

Try out your thought experiment with others who are familiar with the research setting to see if your intuitions jive with theirs. If not, figure out why not.

Converting an argument into a thought experiment is also a good way to *clarify* an abstract or otherwise ambiguous causal argument. Sometimes these are called "magic-wand experiments" since they involve fanciful experiments that probably could never be carried out (at least not in an affordable and ethical fashion). Their purpose is not to work out a practical research design but rather to make explicit the envisioned treatment (embodying the causal factor of theoretical interest), the outcome, and the background conditions (features that stay constant) implicit in any causal argument.

If you think that low wages and sweatshop conditions in the developing world are a product of mobile capital, what is the (real or fanciful) experiment that could test this theory? If you think that a weak civil society is responsible for democratic backsliding, what is the imagined experiment that could test this theory? If these questions cannot be adequately answered your theory is not very clear – at least not in a causal sense.

Causal Effects and Causal Mechanisms

For any causal effect ($X \rightarrow Y$) there is a causal mechanism (aka pathway), M, that connects X to Y (see Figure 1.1). Although these elements of causality are intertwined, they suggest different approaches to exploratory research.

Research focused on *causal effects* often begins with an outcome of concern in an attempt to understand its causes. Occasionally, researchers start with a cause in a bid to understand its effects. In either case, the goal is to understand X's relationship to Y. At some point, this will involve grappling with the causal mechanism(s) at work in this relationship, though this may be dealt with only speculatively.

Another approach to exploratory research begins with a *mechanism* that is thought to have far-reaching applications. (This approach is *theory-centered* since mechanisms lie at the heart of any causal theory.) At some point, the researcher will be obliged to tackle the question of causal effects (To which X/Y relationships does the mechanism apply? To what population of cases?) though this might be accomplished in a more speculative fashion. Famous examples of this kind of work include Elster's writing about social mechanisms (Elster 1989, 1998, 2015), and Tilly and Tarrow's (2001) work on contentious politics.[13]

For a more focused set of examples about how interesting research can build either from interest in causal effects or from attention to causal pathways, consider the literature on inequality in politics. A causal-effect centered concern with the importance of the broad and abstract variable of inequality motivates interesting research on (a) processes of socialization, skill acquisition, and political mobilization related to education (Gallego 2010), (b) the dynamics of politicization and skill acquisition in religious activity (Smith 2017; Verba, Schlozman, Brady 1995), and (c) the ways that wealthy citizens' donations and social networks can shape the political environment (Cook, Page, Moskovitz 2014).

Moving in the opposite direction, questions about the causal process of political persuasion and manipulation in specific campaigns generated large literatures about the causal effects of variables such as timing, source credibility, repetition, and the quality of persuasive messages in framing public opinion (Chong, Druckman 2007; Matthes 2012).

---

[13] See also Hedström, Swedberg (1998).

In summary, projects may be motivated initially by interest in a causal effect or a causal process. But eventually, research must consider the other element, as both are implied by the concept of causality.

Cases and Samples

Social relationships may be viewed through the prism of individual units, for example, persons, groups, organizations, or states. This is the case study approach to social science (Gerring 2017). Or they may be viewed through the study of large samples, perhaps even entire populations. This may be referred to as a "statistical," "large-N," or "cross-case" approach to social science.

Consider the topic of *democratization*. In some studies, this phenomenon is apprehensible through the study of key cases – generally countries that have undergone some sort of regime transition – toward democracy or toward autocracy (O'Donnell, Schmitter 2013; Rustow 1970). In other studies, democratization is approached with a global sample of countries, explored statistically (Przeworski, Limongi 1997).

While these two ways of thinking sometimes seem opposed, each implies the other. If a case-level relationship is general, it must apply to a larger population. If a sample-based relationship is general, it must apply to most cases in that population (though not necessarily to all). Unit-level relationships imply population-level relationships and population-level relationships imply unit-level relationships.

Naturally, there are reasons for why topics are often approached in a particular way and not another. Case studies tend to be employed in situations where a dramatic change in X and/or Y occurs within one or several cases (where the variation of theoretical interest is rare), where it is difficult to collect data across a large number of cases, or where the large-N data is prone to confounding. Large samples tend to be employed in situations where these features are reversed (Gerring 2017: Ch. 11).

Even so, the reciprocal nature of cases and samples suggests that it may be fruitful to *flip the switch*, that is, to reverse whatever is the usual mode of thinking on a topic. For causal relationships that are typically understood across a large sample of cases it may be helpful to focus on a single case or a small set of cases. For causal relationships that are typically approached in a case study format it may be helpful to examine a large sample of cases.

Bear in mind that our objective at this stage is to gain insights, to develop hypotheses, not to provide definitive tests. One should not be too concerned with the possibility of spurious relationships when the goal is discovery. False leads are to be expected.

Hermeneutics

A well-established technique of discovery is empathic, or (to invoke the philosophical jargon) *hermeneutic* (Gadamer 1975). Here, one attempts to enter into the world of the actors who are engaged in the activity of interest – playing ball, drafting a bill, casting a vote, murdering opponents, and so forth – in order to understand their perspective on the phenomenon.

This is easier when the actors are our contemporaries and can be studied directly, that is, ethnographically or through interviews and surveys. David Gordon (1998: 117) reports his experiences interviewing trade unionists and factory workers in the 1970s. In light of the phenomenon of "stagflation," Gordon and his colleagues expected workers to be preoccupied with issues of job security and inflation. Instead, "They were more interested in talking about problems they were constantly experiencing with their bosses on the job. They complained that their supervisors were always on their case, that bureaucratic harassment was a daily burden." This led to a new research agenda in labor economics focused on the "intensity of supervision." Further research revealed, as Gordon tells it, that "the ratio of nonproduction and supervisory workers to production and nonsupervisory workers had been rising dramatically in the United States," making this country one of the most bureaucracy-heavy economies in the OECD.

You can learn a lot by listening with an open ear to your research subjects. Of course, doing so is harder if the actions took place long ago or are removed from direct observation, and must be reconstructed. However, this is precisely where hermeneutic skills are most needed, and where those skills must be most highly developed.

Social science begins with an ability to re-create or re-imagine the experiences of those actors whose ideas or behavior we wish to make sense of. Somehow, a link must be formed between our experiential horizons and the horizons of the group we wish to study. This may involve a form of role-playing (What would I do in Situation *X* if I were Person *Y*?).

To do this effectively requires some degree of sympathy with one's subjects. This may be difficult to muster if the subject is grotesque. No one wants to empathize with Nazis. But the hermeneutic challenge remains; some way must be found to enter into the lives and perceptions of these historical actors in order to explain their behavior. The stranger that behavior, the greater the need for intuition.

Human action must make sense (on some level) to the actor. The actor's behavior need not be rational (however that vexed concept might be defined). But it must make sense, in some fashion. There are reasons why individuals do things. And wherever large numbers of people do things together these reasons are likely to be carefully considered and articulated. To understand their behavior, and their reasons, is not to excuse it.

Hermeneutic understandings are hypotheses. Like other sorts of hypotheses, they are prone to error. We should not assume that our intuitions about the "native's point of view" (Geertz 1974), or even our own point of view (Nisbett and Wilson 1977), are correct. After all, the world is filled with self-serving, but misleading, rationalizations. Indeed, for any individual there are probably multiple reconstructions that could make sense of their activity. Ideally, these generate testable hypotheses.

For example, in the 1990s, there was a widespread view among left-leaning actors that presidents in Latin America pursued privatization of state-owned enterprises for fundamentally corrupt reasons: they would get some kind of payoff or other personal reward from wealthy individuals and corporations in exchange for the sale of government property. Susan Stokes (2001) considered this perspective, but also another: perhaps presidents adopted privatization and other "neoliberal" policies, even after promising not to do so, because they sincerely believed that they were the best solution to their countries' problems, and because they anticipated reaping an electoral reward at the next election. She then explores at length what a president would be expected to believe or do under these alternative interpretations.

Sometimes, interpretation is regarded as a specialized skill, one possessed by ethnographers (Geertz 1973, 1974) and historians (Walters 1980). We have no doubt that some individuals are uniquely gifted in this capacity. But, like any skill – for example, statistics or formal theory – interpretation can be practiced and improved upon. Indeed, this skill is so central to the social-scientific enterprise that it cannot be dispensed with and is probably employed on an everyday basis even by those who would eschew the labels "interpretivism" and "hermeneutics."

Abstraction

To affirm that "we are all interpretivists" does not imply that theorizing should focus *only* on the meanings ascribed to actions by the actors themselves. Sometimes, actors are unwilling to admit the true reasons for their actions. Sometimes, they are unaware. Indeed, many theories – for example, the cost-benefit theory of fertility, discussed previously – stretch far outside the perceptions of actors.

Making sense of a phenomenon in ways that are useful for social science usually means abstracting from the reality of lived experience to a more theoretical perspective. What is *really* going on here? What is the deeper meaning?

In this fashion, Clifford Geertz (1973) proposes that a Balinese cockfight exemplifies much more than a betting game (its ostensive meaning); it embodies a search for status and membership within a highly stratified Balinese society. Interpretivism, in Geertz's vision, does not mean one must accept the perspective of one's interlocutors, though it does mean that the proposed explanation should incorporate – make sense of, be consistent with – the subjects under study.[14]

To help this process along, you might try the following exercise.[15] Describe a phenomenon without using any of the particulars of the case. Or, in words made famous by Przeworski and Teune (1970), "omit proper nouns." By following this stricture, one is forced to abstract from the particulars to the general case.

Another way to abstract from reality is to reconfigure that reality through the lens of *ideal-types* (Weber 1949). Ideal-types exhibit features of the world in a more perfect, ideal, or extreme form. They are specifically recommended by Weber as heuristic devices, and are not intended to be entirely realistic (Swedberg 2014a: 62–63). As such, they are useful tools for thinking, aka "stylized facts."

When considering the possible impact of the middle class on democracy (Lipset 1959), one might consider the concept of "middle class" as an ideal-type,

---

[14] Granted, some writers propose to limit explanation to the explanations offered by the subjects themselves, or those they would recognize and approve. But this perspective is not very popular in social science (outside of anthropology, which we have not included in our definition of social science) and seems antithetical to a generalizing science.

[15] Credited to Bernie Beck, and described by Becker (1998: 126) and Swedberg (2019: 11).

including all those features that seem to distinguish middle classes from other classes.

When considering the possible impact of the demographic transition on development (Dyson 2001; Kirk 1996), one might consider the concept of "demographic transition" as an ideal-type, including all those features that seem to distinguish this point in time from the pre- and post-transition eras.

One may commit these acts of cogitation even if the posited traits are never found together in one place, that is, if the type remains ideal that is never entirely realized in practice. Note that we do this habitually with lots of social science concepts. "Social equality" has a meaning even though no perfectly egalitarian society has ever been identified. In this instance, and many others, an ideal-type allows us to abstract from reality to more clearly identify relationships that would otherwise remain obscure.

A final abstracting heuristic is the *paradigm-case*. These are cases that, by virtue of their theoretical or everyday prominence, help to define a phenomenon. Consider the way the French Revolution defines revolution, the American civil rights movement defines social movements, the Holocaust defines genocide, "9/11" defines modern terrorism, and the Soviet Union defines communism. Paradigm-cases exist in virtually every realm of social science inquiry. They often provide good points of entry into a topic because they are overloaded with attributes. In this respect, they operate like ideal-types.

Of course, at the end of the day we must remind ourselves that ideal-types are theoretical constructs, and paradigm-cases may be far from normal. Generalizing from these stylized facts may be fraught. But our concern at present is with theory-generation, not theory-testing. Just as physicists talk about relationships among objects in perfect vacuums (which do not exist anywhere), we may talk about entities in their "ideal" or "paradigmatic" forms.

Failures

Not all ideas pan out. Perhaps the hypothesis is incorrect or is not generalizable, or the method is not as tractable as anticipated. While this might seem like the worst possible outcome it is important to recognize that a key component of academic work – or any sort of problem-solving – is being *wrong* (Firestein 2015; Schultz 2010).

Acknowledging a mistake requires courage. Most researchers will go to great lengths to avoid taking positions on matters they are not absolutely certain of. Once they have made a public statement on a subject, they are likely to defend themselves vigorously against any suggestion of error. For error is viewed as a sign of stupidity, carelessness, bias, or fraud.

This has led to a species of academic *timidity* (with respect to propounding new ideas) and *obstinacy* (with respect to defending ideas one has propounded) that is not conducive to scientific progress. In these respects, our quest to avoid error hampers our collective capacity to move closer to the truth.

Granted, some mistakes are the fault of the author. They could, and should, have been rectified. Some faults are egregious. Researchers who commit fraud are rightly excoriated and driven out of the profession.

However, most mistakes – the vast majority, we believe – are honest mistakes. The idea was highly plausible, and method of testing and reporting was not intentionally biased. The author did their level best.

We must recognize, with Karl Popper, that all truth is uncertain, and new ideas especially so. We must also recognize, with Popper (and nearly every other philosopher or historian of science), that science is a communal activity. As such, we must trust ourselves to put new ideas forward, while acknowledging their uncertainty. And we must trust others to regard this effort charitably, as an occasion for communal brain-scratching rather than one-upmanship.

In a humorous missive, Nisbett (1990: 1079) takes note of the intellectual atmosphere of a "well-known East-coast department" of psychology where,

Every student lived in terror of the faculty's critical skills. Each member of the faculty could find six flaws in every design, 12 artifactual explanations for every finding, and 24 predecessors for every alleged original idea. Every student adopted that same stance toward his or her fellows. And, most important, that critical stance became part of the scientific conscience of every student.

This sort of environment, common on university campuses, is not conducive to creative thinking.

Again, one must remember that the progress of science is assisted by arguments that prove true as well as arguments that prove false. Sometimes, it is easier to disprove a (false) hypothesis than to prove a (true) hypothesis. In this manner, the set of plausible truths – for example, the possible explanations for a given outcome – is narrowed. These are occasions to celebrate, and the propounder of the false hypothesis should receive their share of the acclaim.

Einstein remarks, "Science can progress on the basis of error as long as it is not trivial" (quoted in Simonton 1995: 91). This recalls Bertrand Russell's witticism: it is better to be definitely wrong than vaguely right (paraphrased by Kaplan 1964: 345). It follows that a key element of working in a creative mode is making mistakes. Give yourself license.

If a project has been completed (there is something that could be called a "result"), do your best to publish it. If no journals or presses are interested, post it as a working paper on SSRN or some other site. This is essential. Failures can contribute to progress only if they are known. (Of course, you the author have benefited but one would like the discipline at large to benefit from that knowledge as well.)

If a project fails prior to completion, you must acknowledge this fact. This is a hard truth to reconcile oneself to, especially if one has made a substantial investment in the project and if (as is likely) one feels emotionally committed to it. However, once you realize that a project is unlikely to pan out you must move on – presumably, to other project ideas.

Sometimes, the lesson from repeated failure is to persevere. Keep trying 'til you get it right. However, there is a danger of interrogating the data until it confesses or continuing to adapt a theory in an ad hoc fashion until it fits the data. The result may have little generalizability. It may not even make sense of the data generating process at hand.

Try your best to avoid the fallacy of sunk costs. Even if you have invested considerable time and energy in a topic, the relevant question is not what you have already done but what you might do, going forward. If a project seems like a quagmire, don't wade further into the muck. Every successful scholar who has been around for a while has left plenty of so-called failures behind. It is the unsuccessful scholar who continues to flog a failed project.

To Henry Ford, "Failure is the opportunity to begin again more intelligently." Simonton (1995: 91) points out that "the most successful creators tend to be those with the most failures." Indeed, without failure, there is no success. This is true as a matter of logic and as a matter of practice.

In the business world, entrepreneurs have come to view failure as prologue to future success. We in the social sciences would do well to adopt the same attitude – especially as there is generally a lot less money at stake. Moreover, many academics enjoy job security. Failure to prove a hypothesis is not a fireable offense. Thank goodness.

Conclusions

In this chapter, we have set forth a series of heuristics that may help researchers find areas of ignorance – if you prefer, "areas of greater than usual ignorance." This is in recognition that science thrives on the unknown (but hopefully knowable). George Bernard Shaw once remarked, "Science is always wrong. It never solves a problem without creating 10 more" (quoted in Firestein 2012: 28). That is a good description of a productive field, which poses more questions than answers. A dead field is one where all the questions worth answering have already been answered or have been given up as unanswerable. So, try to choose a field or a question that is drowning in ignorance.

But do not imagine that ignorance will turn to solid knowledge in the blink of an eye. When thinking about scientific discovery most people imagine a "Eureka" moment, when the pieces of a puzzle fall into place and the key to a phenomenon becomes apparent to the researcher.[16] Frederic Holmes (2004: 172–173) provides some illustrative examples from the history of natural science.

The most famous of these are the accounts by August Kekulé of the dreamlike state in which he first envisioned atoms linked together in chains while riding on an omnibus; and that by Henri Poincaré of his recognition, just at the moment when he put his foot on the step of an autobus, that the transformations he had used to define what he called "Fuchsian functions were identical with those of non-Euclidian geometry." Charles Darwin testified that when he happened to read Malthus on *population*, "it struck me that under these circumstances favourable variations would tend to be preserved and unfavourable ones destroyed. The result would be the formation of new species. Here, then, I had at last got a theory by which to work." Concerning the "tendency in organic beings … to diverge in character as they become modified," Darwin wrote, "I can remember the very spot in the road, whilst in my carriage, when to my joy the solution occurred to me." More recently, the immunologist Niels Jerne has related that the idea for the selection theory of antibody formation came to him while he was walking home in Copenhagen, and James Watson has described the moment when, while tinkering with a mechanical set of the four bases contained in DNA, he became aware that they fitted together in two pairs, each of the same overall dimensions.

---

[16] See Irvine (2015), Klein (2013), Koestler (1964).

Nearly half of the respondents to our faculty survey reported a "lightbulb" moment when the pieces of a project came together (see Figure 2.6), so this vision of scientific discovery may not be so unusual.

On the other hand, it is possible that our survey respondents suffer from hindsight bias. Perhaps, intellectual developments were not quite so sudden or dramatic as later described (Gruber 1989). From this perspective, progress in social science is akin to Max Weber's (1946) description of politics – "a strong and slow boring of hard boards."

In seeking discovery, we should not expect sudden revelations in which the heavens open and truths are revealed. By our reckoning, insight usually occurs in a more gradual fashion. But this should not discourage the search for innovation or the leap for unexpected truths.

Part III

Playing with Data

In Part II, we offered suggestions about how to play with ideas – the ideational angle. In this part of the book, we focus on data – the empirical angle. By this, we do not mean testing – the usual way of thinking about empirics. Instead, we mean data exploration, the use of data to suggest hypotheses.

One such approach centers on individual cases, which can usually be mined for information more readily than large samples. Chapter 6 offers a menu of options for *selecting cases* when the goal is exploratory, rather than confirmatory.

Another approach centers on methods of analysis. Chapter 7 offers three general techniques for *soaking and poking*. We categorize these as ethnographic, archival, and statistical. Each is approached as a mode of generating ideas for new projects.

6   Case Selection

Immersion in the particular proved, as usual, essential for the catching of anything general.

Albert Hirschman (1967: 3)

One way to explore a topic is to focus on one or several examples of a phenomenon, a *case-based* approach to exploratory research. Here, the case serves as a heuristic tool to identify a fruitful causal hypothesis.

To do so, one must first select a case, or a small set of cases, for in-depth analysis. A case might be an individual, community, organization, event, country, or any relatively bounded unit.

For exploratory purposes, several case-selection techniques are plausible. These may be classified as *extreme, index, deviant, most-similar,* or *diverse.* Their essential features are summarized in Table 6.1.

These five case-selection strategies are designed primarily for identifying a new causal factor (X) that may explain an outcome of theoretical interest (Y). Occasionally, the researcher may begin with X and proceed to Y – a new outcome that X explains. But this is much less common. Most exploratory work begins with an outcome of interest.

Importantly, if the researcher's principal goal is to identify the *mechanisms* connecting X to Y (a known causal relationship) then a different case-selection strategy is probably advisable.[1] Likewise, if the researcher's goal is *descriptive*, other approaches are needed.[2] For the moment, we assume that the goal is causal.

It bears emphasis that the five case-selection strategies outlined in Table 6.1 are intended to serve an exploratory role. Once a hypothesis is identified it should be tested in a more systematic fashion. This might involve the selection of additional cases or perhaps an entirely different (non-case study) design. (Strategies of testing lie beyond our purview.)

---

[1] See discussion of *pathway* cases in Gerring (2017: Ch. 5).
[2] See discussion of descriptive case studies in Gerring (2017: Ch. 4).

Table 6.1 Exploratory case-selection strategies

Label	Cases	Criteria
Extreme	1+	Cases exemplifying the most extreme or unusual value for Y (occasionally, for X)
Index	1+	Cases exemplifying the first instance of Y (occasionally, X)
Deviant	1+	Cases poorly explained by Z
Most-similar	2+	Cases similar on Z but different on Y
Diverse	2+	Cases exemplifying all possible configurations of Z

X = causal factor(s) of theoretical interest. Y = outcome of interest. Z = vector of background factors that may affect Y.

For this reason, we do not concern ourselves with problems of generalizability and replicability. These issues should be front-and-center in the confirmatory research that follows once a specific hypothesis has been identified. At the exploratory stage, the flexibility and context-rooted nature of a case study is a feature rather than a bug, allowing the researcher to think through issues, and collect relevant data, in a fashion that would be difficult to achieve across a large sample.

Extreme

An *extreme* case design maximizes variation on a variable of theoretical interest, either X or Y.[3] This may be achieved by a single case or by a set of cases that, together, exhibit contrasting outcomes. William James writes that "moments of extremity often reveal the essence of a situation" (quoted in Singh 2015). It is not entirely clear how to understand "essence" in a social science context. Nonetheless, one may take the point that substantial variation in X or Y makes a relationship more transparent, and thus helps to identify hypotheses for further research.

Extreme cases are often regarded as prototype cases or paradigm-cases. This is because concepts are often defined by their extremes, which may also be understood as the partial embodiment of an ideal-type. German fascism defines the concept of fascism because it offers the most extreme example of that phenomenon. The Jewish Holocaust defines genocide because it offers the most (or at least one of the most) extreme examples of that phenomenon.

---

[3] The "extreme" case approach to case selection (Seawright, Gerring 2008) is understood here as a subtype of "outcome" case strategy.

Table 6.2 Extreme case exemplars

Study	Phenomena
Caldwell (1986) *Routes to Low Mortality*	Mortality
Curtiss (1977) *Psycholinguistic Study of "Wild Child"*	Human development
Fearon, Laitin (2008, 2014, 2015) *Random Narratives*	Civil wars
Goldstone (1991) *Revolution and Rebellion*	Revolutions
Harding et al. (2002) *Study of Rampage School Shootings*	School shootings
Johnson (1983) *MITI and the Japanese Miracle*	Industrial policies
Kindleberger (1996) *World Economic Primacy*	Economic development
Linz, Stepan (1978a, 1978b) *Breakdown Demo. Regimes*	Democratic breakdowns
Peters, Waterman (1982) *In Search of Excellence*	Firms
Porter (1990) *Competitive Advantage of Nations*	Economic development
Sagan (1993) *Limits of Safety*	Nuclear accidents
Skocpol (1979) *States and Social Revolutions*	Revolutions
Tilly (1964) *The Vendée*	Counterrevolutions
Vaughan (1996) *Challenger Launch Decision*	Space launches
Veenendaal (2015) *Microstates*	Democracy

Sweden defines the welfare state because it offers one of the most developed examples of that phenomenon.

Extreme cases may also be intrinsically interesting – perhaps even strange, exotic – by virtue of their extremity or rarity. However, the prime methodological value of the extreme case derives from its promised variation in X or Y.

Table 6.2 lists fifteen extreme-case studies. These exemplars stretch across the social science disciplines and cover a range of topics including democracy, economic development, human development, industrial policies, mortality, nuclear accidents, space launches, revolution, school shootings, and the success/failure of firms.

Most are focused on variation in Y, rather than X. The exception is Wouter Veenendaal's (2015) study of microstates, chosen on the basis of their diminutive size. Veenendaal is interested in how size affects the nature of politics, with particular attention to outcomes related to democracy. To do so he chooses four tiny countries – Palau, St Kitts & Nevis, San Marino, and the Seychelles – which are then examined intensively through interviews, ethnography, and secondary sources. While extreme cases on X are perhaps less common than extreme cases on Y, they can be valuable for exploratory purposes and perhaps deserve more prominence in applied research (Seawright 2016b).

Looking more closely, one may discern three versions of the extreme-case. The first exhibits extreme values on X or Y (or ΔX or ΔY). In this vein, studies of welfare state development often focus on the world's largest welfare states. Studies of war often focus on one of the two world wars. Studies of altruism focus on those who risk their lives to save others (Monroe 1996), rather than those who make small donations to a cause. Companies that are supremely successful (Peters, Waterman 1982), or supremely unsuccessful, attract more attention than companies that follow a middling trajectory. Countries with extremely high growth rates (Johnson 1983), or negative growth rates, are more likely to be studied than countries with modest growth rates. Countries with an extremely high (e.g., Guatemala), or extremely low (e.g., Japan), rate of violent crime are most likely to form the basis of case studies. And so forth.

A second version applies when an input or output is conceptualized in a binary fashion and one value is especially rare. Case studies of war generally focus on wars – peace being the more common condition. Case studies of democratization generally focus on regime transitions – continuity being the more common condition. Case studies of revolution generally focus on revolution – non-revolution being the more common condition. Case studies of space launches focus on failures (Vaughan 1996). The more unusual the occurrence the more valuable that extraordinary case becomes. Harding, Fox, and Mehta (2002) study "rampage" school shootings, noting that these events are extremely rare, numbering only 30 to 50 (depending upon how the event is defined) over three decades across the United States. This reinforces the authors' determination to focus on instances where the awful event occurred. (It would make little sense to study a school without violence.)

A third approach to achieving variation in the outcome is to choose cases lying at *both* tails of the distribution, that is, *polar* cases. Here, comparisons can be made directly across the chosen cases. For example, a study of war may focus on cases exhibiting peace *and* war (e.g., Fearon, Laitin 2008, 2014, 2015).[4] Superficially, the polar case is quite different from the extreme or rare case since variation is built in to the research design. However, one must bear in mind that studies focused on cases that lie on one side of the distribution are never focused exclusively on the chosen case(s); they always make implicit or explicit contrasts to other cases that have less extreme/rare values, which may be regarded as "shadow" cases.

---

[4] In practice, we find that researchers generally focus on only one tail of the distribution. This, in turn, could reflect a persistent feature of the world. Long-tailed distributions – with especially large variance scores – may be accompanied by skew (to the right or the left). This is true by construction for phenomena such as income or mortality, both of which are bounded at zero.

All versions of the extreme-case design maximize variation on X or Y, preferably observable through time (ΔX or ΔY). To identify such case(s) from a large population of potential cases an informal approach may be sufficient. Skocpol knew where revolutions had occurred and where they had not. But not all settings are self-evident. Here, one may employ an algorithm, selecting a case(s) that lies farthest from the mean, median, or mode of the distribution, or cases that lie on both tails of the distribution.

Index

An *index* case is the first instance of a phenomenon. In epidemiology, it refers to the first patient to contract a disease. Identifying the index case is useful for understanding the origin and spread of disease and for that reason a good deal of effort goes into the search for *patient zero*.

In other social science disciplines, the focus on index cases is also motivated by the desire to understand the origins of a phenomenon. The presumption may be that the index case plays a causal role – as a prime mover or as an illustrative or standard-setting case, establishing a practice to emulate or avoid. The primacy of "firsts" is imprinted in natural language and in the scientific lexicon, where new phenomena are often named after the person, place, or event of their first occurrence. In this fashion, the first instance of a case comes to *define* the case.

Six index case studies are listed in Table 6.3. These involve the discovery of democracy (Athens, sixth century BC), the deployment of nuclear weapons (the United States, 1945), the imposition of limited government (England, sixteenth century), revolution (Britain, seventeenth century), class formation (Britain, nineteenth century), and tax revolts (California, 1973). The

Table 6.3 Index case exemplars

Study	Phenomena
Alperovitz (1996) *Decision to Use Atomic Bomb*	Nuclear deployment
Martin (2008) *Permanent Tax Revolt*	Tax revolts
North, Weingast (1989) *Constitutions & Commitment*	Limited government
Pincus (2011) *1688: First Modern Revolution*	Revolutions
Raaflaub et al. (2007) *Origins of Democracy*	Democratization
Thompson (1963) *Making of English Working Class*	Class formation

prominent position of historians, and British historians in particular, in the genre of index cases will not be missed.

Deviant

A *deviant* case deviates from an expected causal pattern, as suggested by scientific theories or common sense, thereby registering a surprising result. The study of deviance may also be framed as the study of *anomalies*, which are widely acknowledged to play a central role in scientific progress (Elman, Elman 2002; Lakatos 1978).

Note that while extreme cases are judged relative to the mean of a single distribution (X or Y), deviant cases are judged relative to a general model of causal relations including Z (a background factor or set of background factors). The deviant-case method selects cases which, by reference to a general cross-case relationship, demonstrate a surprising value. They are "deviant" in that they are poorly explained by existing frameworks.

In a regression model, deviance can be measured by the residual for a given case. If there is considerable distance between its predicted value and its actual value, we may feel justified in calling it deviant. Since deviance is usually a matter of degrees, the residual provides a convenient method of evaluating relative deviance among a large number of cases.

Because deviance can only be assessed according to a general (quantitative or qualitative) model, the relative deviance of a case is likely to change whenever that model is altered. For example, the United States is a deviant case with respect to its "laggard" welfare state when a causal model includes only per capita GDP. But it is no longer deviant when certain additional factors measuring social and political institutions are included in the model. Deviance is always model-dependent, even if the model is of an informal (qualitative) sort. Thus, when discussing the concept of the deviant case it is helpful to ask the following question: *Relative to what general model* (set of background factors) is Case A deviant? This feature is an advantage in longer research cycles; the set of deviant cases can shift as knowledge progresses, facilitating fresh case selection across multiple rounds of research.

The purpose of deviant-case analysis is to probe for novel explanations, that is, new causes of Y. Thus, the deviant-case method is only slightly more determinate than the extreme-case method. It, too, is an exploratory form of research. The researcher hopes that evidence found within the deviant case will illustrate some causal factor that is applicable to other (deviant) cases.

This means that a successful deviant-case study culminates in a general proposition – one that may be applied to other cases in the population.

As soon as that proposition is discovered, the case is no longer deviant; it has been explained. If the new explanation can be accurately measured as a single variable (or set of variables) across a larger sample of cases, then a new cross-case model is in order. In that cross-case model, the previously deviant case should receive a smaller residual. It is pulled toward the regression line.

Alternatively, the study of a deviant-case may suggest a revision to the scope-conditions of a theory. It may be determined that cases of Type *O* are not affected by *X* (and thus lie outside the population of the theory) or are differently affected by *X*, depending upon the existence of some moderator, *D*.

Of course, deviant-case analysis does not always culminate in a new, generalizable explanation for *Y*. It might culminate in the researcher's conclusion that the chosen case is deviant for idiosyncratic reasons – reasons that are accidental or do not apply to other cases. This would be a less satisfactory conclusion from the perspective of building theory. But it may be true to the facts, and in this sense plays an important role in the development of social science knowledge. Some deviant cases are just different.

Nine deviant case studies are listed in Table 6.4. These encompass various fields and topics including economic development, welfare state development, capitalism, socialism, ethnic conflict, union democracy, and fertility. Most of these studies choose cases in an informal fashion and incorporate only one or two deviant cases in the analysis.

Table 6.4 Deviant case exemplars

Study	Phenomena
Acemoglu et al. (2003) *African Success Story*	Economic development
Alesina et al. (2001) *Why Doesn't US Have Welfare State?*	Welfare state
Amenta (1991) *Theories of Welfare State American Experience*	Welfare states
Aymard (1982) *From Feudalism to Capitalism in Italy*	Capitalism
Lieberman (2003) *Politics of Taxation Brazil, South Africa*	Fiscal policy
Lijphart (1968) *Politics of Accommodation*	Ethnic conflict
Lipset et al. (1956) *Union Democracy*	Union democracy
Pearce (2002) *Integrating Survey & Ethnographic Methods*	Fertility
Sombart (1906) *Why No Socialism in United States?*	Socialism

One study, by Lisa Pearce (2002), approaches the subject in an algorithmic fashion. Pearce begins her study of childrearing choices in Nepal with a standardized survey of ideal family size. The survey was conducted in the Chitwan Valley of south-central Nepal in 1996 and contains 5,271 respondents. Based on extant research and theoretical priors she constructs an initial model to predict preferences in family size. The model includes measures of religious and ethnic identity, gender, age, number of siblings, education, parents' education, media exposure, travel, distance to nearest city, and expectations of an inheritance. With this regression model, she identifies respondents whose preferences are not well-predicted by the model. From these outliers, she chooses twenty-seven subjects for in-depth analysis. These are the deviant cases. Following her theoretical interests, she chooses outliers that fall above the predicted line (they desire more children than the model predicts), possessing standardized residuals of at least six.

For each subject, she conducts in-depth interviews with open-ended questions designed to gauge unmeasured factors that may influence family planning (Pearce 2002: 114). Insights gained from these interviews are then used to re-code features of the survey and re-specify the regression model. For example, Pearce is impressed with the degree to which religious practice centers on the family. Accordingly, she constructs indices from the survey to measure religious practices and beliefs at the household level. This becomes an important predictor in the revised model, which improves the overall fit and reduces the "deviant" status of her research subjects.

Most-Similar

Often, fruitful analysis begins with an apparent anomaly: two (or more) cases are apparently quite similar and yet demonstrate surprisingly different outcomes. The hope is that intensive study of these cases will reveal one – or, at most, several – factors that differ across these cases and are plausible causes of Y.

This is the intuition behind the *most-similar* research design (aka Method of Difference), when employed for exploratory purposes.[5] These cases exhibit

---

[5] The most-similar method (Przeworski, Teune 1970) may also be referred to as the *method of difference* (Mill 1843/1872), the *comparable cases* method, or the *comparative* method (Collier 1993; Glynn, Ichino 2015; Lijphart 1971, 1975). Frequently, this topic is addressed in tandem with other techniques for small-n cross-case selection and analysis under the rubric of *controlled comparison, paired comparison,* or *Mill-ean* methods (Adcock 2008; Cohen, Nagel 1934; Gisselquist 2014; Meckstroth 1975; Sekhon 2004; Slater, Ziblatt 2013; Tarrow 2010).

Table 6.5 Exploratory most-similar case design

		Variables		
		X	Z	Y
Cases	A	?	0	1
	B	?	0	0

Exploratory most-similar design with binary factors, an
exemplary setting. X = causal factor of theoretical interest (to be
determined). Z = vector of background factors. Y = outcome.
Note that the assignment of 0s and 1s is an arbitrary coding
choice. The key point is that cases A and B share the same
values on all Z and differ on Y.

similar background conditions (Z) and different outcomes (Y). Knowing
valucs for Z and Y, the researcher hopes to uncover the identity of X –
a previously unknown cause of Y. Specifically, by exploring all possible causes
of Y, it is hoped that the researcher will stumble upon a factor that differs
across the cases and also seems – on theoretical grounds – like it might serve
as a cause of Y. This is regarded as the putative cause.

If factors of theoretical interest are *binary,* they may be represented in
a simple diagram as shown in Table 6.5. Note that Z and Y are coded while
X remains a mystery. That is the question posed by the exploratory case study.

If the factors are ordinal or interval, the researcher must seek to *maximize*
variance on Y (the outcome) and *minimize* variance on Z (background
factors that might serve as confounders) across the chosen cases.

Naturally, a most-similar case study may uncover *multiple* factors that
differ across the cases and seem like theoretically plausible causes of Y. In this
circumstance, the most-similar design is not very helpful. Indeed, it is not
a most-similar design but rather a *sorta-similar* design. Even so, the study
may be able to pare down the number of plausible suspects.

Seventeen most-similar case studies are listed in Table 6.6. Exemplars
include all major social science disciplines and a wide range of topics,
signaling the relative popularity of this form of analysis.

Consider John Snow's initial report on cholera in London, published in
1849, with a second greatly expanded edition in 1855.[6] At the time,

---

[6] The 1855 edition features Snow's map of London showing cholera incidents in London, reproduced in
Figure 10.5. Our account follows Vinten-Johansen et al. (2003: 206–210). For other accounts see
Freedman (1991), Hempel (2007).

Table 6.6 Most-similar (exploratory) case exemplars

Study	Phenomena
Alston et al. (1996) *Property Rights*	Brazilian states
Cornell (2002) *Autonomy as a Source of Conflict*	Ethnic groups
Dreze, Sen (1989) *China and India*	Economic development
Epstein (1964) *A Comparative Study of Canadian Parties*	Party systems
Fiorina (1977) *Congress*	US legislative districts
Geertz (1963) *Peddlers and Princes*	Towns
Heclo (1974) *Modern Social Policies in Britain and Sweden*	Social policies
Key (1949) *Southern Politics in State and Nation*	US States
Lange (2009) *Lineages of Despotism and Development*	Economic development
Luebbert (1991) *Liberalism, Fascism, or Social Democracy*	Regime-types
Mahoney (2002) *Legacies of Liberalism*	Regime-types
Miguel (2004) *Tribe or Nation: Kenya v. Tanzania*	Nation-building
Putnam (1993) *Making Democracy Work*	Italian regions
Rosenbaum, Silber (2001) *Matching*	Patients
Sahlins (1958) *Social Stratification in Polynesia*	Societies
Snow (1855) *Communication of Cholera*	City blocks
Ziblatt (2004, 2008) *Rethinking Origins of Federalism*	Centralization

physicians knew little about the source of this ghastly epidemic. Several theories were in circulation, including one based on the quality of the air (miasma). Snow conjectured that the source of contamination might be the water supply, so he had a working hypothesis. However, his initial selection of cases was not based on varying water sources (X). Instead, Snow compared city blocks where the disease was rampant with neighboring blocks where it was not – selection on Y, holding Z constant. Note that geography serves as a proxy for background factors that might affect the outcome of interest. People living cheek-by-jowl are assumed to share many characteristics – a common assumption in most-similar research designs, whether the spatial units are blocks, neighborhoods, cities, or countries. In any case, the work of the case study consisted of delving into these incidents of the disease – interviewing medical practitioners, residents, water companies, and through direct observation of the sites themselves, which sometimes consisted of neighboring courts – in an attempt to rule out features that were common (Z), and therefore unlikely to cause the disease, and to isolate the discriminating feature (X), which Snow concluded was the water supply.

A second example of a very different sort is provided by Leon Epstein's (1964) study of party cohesion, which focuses on two neighboring countries. The two cases, United States and Canada, are assumed to share a large number of background characteristics – for example, vast expanses of land rich in mineral and agricultural resources and lightly populated by indigenous peoples, a British colonial heritage, weak socialist traditions, heterogeneous populations, federal constitutions, and first-past-the-post electoral districts. Yet, Canada has highly disciplined parties whose members vote together on the floor of the House of Commons while the United States has comparatively weak, undisciplined parties, whose members often defect on floor votes in Congress. In explaining these divergent outcomes, persistent over many years, Epstein points out that the two countries differ in one potentially important constitutional feature: Canada is parliamentary while the United States is presidential. It is this institutional difference that Epstein identifies as the probable cause.

Diverse

A final exploratory case-selection strategy identifies a variety of possible causes of Y, exploring each of them in order to determine which might be true. The assumption is that the true causal factors (X) are to be found among the putative causal factors (Z).[7] To achieve this, the researcher identifies cases that exemplify variation on each causal factor, including relevant interactions.

George and Smoke, for example, wish to explore different types of deterrence failure – by "fait accompli," by "limited probe," and by "controlled pressure." Consequently, they need cases that exemplify each causal factor.[8]

Where the potential causal factor is categorical (on/off, red/black/blue, Jewish/Protestant/Catholic), the researcher would normally choose one case from each category. For a continuous variable, one must construct cutoff

---

[7] This method has not received much attention on the part of qualitative methodologists; hence, the absence of a generally recognized name. It bears some resemblance to J. S. Mill's Joint Method of Agreement and Difference (Mill 1834/1872), which is to say, a mixture of most-similar and most-different analysis, as discussed below. Patton (2002: 234) employs the concept of "maximum variation (heterogeneity) sampling."

[8] More precisely, George, Smoke (1974: 522–536, Ch. 18; see also discussion in Collier, Mahoney 1996: 78) set out to investigate causal pathways and discovered, through the course of their investigation of many cases, these three causal types. Yet, for our purposes what is important is that the final sample include at least one representative of each "type."

points (based on theoretical understandings of the phenomenon or natural breakpoints in the data), for example, dichotomizing or trichotomizing the variable, and then choosing cases with each discrete value.

If one suspects that causal factors interact, then one will look for cases that represent intersections of these variables (understood as categorical variables). Two dichotomous variables produce a matrix with four possible cells, for example. If all variables are deemed relevant to the analysis, the selection of diverse cases mandates the selection of one case drawn from within each cell – assuming there are members in each cell. Let us say that an outcome is thought to be affected by sex, race (black/white), and marital status. Here, a diverse-case strategy of case-selection would identify one case within each of these intersecting cells – a total of eight cases. In this setting, the logic of diverse-case analysis rests upon a *typological* logic (Elman 2005; George, Bennett 2005; Lazarsfeld, Barton 1951).

In choosing a small basket of diverse cases from a large population of potential cases the researcher may draw on qualitative comparative analysis (QCA) algorithms to identify the various possible conjunctures, selecting case(s) from each configuration (Schneider, Rohlfing 2016). Alternatively, within a regression framework, the researcher may explore various interaction effects, choosing cases that exemplify disparate interactions.

Eleven diverse case studies are included in Table 6.7. All stem from the fields of political science or sociology, and many fit the description of *comparative-historical analysis* (Mahoney, Rueschemeyer 2003).

Table 6.7 Diverse case exemplars

Study	Phenomena
Bunce (1981) *Do New Leaders Make a Difference*	Succession
Collier, Collier (1991) *Shaping the Political Arena*	State-labor relations
Downing (1992) *Military Revolution and Political Change*	State-building
Evans (1995) *Embedded Autonomy*	Economic development
George, Smoke (1974) *Deterrence in US Foreign Policy*	Crises
Kohli (2004) *State-Directed Development*	Industrial policies
Levi (1988) *Of Rule and Revenue*	Fiscal policy
Moore (1966) *Social Origins of Dictatorship and Democracy*	Regime-types
Rueschemeyer et al. (1992) *Capitalist Development*	Regime-types
Tsai (2007) *Accountability without Democracy*	Village governance
Wood (2000) *Forging Democracy from Below*	Regime-types

Table 6.8 Diverse cases in Moore (1966)

	Routes to modernity			
	1		**2**	**3**
	UK, USA	**France**	**Germany, Japan**	**Russia, China**
Common starting point	Agrarian bureaucracy		Agrarian bureaucracy	Agrarian bureaucracy
Key variable clusters				
Bourgeois impulse	Strong	Strong	Medium	Weak
Mode of commercial agriculture	Market	Labor-repressive	Labor-repressive	Labor-repressive
Peasant revolutionary potential	Low	High	Low	High
Critical political event	Bourgeois revolution		Revolution from above	Peasant revolution
Major systemic political outcome	Democratic capitalism		Fascism	Communism

Reproduced from Skocpol (1973: 10).

Of these studies, one stands out as especially influential, and thus serves as our in-depth exemplar. Barrington Moore's (1966) *Social Origins of Dictatorship and Democracy* is sometimes regarded as the fountainhead of modern comparative-historical inquiry, influencing a generation of scholars in the adjoining fields of sociology and political science. The study is extraordinarily ambitious – the subtitle reads "Lord and Peasant in the Making of the Modern World" – and written with a vivid narrative that manages to weave events and analysis together in a lucid fashion. Although lengthy, this book is readable to an extent that few works of social science in the contemporary era can match. No doubt this helps to account for its enduring influence. With respect to case-selection, we follow Theda Skocpol's (1973) synopsis of the book, summarized in Table 6.8. This shows that there are essentially three routes to modernity, with two or three cases serving to represent each route in Moore's study.

Conclusions

In this chapter, we have laid out a menu of case-selection strategies suitable for causally oriented exploratory research. These are classified as extreme, index, deviant, most-similar, and diverse. If one is looking for a way to identify potential causes of an outcome, this is often a good way to start.

To elucidate each approach, we listed a number of exemplars. Here, we are making an important assumption: that the authors used the chosen cases to develop their theories. An alternative reading of these works is that the authors developed their theories ex ante, using the cases in a confirmatory fashion (to test the theory). If so, these studies are mis-classified. Regrettably, it is often difficult to say for sure what the authors knew and when they knew it. However, for illustrative purposes our exemplars are well-chosen. Cases employed in these studies *could have* played an exploratory role.

While listing the desiderata of each case-selection method, we are acutely aware that other desiderata may also come into play. Foremost among these is access to the chosen case and the availability of evidence pertaining to one's research question. There is no point in choosing a case that is inaccessible or for which records – or informants – are unavailable. Other logistical concerns may also play a part in case selection – convenience, familiarity to the researcher, and so forth. Case selection is complicated, and we don't mean to minimize the complexity of the task (explored at much greater length in Gerring 2017). However, many of these additional criteria are fairly commonsensical. As such, the short primer offered in this chapter may be serviceable, at least as a point of departure.

One methodological issue bears further discussion. The reader will have probably noticed that exploratory case-selection strategies often select cases based on the outcome of interest, Y, violating a well-worn piece of social science folk wisdom not to select on the dependent variable.[9] However, the literature on selection bias and other concerns about selecting on the dependent variable suppose that the scholar is engaged in statistical estimation or theory testing; in contexts of exploration and project-finding, there is no obvious drawback to selecting on the dependent variable.

As is well known, selecting on the dependent variable is indeed problematic if a number of cases are chosen, all of which lie on one end of a variable's spectrum (they are all positive *or* negative), and the researcher subjects this sample to cross-case analysis as if it were representative of a population.[10] Suppose that Theda Skocpol (1979) examined three revolutionary countries – France, Russia, and China – comparing them to each other in a quest to understand revolution. Or suppose that Peters and Waterman (1982)

---

[9] Geddes (1990). See also discussion in Brady, Collier (2004), Collier, Mahoney (1996), Rogowski (1995).
[10] The exception would be a circumstance in which the researcher intends to disprove a deterministic argument (Dion 1998).

examined forty-two highly successful firms, comparing them to each other to understand the causes of success. Results for these analyses would assuredly be biased (Collier, Mahoney 1996). Moreover, there will be little variation to explain since the outcome values of all cases are explicitly constrained. They are all "positive" or "negative" cases.

However, this is not the usual employment of cases chosen in an exploratory fashion. First, when cases are selected on the outcome it is usually *change* in the outcome (ΔY) that is of primary interest. Skocpol looks at pre-revolutionary, revolutionary, and post-revolutionary periods for each chosen country. Peters and Waterman examine firm histories – how each firm achieved success.

Second, case study designs often incorporate cross-case variation in Y in a less explicit fashion, as *shadow* cases. Thus, Skocpol compares revolutionary cases to cases of non-revolution or partial revolution and Peters and Waterman compare successful firms to unsuccessful firms.

Accordingly, the problem of "selecting on Y" may not be as severe as some writers have imagined. To be sure, selecting on Y is not the best way to select a representative sample. But this is not a primary concern at a very preliminary stage of research. Indeed, when the goal is exploratory, it is difficult to envision a viable case-selection strategy that takes no notice of values for the outcome of interest.

Imagine a geologist who is trying to understand earthquakes but has no particular hypothesis in mind as they seek to discover the cause(s) of these cataclysms. In their quest to avoid a biased sample they refuse to consider the prevalence of earthquakes in their selection of a research site, ending up in Kansas – one of the world's more stable geological locations. Time spent in Kansas might be fruitful. However, it seems less likely to yield clues into the behavior of earthquakes than locations that lie along a major fault line, where geologic activity is frequent and leaves many observable traces.

Thus, we enthusiastically endorse "selecting on Y" as a strategy of exploratory case-selection, while cautioning against its use in confirmatory research designs. That said, even in exploration, it might sometimes be better to select on an adjusted version of Y, as with deviant cases. Such approaches can subtract out the effects of already-known phenomena, allowing scholars to better focus in on novelties (Seawright 2016b).

7 Soaking and Poking

What the devil is going on around here?

Abraham Kaplan (1964: 85)

Sometimes, a project begins with a general topic of interest or a setting which is intriguing in as yet undefined ways. The researcher may have some general sense of what they are looking for, of the kind of contribution they want to make, or of the case or cases they want to make sense of. However, this general sense of the topic may be rather diffuse. There is much ground to be covered before they can arrive at the level of specificity and detail needed for a research design.

For example, research often begins with an outcome of interest, but with a limited sense of the causal hypothesis or hypotheses that will eventually structure research, of the cases that will provide empirical evidence, or even of the specific contrasts on the outcome that will motivate the explanatory puzzle. Untold numbers of research projects have started from a general interest in the causes of inequality, democracy, national economic development, racism, war, and so forth. Having this kind of broad topic of interest is valuable; it is the seed of a project or even a series of projects, and it can be nurtured into a full-scale research question and design. However, it does not sprout of its own accord.

Other projects start with a core interest in a specific case or set of cases. A researcher may want to make sense of the conflict in Syria, the breakdown of Venezuela, the election of Donald Trump, the victory of Brexit, or the economic development of China. Or perhaps the situation is even less well-formed; instead of a case of conflict, breakdown, development, and so forth, the starting place may be a research context that is broadly intriguing. What is going on in Quebec, or Botswana, or rural Wisconsin, anyway? As with an outcome, a case or research context of interest is a valuable starting resource for building a project. But that resource needs to be developed.

In such situations, one valuable strategy for building a full-fledged project is raw induction: rummaging around in a research site, an archive, or a data set to see what is there and thereby expose oneself to novel evidence that may spark new ideas. Unexpected categories, unanticipated relationships, or unfamiliar arguments can often provide the impetus for turning a broad interest into a full-scale research project that moves the scholarly conversation forward. Several branches of methodology have clear value in helping researchers expose themselves to serendipity in these ways. In this chapter, we consider (a) ethnographic, (b) historical, and (c) statistical approaches to inductive play with evidence and data, discussing for each how they are done and why they can be valuable to the process of finding a project – above and beyond their value in exploratory or confirmatory styles of research.

For each of the families of methods discussed in this chapter, there are scholars who argue cogently that the techniques discussed here as ways of discovering new concepts, theories, and relationships can also play important roles in causal inference, theory testing, and other aspects of social science. Ethnographic research can support descriptive and causal inferences, alongside its perhaps more prototypical goal of revealing other ways of thinking about and seeing the world. Historical research in its home discipline as well as in associated forms such as comparative-historical social science or American political development, clearly offers process-tracing tests of causal claims and broader theories. Finally, it is a commonplace that statistical methods can, with proper research design, illuminate causal effects. Discussing ways these methodological traditions can be deployed to find research projects in no way diminishes their value for later stages of scholarship.

Each of these families of techniques has more and less structured versions. In distinguishing between the phase of finding a project and exploratory/confirmatory research, a dimension of flexibility versus structure is of the essence. For confirmatory research, each research tradition has expectations regarding documentation, procedure, and other formalities. Within statistical research in particular, scholars have developed a set of expectations designed to avoid false inferences based on excessively flexible patterns of data analysis. Thus, depending on the specific research community a scholar belongs to, they may be expected to preregister their research, adjust results for multiple comparisons, split data into training and test samples, and so forth. Exploratory research is, of course, more inductive but nonetheless has important formal norms related to reproducibility, transparency, and statistical techniques aimed at reducing the rate of false discovery. Historical and ethnographic scholarship have different formalities associated with exploratory and confirmatory research, but concerns about clarity of citations, transparency of interpretation, considering positionality, and a range of other issues similarly mark research aimed at speaking in an authoritative way to the scholarly and broader community.

By contrast, when the aim is to discover an interesting research question and an associated design, such concerns are essentially beside the point, and flexibility is a prime virtue. After all, the origin story of a good research project has no need to be replicable; no scholar need ever rediscover a project. Likewise, issues of false discovery, misinterpretation, and so forth are not primary concerns here. Good questions and interesting research designs retain their value even if the answer is other than the researcher initially expected. Instead, when using these methods for finding a project, the best practice is to follow interesting paths at high speed and switch directions often. Flexibly exploring more ideas, more angles, and more surprises creates more moments in which creativity and inspiration may spark.

Ethnography

Scholars in a variety of intellectual traditions across the social sciences have long recognized the special advantages of immersion and proximity to an event, culture, institution, or other object of study. Breathing in the subject matter day-to-day, deliberately encountering unfamiliar perspectives, and allowing an experience of a different reality to confront preconceptions formed in everyday life or from the scholarly literature has obvious advantages for discovering new concepts, building new theories, and generating original research.

Scholars representing a variety of intellectual and methodological traditions have discussed the advantages of immersion and hands-on experience in finding new insights that can generate projects. From the statistical causal inference perspective, Campbell argues that, "the social scientist undertaking an intensive case study, by means of participant observation and other qualitative common-sense approaches to acquaintance, ends up finding out that his prior beliefs and theories were wrong" (Campbell 1975: 182). Within the tradition of macro-comparative politics, Collier emphasizes that qualitative approaches based on deep knowledge of a single context serve "as a source of new ideas, hypotheses, and research agendas, and not just as a source of data for broader comparative research" (Collier 1999: 4). Fenno, an early practitioner of participant observation in the study of elite politics, writes that in close qualitative interaction with the people who are the subject of study, a fundamental intellectual transformation takes place: "If something is important to them, it becomes important to you. Their view of the world is as important as your view of that world. You impose some research questions on them; they impose some research questions on you" (Fenno 1986: 3).

Thus, social scientists from a wide range of intellectual backgrounds have expressed an appreciation of the role of close qualitative experience of a case, a context, or a community in finding new projects. However, in the social sciences today, ethnographic research traditions in sociology, anthropology, and increasingly political science are the center of gravity for these kinds of research activities. Ethnographers have developed impressive and diverse collections of tools for facilitating discovery based on immersion in an unfamiliar context, and they have also highlighted the ways that political and normative engagement can not only make such research more ethical but also enhance the power and novelty of resulting ideas and scholarly interventions.

It would be impossible for this chapter to fully discuss all traditions and methodologies for discovery and framing of projects within ethnography – or, indeed, within history or statistics. For each of these research traditions, pioneering scholarly voices in the tradition have provided textbooks, methodological introductions, and other intellectual roadmaps, and the present text probably serves best as an appetizer and an invitation to further engage with those resources. Nonetheless, it is useful to highlight at least some of the commonly used tools within each tradition.

From the broadly ethnographic perspective, we will highlight clusters of ideas and techniques related to observation, interviewing, and focus groups. These approaches offer a diversity of ways of finding new ideas and perspectives, and they have each produced success stories as a way of finding projects in the social sciences.

In many ways, methods related to observation lie at the heart of people's preconceptions of ethnography. Ethnographers are often imagined watching a cultural event and taking close notes, or even throwing themselves into the moment and recording their experience afterwards via detailed journaling. Such activities are stereotyped as being primarily about understanding and documenting cultural difference, perhaps with an emphasis on the study of hunter-gatherer societies in places far from one's home university.

These stereotypes are limiting, at a minimum, and to some extent entirely out of date. Ethnographers contribute to contemporary intellectual debates about economics, social policy, health care, political participation, genocide, and a huge range of other issues. They also study phenomena in contexts that are close to, as well as far from, home. So, we should have no sense that methods related to participant observations are limited in terms of subject matter or social domain.

How should a scholar approach the task of using participant observation and related methods in order to discover a new project? It is useful to frame an answer in highly practical terms. First, the researcher must identify a research site or a set of sites. Next, it is important to work out the conditions of access to each site. Finding some initial informants who can help orient the research and introduce the researcher to the community is a valuable step, as is self-reflection regarding the researcher's preexisting expectations and positionality. Participation in the planned events at each site must be combined with careful documentation. Finally, extended critical reflection on the overall experience provides the best opportunities for discovering new ideas and projects.

Choosing a research site is a critical moment in ethnographic exploration. Processes of discovery are not bound by strictures related to external validity or even causal inference, so concerns about case selection related to representativeness or selection bias are probably misplaced. Instead, selecting a research site routinely focuses around a balance between accessibility and relevance (Walford 2001).

Considerations of accessibility are obvious and inevitable. At the extreme, it is impossible to do ethnography in past or future societies, and it can be extremely challenging to engage in participant observation in contexts where some dimension of the researcher's identity is unwelcome. Some research sites involve learning new languages or require difficult and expensive travel; others play to a scholar's existing strengths. There is nothing inherently wrong with selecting research sites that are easy to access, but this should not be the only or necessarily the primary criterion.

Alongside accessibility, it is a good idea for scholars to select research sites in which something interesting is going on. As Walford argues, "it is usually necessary to select research sites which are important for themselves and for their historical and strategic role" (Walford 2001: 162) in producing some kind of event, process, or transformation. Even when the researcher has not chosen a main dependent variable or even settled on a final research question, it makes more sense to spend time exploring a context in which something important is definitely going on than one in which nothing is happening.

Of course, what counts as an important research site will depend fundamentally on the interests, intuitions, and life experience of the researcher. Pachirat (2011) saw slaughterhouses as important sites of violence, authority, and hierarchy, and Cramer (2016) found similar value in rural Wisconsin political discussion clubs. Discovery will perhaps come most readily from engaging with research sites that strike each individual researcher as potentially interesting, unsettling, or exciting.

Abby Wood works at the intersection of law and politics. She reports (in open-ended answers to our survey) that her expertise derives from interfacing with practitioners – in her case, lawyers, judges, and activists engaged in setting and contesting policies related to transparency and corruption. She advises contacting whatever sort of practitioners are engaged in your sort of work.

Take them to coffee and ask about their work, without an agenda. Sometimes they can steer you away from a bad question, but often you'll learn more just by asking about the most interesting thing on the horizon for them and what challenges they anticipate. As they answer, think about data you could either find or create (including via interviews) to help form a project.

Researchers are not guaranteed access to a site simply because it interests them, and even seemingly easy sites can sometimes prove challenging. Groups may not cooperate, government offices may deny permission, meetings may be closed to the public, and people may ask you to leave. Such events are by no means guaranteed, and scholars have sometimes obtained surprising degrees of ethnographic access to gangs, political party machines, and other seemingly secretive organizations. Patient bargaining and simple transparency about research goals can sometimes help. Furthermore, a failure to gain certain kinds of access can itself serve as a source of information; following up to try to learn why a group or individual does not want to cooperate can generate valuable leads for forming new projects.

As relationships are formed with informants, organizations, and other relevant actors, ethnographers are strongly encouraged to engage in intellectual and ethical reflection regarding their own role in the situation at hand. It is self-evident that an outsider acting as a researcher is a participant in any social event, and that participation inevitably changes the dynamics of the event in question; there is no such thing as neutral ethnographic observation. Hence, at a simple intellectual level, it is essential to ask why people react to the researcher in the way that they do, and to consider how the researcher's behavior, traits, and self-presentation influence the events under study.

This is not a defect in ethnographic exploration; serving as a (major or minor) disruption to the social system and dynamics of interest may help make visible aspects of the situation that would otherwise be obscure. Yet it is important to take into account – and to carefully consider the ways in which scholarly intrusion distribute costs and benefits across the people who serve as subjects of research.

A crucial part of the ethnographic tradition is the maintenance of detailed daily notes on fieldwork events and observations. These notes capture moments and experiences that may otherwise be forgotten or distorted by memory over time, and scheduling a significant daily session for private note-taking gives a researcher an excellent opportunity to reflect on recent events. Considering which events are unusual enough to merit extra exploration, which statements by informants or actors seem confusing or unexpected, and generally where the areas are that make the least sense to the outside observer given prior knowledge, theory, and preconceptions offers an excellent opportunity to discover the starting points of a new research agenda.

For an example, Lisa Wedeen's (1999) research on the politics of domination in authoritarian Syria began with a set of research ideas connected with how dictators use education for purposes of political socialization. Yet upon arriving in Syria and beginning participant observation, Wedeen quickly discovered that many of the propaganda materials that interested her were discussed with evident sarcasm. If there was little evidence of sincerity in how regime messages were discussed, how important could they be in socialization? In the light of this intellectual impasse, Wedeen found an alternative project by creatively confronting her early ethnographic insights related to insincerity with an unrelated text by Stephen Greenblatt, in which Greenblatt described how self-evidently insincere praise of a monarch demonstrated the monarch's power: if everyone could be forced to praise the monarch in ways that everyone knew to be false, the real message of the obviously insincere and hyperbolic praise was ultimately one of submission rather than defiance. Perhaps sarcastic propagation of regime propaganda played a similar role, conveying acceptance of the awesome power of the dictator even as it expressed disbelief in his messages. This idea became the foundation for a research project that altogether replaced the earlier, unsuccessful effort.

Zooming in substantially, a key element of ethnographic work, and of qualitative project-finding, exploration, and discovery more generally, is the unstructured or semi-structured interview. Research has long depended on evidence gathered through extended conversations with informants, survey respondents, and the like.

Sometimes, interviews are relatively unproductive. Researchers may hear primarily what they already know, and the other participant in the interview may stick to homilies and other banalities. Other interviews, however, singlehandedly reframe projects, uncover concepts, or suggest previously unimagined relationships. Certainly, some of the differences between productive and useless interviews involve luck or circumstances outside the control of the researcher.

Yet there exists a wealth of practical and intellectual advice for how to make unstructured and semi-structured interviews as productive as possible. Fujii's (2018) book on relational interviewing captures much of the state of the art. Good interviewing, Fujii teaches us, involves active listening, learning the new lexicon of our interlocutors, learning from mistakes, and treating people with respect and dignity (Fujii 2018: 3–7). In order to maximize the value of interviews, it is necessary to construct a working relationship with our informants, recognizing that they have goals and objectives in the conversation that are at least as important to them as ours are to us (Fujii 2018: 12–15). Working through the available evidence to understand those goals may provide insight that opens the door to new projects, just as much as the actual explicit contents of the interview.

Selecting people to interview raises several of the same themes as selecting sites for ethnography. When the goal is discovery, there need be no well-defined population, and thus interviews should not be seen as a sample. Instead, researchers can productively interview a diverse set of people who seem connected to a broad topic of interest. Fujii constructs a useful example, imagining a scholar interested in studying how students at elite universities think about "eliteness" (Fujii 2018: 35–36). One approach might be to interview all the students at a given elite university – an approach that would consume a great deal of time and resources. Instead, the researcher decides to select informants from different social and economic backgrounds, in order to discover whether there are patterns in which different life experiences lead to different ways of thinking about a university's elite status. With such an approach, the process of recruiting new interview subjects can flexibly follow the lines of social division that appear most interesting in practice, and the social science content of the study can emerge from the interviewing process itself.

The actual process of interviewing involves a series of important skills and decisions. First, is it necessary and/or helpful to record the interview? In less structured interviews, it is essential that the interviewer be fully present in the conversation and attentive to pick up on interesting or unexpected information and to manage the direction of the discussion (Fujii 2018: 22–29). For some researchers, recording the interview will facilitate such attentiveness, while others will be helped more by the need to take ongoing notes. Whichever solution is adopted, the key is to pay full attention to the twists and turns of the conversation and to convey that attentiveness fully to the person being interviewed.

In the actual moment of the interview, how should the conversation take place? Show the knowledge you have of situations, but also reveal your ignorance. If the conversation pushes in the direction of an argument, don't be afraid to engage. After the ice is well and truly broken, lean into open-ended questions that ask for stories about the informant's world and life experience.

For scholars who are interested in acquiring the skill of conducting open-ended qualitative interviews, valuable resources can be found in Monroe's (2004) book on the moral calculus of people who chose to rescue Jews during the Holocaust, those who chose to watch from the sidelines, and those who chose to support the Nazis. Monroe not only offers an engaging theory of why people made these choices and a valuable interpretive analysis to support that theory, but also provides extensive verbatim quotes from the interviews that she did to develop the project. In those interviews, a researcher new to such methods can effectively observe a highly skilled practitioner at work and thus gain invaluable indirect experience in how to use conversations in order to encounter other people's experiences of politics.

Of course, ethnography and related modes of qualitative, close-range encounters with the world need not be limited to interviews with one person at a time. In recent years, there has been increasing attention given to the option of creating artificial conversations, using focus groups, as a way of generating insights into shared beliefs, identities, culture, and other collective social phenomena.

Focus groups consist of carefully constructed group conversations, in which the researcher introduces questions, topics of discussion, and activities as a way of prompting participants to discuss their areas of agreement and debate within a topic domain. Such research is often used as a source of qualitative theory-testing evidence (Cyr 2019), but it can also be a productive way to find a project. If there is a broad topic of interest, then gathering a group of people who have life experience related to that topic and prompting discussion can generate a wealth of possible ideas. Projects can be constructed around surprising areas of agreement among participants in a group; alternatively, areas of disagreement can point to disagreements and dimensions of conflict. Intriguing elements of consensus or surprising domains of disagreement can each serve as a conceptual springboard for a research project explaining causes and/or effects of such ideational factors.

Across these many forms of ethnographic project-finding, a persistent key is to find contrasts between what is common sense to people participating in a society or phenomenon of interest and what is received wisdom in the academic literature. Intriguing projects can be built around translating concepts or relationships that are evident to people in the situation under study into academic theoretical language and exploring the ways in which they raise tensions with widely held beliefs among scholars. Alternatively, a good project can rely on using scholarly literature and intellectual insights to problematize and throw light on elements of life that are unremarkable and self-evident to people living them but that can highlight intriguing elements of politics and society.

Ethnographers often write in celebration of the playful, transgressive, undisciplined nature of ethnographic and related methods. Such an intellectual attitude of enthusiastic openness to messy reality, to contradiction of expectations, and to opportunities to unsettle received wisdom is well worth cultivating in exploring any new project.

Archives

For scholars in comparative politics, American political development, and some traditions within international relations and sociology, there is no research activity more iconic than spending time in an archive. In reality, actual reading in an archive is unlikely to produce a valuable project without reflective engagement with a broader set of ideas. We always experience primary sources in the context of our previous reading in the historical literature and in related texts. Indeed, most primary sources would be difficult to understand or appreciate without that prior engagement. Hence, it is useful to think about the process of finding a project with archival and other primary sources in terms of a dialogue between ideas from the literature and a given set of texts or other archival materials.

Furthermore, it is good to have a certain amount of resistance against the temptation to build a project around emphasizing a peculiarity discovered in the history of a single case. With the proper context, one odd or unusual case can generate interesting and fruitful projects and even broader debates. Odd facts about cases routinely generate opportunities for the discovery and analysis of natural experiments, for example. Posner's (2005) knowledge of the idiosyncratic process of drawing boundaries between Zambia and Malawi enabled a highly influential research trajectory related to the emergence of ethnic identities and cleavages. Angrist and Lavy (1999) used the fact that medieval Jewish scholar and theologian Maimonides had influenced education policy in Israel to generate a research project that produced high-quality estimates of the effect of class size on educational attainment. Brady and McNulty (2011) took advantage of their awareness of budget constraints during Arnold Schwarzenegger's California gubernatorial election to build a project testing the paradox of voting literature.

What these examples crucially share is that the scholars in question used idiosyncratic historical facts in transformative ways in order to build a broader project. For each of these examples, the unusual facts uncovered by knowledge of history becomes the source of an as-if random assignment. Arbitrarily drawn borders between Zambia and Malawi as-if randomly assign people living nearby to one or another institutional context; a rule about the maximum permissible number of students under a single teacher as-if randomly assigns large or small class sizes to children in groups just above or just below that maximum; and a state's budget crunch forces it to as-if randomly close two-thirds of polling places, thereby increasing the costs of voting for a probably-representative sample of voters.

This conceptual translation, from an interesting singular fact about a case into a basis for broader research, is almost universally necessary if historical work is to become the foundation for a research project. Often, the translation will not follow these examples in generating the statistical analysis of a natural experiment. However, it is almost always essential to make some kind of intellectual move that gives facts discovered through history a broader purchase and meaning if those facts are to anchor a project. Without such a move, historical details and oddities often serve only to confirm yet again the wild variety of human existence.

Thus, when seeking to build a project using historical materials, it is even more valuable than usual to start by reading deeply and broadly. The background necessary to build a project in this way certainly includes some degree of baseline familiarity of the case or cases where you intend to explore the archives. Otherwise, it can be difficult to even make sense of the historical materials. However, it is also important to build an intellectual repertoire of the ways previous scholars have transformed odd historical facts into projects. Thus, a broad but probably worthwhile exploration of diverse methodological and substantive research that contacts with history is a useful step.

One common approach that turns an interesting document, interview, or other single piece of evidence into a broader project is to ask how prevalent the particular theme that makes the initial finding interesting is across a broader body of evidence. If the decision in one case argued before Argentina's Supreme Court contains remarks about owing deference to the president, that is perhaps unremarkable. However, finding a pattern in which that Supreme Court sometimes but not always expresses deference to the president – and in which the Brazilian Supreme Court rarely if ever explicitly defers to the president in its decisions – turned out be a substantial part of a major research project (Kapiszewski 2012). The risk here is that, if there turn out to be few or no additional examples of the phenomenon that raised initial interest, the project may need to be reworked or even fizzle.

An alternative approach is to conceptualize the striking fact that has been found as a puzzle to be explained in light of a broader understanding of the case and the historical context. Here, becoming aware of an unusual fact from history becomes an opportunity to use broader historical knowledge, theory, and research design to clarify something that was initially hard to understand given your background or understanding. A fact need not be common in order to pose an interesting puzzle – and such a puzzle can certainly generate an interesting project, as long as it turns out to involve unexpected causes, effects, interactions, or other theoretical combinations.

Large and influential literatures have launched in exactly this way. Why did the United States build early and relatively robust welfare state institutions for former soldiers and for mothers, given that it lagged far behind many other developed countries in general welfare state institutions (Skocpol 1995)? Why did Western European socialist parties rarely meet or exceed 50 percent of the vote (Przeworski and Sprague 1986)?

These questions are motivated by facts from history that become worth explaining for two reasons. First, they are to some degree surprising given theory and other historical literature. In light of the well-known argument in the literature on comparative welfare states that the United States has a far smaller welfare state than most other advanced industrial democracies, the existence of a segment of robust welfare institutions throws some doubt on existing literature and becomes a puzzle worth solving in its own right. Likewise, given the belief in widespread class voting in Western Europe during much of the twentieth century, as well as the evident fact that the working class is larger than the upper class, the lack of majoritarian socialism in most of Western Europe becomes a path into understanding deeper tensions of class-politics strategy for socialist parties.

Second, both facts can potentially connect with a wide range of other theoretically loaded variables, techniques, and broader ideas. Skocpol's project contributes to broader discussions related to institutional development, identity, ideology, and American political history; scholars who are not interested in the details of welfare policy can still connect to the project because of the many other variables that become part of the story. Likewise, Przeworski and Sprague's project is of interest to readers who care about party strategy, about class identity and politics, and about the application of rational-choice ideas in sociology and political science.

Thus, when building a project around an odd feature of a case discovered through historical research, it is essential to adopt a strategy for broadening out the story. This may be achieved by asking how common the unusual finding is across a broader set of cases and then by trying to explain when, why, and how a pattern of differences exists. Alternatively, you can build an exciting project by problematizing the fact that has interested you in light of existing scholarly literatures and debates and then you can build an explanatory framework that incorporates a wide range of normatively or intellectually attractive ideas. Either strategy requires a kind of pivot from the narrow facts of the archive to a broader conceptual space – and thus relies heavily on your prior reading, research, and general intellectual preparation.

Some approaches to finding a project through engagement with history rely far more centrally on engagement with scholarly literature instead of archival efforts. Some projects are discovered by finding elements in historical or historically oriented social science literature that spark confusion, disagreement, or a sense of mystery on the part of previous authors. When scholars disagree about the meaning or details of an important event, there is an opportunity to build a project.

The key here, of course, is to avoid framing the project as simply filling in details in a picture that has been largely worked out by previous scholars. Instead, it is a good idea to ask why confusion lingers even after all the research that has been done to date. Sometimes, a literature becomes confused because different scholars treat a multifaceted phenomenon as if it were necessarily all one thing or all another. For example, R. B. Collier (1999) showed that research on transitions to democracy had become muddled by an argument that class mobilization and protest was essential to the process of regime change either in all cases, in none, or only in historically early cases – but that in fact transitions to democracy in both Western Europe and Latin America sometimes showed patterns of class-based mobilization and sometimes did not. From this position, a clear project emerges with a focus on explaining why some countries experienced one pattern as opposed to the other. More generally, good projects can often be built by turning debates from historically oriented literature about whether all cases experience one version or another of a phenomenon into a focused analysis of why some cases experience one version and some the other.

In other instances, there is a muddle in the literature because the primary sources disagree. Here, a productive move is to ask why they disagree, and whether there is anything to be learned from the disagreements preserved in the historical record.

Regardless of the specific approach taken, it is important to remember that interesting facts in historical documents, unresolved debates in secondary sources, or other intriguing historical discoveries do not spontaneously generate a good research project. An intellectual pivot is almost always needed from the concrete details of documents and historiography toward a question that invites multiple audiences of scholars to engage with your research. Conveniently enough, such a pivot also invites engagement with the ideas of conceptualization, theory, and research design that characterize social science more generally.

Statistics

Statisticians and quantitative practitioners have for decades maintained a distinction between exploratory analysis – designed to discover interesting concepts, patterns, or trends – and confirmatory analysis – designed instead to provide (ideally rigorous) tests of well-specified hypotheses. There is perhaps a strong elective affinity between exploratory analysis and finding new projects; however, there are also productive frameworks in which an existing confirmatory analysis offers a jumping-off place for a new and sometimes a transformative project.

We will begin by reviewing the classic, and perhaps still in practice underrated, approach to discovering projects using statistical data: graphical exploration. Next, attention turns to methods for exploring patterns of missingness as a prompt to discovery and project creation. Then, we will discuss cluster analysis and related methods for finding groupings of multidimensionally similar cases, with an eye to the ways such methods can prompt creativity and project formation. At this point, the discussion will shift to a category of methods that bridge between exploratory and confirmatory analysis: regression-type and machine-learning methods for systematic analysis and exploration of relationships between variables. Finally, we will discuss ways that existing confirmatory statistical analysis can serve as a starting point for creative new projects, with a focus on exploring outliers and extreme cases.

It should be clear that all of these methods require the prior existence of some kind of quantitative data. This is no longer a high bar for most researchers; vast collections of data about politics and other social behaviors exist at many levels of analysis and of aggregation. Often, the existing data are incomplete, error-prone, or otherwise imperfect in ways that would hamper confirmatory analysis, but these problems need not be a major obstacle to the kinds of exploration that generate new research; indeed, they can serve as the impetus to the creative moves necessary to find a project.

However, even in the now-unusual situation that no relevant data about a particular topic or theme exist at all, it is sometimes possible for the researcher to do some preliminary coding of their own – in a provisional fashion. This may, for example, involve creating a rank ordering or a simple yes/no coding scheme, focusing upon a small number of cases and variables of interest. Suppose one is attempting to determine why some countries in sub-Saharan Africa have democratized while others have not in the decades since independence. One would begin by coding the dependent variable (autocracy/democracy), and proceed to add possibly relevant causal factors, for example, economic growth, urbanization, landlocked status, colonial history, and so forth. Some of these factors might be binary, while others could be coded continuously or reduced to a binary format (e.g., high/low). Some of these factors are likely to be easy to code ("objective"), while others may involve considerable judgment on the part of the coder ("subjective"). In any case, these simple data could then be examined using tables or simple graphs.

The standard recommendation of the literature on exploratory data analysis is to make heavy use of graphs to search for patterns in the data (Tukey 1977; Tufte 2001). Such exploration is rarely described in published scholarly reports, and there is room for a reasonable suspicion that the advice is, as the saying goes, more honored in the breach than the observance. Furthermore, when graphical explorations of statistical data are reported, they very often take the form of histograms or bivariate scatterplots.

In fact, contemporary statistical computing offers graphical tools for exploring data that go beyond these simple starting points. Statisticians and computer scientists have offered a wide range of exceedingly sophisticated and creative tools for the multidimensional graphical exploration of data (Chan 2006), but most of these may be somewhat unfamiliar to social scientists and thus present relatively high barriers to entry. Two, however, are simple twists on widely used tools that allow for quick and effective exploration.

First, researchers can quickly see basic patterns of relationships across a wide range of variables using a simple modification of the variance-covariance or correlation matrix. Specifically, adding a heat map that scales from blue (for covariances/correlations close to 0) to red (for those with the largest absolute values) allows the strongest pairwise relationships to visually pop from the mix and gives a very quick sense of the overall structure of multivariate data. By facilitating a quick but comprehensive view of the overall pattern of strong and weak (and potentially positive and negative) relationships in the data, such a matrix with a heat map provides a powerful tool for deepening researchers' understanding of overall data structures. Furthermore, attention to surprising patterns of relationships among variables or striking juxtapositions of strong and weak correlations may serve as the spur to innovation needed to launch a successful new project.

Figure 7.1 offers an example of a heat map applied to a correlation matrix. The data here are the Quality of Governance data set for 2017. For this figure, and throughout this section, the dependent variable of interest is the infant mortality rate. What, if any, are the political-economic causes of cross-national differences in infant mortality? There is a literature on this topic (e.g., Navarro et al. 2003; Zweifel and Navia 2000; Shandra et al. 2004); however, throughout this section we will approach the question from a position of intellectual naivete, with the goal of seeing whether statistical tools for data exploration can provoke interesting research ideas.

In fact, the heat map in Figure 7.1 already suggests some interesting ideas. The bottom row shows us that the strongest positive predictor of infant mortality is the country's perceived level of corruption; only the relatively obvious variable that measures the rate of medical attendance at births has a stronger relationship. Furthermore, the next row up shows us that a common measure of democracy is a good predictor of perceived levels of corruption, with a substantial negative relationship. Finally, there is a substantial negative relationship between corruption and the percentage of births that are attended by medical professionals. This

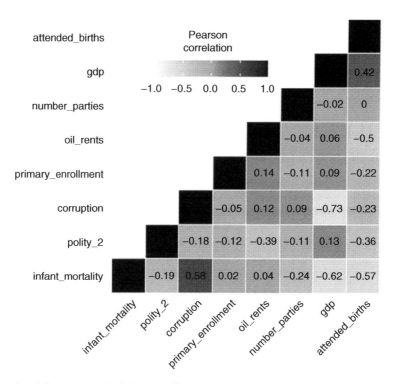

Figure 7.1   Correlation heat map for infant mortality

suggests a possible hypothesis in which democracy starts a causal chain leading to reduced infant mortality by cutting the level of corruption, which in turn frees up resources for medical personnel to attend more births. Obviously, this idea might be true or false. Nothing about the correlation heat map provides a compelling test of the hypothesis. Nevertheless, the heat map facilitates finding these kinds of interesting potential linkages, which in turn can motivate a project.

Second, there is a fascinating generalization of scatterplots, called trellis scatterplots, that allows for comparatively easy examination of relationships between two variables controlling for the value of up to two others. The idea with these plots is to produce several bivariate scatterplots between a pair of chosen variables, organized into a grid. The grid provides information about the value of two variables; scatterplots are organized left to right according to the value of one of those variables, and top to bottom according to the value of the other. The scatterplot explicitly presents the value of two variables, conditional on the variables that define the grid.

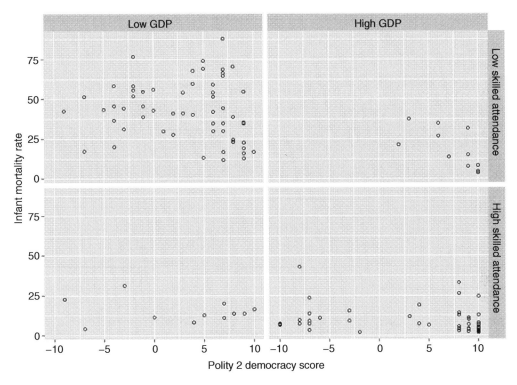

Figure 7.2   Trellis scatterplot of democracy and infant mortality

For example, the simple trellis plot in Figure 7.2 explores the relationship between democracy and infant mortality, conditional on per capita GDP and the proportion of births that are attended by a skilled medical professional. To keep things simple, the two conditioning variables have been dichotomized at their medians. Thus, the left column shows countries with a 2017 per capita GDP below the world median and the right column shows countries at or above that median. Likewise, the top row shows countries with rates of professional medical attendance at births below the 2017 world median, while the bottom row shows those above the median.

The scatterplots in each box show the relationship between democracy and infant mortality for each combination of conditioning variables. The plot immediately shows some features of the data. For example, there are comparatively few countries with high GDP and low rates of skilled attendance at births, and also not too many with low GDP but high skilled attendance. Mortality rates are higher and more variable in countries with low skilled attendance, highlighting the key significance of that variable.

More subtly, the scatterplots within each window suggest somewhat different pictures. Countries with high skilled attendance show no obvious relationship between democracy and infant mortality. The relatively small set of countries with high GDP but low skilled attendance suggests a possible negative relationship between democracy and infant mortality rates, although if there is a pattern, it largely involves countries with very high levels of democracy. Looking at the set of countries with low GDP and low skilled attendance, there may also be a drop in infant mortality rates connected with very high levels of democracy. Thus, the trellis plot suggests a potentially interesting question: Do high levels of democracy somehow connect with lower levels of infant mortality among countries (rich or poor) with limited health care support at birth?

Graphical exploration of data sets can help expose this sort of detailed and specific question, which in turn can serve as the starting point for interesting and creative broader projects. Indeed, there is a marked tendency in the literature on statistical exploratory data analysis to emphasize just such graphical analysis. This tradition notwithstanding, there are important alternative statistical tools that can be equally productive in discovering the starting point for new research projects.

One relatively unusual approach to discovering a new project is to examine patterns of missing data in an existing data set. Standard statistical analysis requires assumptions regarding missing data, which typically must be missing either completely at random or at random conditional on some control variables. These assumptions are typically treated as technical obstacles to be overcome along the path to valid statistical analysis, but at an earlier stage of research it is valuable to regard patterns of missing data as a puzzle to be explored.

Forming a list of cases with missing data (or with the most missing data for panel/cross-section time-series data structures) can suggest substantive research puzzles and even provoke novel new hypotheses. A list of countries, candidates, parties, or other units with significant missing data may suggest candidate explanations for missing data related to strategy, capacity, or other social dynamics.

In addition to, or for some kinds of data where case identifiers are uninformative instead of, generating a list of cases, it can also be productive to explore differences between cases with missing and complete scores in terms of their average values on a range of other variables. Producing a table with a list of the means on a diverse set of variables for cases with no missing values on a variable of interest, the means for cases with missing values, and a difference in means test can reveal patterns that suggest potential stories about the motives or resources behind failures to report. These, in turn, can motivate new research trajectories.

To continue with the example related to national rates of infant mortality, the World Development Indicators data for 2017 show only three countries that failed to report: Taiwan, North Korea, and Lichtenstein. One may suppose that North Korea does not report infant mortality because it broadly refuses to report statistics to global institutions as an act of defiance, and the Quality of Governance data set (which includes the World Development Indicators and many other data sources) indeed show North Korea missing data for many variables: the cross-sectional data set has 1,562 missing values for North Korea out of 1,985 variables. Taiwan presumably has missing data because of its disputed international status, and this shows up across a wide range of variables with 1,320 missing values in the Quality of Governance.

Lichtenstein has a substantially larger list of missing values, however; it is missing 1,661 out of 1,985 possible variables. This pattern of extensive missing data does not correspond with disputed international status or with a rogue state reputation. Perhaps Lichtenstein fails to report so broadly because it is a very small country, with fewer than 40,000 citizens? Additional exploration of the data reveals that the average number of missing variables in the Quality of Governance data set for countries with a population below 100,000 is 1,420 out of 1,985 – vastly higher than the average for larger countries. This is the case even though several very small countries are quite wealthy. Why, then, is their data reporting so poor? Are important findings in comparative politics and international relations distorted by the consistent omission of these countries?

Some kinds of multivariate statistical analysis can be equally as provocative at the phase of finding a project. Such preliminary analysis is distinguished from confirmatory statistical work because there is no need to define and defend a statistical model. Instead, as with the kinds of exploratory graphical analysis used as a tool for finding projects above, the emphasis is on data-intensive modes of analysis that present relationships in ways that make unexpected aspects of the data easy to recognize.

One useful and perhaps underutilized tool for this kind of multivariate data-driven creativity enhancement is cluster analysis, which is a family of tools designed to efficiently group cases in complex multidimensional spaces. This provides a range of useful opportunities for substantively fruitful surprise and inspiration. Most notably, if seemingly dissimilar cases turn out to be grouped in the same cluster across multiple dimensions or if seemingly similar cases are in very different groupings, these unexpected groupings constitute an empirical invitation to puzzle-solving in a way that can produce interesting projects.

Continuing with the example using data on infant mortality, as a way of throwing light on possible surprising patterns in the data we carried out a K-means cluster analysis using a collection of interesting if somewhat arbitrary variables from the cross-sectional Quality of Governance data. While the choice of clustering algorithm can be highly consequential for the content and details of classification schemes, it is perhaps less critical when the goal is simply to encounter surprising and intellectually provocative patterns; so also, the selection of specific variables can be motivated by curiosity more than rigorous prior theory at this phase.

Preliminary analysis suggests that six meaningful clusters exhaust most of the meaningful variance. Table 7.1 shows the average scores of the resulting clusters. The results show, perhaps unsurprisingly, that wealthy democracies and very wealthy authoritarian countries have low rates of infant mortality. The third cluster is perhaps more intriguing, consisting of a set of thirty-three countries with reasonably low levels of infant mortality despite relatively low per capita GDP – but in conjunction with fairly high levels of democracy. The sixth cluster suggests that highly democratic upper-middle-income countries may have infant mortality levels that compete with those of the most developed countries. These results raise the possibility that regime type may matter for understanding levels of infant mortality, but that the connection exists largely in countries in the middle-income range. This result is odd and may well suggest hypotheses worth further development and testing; if so, the analysis is a success.

Table 7.1 Cluster means

Cluster ID	Infant mortality (WDI)	Democracy (polity)	Gende (V-Dem)	Air pollution	Per capita GDP (PPP)
1	4.40	5.19	0.82	87.68	51215.51
2	3.73	−0.67	0.71	83.40	98526.37
3	14.21	4.30	0.78	87.79	16927.95
4	24.99	4.27	0.76	91.28	8288.30
5	47.56	3.40	0.70	93.48	2407.73
6	7.44	7.75	0.86	86.65	31008.94

Projects often emerge from the discovery of an unexpected or seemingly inexplicable statistical relationship among a set of variables. Methods that allow for efficient multivariate exploration of data can facilitate this kind of discovery. What is wanted here are methods that are sensitive to unexpected relationships, allow for complexity, and are relatively unlikely to highlight random noise as if it were a real clue to interesting phenomena in the world. These traits increase the probability of learning something new that sparks creativity or discovering hidden nuances that open doors for problematizing existing ideas, but without wasting time on results that turn out to be simple chance features of the data.

Fortunately, a variety of methods from machine learning and related statistical fields combine these properties. LASSO regression (Tibshirani 1996) methods allow a scholar to run a regression analysis relatively efficiently using very large numbers of predictor variables by adding a penalty that shrinks the coefficients of unhelpful variables to zero. Thus, it lets scholars include many or all possibly relevant variables in a single, unified analysis, efficiently separating them into a set that are promising predictors of the outcome and an often much larger set of those that are less intriguing.

While LASSO regressions can work well in uncovering interactions and other kinds of nonlinear relationships (Bien, Taylor, Tibshirani 2013), other algorithms are designed specifically with these kinds of patterns in mind. Perhaps the most famous involves the tradition of random forests (Breiman 2001). In these techniques, a potentially wide range of independent variables are used to predict values of the dependent variable.

A random-forest analysis starts by finding the single split of the data in terms of one independent variable that produces the largest possible difference in means on the dependent variable. That split is recorded as the first branch in a tree. The process then iterates, finding the best available splits for cases on each side of the initial branch, and deepening the tree until there are either too few remaining cases or a high level of homogeneity on the dependent variable. Random forests generalize this process by generating multiple trees, each on a random subset of the original set of cases and of independent variables, and then averaging important results together. This averaging process reduces the degree to which results are found that capitalize on chance.

Scholars can discover the key ideas which generate new projects through these and other intensively inductive tools for data analysis. The relevant research design is as follows. First, collect a viable statistical measure of the outcome variable, as well as the broadest feasible set of possible independent variables. Second, comb through the set of independent variables to eliminate any which might function as alternative measures of the outcome; otherwise, the analysis is likely to produce the rather uninspired finding that the outcome is related to itself. Third, choose LASSO regression, random forests, or a similar technique and apply it to the data. Finally, read through the results, paying special attention to odd or hard-to-interpret variables that nonetheless play a meaningful role in predicting the outcome.[1]

Returning to the example of finding a project related to cross-national infant mortality rates, both LASSO regression and random forests offer interesting suggestive clues. In order to use these techniques, a certain amount of preprocessing is needed. Starting from the Quality of Governance data set, some variables have to be removed as alternative measures of the outcome (or partial measures of the outcome, or measures that include the outcome as part of an index). These include the World Development Indicators measures of male and female infant mortality, neonatal mortality, and mortality rates under five years old (including male and female variants); OECD and World Health Organization measures of infant mortality, neonatal mortality, and mortality under five years old; and the Sustainable Governance Indicators health policy index, which includes infant mortality as a component. Also excluded are country names and codes, years, and a set of variables that measure party-system change which have effectively zero cross-sectional variation.

After removing these variables, one serious problem remains. Across the 1,967 available predictor variables, at least one has a missing value for each country. Either an imputation technique must be used to deal with missing data, or scholars would be forced to undermine the project of discovery by excluding large numbers of variables, countries, or probably both. To avoid this undesirable outcome, we used random-forest-based missing data imputation (Stekhoven, Buehlmann 2012).

After preprocessing was completed, a LASSO regression analyzed the relationship between all 1,967 available predictor variables in the Quality of Governance data set and the outcome of infant mortality. The results are shown in Table 7.2.

In reading through these results, it is helpful to remember that the variables shown here have results after the algorithm considered the much broader set of options in the entire data set; thus, these are the most

---

[1] For an applied example of this process, with explicit transparency about the steps taken along the way toward theory discovery, see Seawright (2018).

Table 7.2 LASSO regression results

Variable	Coefficient
(Intercept)	158.1293512380
International Treaty Transition	0.8939695871
Slavery Allowed by Constitution	0.0006057451
Legislative District Magnitude	−0.0003620441
Are Multiple Parties Legal?	−0.1126114723
Business Tax Burden	−0.0404361546
Frequency of Bribes to Tax Authority	0.2083695380
Drinking Water Access	−0.0416680263
Irrigation of Agricultural Land	0.0366764662
Availability of Handwashing in Cities	−0.0146703133
Urban Drinking Water Services	−0.0154903841
Price Level of Consumption Goods	0.7464562439
Human Resources Rating	−2.8838493030
Adult Literacy Rate	−0.0780267999
Gender Equality Rating	−0.7963675810
Percent of Women with Secondary Education	−0.0092604094
Male Self-Employment	0.0206559826
Births Attended by Medical Staff	−0.0189278521
WDI Female Life Expectancy	−1.2374006614
Female Adult Mortality Rate	0.0072178365
WHO Female Life Expectancy	−0.1381510689
Maternal Mortality Rate	0.0095556766

promising predictors across a vast array of options. Many of them are unsurprising results, showing connections among maternal health, overall quality of health care, and infant mortality. Some results, however, show intriguing relationships of political and broader social-scientific interest. Infrastructure related to water supplies matters a great deal in a variety of ways, for example. Gender equality also has an intriguing negative relationship with infant mortality. Furthermore, the results also feature a range of explicit variables measuring practices of corruption, taxation, elections and party-system structure, and the legality of slavery. These results could motivate the development of a project that, for example, looks at how the politics of taxation are connected with infant mortality rates, or alternatively at why single-party authoritarian regimes are singled out as having worse infant mortality rates.

Table 7.3 Random forest variable importance

Variable	Importance
WDI Life Expectancy	15078.57
WDI Female Life Expectancy	9760.04
WHO Life Expectancy	8294.45
WHO Female Life Expectancy	7088.19
WHO Healthy Male Life Expectancy	4223.74
WHO Healthy Female Life Expectancy	4217.13
WHO Healthy Life Expectancy	3106.15
Maternal Mortality	2850.74
WHO Male Life Expectancy	2520.86
Lifetime Risk of Maternal Death	2415.82
Rural Access to Handwashing Facilities	1537.06
WDI Female Mortality Rate	1371.92
WDI Crude Death Rate	1020.93
Female Tertiary School Enrollment	891.18
Urban Access to Handwashing	870.77
GDP Per Capita in 1700	778.12
WDI Male Life Expectancy	767.18
Gender Inequality Index	715.04
IHME Female Life Expectancy	685.14
Sanitation and Drinking Water Quality	639.76

Applying a simple random-forest analysis to the same preprocessed data yields some similar results, but also a narrower focus. The importance scores for each variable, shown in Table 7.3, represent a combination of how often each variable was included in the analysis across various random samples from the data and the set of competing variables, but also how high up each variable appears in the tree. Thus, a variable with a high importance score, such as the World Development Indicators Life Expectancy measure, appears near the top of virtually every analysis.

The first several variables that appear in the table show that infant mortality is closely connected with death rates in general. This may be interesting to some people, but others will find it a bit self-evident and may wish to repeat the analysis excluding those variables. Alternatively, we could read a bit further down the list and find once again that access to water and handwashing facilities are strong predictors of infant mortality, as are female equality and access to education. Many of the intriguing explicitly political variables from the LASSO regression are not to be found here, but there is a strong emphasis on water infrastructure and on gender equality, both of which point in the direction of interesting research projects. For example, it would be intriguing to set up an experiment in which the treatment group is informed about the statistical connection between gender equality and infant mortality, while the control group is not. Would this treatment, connecting gender equality with the lives of babies, shift attitudes about women in politics or other interesting beliefs and values connected with gender?

Using highly inductive techniques such as LASSO regression and random forests can clearly help discover relationships and thereby build a research project. Often, the relationships that are highlighted in such analysis will be unexpected and will drive subsequent research in novel directions. However, these advantages notwithstanding, such intensive data exploration often makes social scientists nervous. Surely, they worry, this kind of data mining will produce a huge number of meaningless, chance findings that will pollute the research project as a whole?

In fact, both LASSO regression and random forests have features that help mitigate this concern. The penalization of non-zero coefficients in LASSO regression and the random selection of subsamples of cases and variables in random forests both serve to reduce the probability of false discoveries. Furthermore, principled use of these techniques avoids much of the specification searching process that gives inductive research a bad name. Because LASSO regression and random forests allow scholars to simply include all potentially relevant independent variables, they can help mitigate the undesirable researcher degrees of freedom involved in selecting a narrow subset of those variables to include in an analysis, thereby increasing transparency and likely reducing the rate of false discoveries.

However, in situations where avoiding false discovery is unusually important, there are techniques which can provide additional help. In particular, cross-validation for the selection of hyperparameters[2] and the practice of splitting the data beforehand so as to evaluate the final estimator with an as yet untouched test sample (James et al. 2013: 176) can serve to substantially reduce the concerns about false discovery that give data mining a bad name.

Finally, turning beyond the limits of strictly quantitative technique, there is a long history of social scientists finding interesting projects by examining cases that fit uncomfortably within existing statistical results. O'Donnell's (1988) work on bureaucratic-authoritarian regimes during the 1970s arose

---

[2] In random forests, this is typically done through out-of-bag validation (Breiman 1996).

from a concern with the way that Latin American countries during the Cold War were not becoming more democratic as they developed economically – in contradiction with famous statistical results showing a positive link between economic and political "modernization." Dunning's work on oil and democracy (Dunning 2008) starts from the puzzle that Venezuela became more stably (if not deeply or substantively) democratic as its oil industry matured. A huge literature derives from the observation that the development of the US welfare state is out of statistical step in relation to its economy in comparison with other advanced industrial democracies.

Each of these research trajectories begins with the recognition that something is odd about a given case. Looking deeper into that case using diverse mixes of qualitative and quantitative data and tools led to the ideas and research designs that became influential studies and even research traditions. The sense that a case does not fit the existing statistical relationship can be formalized: cases that are awkward fits with a broader relationship are almost always either outliers or extreme cases (Seawright, Gerring 2008; Seawright 2016b). Outliers are cases that are poor statistical fits with a regression or similar statistical model; they are cases with large residuals, and thus those that diverge most dramatically from the broader pattern. Extreme cases are simply unusual fits with the broader data set on a single variable: they have an unusually high or low score on a supposed cause of interest or on an outcome. Because these two kinds of cases are unusual in one way or another, they are particularly good contexts in which to discover new projects. It can thus be productive to find an existing data set, mock up a regression-type analysis that comes as close as possible to capturing the current state of the art for a given literature in terms of substantive knowledge and statistical technique, and then to look closely and curiously at the cases that fit poorly with the resulting model.

The key point of these adventures in data exploration is to reveal new hypotheses and to expose one's hunches to preliminary tests, as quickly as possible. Do not be afraid to deal in stylized facts – rough guesstimates about the reality under consideration. More systematic testing procedures can wait for a later stage of the process. Data exploration should be understood as a series of plausibility probes (Eckstein 1975).

Conclusions

There are no formal rules for methods used in discovering a project. Excellent ideas and research designs can emerge from the use and abuse of any of the tools discussed above. Nevertheless, the methods reviewed in this chapter play a highly useful role because they offer a package of scripts that can be followed when ideas have not yet fully crystalized.

Whether the initial empirical encounters that help generate a research project are ethnographic, historical, or statistical in orientation, some intellectual attitudes and orientations are valuable across the board. It is a good idea to enter this kind of research activity with a flexible attitude about the topics that are under consideration. A concept that initially appears as a puzzle to be explained may ultimately be more interesting as a cause to test, and a research context that at first seems to exemplify one phenomenon may turn out to be better described in terms of something else. Analytic flexibility lets the data speak more loudly in the process of project discovery, which in turn can make it easier to find something that ultimately helps define your unique scholarly voice.

Likewise, an eye for surprise and the counterintuitive is valuable at this phase. Evidence that fits with academic preconceptions can be interesting and useful, but it may not help you find a project that adds new ideas and results to the literature. By contrast, moments in the data that raise a sense of shock or confusion will require additional effort to form into a usable project – but the resulting project is more likely to move debates forward. The extra effort to creatively highlight and interpret oddities is deeply worthwhile as a way of forming a project.

Part IV

Playing with Theories

Part II of the book focused on the ideational components of exploration and Part III on the empirical components of exploration. In this part, we focus on the theoretical components.

Chapter 8 serves as our entrée into this topic. Here, we offer a smorgasbord of theoretical frameworks that are commonly invoked in the social sciences.

Chapter 9 reviews explanatory challenges – what a good theory is, different ways of approaching cause and effect, the opportunities and pitfalls of causal mechanisms, and the units-of-analysis problem.

Chapter 10 offers tools and tips for theorizing. This includes various modes of articulating a theory (speech, prose, pictures, key cases, and formal models), general guidelines, the development of hypotheses, dealing with alternate explanations, and achieving empirical tractability.

8 Theoretical Frameworks

The word was theory, pronounced reverently, growing larger with the telling – theory, THEORY – only to recede wistfully into the distance as soon as it came into focus. Always alluring, forever, except for the favored few, unreachable. Gradually it dawned on us that if having knowledge of theory were akin to predestination – either you had it or you did not – there was no point in worrying about it or studying for it. Sensing that theory explained whatever was worth explaining but unable to figure out what form it took (a common put-down at the time was to say that some work lacked theory or that someone would not know a theory if he ran into one), we retreated to something admittedly less satisfactory but eminently more practical, namely, who said what. If we could neither recognize nor create theory, we could pass our doctoral exams by telling our professors what the greats and near-greats whose books had been assigned to us had said.

Aaron Wildavsky (1993: 28)

Social science is not a theoretically unified endeavor. Indeed, it is often criticized for having a superfluity of theories. For any outcome, there seem to be myriad explanations, none of which can be decisively proven or disproven. Even so, most of these causes fit into a small number of explanatory frameworks that are invoked (implicitly or explicitly) again and again across the disciplines of social science.

Note that when we use the term *cause*, we refer to a single factor or perhaps a vector that could – at least in principle – be manipulated. A *framework*, by contrast, is a larger theoretical scaffolding that is not manipulable and that fits together logically, subsuming a variety of causal factors. The mutation of a gene is a cause; evolution is a framework. Causes are generally falsifiable; frameworks may not be. But since their goal is to help us theorize that is not a serious problem. Of a cause we want to know its *truth*-value. Of a framework we want to know its *use*-value: how useful is it in constructing theories?

Theorizing often begins with broad, theoretical frameworks. Scholars discover projects by pushing themselves to imagine ways that a particular theoretical framework could fit with disparate subjects. Scholars may also

Table 8.1 Explanatory frameworks

MOTIVATIONAL
- **Interests** (that which benefits an actor)
- **Norms** (values, beliefs, ideology, culture, identity)
- **Psychology** (cognition, emotion, personality, genetics)

STRUCTURAL
- **Material factors** (financial resources, geography, technology)
- **Human capital/Demography** (health, mortality, education, skills, migration, life-cycle events)
- **Institutions** (formal rules and organizations)

INTERACTIVE
- **Adaptation** (feedback, competition, selection, evolution, efficiency, functionalism)
- **Coordination** (collective action, externalities, credible commitment, transaction costs)
- **Diffusion** (demonstration effect, exposure, ideas, information, knowledge, exposure)
- **Networks** (informal associational structures, social capital)
- **Path dependence** (contingent moments [critical junctures] leading to fixed trajectories)

construct an inventory of explanations for a given phenomenon based on diverse frameworks as a preface to further theorizing and testing. For the moment, our task is to introduce a collection of common social science theoretical frameworks, which should provide a palette for composing new ideas and novel projects.

Our three-part typology of explanatory frameworks is summarized in Table 8.1. *Motivational* frameworks include interests, norms, and psychology. *Structural* frameworks include material factors, human capital/demography, and institutions. *Interactive* frameworks include explanations grounded in adaptation, coordination, diffusion, networks, and path dependence.

In the following sections, we lay out each framework along with a few illustrative examples. The final section of the chapter adds important clarifications to this scaffolding, discusses how the various frameworks might be combined to provide a coherent overall explanation, and returns to the question of how theoretical frameworks can assist in exploratory research.

Motivational Frameworks

One set of explanations center on motivations, that is, what impels people to behave in certain ways or to think about things in certain ways. Three motivational frameworks predominate in the work of social science: *interests*, *norms*, and *psychology*.

One need not worry about which of these frameworks is "rational" or "irrational." (Whatever conclusions one might draw would depend upon how one chooses to define that complex term.) The point is that they motivate, and thereby help to explain, human attitudes and behavior.

Interests

Attitudes, preferences, and behavior are often the product of interests, that is, what it is in the interest of a person or group to think or to do. That includes material factors (e.g., money), power, or status.[1]

Interest-based explanations play a key role in Aristotle's *Politics* and are also a hallmark of Marxist theory and of studies that adopt an economic interpretation of human behavior, including work by Charles Beard, Gary Becker, and the collaborative team of Daron Acemoglu and James Robinson.[2] Accordingly, if one wishes to explain why elites generally resist revolutionary change, and why members of the landless proletariat occasionally support fundamental change, one might begin with the notion that each group has something to gain by the positions they take in this struggle. Likewise, if one wishes to explain why rich people generally support conservative parties and poor people generally support liberal or left-wing parties, one might suppose that these well-established partisan preferences are grounded in the divergent interests of these social classes – in the one case for property rights and limited taxes and in the other case for redistribution of wealth. By the same token, a reasonable starting point for any analysis of interstate relations is that each state has a set of interests – for example, land, resources, power – that it wishes to protect, and if possible expand. This is the foundation of the *realist* paradigm of international relations. And finally, in understanding the behavior of politicians a reasonable starting point is the assumption that politicians desire to attain public office and, once in office, desire to maintain their position.

Interest-based explanations are often self-evident, a primal explanatory trope. When we are asked to explain a phenomenon, we are apt to look first to self-interest as an explanation. However, this sort of explanation is not always as clear-cut as it may seem.

---

[1] A broader definition, including whatever individuals define as worthwhile, becomes so diffuse as to lose its explanatory power or merges into a preference-based analysis, as discussed at the end of the chapter.

[2] E.g., Acemoglu, Robinson (2012), Beard (1913), Becker (1976).

First, the various goals assembled under the rubric of interests – money, power, and status – are not always in synch. For a politician, staying in office may maximize their power while leaving office may enhance their pocketbook (if more remunerative jobs are available in the private sector). Here, two interest-based explanations collide.

Second, short- and long-run interests may conflict. For example, it may be in one's short-term interest to purchase consumption goods and in one's long-term interest to invest. To take another example, one may maximize short-term gain by stealing; but long-term financial gain is probably maximized by working hard and following prevailing rules and norms. Different temporal frames thus suggest different courses of action, and the choice between the two will depend upon other (non-interest based) factors.

Third, actors often find themselves with conflicting interests based on different social identities. To simplify, let's think of interests as referring solely to money. If a person sacrifices to pay for their child's education, they are sacrificing their interest as an individual but satisfying their interest as a parent. Likewise, one's financial interest as a member of one group (say, an ethnic group) may conflict with one's financial interest as a member of another group (say, a social class).

Fourth, since interests are often unclear, actors in the same objective position may nonetheless have different ideas about their (true) interests. For example, some members of the working class may believe their interests are best served by a socialist program while others believe their interests are best served by a conservative or liberal program. Karl Marx regarded members of the working class as victims of "false consciousness" if they did not support the communist cause. Others might argue that working classes rarely stand to benefit from communist revolutions, and thus their true interests lie with capitalism.

To sum up, it is often possible to infer attitudes and behavior from an individual's (or group's) position by assuming that people are acting to maximize their perquisites, power, or status (according to some definition of what that is). There is almost always a self-interest explanation for a persistent pattern of behavior. However, the plasticity of the concept of self-interest – the multitude of things that seem to satisfy this explanatory framework – should give one pause. There is a sense in which self-interest explains everything, and nothing.

Norms

Interest-based explanations are often contrasted with those based on norms. By this, we mean to include values, ideologies, beliefs, belief-systems, philosophies, worldviews, religions, cultures, identities, and other related concepts. When we use these terms, we suppose that the norm in question is not simply a reflection of interests (as described above) or of factual information about the world (as described under the rubric of diffusion below). We also suppose that a norm carries special force. It is what we *ought* to do, that is, what is expected of us (by some reference group whose opinions we value). Norms follow a logic of *appropriateness*.

Norms may be regarded as specific to a particular action such as the norm against incest. They may also be understood as part of a broader ideational *system* – an ideology, culture, belief-system, or value-system. For those who define themselves in religious terms the norm against incest would be understood as an element of their (Christian, Muslim, Buddhist, et al.) belief-system rather than as an isolated proscription. Identification with a social group (e.g., an ethnic group, national group, professional group, or college cohort) entails sharing the beliefs and values of that group. It is this set of norms that help to define the collectivity.

Norms may be set out in a formal manner, for example, the Old Testament's Ten Commandments, or they may take the form of informal understandings. The point is that they are shared and that they command obedience for reasons that reach beyond the interests of the actor. One feels a sense of obligation to a norm; if there is no such obligation then it is not a norm.

However, our use of the term presupposes that there is no explicit sanction for misbehavior or organization charged with maintaining that sanction. This is what distinguishes a norm from an *institution* (discussed below). For example, an electoral norm discourages politicians from lying to constituents in order to get elected. An electoral rule forbids politicians who are not citizens of a country from running for office. Infringement of the first brings no specific sanctions. Infringement of the second brings disqualification. This, in a nutshell, is the difference between a norm and a rule or institution, as we use these terms.

Psychology

In addition to interests, norms, and information, a person's attitudes and behavior may be affected by the way in which stimuli are processed. We shall refer to this set of explanatory factors as the realm of psychology.

Arguably, all individual-level behavior rests on some sort of psychological explanation. Sometimes, this explanation is so simple that we don't bother to delve into "psychology." When a consumer purchases a product after the latter is discounted this sort of behavior is consistent with an interest-based explanation and requires little comment. However, we could imagine a psychological explanation that would construct a micro-level foundation for this behavior. Someday, it may be possible to trace these micro-foundations with indicators of brain activity, as we can already do in a crude fashion with some emotions and cognitive faculties.

When writers invoke psychology, it is usually to explain behavior that doesn't seem to be based solely on a calculation of self-interest, the logic of appropriateness, or the inherent truth of an idea (as revealed by some diffusion process). For example, in understanding conflict of a violent nature it may be important to understand the emotions of the actors in that conflict, emotions such as hatred, fear, or resentment. In understanding the role of information, it may be important to understand how individuals calculate uncertainty. Research has shown, for example, that most people count losses more than gains, that they discount the future heavily, and that information is more believable if it is propounded by someone from their own social or political group or from a trusted authority.

Some psychological factors are widely shared among members of the species; they are universal, or nearly so. Other psychological factors may be specific to men or women or to persons of a specific age group. Others may be specific to individuals who occupy certain roles (e.g., leaders), inherit specific cultural traits (e.g., individualism), or have cognitive predispositions that set them apart from others (e.g., risk aversion). The notion of a *personality type* is intended to distinguish categories of people according to their way of processing information and reacting to the world.

Psychological characteristics may be hardwired in a person's genetic makeup. These features are often referred to as *cognitive* or *innate*. A lively research agenda within the social sciences focuses on cognitive features that influence attitudes, preferences, and behavior that we observe in the world today. Other psychological features are the product of a person's culture, family, neighborhood, or some other aspect of their lived experience (perhaps in interaction with their genetic endowments). This is *learned*.

The *nature/nurture* distinction is an important one. However, we should be wary of treating it as a dichotomy. Research suggests that our genetic makeup is not entirely fixed at conception and may evolve over time through lived experiences. In some respects, our nature is nurtured.

Structural Frameworks

A second set of explanations center on structural features that condition the perceptions, motivations, and capacity of actors. Three structural frameworks are common in the work of social science: *material factors*, *human capital/demography*, and *institutions*.

Material Factors

Material factors enable and constrain what humans can do. They include financial resources (e.g., income or capital), geography, and technology. An explanation based on material factors may be described as *materialist*. While materialist structures often work in tandem with interest-based motivations, as discussed above, they are not identical, as will become clear.

Individuals with lots of financial resources have the capacity to attain many goals that are beyond the reach of those without such resources. Moreover, those with and without money may see things differently, and behave differently, by virtue of their social class position. The poor usually vote differently from the rich; they are more likely to support redistributive policies; and they are more likely to commit violent crimes. Social class matters, as researchers since Karl Marx have reminded us. The primordial question of social science, Marxists would argue, is *who has what?*

Material explanations may also hinge upon the *distribution* of a good within a population, that is, who has *more*. Sometimes, the distribution of a good matters more than its absolute level. For example, happiness may depend more upon one's standing relative to others than one's actual (absolute) income. Here, income becomes a marker for success and thus determines one's social status. It is not having a car that matters but rather whether others in the neighborhood also possess cars, or whether they possess fancier cars than you do.

Just as rich people are different from poor people, rich societies are different from poor societies. Work in the modernization paradigm may be understood as an exploration of all the ways in which the advance of material development affects society, culture, and politics. An intriguing (but also controversial) example is "mother love" – the bond of attachment between a mother and child. Nancy Scheper-Hughes (1992) argues that the strength of this bond is to some extent determined by infant mortality rates within a society. As rates fall and infants are expected to survive through the perilous period of childhood, parents begin to invest emotional energy in their children at an earlier age. If so, mother love – seemingly, the most natural emotion of all – is explained as a product of material conditions.

Geography provides another type of material explanation. If one lives in a mountainous or heavily forested area that is distant from the sea or a navigable river one is likely to be relatively isolated. Over time, such isolation may prevent development and preserve long-established cultural practices. Marvin Harris's (1974) book, *Cows, Pigs, Wars & Witches*, explores the role of geography and other material factors in the development of cultural practices around the world. Jared Diamond's (1992) more recent synthesis, *Guns, Germs, and Steel*, explores the ramifications of geography for long-run development.

Technology is a third type of material factor, referring to tools that help produce or achieve an outcome. A generous reading of "tool" includes everything from the invention of writing to biogenetic compounds and prophylactics (birth control). As such, technology represents a key factor in the arts, in the economy, and in all aspects of human life. Some technological factors operate over long periods of time and in ways that are scarcely apparent to those of us who inherit their historical effects. Alesina, Giuliano, and Nunn (2013) argue that "the descendants of societies that traditionally practiced plough agriculture today have lower rates of female participation in the workplace, in politics, and in entrepreneurial activities, as well as a greater prevalence of attitudes favoring gender inequality." If the authors are correct, the timing of a technological advance in agriculture – namely, the plough – has an impact on gender roles many centuries later.

Human Capital/Demography

Human capital and demographic explanations focus attention on individual attributes such as education, skills, health, migration, age, and life-cycle events such as birth, marriage, and death. These attributes may also be aggregated up to describe a population. For example, one can speak of the educational attainment of an individual or the (average) educational attainment of a population.

Education is generally acknowledged to be a strong predictor of success, at all levels. Individuals with more education earn more than individuals with less education. Businesses with a lot of smart, well-trained people are likely to out-perform businesses with weaker employees. Countries with high human capital are thought to enjoy a significant advantage over countries with high illiteracy. Economists have also found that measures of health show a strong relationship to individual- and country-level achievement. Demographers have explored the various causes of high and low fertility across societies, and the impact of fertility on gender roles, infant survival, and cultural attributes such as individualism. The so-called demographic transition – a point in time when mortality rates fall, and birth rates fall – is thought to have vast implications for society and is widely regarded as a key element of economic and social development.

It seems clear that human capital/demography explains a lot about human attitudes and behavior, at individual, group, and societal levels.

Networks

Wherever a stable pattern of communication among individuals (or groups) exists the resulting network may be mapped, that is, drawn in a diagram or represented in a matrix. The network configuration may include additional information concerning the frequency of contact within a dyad, the duration of the event or the interconnection, the direction of the relationship, the substance of the communication, or attitudes toward others (inside and outside the network). Armed with this information, it may be possible to characterize ties as strong or weak and nodes in the network as central or peripheral.

The premise is that one can explain individual-level outcomes by examining the position of individuals within a network. For example, those with greater centrality may be more likely to receive information, to influence the behavior of others, or to fall victim of a communicable disease. At a system level, it may be possible to explain the relative speed or extent by which ideas, institutions, germs, technology, or some other factor of interest diffuses through a network.

Social capital explanations focus on the relative density of social networks. In a community where individuals have lots of interconnections that extend beyond their immediate family and workplace, there is high social capital. This sort of interaction is thought to foster social trust (and is in turn the product of social trust), political engagement, and employment opportunities. At an aggregate level, social capital is often seen as a key feature in economic development and good governance.

Institutions

Institutions refer to humanly created rules and the organizations that establish and maintain those rules. Together, they create incentives that condition preferences and behavior – and may, over time, affect the construction of norms.

A *rule* is understood as formal, explicit, and (usually) written, and is connected to sanctions or rewards for good/bad behavior. For example, electoral law establishes the context for elections, affecting the behavior of candidates, parties, and voters. Property law establishes the context for the operation of markets, affecting the behavior of investors, producers, and consumers. Those who do not abide by these rules are subject to prosecution.

Rules are enforced by *organizations*, which is why we incorporate both elements into our definition of an institution. An organization might be religious (e.g., the Catholic church), economic (e.g., a firm), political (e.g., a government), or social (e.g., a kin-group). In order to qualify as an organization, a group must have relatively clear boundaries, explicit criteria for membership, a set of rules, and officials who make and enforce the rules. A nation-state is an organization because it possesses all of these attributes. A nation without a state, by contrast, is less organizational. It is not clear for example who is a member of the Kurdish nation, how one gains or loses membership in this body, or who is responsible for making and enforcing the rules.

Our definition of institutions is a fairly narrow one, intended to help distinguish among rival explanatory frameworks. A broader definition of the subject would encompass many of the other explanatory frameworks explored in this chapter. ("Institutions" is one of the more malleable words in the social science lexicon.) Therefore, for present purposes a narrow definition is more useful.

However defined, social science work often focuses on the role of institutions – so much so that we are at a loss to provide specific examples for this section of the chapter, as they would encompass a majority of work in economics, political science, sociology, and related fields.

The popularity of institutions is not because institutions are necessarily more important than other explanatory factors. It is, rather, because institutions are the one explanatory factor that is solidly within our power – collectively – to change. Insofar as we want to improve society, we are likely to focus on institutional theories about how society works, for they are more relevant than factors over which we have little direct influence. When societies seek to change factors like resources, human capital, or motivational features of human existence, they do so by changing institutions that structure these outcomes. To change the distribution of resources we might propose a change in the tax code, for example. To improve the quality of human capital we might propose an increase in spending on educational programs. In this respect, institutional factors can claim primacy over other explanatory frameworks.

Interactive Frameworks

Sometimes, human attitudes and behavior is best explained as a dynamic interactive process rather than as the product of a single factor. Interactive frameworks include *adaptation, coordination, diffusion, networks,* and *path dependence*. Here, outcomes are understood as the product of interactions among people over time. Interactive factors thus combine elements already introduced as motivational or structural, building upon previous sections.

Adaptation

Adaptation focuses on the way in which individuals and groups adapt to a given environment. The notion is that, over time, the most efficient (fully adaptive) form will be achieved, with *efficiency* understood according to the preferences of the actors or by measuring success or survival.

Likewise, the attitudes and behavior of individuals and groups within a society may be understood according to the roles they play, that is, the functions they perform within that larger society. This *functionalist* view of social relations has a long history in anthropology and sociology stretching back to Emile Durkheim.

Sometimes, the adaptive (efficient) result is obtained through a process of *feedback*. When an individual pursues a strategy (e.g., to get elected or to sell a product) they receive feedback (from voters or from consumers). Based on this feedback they may decide to change their strategy.

Sometimes, the adaptive result is obtained through a process of *competition*. In a market economy, firms compete with one another for profits and market share. Competitive pressures – Adam Smith's *invisible hand* – may prompt firms to lower costs, improve their product, or adjust their sales strategy. Likewise, in a political market, parties (and politicians) compete for votes. Competitive pressures may prompt parties to alter their platforms, change their behavior, or adopt different campaign strategies. At a national level, one might regard nation-states as engaged in a similar battle for survival, prompting adaptive changes in organization. The implicit selection mechanism at work here – with firms, parties, or states – is survival. Organizations that do not adapt may disappear. This explanatory trope is modeled on Charles Darwin's theory of *evolution*, in which a process of natural selection rewards species that successfully adapt to their environment and punishes (by extinction) species that do not.

Sometimes, adaptation happens because individuals choose outcomes that benefit them. Here, adaptation maximizes utility. Efficient outcomes might take the form of a formal contract (e.g., between a buyer and a seller) or an informal understanding (e.g., between a patron and a client). One may also regard larger societal outcomes as efficient if they maximize the preferences of members in that society. For example, it might be argued that the spread of the nation-state throughout the world in the past several centuries is due to the fact that this particular form of political organization is the most efficient way to resolve conflict and provide public goods (though not everyone agrees with this premise). In any case, adaptive explanations presume a group – which may be as small as a family or as large as a country – for whom the arrangement is efficient.

Coordination

Coordination explanations focus on the failure to achieve efficient outcomes. Specifically, they focus on situations where the pursuit of individual preferences leads to suboptimal outcomes for those concerned. In this sense, all coordination problems may be described as *collective action* dilemmas.

One common coordination problem occurs when individuals find it in their interest to *free ride* on others. For example, citizens may prefer not to pay taxes even though they benefit from the services that government provides. Likewise, states may prefer not to lower tariffs on foreign goods even though they benefit from global free trade.

Table 8.2 Prisoner's dilemma

| | | Prisoner B | |
		Silence	Confession
Prisoner A	Silence	A: 1 year B: 1 year	A: 3 years B: 0 years
	Confession	A: 0 years B: 3 years	A: 2 years B: 2 years

Years: sentence to be served in prison.

Another sort of coordination failure is the *prisoner's dilemma* – where the payoffs from a situation give each player an incentive to defect from a cooperative outcome that would benefit both parties. Consider the following stylized scenario. Two prisoners arrested for the same crime are placed in separate cells and offered the same choice by the district attorney: confess (and implicate the other defendant) or remain silent. The payoffs for each set of decisions (length of sentence in prison), as stipulated by the district attorney, are listed in Table 8.2. Note that the optimal outcome for both prisoners – considered collectively – is to stay silent, which will mean they serve only a short, one-year term in prison. However, each prisoner is better off confessing than remaining silent, regardless of what the other prisoner decides. Defecting (confessing) is therefore the rational choice in a situation where prisoners are unable to coordinate with each other.

This hypothetical game has spawned a thousand others, each with modifications to the payoff structure, the number of players, the degree of communication allowed, the sort of rewards or punishments offered, and so forth. For our purposes, the key insight is that many social settings seem to exhibit coordination failures – where a suboptimal outcome is achieved because individuals (or groups) cannot successfully coordinate their activities.

A third sort of failure involves inter-temporal coordination failures such as those arising from the inability to make a *credible commitment* to a policy. Here, one party wishes to make a promise to another party but has no means of convincing the other party that the commitment will be upheld. An oft-cited example is the dictator who promises to respect property rights. In this scenario, investors have no assurance that the dictator will remain true to his/her promise in the future because a dictator – by definition – can change the rules whenever it suits him or her to do so.

A fourth sort of coordination failure (or impediment) involves *transaction costs* among individuals seeking to reach an agreement (or contract). These refer to any sort of barrier that increases the costs (on either party) of exchanging a good or service. This might involve information costs (relative to the substance of the agreement or the product being purchased), bargaining costs, or enforcement costs. While the transaction-cost framework was originally developed to understand the behavior of markets it has also been applied to politics, social institutions, and other venues.

Problems of coordination bedevil all social settings and are especially valuable in explaining the formation of institutions and in designing new institutions. Indeed, for some writers the concept of an institution is inseparable from the coordination problem it is designed to solve. It is often argued, for example, that the primary function of government is to solve collective action problems, for example, by internalizing costs and benefits and preventing free riding. Likewise, some state structures may enjoy an advantage because they solve a particular coordination problem. For example, since democratically elected rulers are constrained by a constitution and an independent judiciary, as well as by an electorate (who can vote out the incumbent), democracies may be better situated to solve problems of credible commitment – assuring investors that their property will be respected in the future.

Diffusion

Some phenomena are so irresistible that their spread can be explained simply by exposure. This process is often labeled diffusion. It might apply to especially appealing ideas, new information that affects the way we think about a topic, or new technologies that promise great returns. Here, a *demonstration effect* of prowess is sufficient. Since information expands knowledge and facilitates learning, *knowledge-* and *learning*-based explanations are integrated into this discussion.

Consider the choice between dropping out of school and remaining in school. This choice is presumably affected by one's understanding of the payoffs to each course of action. One might know with a high degree of certainty that one can get a job and the wages that job would bring, and one might be highly uncertain about whether one could get a higher-paying job if one continued one's education. Changes in this information – gained, say, by talking to recent graduates or reading a study following the fortunes of recent graduates – are likely to affect one's decision. The same is true for other decisions, for example, purchasing a good, casting a ballot, joining an insurrection, committing a crime, or procreating.

Not surprisingly, attempts to change behavior often take the form of information campaigns. To combat the spread of HIV/AIDS, people are informed about how the disease is spread, the consequences of contracting the disease, and methods of protecting themselves. To combat the use of tobacco and other drugs (especially among youth), people are informed of their highly addictive qualities and the consequences of long-term use. To promote a candidate, voters are informed of the candidate's background, their achievements to date, and their proposed program of action, which may be directly contrasted with their opponents' qualifications and policy commitments. Likewise, a promotional campaign for a new product may convey important information about that product.

Granted, information campaigns are generally not limited to information. There may also be a good deal of extraneous material, some normative appeals, and perhaps some downright falsehoods. Moreover, discerning information (truth) from lies is not always easy. This is why writers sometimes prefer to speak of *ideas* rather than information. In any case, the point remains that information (or ideas) about a subject often affects what an actor thinks and does.

The diffusion framework is so simple that it requires little elaboration. Suffice to say that causal explanations usually have a second focus – on the factors that encourage or discourage exposure. For example, diffusion of an idea might be enhanced by a network of communications, which in turn may be affected by communications technology (e.g., the availability of phone, email, or web-based connections). This leads to our next topic.

Path Dependence

A critical juncture is an event that is in some respect stochastic (random), that is, it could have been otherwise and cannot easily be explained by some other factor. Sometimes, an event of this sort has enduring consequences that flow in a structured way from the event. Here, we may refer to the resulting trajectory as path-dependent. This is the loose sense in which the terms critical juncture and path dependence are usually employed.

A narrower definition of path dependence refers to a situation in which an initial event is followed by a positive feedback loop ("increasing returns" or "lock-in") that works to entrench the original event. Unfortunately, it is often difficult to tell when a weak or strong version of the framework applies. And many writers do not have this more restrictive condition in mind when they use the term. Thus, we adopt the looser, more encompassing definition.

An instance of critical juncture/path dependence (by any definition) is the location of the keys on a standard English keyboard, which spell out the sequence QWERTY. The reason for this arrangement is largely accidental. An early typewriter assumed this format and later keyboards followed suit, for the simple reason that consumers (it was assumed) would not wish to learn a new system. It is, however, not highly adaptive (see discussion above), as typing speed would increase if the keys were arranged in a different fashion (once people learned the new system). But we are unlikely ever to realize that new arrangement because of sunk costs, that is, path dependence.

Institutions usually involve a degree of path dependence. Consider that every public policy involves a set of beneficiaries and a larger set of actors whose incentives are affected by the law. For example, the passage of the Social Security Act in 1935 established a new class of government beneficiaries (old people) and a larger class of individuals (including Americans of all ages) who base their retirement and investment decisions on the existence of this policy. Once a society has adjusted to this reality it becomes very difficult to change. Other policy solutions become less feasible (Derthick 1979).

Large and abstract institutions are also heavily path-dependent. Once democracy has become established in a country people accustom themselves to this form of government. Leaders gain material stakes in the system. Everyone's behavior and norms change. Consequently, democracy develops staying power. This is one way to explain the fact that few countries revert to autocracy once they have experienced several decades of democratic rule.

Importantly, path-dependent explanations are not always efficient (in the sense of maximizing the long-run preferences or interests of all concerned). Sometimes, a low-equilibrium outcome will persist even though it is not serving anyone very well. An example would be the QWERTY keyboard. Some might argue that in the context of an aging society the shape of social security policies also qualifies as an example of a non-efficient outcome.

Clarifications

Having introduced a typology of explanatory frameworks, summarized in Table 8.1, we need to clarify several points that have been left dangling.

First, the typology is not intended to be exhaustive. Indeed, the notion of a comprehensive set of explanatory frameworks would presume a comprehensive typology of human behavior – an unlikely prospect.

Second, each of the frameworks listed in Table 8.1 is broadly defined so as to encompass a wide variety of specific theories. Readers should not suppose that there is only one sort of materialist framework or that writers invoking material explanations agree with one another about the way the world works. There is a good deal of diversity within each framework, as we have sought to demonstrate.

Third, most of the frameworks listed in Table 8.1 can be applied at the individual or group level. For example, a person may be subject to material constraints as well as a social group, organization, or an entire nation. A group, after all, is a collection of individuals. Likewise, different explanations may apply at different levels. For example, individual behavior may respond to material incentives while group behavior is best explained by institutions.

Fourth, the outcomes of a causal theory – the phenomena one is ultimately concerned to explain – may be variously defined. Specifically, a theory may be designed to explain *attitudes* (what people think or feel), *preferences* (how people prioritize across options), *behavior* (what people do), or *conditions* (how people live or die).

Fifth, any number of possible interrelationships may be envisioned among the various frameworks. For example, a materialist theory may be enlisted to explain an institutional outcome. In this case, one framework serves as the cause, and another serves as the outcome.

Finally, these frameworks often play complementary roles. Indeed, a complete causal explanation for any social phenomenon generally incorporates more than one of the frameworks listed in Table 8.1. An explanation might enlist coordination logic to explain a set of institutions; these institutions might establish material incentives; and these incentives, in turn, may serve to motivate behavior. Here, diverse frameworks are woven together into a single narrative. So, causal frameworks are not always rivals. Sometimes, they are building blocks that combine to form a coherent causal explanation.

An Example: *Birth*

As an example of how different explanatory frameworks interweave let us consider the decision to have a child, which we have classified under the rubric of demography in Table 8.1. At group levels, this decision is typically measured as the total *fertility rate*, the average number of children born to each woman within a group or society during her childbearing years.

Some societies have high fertility rates. In sub-Saharan Africa, several countries have fertility rates of seven or more. Advanced industrial societies generally have fertility rates of two or less, below the rate at which a population can sustain its current level (without in-migration). Fertility rates in Hong Kong and Macao are now at about one child per woman, an astounding fact in light of human history. Only a century ago, fertility rates in most countries were close to those found today in the developing world. Indeed, fertility is an area where enormous change has occurred over a relatively small period of time, with immense consequences for humankind and for the natural environment.

A range of theoretical frameworks have been enlisted to explain fertility. Interest-based explanations regard procreation as a choice based on a calculation of costs and benefits. Fertility goes down when the costs of bearing a child go up relative to the associated benefits. This, in turn, is affected by the material situation in which adults find themselves, calling forth materialist explanations. Urban dwellers are less likely to need the labor provided by their children than those living in the countryside; likewise, space is scarcer and more expensive. Both of these factors alter the calculus of childrearing as the process of urbanization moves forward. Likewise, social insurance policies designed to care for adults in their old age lessen the need for children to serve as caretakers; in this fashion, the long-term payoff provided by children is lowered. Finally, as child mortality rates fall (as they have virtually everywhere in the world), the number of births required to achieve a given family size also declines. Here, mortality alters fertility.

However, varying fertility rates around the world do not seem to be solely the product of material considerations. Indeed, families are much larger in some parts of the world – especially in sub-Saharan Africa – than would be explainable on the basis of a narrow conception of self-interest. One possibility is that people are not correctly calculating the costs and benefits of having a child under current conditions; instead, they may be following norms of behavior that were established some time ago, under very different conditions (e.g., when child mortality was high). Perhaps norms lag behind objective circumstances. If so, we may think of material factors as the ultimate cause and norms as the proximate cause of behavior. If so, a change of norms may be required to affect fertility rates in a society.

Another possibility is that adults are not thinking about procreation in a cost-benefit framework at all; choices about when to marry, when to engage in sex, and whether to use birth control are instead based on deeply rooted cultural norms (including religious prescriptions) about what is expected, that is, a logic of appropriateness.

A third approach to fertility focuses on institutions. Public policies may prohibit or encourage the use of contraception and abortion. Policies may explicitly discourage large families in countries where the government wishes to depress the birth rate (e.g., the one-child policy in China) or encourage larger families in countries where depopulation is regarded as a problem (e.g., child allotments, offered in many advanced industrial countries).

A fourth approach focuses on psychological factors affecting the decision to have intercourse, utilize contraception, nurture a fetus to term, and seek appropriate medical assistance. A fifth approach considers fertility from within an adaptive framework. In some settings, groups are thought to engage in fertility competitions, in which only the most fertile groups survive. A sixth approach might enlist a coordination framework. Arguably, high fertility is a product of situations where the costs of a child are dispersed across a community while the benefits are centered on the child's biological parents. A communal setting of this sort establishes a collective action problem in which individual incentives are not aligned with community interests.

Other explanatory frameworks can easily be imagined. The point is, for any given outcome there are usually many possible explanations. Some may be truer than others; in this respect, explanatory frameworks are rivals. But all may be true, in varying degrees, or at different levels. If so, the various causal factors at work are likely to be interrelated in a complex fashion. Institutions may affect norms, and norms may also affect institutions, as seems likely in the previous example.

Conclusions

How can scholars use this collection of explanatory frameworks to construct a new research project? We can offer three affirmative suggestions, as well as several warnings.

Let us begin with the warnings.

First, one must be wary of theoretical frameworks that simply redescribe what is already known with a different vocabulary. There is some value in triangulating, but only if each perspective adds something to our understanding of the topic. This is sometimes difficult to evaluate since there are many dimensions of theoretical adequacy (outlined at the beginning of Chapter 9). Accordingly, the researcher will need to carefully consider various theoretical frameworks that have been invoked as explanations of Y to see which are superior along different dimensions (if they have unique strengths and weaknesses), and if there is any which is superior overall (taking all dimensions into consideration). Just as we want to avoid playing musical chairs with concepts (Sartori 1975) we must avoid playing musical chairs with theories.

Second, it can often be a bad idea to try to build a project that competes in the same intellectual niche as a prominent existing study, and trying to do so in a way that makes a contribution can end up creating tension with the just-discussed need to avoid theoretical musical chairs. It can be attractive to demonstrate that a new project is building closely on existing work – but if such a project is to be innovative and influential, it will need to make notable changes to the existing framework that are compelling and closely motivated by evidence. Consider Collier and Collier's (1991) renowned study using the path-dependence framework to explain how contrasting state approaches to legalizing labor unions in Latin America generated different party-system structures and concomitant trajectories of regime conflict. Roberts (2014) was able to construct a highly influential research project by asking whether that same framework applied to a subsequent set of political-economic changes in Latin America. Yet to make his project successful and intellectually exciting he had to apply the framework in very different ways, emphasizing very different causes and an entirely novel typology of outcomes. Furthermore, his sources and use of evidence was substantially different. In other words, in order to put together a successful project that follows in the footsteps of a famous piece of work and that uses the same explanatory framework it will generally be necessary to find sources of project-defining novelty. The major task then becomes justifying why those sources of novelty are productive and contribute to understanding – little in academic life is as tedious as change for its own sake.

Third, it is important to recognize that theoretical frameworks are seductive. Those in the business of constructing explanations are always on the lookout for master theories. By training and by inclination, we want to explain. And the greater the parsimony of our theories, and the more they seem to explain, the happier we are. Ideally, all the facts fit together into a coherent theory about "how the world works."

There is nothing wrong with this ambition. Indeed, it is highly functional. But we must remind ourselves that frameworks are famously loose. As such they are not really falsifiable, at least not in a strict sense. If someone claims that "norms, rather than institutions" affected an outcome it is doubtful that this sort of statement – at such a high level of abstraction – can be definitively proven. What is falsifiable is the *specific norm* that the author identifies.

Now, on to the suggestions.

First, avoid becoming too attached to a broad theoretical framework at the outset of a project, as it may lead one astray. Instead, look upon theoretical frameworks as aids to thinking. Reflection at an abstract level can sometimes help one to generate new ideas about an old topic, or about a new topic for which the literature is thin. It is these hunches, eventually developed into specific hypotheses, that form the basis for an argument and that can be tested once the research enters a confirmatory mode.

Second, scholars often create interesting projects by combining an explanatory framework with a real-world domain to which it seems unlikely to apply. This forces the creative task of imagining how that framework could contribute, a challenge that sometimes generates deeply counterintuitive theories and can point toward unexpected forms of empirical evidence. A classic example of this approach is Becker and Murphy's (1988) research on rational addiction. It seems hard to imagine a topic less conducive to interest-based explanation than drug addiction; surely it involves self-destructive behavior that disregards the rational mind? By disregarding this evident incompatibility and pushing interest-based explanation as hard as they can, Becker and Murphy propose an explanation of much addictive behavior that uncovers new, testable implications related to price shocks and addiction, the effects of divorce and unemployment on drug use among addicts, etc.

Many unusual combinations of explanatory framework and substantive domains can be imagined. What would a demographic theory of political apathy look like? A path-dependent theory of the democratic peace? An adaptation-based theory of money in politics? Such combinations may well prove unworkable, but the effort to creatively explore such juxtapositions can sometime generate insightful projects.

Third, projects can emerge from creative combinations of two different explanatory frameworks. Creative thought about how causes drawn from two disparate kinds of traditions can point the way toward interesting and original explanations, and toward broader projects. For example, Tilly's (1992) work on the origins of the modern state combined ideas drawn from the adaptation and interest paradigms: states became the predominant political actors in Europe and beyond because they had traits which made them capable of defeating rival forms of political organization in war, but the specific traits which made different states fit in this evolutionary sense depended on the degree to which they were dominated by the interests of trade-oriented cities. Such hybrid explanatory projects can help generate theories that have disciplined complexity, uniting diverse variables in principled and coherent ways.

Fourth, some projects originate in efforts to apply a wide range of explanatory frameworks to a new problem area, with a special spark coming from the question of which of these well-worn traditions will work best in breaking new empirical ground. For this kind of project to work well, it is essential to start with a broad and deep grounding in the various theories at issue. Deploying a subpar version of one explanatory framework against a well-developed version of another frameworks invite accusations of "straw-man" arguments (defeating a theoretical opponent by stating an extreme or weak version of the theory). Thus, it is best to start such a project from a perspective of interest in and enthusiasm about a wide range of divergent explanatory frameworks.

In any case, a combination of a broad interest in applying diverse theoretical perspectives with a new empirical context can create a fascinating project. Because the subject matter is novel for scholarship and because the application of explanatory frameworks is evenhanded, there is a substantial opportunity for influential new evidence about the usefulness of different frameworks – and therefore an inherent hook for readers.

Explanatory Challenges

In the early days of the Nazi regime a gang of thugs cornered a Jew and demanded of him who was responsible for Germany's troubles.
"The Jews," he promptly replied, "and the bicycle riders."
"The bicycle riders! Why the bicycle riders?"
"Why the Jews?"

Abraham Kaplan (1964: 331)

In the previous chapter, we introduced a variety of commonly used theoretical frameworks, classified as motivational, structural, or interactive. Our hope is that this itinerary is helpful in thinking through possible explanations for a phenomenon of interest, or perhaps even as a point of departure (if one is interested in the empirical implications of a specific framework).

In any case, a framework is not an explanation. One cannot simply adopt a framework and slap it onto a causal effect. Explanation is not a multiple-choice exercise.

What does it mean to explain? Previous chapters offered advice on how to come up with ideas for a topic. We emphasized that ideas often arise initially in an inchoate form – as hunches, intuitions, predilections, "tacit knowledge" (Polanyi 1966). Regardless of their source, a hunch must be nurtured. You will need to play with it, elaborate it, reconfigure it so that it begins to resemble a cogent explanation.

Little has been written on the problem of how to turn ideas into theories. Morrison and Morgan (1999: 12) note, "When we look for accounts of how to construct models in scientific texts we find very little on offer. There appear to be no general rules for model construction in the way that we can find detailed guidance on principles of experimental design or on methods of measurement." To be sure, there is an extensive philosophical literature on the meaning and workings of theories and models, a literature on formal models and a literature on social theory (see our review of sources at the end of Chapter 1). But few studies offer practical advice about theorizing that is not tied to a particular school or framework.

We begin this chapter by introducing the general desiderata of a good theory, and trade-offs that flow therefrom. Next, we discuss various complexities of theorizing – the number of causes and effects embraced by a theory, the specification of mechanisms, and defining units and levels of analysis.

Criteria of a Good Theory

What is a good causal theory? Why should we prefer one explanation of Y over another?

A good theory should strive for clarity, manipulability, separation, independence, impact, mechanisms, precision, generality, boundedness, parsimony, coherence, commensurability, relevance, tractability, and truth. These generic features of theories are summarized in Table 9.1.[1] Along these dimensions, one may judge one theory superior to another.

Of course, these criteria are often in conflict with each other. Maximizing one criterion may entail sacrificing another. In these instances, one theory is not obviously better than another; they are, rather, prioritizing different goals. Several trade-offs are especially ubiquitous: (a) parsimony v. impact, (b) abstraction v. realism and (c) precision v. generality.

Parsimony v. Impact

Theories aim at parsimony; this is, one might argue, their most distinctive trait. However, they also aim for impact. Often, these desiderata pull in different directions.

Typically, a concise theory explains only a small portion of the variance on Y, while a more turgid theory, with multiple moving parts, encompasses more of the variability.

Consider the contrast between two theories of democratization. One rests on the distribution of resources (measured by income, wealth, or land), which may be understood as a monotonic relationship (more inequality → less democracy [Boix 2003]) or a curvilinear relationship (where the probability of a democratic transition is maximized at a moderate level of

---

[1] For further elaboration see Gerring (2012b).

Table 9.1 Criteria of a good causal theory

Clarity (*antonym*: ambiguity)
What is the envisioned variation on X and Y, the background conditions, and the scope-conditions of the argument? Can X and Y be operationalized?

Manipulability
Is the causal factor manipulable (at least potentially)?

Separation (differentiation; *antonym*: tautology)
How separable is X relative to Y?

Independence (foundational, original, prime, prior, structural, unmoved mover)
Is X independent of other causes of Y?

Impact (effect size, magnitude, power, significance, strength)
How much of the variation in Y can X explain? Is the causal effect significant (in theoretical or policy terms)?

Mechanism (intermediary, mediator, pathway, process)
How does X generate Y? What are the causal mechanisms (M)?

Precision (specificity)
How precise are its predictions (hypotheses)?

Generality (breadth, domain, population, range, scope)
How broad (general) is it?

Boundedness (population, scope-conditions)
How well-bounded is it? Are the scope-conditions theoretically defensible?

Parsimony (concision, economy, Occam's razor, reduction, simplicity)
How parsimonious is it? How many assumptions are required?

Coherence (clarity, consistency; *antonym*: ambiguity)
How coherent internally consistent is it?

Commensurability (consilience, harmony, logical economy, theoretical utility; *antonym*: ad hocery)
How well does it cumulate with other inferences? Does it advance logical economy in a field?

Relevance (everyday importance, significance)
How relevant is it to issues of concern to citizens and policymakers?

Tractability (falsifiability, testability, verifiability)
How testable is it? Can it be verified or falsified?

Truth (accuracy, validity, veracity)
Is it true?

inequality [Acemoglu, Robinson 2005]). Regardless of the functional form, advocates of these theories will probably agree that they explain only a small portion of the variability in democratization as it has occurred over the past several centuries.

A second theory rests on a set of developments summarized as "modernization" (Boix, Stokes 2003; Inglehart, Welzel 2005; Lipset 1959). This includes income, industrialization, transportation and communication networks, education, and broader values. Writers may emphasize different aspects of modernization theory, but in practice – and in theory – they are difficult to disentangle. This makes the theory rather unwieldy, as it is not clear which factors (or which mix of factors) are carrying the freight. However, this omnibus theory also explains more of the variability in democratization than theories centered narrowly on the distribution of resources. It has greater impact.

Abstraction v. Realism

For some writers, the overriding objective of theorizing is *abstraction*.[2] In terms of the foregoing typology, this can be understood as a combination of generality, parsimony, coherence, and commensurability. Fans of theoretical abstraction point out that theories must be abstract if they are to perform the work required of them, namely to explain many phenomena with a few assumptions and, at the same time, linking up to other theories in a logical fashion.

For other writers, the overriding objective of theorizing is *realism* (Glaser, Strauss 1967; Little 1998; Swedberg 2012). In terms of the foregoing typology, this could be understood as a combination of precision, impact, tractability, and a clear specification of mechanisms.

In sociology, this debate is often traced back to a confrontation between Talcott Parsons, arguing for all-embracing theoretical frameworks (in this instance, structural-functionalism [Parsons, Shils 1962]), and Robert Merton, who argued for "middle-range" theories.[3] C. Wright Mills (1959) also castigated Parsons for theoretical overreach. Nonetheless, we can all appreciate the need for theoretical unification, and the associated loss of meaning if every theory floats in its own sea of concepts and assumptions (Wilson 1999).

The modern incarnation of this debate (there are few Parsonians nowadays) concerns rational choice, aka economic models (game theory et al.).

---

[2] See Cartwright (1983), Clarke, Primo (2012), Friedman (1953), Giere (1990), Healy (2017), Hesse (1966).
[3] The debate is nicely described in Rueschemeyer (2009: 10–11).

Those who advocate for abstraction generally have in mind a formal theory of some sort, as described in the next chapter. Critics of rational choice often cite a lack of realism in these models, among other things (Spiegler 2015).

Precision v. Generality

Most causal relationships of concern to social science are affected by background conditions that serve as moderators on the main relationship of interest: X's impact on Y is affected by D (see Figure 1.1). The broader the scope-conditions of a theory the more moderators are likely to be present. Since these are difficult to identify and to integrate, the theory experiences an attenuation in precision. The farther it extends, the less precise it is likely to be – not just with respect to the main causal effect but also with respect to the stipulated causal mechanisms. Since both precision and generality are rightly valued, this qualifies as another persistent trade-off encountered when formulating theories about the world.

Consider modernization theory, which we discussed above. If applied narrowly to the postwar world the theorist can make more precise predictions about the workings of the theory and the relationship between inputs and outputs. If, however, the scope-conditions are broadened – stretching back to the nineteenth century or even to the ancient world – things become more ambiguous. The theory loses precision.

Conclusions

There is no single right way to compose a theory, as the foregoing trade-offs amply illustrate. One may view each of these styles of theorizing as useful for certain purposes and in certain contexts. So, as you craft your theory think about the alternatives, and the strengths and weaknesses of each approach. Your goal as a theorist is to maximize the objectives of theorizing (summarized in Table 9.1), while acknowledging that there may be trade-offs.

With this as background let us turn to other challenges.

Causes and Effects

In constructing a causal explanation, you need to think carefully about what your objectives are. Since this may not be immediately obvious, we shall spend some time discussing the options.

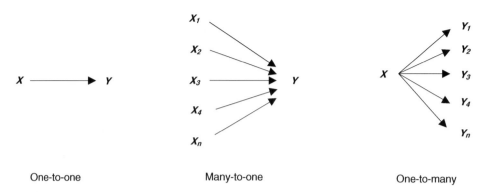

One-to-one   Many-to-one   One-to-many

Figure 9.1   A typology of causes and effects

Causal theories may be categorized according to the number of causes
(X_{1-n}) and effects (Y_{1-n}) the theory encompasses. Viewed schematically,
there are three available options: *one-to-one*, *many-to-one*, and *one-to-
many*, as illustrated in Figure 9.1. (No one undertakes to investigate
many causes and many outcomes; that would be a truly unbounded
enterprise.)

One-to-One Theories

Most article-length work is focused on a single cause and a single outcome,
sometimes described as "effects of causes" (Holland 1986), which we call *one-
to-one*.

For example, in an influential early study of the resource curse, Michael
Ross (2001) examines whether oil wealth (X) diminishes the possibility of a
democratic opening (Y). There is one cause and one outcome (although, to
be sure, X and Y might be measured in a variety of ways).

A one-to-one relationship is the least ambitious sort of theory, and also
easiest to carry out. From the perspective of causal inference this style of
research has great appeal. However, the theoretical payoff is limited.

Many-to-One Theories

A few articles, and many books, are more ambitious, seeking to identify all
the causes – or at least all principal causes – of an outcome. This style of work
is sometimes described as "causes of effects" (Holland 1986), though we
prefer the term *many-to-one*.

Accordingly, many books attempt to grapple in a comprehensive fashion with (all) the causes of democracy. Such works include a discussion of the resource curse but also other factors – economic development, geography, colonialism, education, religion, ethnolinguistic diversity, political institutions et al. – that might impact a country's regime type.[4]

Many-to-one theories are ambitious, but also ambiguous. It is never entirely clear when a truly comprehensive survey of possible causes has been attained. Note that a many-to-one theory entails a categorization of causes such that the resulting typology is mutually exclusive and exhaustive, and a good deal of judgment will be required in establishing such a typology. (What are all the possible causes of democracy, and how might they be categorized in a meaningful fashion?)

Moreover, the author faces the problem of infinite causal regress: How far back should the inventory of causes extend? Poverty may be understood as a product of (a) individual choices, (b) education, (c) family background, (d) discrimination based on ascriptive characteristics, (e) the structure of the economy, (f) patterns of slavery or migration, or (g) geography. Each of these explanatory frameworks constitutes a step backward in causal order. Granted, this is just one way these causes might be ordered, and any such judgment is open to debate. So, when dealing with a plenitude of causes in a many-to-one theory the author is obliged to establish a causal ordering among the various causes and make a convincing argument about which Xs are endogenous to which other Xs. Empirically, the task envisioned for many-to-one theories is even more complicated.

Nonetheless, for all sorts of reasons – theoretical and practical – we often wish to know everything there is to know about an outcome of great concern. And it is vain to suppose we can learn all we need to know simply by surveying a great number of one-to-one studies. This is because causes of Y interact *with each other*. Of course, in the artificial world of experimental designs they can be separated; but in the real world they interact. And since our theoretical and practical concerns center on the real world these interactions cannot be avoided.

One-to-Many Theories

A third format seeks to identify a wide variety of outcomes stemming from a single cause, a *one-to-many* design.

---

[4] See Coppedge (2012), Møller, Skaaning (2012), Teorell (2010).

In this vein, a later study by Michael Ross (2013) examines the impact of oil wealth on regimes, patriarchy, civil conflict, and economic growth. Gerring and Veenendaal (2020) seek to understand the implications of population size for politics. Dyson (2001) looks at the multifarious effects of the demographic transition.

A one-to-many theory is evidently ambitious. There is, to begin with, the problem of identifying all the effects stemming from a given cause. At the same time, there is less pressure to be comprehensive because the omission of an outcome does not compromise the objectives achieved by the outcomes that *are* under study. One can grapple – theoretically and empirically – with $X \rightarrow Y_1$ without understanding $X \rightarrow Y_2$. In effect, the one-to-many design is an iterated version of the one-to-one design.

It should be pointed out that the theoretical payoff of a one-to-many theory is enhanced if there are some core mechanisms that apply to all (or most) outcomes. This is not always achievable, however.

Mechanisms

Now let us consider the role of mechanisms in a causal theory. To most people, this is the heart of the theory. Indeed, it is virtually indistinguishable from the theory because only in specifying the mechanisms operative between X and Y are we able to provide an answer to the "Why?" question.

For any given causal relationship there are usually a number of plausible explanations. This is especially likely to be the case if X bears a distal relationship to Y. As a point of departure, the researcher is well-advised to compile an inventory of possible pathways that is as comprehensive as possible. To do so, they might consider (a) extant literature, (b) how scholars with markedly different perspectives might view the subject, (c) how the actors under investigation make sense of their own actions (hermeneutics), and (d) widely used explanatory frameworks (Chapter 8).

With this inventory in hand, one can now consider which mechanisms, or which concatenation of mechanisms, is most likely. In the *simple* case, X and Y are connected by a single mechanism, M_1. A *sequential* pathway is composed of a sequence of mechanisms, illustrated as $M_1 \rightarrow M_2 \rightarrow M_3$. A final option identifies *parallel* pathways, M_{1-3}, each of which operates as an independent mechanism through which X affects Y. These three archetypes are illustrated in Figure 9.2.

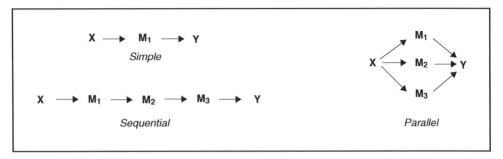

Figure 9.2   A typology of mechanisms

Of course, these options may be combined. And more complex mechanisms may be contemplated. Indeed, there are an infinite number of different diagrams that could be drawn to indicate possible connections between X and Y.

A Cautionary Note

The prospect of a mechanism-centered social science has elicited great enthusiasm.[5] For one thing, mechanisms are sometimes more generalizable than causal effects; in this respect, they function as the building blocks of general theory. Writers also point out that clarity often comes from scoping down – from causal effects to the mechanisms at work in those relationships. In the case of modernization theory, it would be helpful to know which (if any) of the stipulated mechanisms are responsible for the effect.

And yet, there are also reasons to doubt the utility of a mechanism-centered social science (Gerring 2008, 2010).

To begin with, mechanisms are often difficult to measure. If something cannot be measured, or can be measured only for a few cases, it will be hard to test, and the result of that test may be difficult to generalize from.

Second, there are often multiple ways in which X can affect Y, and these pathways are often intertwined. They may affect each other, or be difficult to disentangle, empirically and conceptually. Consider the pathways from economic development to democracy (which for the moment we shall assume is causal). Economic development may stimulate greater education, greater equality, and changes in values and norms. Each may

---

[5] See Bunge (1997), Hedström, Swedberg (1998), Little (1998), Mahoney (2001).

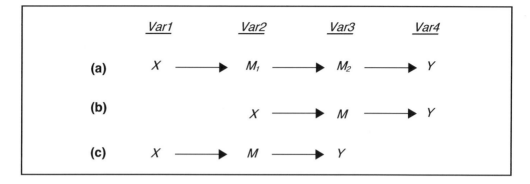

Three causal arguments that define causes, mechanisms, and effects in slightly different ways by focusing on different portions of a larger causal chain. The variables are the same but their role is different.
X   Causal factor of theoretical interest ("treatment")
M   Mechanism, aka pathway, intermediate variable, mediator
Y   Outcome of theoretical interest

Figure 9.3   The residual status of mechanisms

serve as a pathway from economic development to democracy. However, these pathways undoubtedly affect each other, and in ways that would be difficult to diagram.

Third, mechanisms are rarely manipulable, and thus cannot be explored experimentally. Accordingly, mediation analysis involves all the assumptions usual to causal inference *plus* additional assumptions (Imai et al. 2011).

Fourth, it should be pointed out that the very terms themselves – causal effect, mechanism – are the product of a researcher's imagination. It is they who define which variables are labeled causes, mechanisms, and outcomes. This makes the study of mechanisms a fragile endeavor, for it is parasitic on the definition of X and Y.

Consider the three causal diagrams illustrated in Figure 9.3, labeled (a), (b), and (c). Now imagine that that variables in each column – *Var1–Var4* – are identical. Each of these three causal diagrams lays out a different set of hypotheses: the cause, mechanism(s), and outcome are different in each instance. However, they involve the same variables. This game can be extended indefinitely as there are (in principle) an infinite number of mechanisms in between a putative cause and its effect, and there is an infinite number of antecedent causes for every stipulated cause. In principle, any cause can serve as a mechanism or effect; any mechanism can serve as a cause or effect; and any effect can serve as a cause or mechanism.[6]

This is not to denigrate research into mechanisms. It is, rather, to call attention to the *residual status* of mechanisms, which assume meaning only in the context of a particular causal relationship. Since the latter can be reconfigured in any number of ways it follows that the nature of the mechanism can change in any number of ways. A mechanism-centered social science refers to "whatever happens to fall in between X and Y" in the work of social science.

The more distal the relationship between the cause and effect the more crucial – and, at the same time, mysterious – is the mechanism(s) that connects them. The more proximal the relationship between cause and effect the more obvious the mechanism. Some mechanisms are so distal that they must remain highly ambiguous; others are so proximal as to be trivial.

One interpretation of mechanism-centered social science suggests that we should abandon the attempt to reconstruct long causal chains. Instead, we should adopt a tighter focus, defining the causal relationship of interest according to factors that lie close to one another (Green, Ha, Bullock 2010). In principle, this tighter focus ought to shed light on the "nuts and bolts" of social behavior (Elster 1989). However, it is questionable whether close attention to these nuts and bolts will help us reconstruct the larger machines within which they are situated. Micro does not always aggregate neatly into macro – an issue taken up in the next section.

Perhaps the take-home point here is that sometimes it makes sense to shift from macro to micro, that is, from a distal causal effect to a more proximal relationship that is more tractable or at any rate less studied. In Figure 9.3, this involves a shift from (a) to (b) or (c). If we have trouble reaching firm conclusions about the role of modernization in democratization, perhaps we can get traction by focusing on some of the mechanisms supposedly at work in this relationship, treating them as causes (and regime type as the outcome) (Seawright 2019: 32–34). Alternatively, we might look at the relationship between economic development and some of these purported mechanisms, treating them as the outcome of interest.

This is not an issue we can resolve in the general case. But here is some practical advice. If proximal causes are more tractable than distal causes, the researcher is well-advised to travel into the interstices of causality. If

---

[6] This view of mechanisms presumes a "manipulability" approach to the subject (Pearl 2000; Morgan, Winship 2015; Woodward 2005). For contrasting views, see Cartwright (2007).

proximal causes are difficult to disentangle (conceptually and/or empirically) from an outcome, or if they are obvious (and thus not worth investing time in), the researcher is well-advised to move toward more distal causes or more distal outcomes. And if either proximal or distal causal relationships offer a theory with greater breadth, this is also an important dimension to consider. The accordion opens, and closes, revealing different aspects of causation. Where you decide to focus is a highly consequential decision.

Units and Levels of Analysis

Social science theories may be oriented toward explaining individuals or larger aggregates (groups or organizations). The modal psychology theory applies to individuals and the modal theory of international relations applies to states. As always, it is important to clarify the scope-conditions of a theory – in this case, which level(s) it applies to.

But it is not just a question of scope-conditions.

Macro-level explanations presume micro-level relationships. A theory about parties must also make sense of (or at least presume certain things about) the members of that party, as a party does not exist outside of the individuals who comprise the organization. A theory about macro-level economic performance must make sense of (or at least be concordant with plausible assumptions about) the behavior of firms, investors, and consumers. Macroeconomics presumes microeconomics.

Let us consider one further example. Theories of international relations frequently treat states as independent units of analysis with coherent set of interests (Waltz 1979). This is a necessary heuristic tool. But it should not blind us to the fact that states are composed of people, who may or may not share those interests. Indeed, it is common to observe that leaders play two-level games (Putnam 1988), signaling a divergence of goals across different levels. Leadership often works differently at different levels (Yammarino et al. 2005). Thus, macro-level theories must make sense of behavior at lower levels; otherwise, they are not very persuasive.

Likewise, micro-level explanations presume macro-level relationships. This is because individuals are not isolated atoms. They interact with each other and respond to norms and incentives established at a group level. Kenneth Arrow (1994: 4–5) elaborates: "economic theories require social elements as well even under the strictest acceptance of standard economic assumptions . . . individual behavior is always mediated by social relations.

These are as much part of the description of reality as in individual behavior." Even if individuals could be treated as isolated units, it is usually the aggregated effects of individual actions – at a societal level – that we are ultimately concerned with. The "invisible hand" is a useful theory only insofar as it has societal ramifications. So micro-level explanations must be scaled up, transporting one's theoretical rubric from micro to macro.

In summary, although most theories operate predominantly at one level, it is difficult to cleanly separate micro- and macro-level explanations. Each implies the other. From this perspective, all theories involve a micro-macro link.[7]

Sometimes, this link can be theorized in an explicit fashion. In a classic article, Thomas Schelling (1971) argued that racial segregation at municipal levels could be explained by behavior at neighborhood levels. The assumption is that there are shared preferences, for example, that members of a social group would be willing to live alongside members of another racial group but not if they are in the minority. This shared preference leads quickly to a municipal-level outcome of complete segregation. The theory is informative because it produces a result that is difficult to explain except by recognizing the way in which individual preferences can aggregate into societal-level outcomes that, in this case, are neither anticipated nor preferred (in the sense that most individuals, if surveyed, would not choose a completely segregated city).

Of course, this begs the question of what *is* the relevant unit of analysis for evaluating segregation? In Schelling's example it might be neighboring houses, housing blocks, neighborhoods, or cities. (It might even be the state or the nation, though Schelling does not speculate on this.)

Political units with official status and distinct responsibilities are almost always multi-level. For example,

- United Nations (global)
- *European Union* (supra-national)
- *France* (national)
- *Midi-Pyrénées* (regional)
- *Haute-Garonne* (departmental)
- *Toulouse Métropole* (metropolitan)
- *Toulouse* (commune).

---

[7] See Alexander et al. (1987), Blau (1964), Hedström, Swedberg (1998), Little (1998), Raub, Buskens, Van Assen (2011), Schelling (1978).

Sometimes, these units are neatly nested, as in this example. Sometimes, they overlap, as in school districts and counties in the United States.

Evidently, the way in which a spatial unit is defined may determine what appears to go on within that unit. Segregation, viewed at the level of a block, may be quite different from segregation viewed at the level of a neighborhood or city.

There is no clean answer to the question of units, just as there is no clean answer to the question of levels of analysis. The problem – and, one might say, the enticement – of theorizing about society is that everything is connected to everything else, so all distinctions are in some sense arbitrary.

Our point in drawing attention to this arbitrariness is to heighten self-consciousness about an oft-overlooked issue in theorizing. Think about how your units are defined, and how your theory might be affected if you defined those units differently. Think about what levels of analysis your theory operates at, and how it relates to other levels. Scale up and scale down.

Conclusions

Theorizing is not easy, and the task is complicated by the fact that social scientists have different views about how to do it and even about what makes a good theory. In this chapter, we have tried to identify some of these debates.

The good news is that these debates are more about what criteria to prioritize than they are about what makes a good theory (Table 9.1). We can all agree that generality is a desirable feature of theories, though we might not agree on whether, or to what extent, other criteria should be sacrificed for this particular desideratum. And of course, we might disagree about how much generality can be achieved in a given context.

Likewise, there are different ways of structuring causes and effects within a theory, which we have categorized as one-to-one, many-to-one, and one-to-many (Figure 9.1). We can all agree that the first option is easiest, both with respect to theory elaboration and theory testing. But the latter options address important questions that we cannot easily dispense with.

There are also different ways of structuring a set of causal mechanisms, which we have categorized as simple, sequential, and parallel (Figure 9.2). Simple mechanisms are easiest to frame and to test but they may omit a good deal of the action. Again, one faces trade-offs.

Finally, there are inevitable questions about units and levels of analysis. Every theory presupposes a set of micro-macro links, and it is the job of the theorist to make these links as explicit as possible, even if they cannot always be tested.

We hope that this extensive and detailed discussion is an aid to your theoretical deliberations and not a source of frustration. We don't mean to make theorizing more complicated than it already is. The trouble is that these difficulties are *already present*, so one must be prepared to grapple with them. Also, we want to elucidate a full menu of options in theorizing, as we have in other chapters devoted to other subjects. Theorizing can take many forms. Only with a full understanding of those forms is it possible to make an informed choice about what form your theory should take. In the next chapter, we turn to a series of practical tools and tips for guiding the process of theorizing.

Tools and Tips for Theorizing

If carried through with consistency, the enterprise of theorizing might help to usher in a new period of interesting and creative theory in social science. One reason for hoping this is that there is no reason to believe that only a small number of gifted scholars can produce theory. Everyone who can think, can ultimately also theorize; and the project of theorizing is therefore inherently democratic.

Richard Swedberg (2012: 33)

Previous chapters addressed the great variety of theoretical frameworks (Chapter 8) and the challenges of explanation (Chapter 9). Those chapters were pitched at a fairly high level of abstraction. In this chapter, we offer some specific tools and tips for turning incipient ideas into full-blown theories.

William McGuire advocates a "multimodal" approach to the articulation of theories. Describing an idea in different ways "enrich[es] one's grasp of the theory and increase one's likelihood of noticing its implications, of recognizing its similarities and contrasts with other formulations, of detecting its gaps and weaknesses" (McGuire 2004: 179; see also De Chadarevian, Hopwood 2004). From this perspective, presentational issues (What is rhetorically effective?) cannot be separated from heuristic issues (What *is* the theory?).

Building on this oft-cited paper, we suggest a variety of approaches to theory elaboration: (a) oral, (b) written, (c) pictorial (e.g., graphs, causal diagrams, Venn diagrams, multidimensional diagrams, decision trees, maps, networks), (d) key cases, and (e) formal models. In the concluding section we offer some general guidelines for constructing a theory.

The Spoken Word

Let us begin with the spoken word. Speech predates writing and all other forms of complex communication, by millennia. It follows that we might have an easier time expressing a new idea by voice than by any other means.

Speak aloud to yourself, or subvocalize, as you work through your thoughts. Then, try out your idea on family and friends. Work on your "elevator speech." Finally, develop a formal talk that you can present to colleagues.

Articulating an idea in front of an audience should help you understand better what it is you want to say. Keep a close eye on yourself as you speak. See if your presentation of an idea changes as you explain it to different sorts of people.

At what point do you feel most confident, or most uncertain? When do you feel you are bullshitting? These are important signals with respect to the strengths and weaknesses of the project. In this fashion, the process of presenting – aside from any concrete feedback you receive – may force you to reconsider issues that were not initially apparent.

The Written Word

Now let us consider the written word. Crafting sentences on a page forces one to be more explicit than one might when speaking extemporaneously. One cannot use shrugs, winks, and smiles to get through a paragraph. The words must speak for themselves. And this enforces a level of discipline on the thinker (if they are careful with their words).

Writing also allows one to think in a more studied, extended fashion than is afforded by the spoken word. Inevitably, one finds oneself staring at words, reading and rereading sentences, moving text around. While this may seem at the time like a colossal waste of time it should be credited as a form of thinking. In rearranging words, one is also rearranging thoughts.

Some people find that the act of thinking is stimulated by the physical act of holding a pen or pencil and pressing it to a page. Others prefer the apparent freedom of a word processor, which allows endless corrections and edits, wiping away the traces of earlier drafts so that the page remains pristine.

In any case, writing is not a merely mechanical exercise. Getting one's thoughts on paper helps one to craft those thoughts. Wildavsky (1993: 9) declares,

I do not know what I think until I have tried to write it. Sometimes the purpose of writing is to discover whether I can express what I think I know; if it cannot be written, it is not right. Other times I write to find out what I know; writing becomes a form of self-discovery. I always hope to learn more than was in me when I started.

This recalls E. M. Forster's (1927: Ch. 5) quip: "How can I tell what I think till I see what I say?"

At the early stage of a project it may be a mistake to harness oneself to a single *idée fixe* or a detailed outline. Let your prose follow your thoughts. Then, go over what you have written to see how much of it is useful.

Kenneth Arrow (quoted in Kaplan 1964: 289) notes that since language is a social phenomenon, "the multiple meanings of its symbols are very likely to be much better adapted to the conveying of social concepts than to those of the inanimate world." Natural language should be a good fit for social behavior because it is through language that we influence each other and explain our own behavior. We are animals distinguished by our use of language.

Pictures

Although natural language offers a flexible tool of expression its very flexibility can also be an excuse for flatulence. By contrast, drawing a picture may get you – and your audience – straight to the point.

Research in psychology and education suggests that pictures serve an important heuristic function (Larkin, Simon 1987; Novick 2001). They are especially useful for elaborating a theory with many moving parts, for pictures are also highly versatile whenever an idea can be expressed spatially. One can "think" abstractly on paper without falling prey to the constraints of words and numbers. Pictures, finally, offer a highly synoptic format, allowing one to fit an entire argument onto a single figure.

If one is proficient with graphic design, drawing a picture of the relationship of theoretical interest may be handled on a computer screen. For the rest of us, pencil and paper or a whiteboard are the best expedients, at least at initial stages. (Published versions will require fancier technology.)

Evidently, a great many pictorial options are available. In the following sections we touch upon graphs, causal diagrams, Venn diagrams, multidimensional diagrams, decision trees, maps, and networks. Even so, readers will appreciate that we have barely scratched the surface of this vast subject.[1]

---

[1] For further ideas, see Banks (2001), Tufte (2001, 2006), Tufte, Goeler, Benson (1990), Tufte, Graves-Morris (1983), Ward, Grinstein, Keim (2015).

Graphs

Two- or three-dimensional graphs are usually understood as tools for the presentation of data. But they can also be used to present an idea.

As an example, consider the theory of demographic transition (Kirk 1996; Notestein 1945). Every modern society is thought to experience a similar sequence. In the pre-transition stage, high birth rates are matched by high death rates with the result that the population is stable. In the second stage, death rates decline, leading to a period of population growth. In the third stage, birth rates decline, slowing population growth and generating an older population. In stage four, low death rates are matched by low birth rates, stabilizing population growth once again. A hypothetical fifth stage, after the transition is completed, remains unclear. This is a lot of verbiage, and it may be difficult for readers to grasp the main ideas, which are actually quite simple if illustrated in a graph, as shown in Figure 10.1.

Causal Diagrams

If your argument is causal you may want to consider drawing a causal diagram, whose core components were introduced in Chapter 1. This exercise is especially useful wherever there are complex interactions among variables.

For example, in Seawright's (2012) study of party-system collapse, a key part of the argument involves claims that certain kinds of corruption scandals and patterns of underrepresentation cause increased voter scrutiny of politicians'

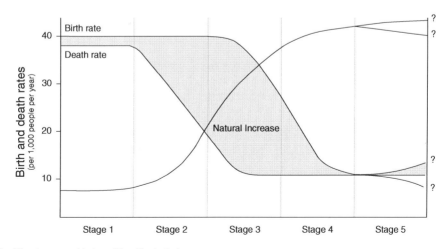

Figure 10.1   The demographic transition illustrated

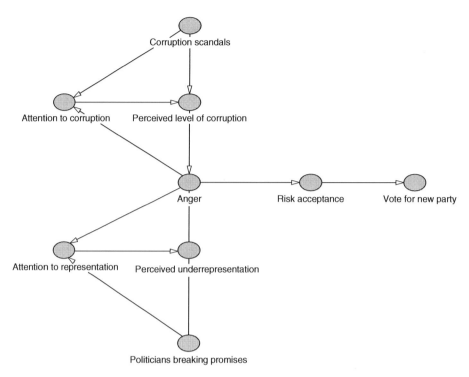

Figure 10.2   A complex set of interactions in a causal diagram
A causal diagram, adapted from Seawright (2012: 12).

job performance in those domains, which in turn is both increased by and increases voter anger. Anger serves as a pivotal variable increasing voters' willingness to take the risk of voting for a brand-new party with no governing track record. This is hard to process in prose and takes pages to adequately spell out. But it is a cinch to diagram, as shown in Figure 10.2.

Drawing a causal diagram will force you to clarify what you mean. Arguably, if an argument *can't* be arrow-diagrammed it is not clear enough to be empirically tested, and is for all intents and purposes unfalsifiable (Van Evera 1997).

So, if there are an intricate number of interconnecting causal mechanisms in your theory, try to map them as nodes in a causal diagram. One can also distinguish between causal factors of theoretical interest and those in the background, for example, rival theories. For this purpose, one might highlight the former in bold, while leaving the latter in regular type. A great deal of flexibility is afforded the author; the only constraint is a two-dimensional grid of nodes tied together by unidirectional or bidirectional arrows.

Bear in mind that to some methodologists these diagrams are viewed narrowly, as a means of mapping a data generating process and thereby achieving causal inference – specifically, keeping track of potential confounders and finding ways to circumvent them. For this purpose, a set of rules associated with "DAGs" (Directed Acyclic Graphs) have been developed (Morgan, Winship 2015; Pearl 2000).

However, causal diagrams are also useful for theorizing as they allow us to sketch out plausible relationships, even those that might be quite complex and that violate techniques of causal inference (e.g., involving feedback loops). This is how we are using the machinery here.

Venn Diagrams

A third pictorial format is afforded by Venn diagrams, a set of circles that establish "within" and "without" relationships. Sometimes, these relationships are understood as necessary and/or sufficient causes (Mahoney, Vanderpoel 2015). More frequently, they are conceptual. For example, in Figure 10.3, a Venn diagram illustrates the relationship between different American Indian identities. On the left is the political identity, requiring an individual to be enrolled in a recognized tribe (a status with its own set of genealogical criteria). On the right is an individual's self-assigned status, determined by whether a person considers themself Indigenous, Native American, or Indian. The intersection of these two circles represents the union of these two sets,

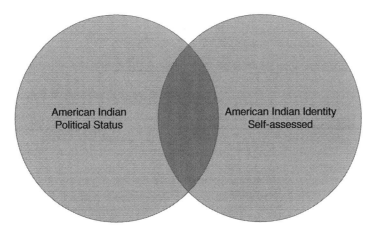

Figure 10.3   A Venn diagram of American Indian identities
American Indian identities, understood as the intersection of political status and self-assessed identity.
Source: Meissner (2018), who builds on Singel (2015).

comprised of individuals who consider themselves, and are considered by the US government, to be Indian. It is a simple point, but difficult to clarify in prose.

Multidimensional Diagrams

A fourth pictorial format is spatial, where each direction in space illustrates a particular dimension (Brady 2011). In political science, it is common to represent ideology along a left-right spectrum, as shown in Figure 10.8 (discussed later in this chapter). Sometimes, however, cleavages do not align neatly on a unidimensional space. Figure 10.4 illustrates two cross-cutting cleavages in American politics, one centered on foreign policy (hawks versus doves) and the other on domestic policy (government versus business). Schattschneider (1960) reasons that the relative salience of these two cleavages had considerable impact on electoral outcomes, and hence on party control and public policy.

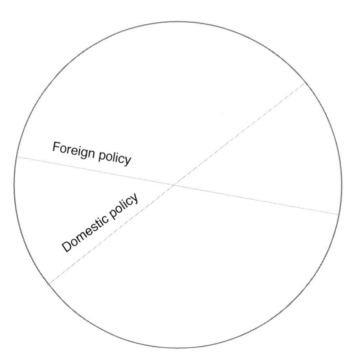

Figure 10.4   Cross-cutting cleavages
Two cleavages in American politics. *Source:* Schattschneider (1960), discussed in Brady (2011).

Decision Trees

A fifth pictorial format is sequential, where each stage of a process is graphed on a decision tree. While decision trees are often associated with game theory and rational choice, they are also used more broadly to think about causation in social contexts. For example, Heemskerk (2002) draws on ethnographic research to propose a theory of why some people in Surinam's portion of the Amazon rainforest engage in potentially environmentally destructive gold-mining activities while others do not. While there is extensive verbal description of the ethnographic evidence and resulting theory, Heemskerk also summarizes it in terms of a decision tree, a somewhat simplified version of which is shown in Figure 10.5.

The decision tree quickly conveys multiple features of Heemskerk's theory of gold-mining decision-making in the Amazon. First, it shows that gendered roles and expectations, as well as an individual's economic circumstances, are

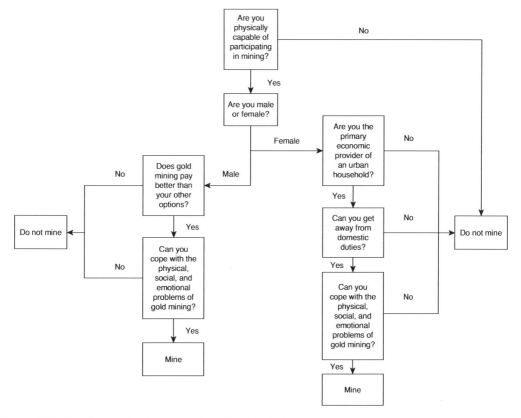

Figure 10.5   Decision tree showing reasons for gold mining in the Amazon
Source: Modified from Heemskerk (2002: 336).

hypothesized to powerfully shape the decision-making in question. Women and men can both end up participating in gold mining, but the tree shows that gender changes the criteria that matter to the decision. For example, men are hypothesized not to consider questions of domestic responsibility, which are seen as decisive for many women. Economic conditions are seen as mattering for both genders, but in different ways. Second, the tree shows that a wide range of potentially important considerations are excluded from the theory. Heemskerk hypothesizes that attitudes about the environment, for example, are simply not a major part of the decision-making process.

Constructing this kind of decision tree can be a helpful tool for building the kind of hypothesis that drives a broader project, as well as being a good way of reporting certain kinds of ethnographic findings (Gladwin 1989). Working through such a tree pushes us to think about how differently situated individuals approach the decision that constitutes our outcome of interest, and encourages ideas about contextual difference and heterogeneity that can generate fascinating research projects. The graphical structure of the tree enhances this thinking both by forcing scholars to make explicit decisions about symmetry across sides of the tree and by helping the audience to quickly understand the resulting, often complex, theory.

Maps

A sixth pictorial format takes the form of a map. Maps depict a phenomenon in a spatial environment, usually with a natural scale – meters, kilometers, and so forth. The scope might be global, national, or very local. Perhaps the most famous map in the history of social science is one drawn at the direction of John Snow, the world's first epidemiologist (Johnson 2006). We discussed Snow's landmark discovery of the source of cholera in Chapter 7. Here, we focus on the medium that allowed him to demonstrate – to himself and to others – the relationship between cholera and impure water. He did so by relating the location of cholera deaths to existing water pumps on a map of London, reproduced in Figure 10.6. The dark squares on this map indicate cholera deaths. At the center of the map, you can see (if you squint) Broad Street and its infamous pump. Note that cholera deaths radiate out in a nearly perfect circle around the pump, a visual suggestion that there might be a causal connection. Indeed, when the pump was shut down, cholera episodes in the neighborhood promptly ended.

Other early and highly influential maps include Minard's rendition of Napoleon's march on Moscow, where the width of the line represents the

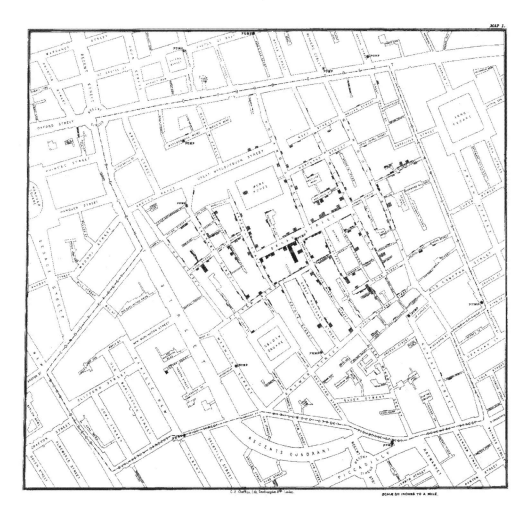

Figure 10.6 Map of cholera outbreaks in London
Source: Snow (1855), drawn from Wikipedia.

size of the army at each location and temperature is plotted along the way. One can see how the army dwindled and the possible role of winter in the demise of the Russian campaign (Rendgen 2018).

In recent years, the advent of Google Earth and OpenStreetMap (which has the added advantage of being open source), along with mapping software such as Arc-GIS and various open-source analogs, have vastly enhanced our capacity to map social phenomena to real space and to combine different elements with that spatial rendition.[2]

---

[2] For work on the use of maps in social science research see Ballas et al. (2017), Dodge, McDerby, Turner (2011), LeGates (2005), Okabe (2016). There are numerous guides to the use of GIS technology, e.g., McHaffie, Hwang, Follett (2018).

Networks

A final species of visual display is the network. In Chapter 8 we introduced networks as a type of theoretical framework. Here, we focus on opportunities for visual display. Consider Figure 10.7, which shows a Facebook social network consisting of individuals and the ties among them. Proximity between nodes and the number of connecting lines indicates frequency of contact. Evidently, patterns of interaction are by no means equally

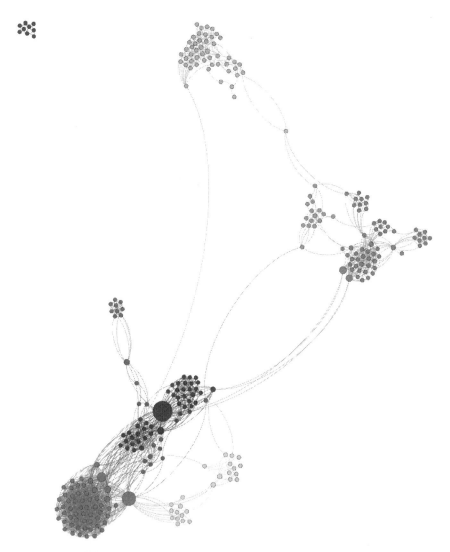

Figure 10.7   A Facebook social network

distributed, and this begs the question of why. A logical next step is to gather further data on the characteristics of each group to see what distinguishes them. This may suggest a fruitful hypothesis, which could then be explored in a more formal manner, perhaps with the use of network models (Borgatti, Everett, Johnson 2018; Knoke, Yang 2019).

Key Cases

Key cases often serve a heuristic role for the theorist and an important presentational device for books and articles. The reason for this is that authors, like readers, tend to think about social science theories as they play out in particular settings. It is difficult to think about an abstract concept like communism, equality, revolution, or democracy without picturing cases that exemplify these concepts. The same is true for full-blown theories. Modernization theory prompts us to think about England, the first nation to fully industrialize. Duverger's theory about the role of electoral systems structuring party competition prompts us to think about the United States, one of the world's oldest first-past-the-post electoral systems and one of the purest two-party monopolies. The role of these paradigm cases is virtually irresistible.

To be sure, paradigm cases can sometimes mislead; one must be careful to distinguish theory elucidation from theory testing. But for the former purpose, reference to key cases is highly advisable. This affords an opportunity to walk the reader through the theory – including the treatment, the mechanisms, and various ramifications. It will put flesh on the bones and may also help you to clarify things in your own mind.

Daron Acemoglu and James Robinson (2005) offer a complex theory of democratization, bolstered by a lengthy formal theory. To ease the exposition, they also offer a short narrative history of four cases – Britain, Argentina, Singapore, and South Africa – chosen to illustrate various pathways identified by the theory. This sort of case may be regarded as a "pathway" case (Gerring 2017). Many readers (ourselves included) are grateful for the interplay of theory with narrative history. Theories are more likely to "click" when they are able to enlist heuristic cases.

If the relationship of interest concerns a small set of identifiable cases – the units that embody the relationship of interest – try constructing a table in which key elements of these cases are summarized. These tables, sometimes referred to as "truth tables" (Ragin 1987), allow one to summarize a great deal of information in a concise manner. If the relationship is causal, one would want to include the causal factor(s) of theoretical interest, any background factors that might serve as confounders or moderators, and the outcome(s). Do not be troubled if these variables must be coded in a rough, provisional way, for example, as "high," "medium," or "low." The point is to summarize the data to the best of one's ability, and thereby inquire into the nature of the possible relationship and potential threats to inference.

As an example, we draw on work by Dirk Berg-Schlosser and Giselle De Meur (1994), which examines possible explanations for the breakdown/ survival of democracy in interwar Europe. Eighteen cases are included in Table 10.1, each of which is coded across five potential causal factors and one outcome. In this instance, coding is binary (0/1) across all factors. Note that because some cases exemplify the same coding they are combined into a single row, a useful reduction and one that involves no loss of information. (This is not always possible, to be sure.)

Sometimes, a plausible hypothesis is suggested by the patterns apparent in a table of key cases. Looking at Table 10.1, one might surmise that three factors were necessary and sufficient for regime survival in interwar

Table 10.1 Table of key cases

| Configuration | Cases | Causal factors: | | | | | Outcome: |
		Developed	Urban	Literacy	Labor	Gov Stability	Survival
1.	Finland, Ireland	1	0	1	0	1	1
2.	Belgium, Czechoslovakia, Netherlands, United Kingdom	1	1	1	1	1	1
3.	France, Sweden	1	0	1	1	1	1
4.	Estonia	0	0	1	0	1	0
5.	Austria	1	0	1	1	0	0
6.	Germany	1	1	1	1	0	0
7.	Greece, Poland, Spain	0	0	0	0	0	0
8.	Hungary, Portugal	0	0	1	0	0	0
9.	Italy, Romania	0	0	0	0	1	0

Key cases and their characteristics, roughly coded. *Source*: Berg-Schlosser and De Meur (1994), as discussed in Rihoux and De Meur (2009: 55).

Europe: (a) development, (b) literacy, and (c) government stability. Of course, one must be wary of overlap between government stability and the outcome of interest, survival, and there are issues of causal order (among the causal factors) to wrestle with. Even so, the table manages to summarize a great deal of useful information and this is what one wants at an early stage of the game.

Formal Models

Sometimes, a theory is stated in formal terms, with an explicit set of assumptions (axioms) upon which a deductive structure is assembled. Formal theories are usually expressed in mathematical language, where a single equation or set of equations (a model) embody the argument. Sometimes, the model can be solved, that is, it offers a single solution or prediction. Sometimes, the assumptions must be narrowed in order to attain a solution. Insofar as it is possible to compute solutions for a formal model using various assumptions (e.g., imposing specific parameter values on the variables), we refer to the exercise as a *computational model* and to the various computations as simulations.

Whether an explanation can be represented in formal, mathematical terms depends upon its simplicity. This is not just a matter of the number of moving parts but also the extent to which each moving part can be understood as a "quantity." Some concepts, like *institutionalization*, are not very amenable to formal treatments.

Formal models often rest on preferences because they are relatively tractable (at least more so than norms and psychology). A preference refers to what an individual (or group) prefers across a range of options. Usually, it is assumed that preferences are *complete*, which is to say that for any two options the actor can decide whether option A is preferred to option B, option B is preferred to option A, or both are regarded as equal. In addition, it is usually assumed that preferences are *transitive*: if A is preferred to B, and B is preferred to C, then A is preferred to C. This allows preferences to be ordered, producing a *utility function*. When an individual's behavior follows this logic, they are said to maximize their utility. (Additional assumptions are sometimes added; but comparability and transitivity are almost always included in a preference-based explanation.) Although this framework may seem complex – and indeed some formulations are extremely technical and involve a great many assumptions – the core idea is quite simple: people's behavior is a product of their preferences.

Let us see how this framework might apply to vote choice. Consider an election conducted with single-member districts (a single candidate is selected from each electoral district) and winner-take-all (aka first-past-the-post) rules, where two parties (Democrats and Republicans) compete. We shall assume that voters' preferences may be understood according to their issue-preferences (about particular policies) and that these policies occupy a unidimensional issue-space from left (liberal) to right (conservative). For illustrative purposes, we also assume that voters are evenly distributed along this spectrum (although this assumption can be relaxed to get the same result). And we shall assume that ideological positioning by the parties is unconstrained by activist members, by their history, by the problem of credible commitment, by changes to voter turnout, or by other factors. Under these circumstances, where should the parties (and their candidates) position themselves?

Early work on voting employed a simple spatial model, illustrated in Figure 10.8, in order to understand why candidates in a general election might move toward the middle – understood as the median voter (that individual whose views lie in the center of the ideological spectrum, with an equal number of persons to their left and right). Consider panel (a), which offers a plausible description of the positions of the parties according to their aggregated personal preferences – with the Democratic party on the left of the spectrum and the Republican party on the right. This setting is not in equilibrium, however, because either party can enhance its position by moving to the center, as the Democratic party does in panel (b). In this scenario, the Democrats win by a landslide simply by moving along the spectrum and thereby capturing more votes in the center. The assumption is that they lose no votes in doing so because voters to the left of the Democratic party have no viable option that lies closer to their ideal-point. Of course, the Republican party may also play this repositioning game. In panel (W), the Republicans move almost all the way to the Democrats, occupying a larger portion of the spectrum and assuring themselves of a landslide victory. This setting is also not in equilibrium because another move by the Democrats – leapfrogging the Republicans – would assure them of victory. Under the terms of our (admittedly simple) model, the only stable equilibrium is one where both parties hug the center, as illustrated in panel (d).

The intuition, then, is that if voters attempt to maximize their preferences (understood as policy preferences), they will vote for the candidate whose policy positions most closely mirror their own. In a two-party competition,

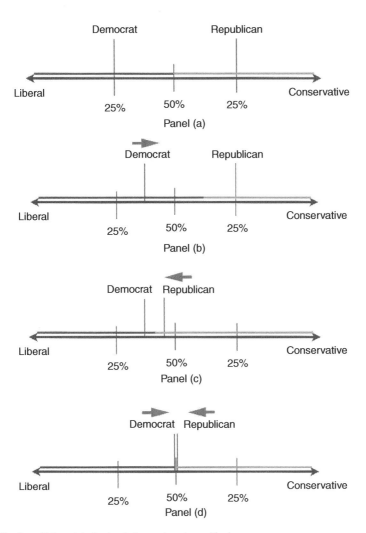

Figure 10.8   A spatial model of vote choice and party positioning

parties (and candidates) maximize their vote-share by moving toward the center, generating a centripetal dynamic.

Here, issue-preferences structure candidate behavior, which in turn structure voting behavior. If most voters behave in this way, we can use this simple folk wisdom to explain the results of an election.

Likewise, if we wish to explain why certain individuals or parties join together in a coalition, we might begin by examining their preferences, with the idea that those with similar utility functions are most likely to form enduring coalitions. The same logic may be employed to explain consumer choice, the structure of markets, the choice of marriage partners, social networks, and many other phenomena of interest to social science.

Of course, inferring what a person's true preferences are is not always an easy matter. One may ask directly (via a survey or interview). But people are not always forthcoming. Sometimes, they tell you what they think you want to hear or what they feel is most acceptable. They will rarely reveal preferences that go against the law or against social mores.

One may also observe an individual's behavior. Typically, preferences predict behavior. If we observe how someone votes we are presumably observing their preferences at work. This approach to measurement is referred to as *revealed preferences*. Sometimes, however, people act strategically. Consider an election contest where three candidates, *A*, *B*, and *C*, compete for a single seat. Let us suppose that Bob's preference-ordering is *A>B>C*. However, he knows (from opinion polls) that *A*'s probability of winning is miniscule. Under these circumstances, Bob might opt for *B* even though *B* is not his first preference. On the basis of Bob's behavior, and knowing something about the situation, one can infer that Bob prefers *B* to *C*. But it is impossible to tell whether he prefers *A* to *B*.

Where asking and observation are impossible or for some reason flawed, one may try to infer preferences from other aspects of a person's situation. This approach may be reasonable if our focus is on the preferences of many people rather than on a single individual. In this case, it does not matter if our guesses about preferences are correct or incorrect for "Bob" so long as they are generally correct for members of Bob's group.

If one is trying to understand a series of decisions (taken by an individual or a group) in a particular sequence, a *decision-tree* model may be applied. This draws on a branch of math and economics known as decision theory. If actions by an individual or group depend upon the actions of others, the resulting model may be described as *game theory*. Here, each player is understood as playing a game insofar as their actions are strategic, with an eye to the probable behavior of others.

Hal Varian (2016: 83), an economist with a great deal of experience in constructing models, declares that all economic models are "pretty much the same."

There are some economic agents. They make choices in order to advance their objectives. The choices have to satisfy various constraints so there's something that adjusts to make all these choices consistent. This basic structure suggests a plan of attack: Who are the people making the choices? What are the constraints they face? How do they interact? What adjusts if the choices aren't mutually consistent?

While this is no doubt an oversimplification, it may provide a useful starting point for those who wish to reconstruct an event or series of events through the prism of a game theory model (formal or informal).

General Guidelines

We have now provided a great many tools for theorizing. This creates a problem, for amid the superfluity of options it may not be readily apparent which set of tools are best suited for the job. "Effective problem solving . . . depends on being able to select a representational tool whose structure matches that of the information to be represented," comments Novick (2001: 282).

If you are unsure, try several of the foregoing options. Each may reveal different aspects of your problem or question. Just as rearranging letters will suggest different words, a key technique in anagrams (Scrabble), a different presentational framework will often suggest different underlying relationships. Allow yourself to play with words, pictures, cases, and formal models to see which one – or which combination – is most satisfactory.

As you do so, consider the following basic guidelines, intrinsic to all efforts to theorize.

First, the goal is to *make assumptions explicit*. Whatever features of the world are needed to support the author's argument – unless they are completely mundane – should be brought forward. What features of the world must the reader subscribe to in order for the theory to be plausible? No one should be left guessing about these core assumptions.

If some assumptions are more essential than others, this should be clarified. Consider the diagram illustrated in Figure 10.9. Here, the path from X flows through M, and then branches out through several capillaries, each of which could – by itself – generate the outcome, Y. In this scenario, M is much more essential than M_{1-3}. If one of the latter fails (is not true), the argument may still hold. But if M fails, the entire theory fails.

Second, theories aim for *parsimony* (Table 9.1). The act of theorizing is an act of reductionism, of simplification. Accordingly, a good theory involves as few assumptions as possible. The fewer the assumptions, the stronger the argument, for there is less that the reader must believe in order to support the argument. So, whenever possible, strip out extraneous material.

Paul Krugman (1998: 144–145) reports on the models of international trade that would eventually earn him a Nobel Prize.

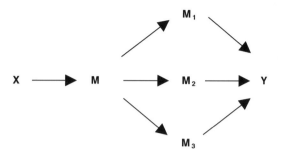

Figure 10.9 A branching theory

The point of my trade models was not particularly startling once one thought about it: economies of scale could be an independent cause of international trade, even in the absence of comparative advantage. This was a new insight to me but had (as I soon discovered) been pointed out many times before by critics of conventional trade theory. The models I worked out left some loose ends hanging; in particular, they typically had many equilibria. Even so, to make the models tractable I had to make obviously unrealistic assumptions. And once I had made those assumptions, the models were trivially simple; writing them up left me no opportunity to display any high-powered technique. So one might have concluded that I was doing nothing very interesting (and that was what some of my colleagues were to tell me over the next few years). Yet what I saw . . . was that all of these features were virtues, not vices, that they added up to a program that could lead to years of productive research.

In Krugman's telling, his work repackaged ideas that critics had been articulating "for decades." Yet, their criticisms were not taken seriously by mainstream international economics until they had been properly formalized. "The new monopolistic-competition models gave me a tool to open cleanly what had previously been regarded as a can of worms," he writes (Krugman 1998: 145). It was a simpler theory, and therefore more potent.

Third, the articulation of a theory generally works *from the ground up*, from assumptions that are deemed to be unassailable ("axioms" or "primitives") to those that are more questionable – and therefore should be presented as arguments rather than assumptions. The foundation should be stronger than the upper floors. Or, if you prefer analogies to nature, the trunk should be stronger than the higher branches.

For example, it is far better to begin a theory of the behavior of legislators by positing that they care about their ideology and about their chances of reelection than it is to start by positing that they generally seek the wellbeing of a particular social class. The latter may well be true, and there is evidence to support the class-oriented conclusion in some systems; but the idea of class bias is controversial enough that it should be regarded as an argument rather than an assumption.

We turn now from the theory, *sensu stricto*, to a consideration of how the theory fits with the empirical world and with rival explanations.

Hypotheses

In order to be falsifiable a theory must be elaborated in a hypothesis, or a set of hypotheses. These are the observable implications of the theory.

Some theories are close enough to the bone that their hypotheses are inseparable from the theory itself. If one is theorizing about the impact of worker-training programs on employment prospects it is hardly necessary to stipulate the main hypothesis – that attending a worker-training program enhances the prospect of employment.

However, there may be subsidiary hypotheses that are not so obvious and therefore should be laid out in an explicit fashion. For example, the researcher might hypothesize that a longer or more intensive course would have a greater impact on employment prospects than a shorter or less intensive course. They might further hypothesize that this relationship is logarithmic (increases in length or intensity translate into monotonic but sublinear increases in employment prospects). They might hypothesize about background characteristics – for example, sex, race, age, education – that could enhance or mitigate the impact of a worker-training program. They might hypothesize about contextual moderators, for example, the state of the local economy, the overall unemployment rate. One can imagine many nuanced hypotheses that take account of anticipated causal heterogeneity in the relationship between the treatment of interest (worker-training programs) and the outcome (employment).

Ideally, a hypothesis is closely tied to one theory. If the hypothesis is confirmed that theory is corroborated and others may be discarded – at least, as explanations for the chosen outcome in the chosen research setting. If, on the other hand, a hypothesis is observationally equivalent to multiple theories it is less useful, as it will not distinguish between them. This is often the case when theories are broad and diffuse. For example, theories of international relations pitched at the level of "realism" and "idealism" are often difficult to distinguish, as they offer parallel hypotheses about the world. One has the impression that they are explaining the same phenomena, though in different ways. Here, the task of constructing falsifiable hypotheses is truly challenging.

Suffice to say, the more abstract the theory the greater the importance of crafting falsifiable hypotheses.

Leaving aside the theory, let us consider the hypotheses formulated to test that theory. For any theory, testable implications may be stated in very general terms or in very specific terms. Consider the following examples:

H_1: An increase in X is associated with an increase in Y.
H_2: An increase of one point in X is associated with an increase of two points in Y.

Evidently, H_2 is more precise than H_1. It is a stronger statement, and more likely to fail. As such, if H_2 is confirmed by an empirical test it offers stronger confirmation of the theory than a similar confirmation of H_1. (We assume that everything else about these empirical tests is identical. We also assume that the scales in H_2 are fairly precisely calibrated.) By the same token, H_1 may be true even if H_2 is not. The prospect of Type 1 error (rejecting a true null hypothesis) must be balanced against the danger of Type 2 error (accepting a false null hypothesis).

The researcher must decide how to thread this needle. In theory-making, precision is good, assuming all else is equal (Table 9.1). But all else may not be equal.

At an exploratory stage, it probably makes sense to formulate hypotheses in a fairly general fashion – avoiding Type 2 error – and giving your theory the greatest opportunity for success. It can be respecified in a more precise fashion later on.

Alternate Explanations

In natural science there is often one cause that suffices to explain an outcome. By contrast, in the social sciences most outcomes of theoretical interest respond to multiple factors. There are myriad causes of infant mortality, democratization, and economic growth, for example. It follows that in developing a theory and a set of hypotheses one must come to grips with *alternate explanations* that might be offered for the chosen outcome(s).

In drawing up a list of possible causes, the following techniques may be helpful:

- Consult the literature, especially comprehensive literature reviews (Chapter 4).

- Consider how scholars with markedly different perspectives might view your subject (Chapter 5).
- Consider how the actors under investigation make sense of their own actions (hermeneutics).
- Consider widely used explanatory frameworks (Chapter 8).
- Work backward from proximal causes to distal causes, extending the causal chain as far as is possible, and including the mechanisms linking each node in the chain.

Even if some of these putative causes are rather hypothetical, it is helpful to draw up a comprehensive list.

In the course of his book on democratization, Michael Coppedge (2012: 305) constructs a sizable inventory of potential causes of this macro-political outcome. This includes income (GDP), income growth (change in GDP), trade openness, inequality, diffusion, British colonial legacy, length of colonial rule, state failure, civil conflict, Islam, Protestantism, Catholicism, land area, age of country, ethnolinguistic fragmentation, population, presidentialism, and regime history. Scholars familiar with this literature could easily generate another dozen or so potential causes. The point is, one needs to wrap one's head around a causal question, and the more complex it is the more important it is to draw up an inventory of potential causes.

Such an inventory is useful in two respects.

First, it allows one to think about a problem in an encompassing fashion, and forces one to come to terms with how one's preferred explanation, X, fits with – encompasses, contradicts, is subsumed by, or supplements – other explanations. This challenge may be clarified with the language of causal graphs, as laid out in Figure 1.1.

Consider a factor that lies prior to X (causally speaking), designated A. If variation on X is largely explained by variation in A, then A may provide a more meaningful point of focus. In this scenario, X is perhaps better looked upon as a mechanism in the pathway from A to Y. If a factor lies downstream from X, designated M in Figure 1.1, then it should be recognized as a causal mechanism lying in the pathway from X to Y. If another factor is thought to have some independent effect on Y (independent of X, that is), then it should be classified as orthogonal to Y (B) or a potential confounder (C). Alternatively, the researcher may be able to show that it is not a cause of Y at all, and hence may be dismissed.

Second, a thorough inventory of causes may lead to further theoretical development. One might decide to construct a broader theory, so as to embrace additional factors that seem important for Y. One might decide to construct a narrower theory, so as to exclude factors that seem better fitted for alternative theories. One might decide to adjust the scope-conditions of a theory so as to provide a more plausible fit between your theory and the outcome to be explained. In any case, juggling the elements of a theory involves all the alternate explanations for a particular outcome.

Third, related to what we have said so far, this list of potential explanations for Y comprises the set of rival hypotheses that you will be obliged to refute, mitigate, or control for (empirically) in your work. So, it's important to have a sense of what they are – especially if they are close (conceptually and/or empirically) to your favored theory.

Granted, if your work is experimental there are no pre-treatment confounders (by definition). However, for an experiment to have any generalizability the researcher must think carefully about how it fits the real world – the world of things that occur naturally. An experiment is useful only to the extent that it informs us about that world. Consequently, it behooves the researcher to think carefully about what affects an outcome of theoretical concern, even if those other causes do not pose problems of confounding. For example, an experimental study of turnout focused on information presented to the voter should come to terms with how various experimentally manipulated interventions compare to other factors currently at work. A proposed intervention must be evaluated – in terms of cost, ethics, and effectiveness – against other interventions, many of which are already in play.

Finally, one's interpretation of the experiment must consider alternate theoretical frameworks. This is because a single experimental manipulation may be consistent with several overarching theories. For example, a turnout experiment whose intervention consists of providing information about neighbors' voting behavior may be viewed as "informational," "normative" (because the information is thought to activate norms about appropriate behavior), or "social capital" (since information is likely to be more available, and norms stronger, where social networks are stronger). Even experimentalists must think through the data generating process occurring in the real world that their experiment is designed to mimic.

Tractability

Theorizing cannot occur in a theoretical vacuum. *At some point*, the theory will need to be operationalized and tested in order to be counted a contribution to knowledge. It must, eventually, gain empirical traction. That is implicit in our discussion of hypotheses and alternate explanations.

We close this chapter by making the point explicit. A good social science theory is a *tractable* theory, as recognized in the general criteria of theorizing set forth in Table 9.1. A framework may hover in space (see Chapter 8), but a theory should hit the ground.

Matters of research design and testing lie outside the purview of this book. They are the traditional focus of methods texts and courses, so the reader is probably already familiar with the subject. We mention it here as a placeholder.

When constructing a theory you must think ahead to the confirmatory stage of research, when that theory will be tested. The more falsifiable the theory, the better the theory – *all other things being equal*.

We do not want to discourage theorizing that ranges freely across topics of social importance. Many of these topics are apt to be historical or rooted in contemporary phenomena that are not amenable to experimental or quasi-experimental designs. As such, tests are likely to be tentative. Causal inference will rest upon assumptions that may not be provable in the strict sense of the term. This does not make them bad theories.

Yet, they are bad in *one* respect: they are not very tractable. There is a cost to a theory that cannot be decisively proven or disproven. Its contribution to knowledge is ambiguous, at least at the present time. (One can hope that in future years this ambiguity will be resolved.) Researchers must reckon with this cost as they assemble their theory.

Part V

Conclusions

This book has focused on how one might identify a topic for research.

Part II approached the subject ideationally, looking at ways we can play with ideas in order to arrive at plausible topics for research. We focused on general strategies (Chapter 4) and heuristics for discovery (Chapter 5).

Part III approached the issue empirically, looking at various ways in which social scientists play with data. We focused on strategies of exploratory case selection (Chapter 6) and methods of soaking and poking (Chapter 7).

Part IV approached the subject theoretically, looking at ways we play with theories. We focused on general theoretical frameworks (Chapter 8), the challenges of causal explanation (Chapter 9), and tools and tips for theorizing (Chapter 10).

This final part of the book consists of a single chapter. Here, we address the important transition from exploration to testing, contrasting these two stages of research.

From Exploration to Appraisal

When a thing is new, people say: "It is not true." Later, when its truth becomes obvious, they say: "It is not important." Finally, when its importance cannot be denied, they say: "Anyway, it is not new."

William James (attributed)

Exploration comes at the beginning, at a point when the researcher is unsure of what they are studying. It encompasses everything that happens *before* committing to a project.

What is the main research question? What is the main hypothesis, or hypotheses? What is the broader theory that underpins the hypothesis(es)? What is the projected research design? These are the questions exploratory research seeks to answer.

This is the most exciting phase of research as everything is open-ended, unstructured. Like youth, exploratory research promises many potential avenues of development, only some of which will be subsequently pursued.

Exploration is also the most frustrating phase of research. One may cast about for months, perhaps even years, with nothing (apparently) to show for it. One may come upon a great idea only to discover that someone else has gotten there first. One may plan out a perfect research design only to discover that the data is unavailable, the participants inaccessible, or the data generating process marred by unforeseen confounders.

The selection of a good research topic is difficult. This difficulty derives partly from the fact that everyone is looking for the same thing: exciting – and feasible – topics for research, the next breaking wave. This means that the low-hanging fruit is probably already picked. One should not expect a perfect topic to fall into one's lap.

Finding a research topic that is suitable for you, personally and professionally, is likely to require some time. How much, it is difficult to say. Exploration is a process, not an event. Nonetheless, one must face the questions: When does exploration end and testing begin? At what point should one commit to a project? How does one know when to reach for closure? Evidently, there are dangers associated with precipitous decisions as well as with decisions too long delayed.

Consider this familiar scenario, related by Kristin Luker (2008: 18). A student ("you") enters their advisor's office with a hazily framed idea of what they would like to work on. The advisor demands to know what the hypothesis is.

If you flounder around trying to answer this question, he or she may follow up by asking what your independent and dependent variables are. Even more basically, he or she will ask what your research question is. You just go blank, feeling like a rabbit trapped on the roadway with the headlights bearing down on you, as you try desperately to explain what's so interesting about, say, privatized water, or rising rates of imprisonment in America, or adolescent sexuality. When you and your advisor part at the end of the time allotted to you, more likely than not, you part in mutual frustration.

In this setting, the student is probably not ready to identify a research question, much less a specific hypothesis. It is still a relevant question, and the advisor is obliged to raise it. However, in haste to answer this question in a satisfactory way – and escape with self-esteem intact – the student may commit to a question that is not, in the long run, very fruitful. The same thing happens with arbitrary deadlines imposed by the academic calendar – a conference at which one has committed to present, a prospectus defense date, and so forth. This is the Scylla of premature closure.

On the other extreme lies the Charybdis of belated closure. Luker (2008: 19) continues,

Suppose . . . that you have an easygoing advisor, and you are permitted to go off "into the field" . . . without answering his or her questions. An even more dreaded fate may well await you, worse than being tortured into producing independent and dependent variables on demand for your advisor, namely . . . the Damnation of the Ten Thousand Index Cards or the Ten Thousand Entries into your computer-assisted note-taking system. The Damnation of the Ten Thousand Whatevers happens to unwitting graduate students who have spent many years . . . gathering data without having stumbled upon exactly what it was that they were looking for when they first went out to that fabulous field site (. . . or library . . .). There they sit, doomed and damned, in front of the computer screen, wondering how to make a story out of the ten thousand entries. Or, worse yet, they finally do stumble onto a story as they pore yet again over the ten thousand entries, but the single piece of information (or the body of data) which they need to really nail the point beyond quibbles is back in the field and they didn't know they needed it, or it's disappeared, or they can't afford to go back. Or they do find it, and realize that eighty percent of the data they have gathered is irrelevant . . . An in-between outcome . . . is that you may actually find the research question, come up with the data that you need to make the case, and have a compelling and . . . well-written story to tell. The only problem is that you have eighteen boxes of data left over, and the entire enterprise took you . . . four years longer than it should have.

To describe this sort of disaster, Luker (2008: 19) quotes a line from Pauline Bart: "Data, data everywhere and not a thought to think."

One must avoid the Scylla of premature closure as well as the Charybdis of belated closure. Neither will serve the cause of science, or our own careers. Push yourself to find a research question as quickly as possible. But don't settle on something that doesn't seem meaningful to you or to your intended audience.

Once you have settled, draw up a document that articulates your theory, hypothesis, and research design (including, if applicable, a pre-analysis plan). This might take the form of a grant proposal, dissertation prospectus, pre-registered report, Registered Report, working paper, or a published paper in a journal that looks kindly upon exploratory work (as advocated below).

However articulated, this point in time marks an important shift from exploratory to confirmatory research. This distinction also occupies an important place in the philosophy of science, where these contrasting sorts of research are sometimes referred to as contexts of *discovery* and *justification*.[1] The meaning and implications of this fundamental distinction are elaborated in Table 11.1.

This book has been devoted to the first part of the research journey – exploration. We have little or nothing to say about confirmatory research, a topic well-covered by extant methods texts. However, we must say something about this key transition since it is encountered in all research projects and also helps to define our subject matter.

In the first section of the chapter, we discuss various steps involved in vetting and refining a research project. In the second section, we discuss when to go public with preliminary ideas and findings. In the third section, we take up the question of what to reveal about the research process in the final product (presumably, a published article or book). Finally, we consider the turning point from exploratory to confirmatory research and how it affects one's perspective on the task at hand.

---

[1] See Popper (1968[1934]), Reichenbach (1938), Schickore, Steinle (2006).

Table 11.1 Two stages of research

	EXPLORATION	TESTING
Near-synonyms	Discovery, Theory generation	Appraisal, Confirmation, Falsification, Justification, Verification
Question	What is the research question, theory, hypothesis(es), and research design?	How true is the theory and hypothesis(es)?
Theory and evidence	Interactive	Segregated
Process	Unstructured	Highly structured
Error to be avoided	Type 2	Type 1
Attitude	Nurturing	Skeptical

Vetting and Refining

Once you have developed a project idea you must pause to take stock. Vetting a potential project is complicated so we will try to walk you through that process in as much detail as possible.

If you have several project options (as advised in Chapter 5), compare and contrast these ideas to each other, evaluating their strengths and weaknesses. Eventually, you will need to abandon those that seem less fruitful. To ease the pain, consider it a deferral rather than a rejection. You may come back to it later – with better skills, better data, a better research design, a better theory, or more funding.

Within that chosen project there are also choices to make. Typically, a social science project contains many moving parts – a key term or terms, a nascent theory, a set of vaguely defined phenomena, various possible research designs, and so forth. It is vital to maintain a degree of fluidity until such time as you can convince yourself that you have achieved the best possible fit between these elements. The theory must be aligned with the research design; the research design must be aligned with the chosen concepts; etc. As we have emphasized, making social science is a holistic enterprise (Chapter 1).

Of course, all of the elements that make for a successful piece of research are unlikely to fall into place at once, and many seemingly final decisions may yet be changed in the process of conducting exploratory research. And yet, one is obliged to wrestle with them, even – one might say, especially – at the outset.

To avoid endless cycling, it may be helpful to identify one element of the project that you feel most committed to – presumably that which is likely to make the greatest contribution to scholarship. If this element can be identified, it will provide an anchor in the process of continual adjustment. Consider the headline. What is the phrase that you imagine printed in bold in the title or abstract of your published work? Now, work backward to see how it might be achieved.

Making a bet on a piece of research is like making a bet on a horse, a team, or a company. One must try to predict the future. Although the prospect may seem daunting, try to map out how your project will unfold. If everything works out as anticipated, what will the completed thesis/article/book look like?

As with any investment, the payoff depends upon lots of things falling into place in subsequent years. One can never anticipate all of the potential difficulties. But the more one can plan ahead, the better the chance of a payoff when the research is completed. And the better the chance that the research will be completed at all. (Bad ideas are often difficult to bring to fruition; the more they advance, the more obstacles they encounter.)

Costs, Payoffs, and Risks

An important part of the vetting process is a calculation of costs, the money and time that will be required to complete the project. If this is complicated, draw up a budget. If external funding is necessary, consider the probability of securing that funding and a Plan B if your application does not succeed.

Consider, also, the non-financial risks associated with a piece of research. Will you gain access to required research sites, informants, and/or data sources? Will potential collaborators agree to collaborate?

Consider, finally, the potential payoffs. What will be the scholarly impact if you are able to demonstrate your main hypothesis? How will the result be perceived? What will be its value-added? Will it be considered more compelling than extant work on the subject? Will it stand the test of current scholarship and of future scholarship (the "test of time")?

When thinking about payoffs, conversations with others – particularly those who are *not* experts in your chosen field – are invaluable. If a research idea can be explained in ways that bring excitement to people intellectually close to you, but also to those at a greater remove, then it is more likely to have a high payoff.

A particular point of concern is whether your hypothesis will be proven, or disproven, in light of the (yet to be collected) evidence. For some research, both "null" and "rejection of the null" findings are informative. Some topics are so novel, and some research designs are so much stronger than those that came before, that *any* finding is informative. This is ideal from the perspective of the scholar's investment of time and energy, as it cannot fail to pay off. Risk is low, so long as the planned research can actually be implemented (never a sure thing).

More typically, research is exciting only when a novel finding is reached, and this generally involves rejecting the null, that is, showing that there is (or is likely to be) a relationship between X and Y.

Some research is especially high risk insofar as it is considered unlikely to yield the hoped-for result. Risks of this sort must be balanced by very high payoffs.

We do not wish to discourage high-risk/high payoff research. Indeed, we feel that there is too little "Nobel" ambition among social scientists (perhaps because, outside economics, there are no Nobel Prizes for social scientists). The point is that researchers should know what they are getting into, and they should be sure that their professional position is secure enough to warrant a long-term investment, perhaps followed by failure.

Ethics

In vetting potential projects, one must bear in mind ethical norms. Like resources, time, and skills, ethics pose a constraint. (At least, so one hopes …) What this constraint consists of, and where the boundaries between ethical and unethical lie, are not always clear. While this is not the place to offer a full treatment of research ethics, a few points are in order.[2]

First, ethical considerations of one form or another arise in virtually all social science research. Some kinds of research designs are so unethical that they should probably be abandoned outright. Scholars are unlikely, for example, to directly replicate the Stanford Prison Study (Haney, Banks, Zimbardo 1973), given the harms it inflicted on research subjects. Yet, there are other designs that explore the main ideas of that study (i.e., role conformity) in what most would regard as an ethical fashion (e.g., Suhay 2015; Panagopoulos, van der Linden 2016). It is rare for ethical constraints to eliminate an entire research agenda.

This leads to our second point. Although ethics is popularly regarded in a binary fashion – a study is, or is not, carried out in an ethical fashion – it is

---

[2] For fuller treatments see Mazur (2007), Mertens, Ginsberg (2009).

more accurate to think of ethical considerations as involving a number of dimensions, each of which is a matter of degrees. This helps to account for why there is often disagreement over what qualifies as ethical or unethical. Ethical norms vary across fields and subfields, and to some extent across countries. They have also changed considerably over time.

Third, research ethics start, but do not end, with the legal requirements imposed by national laws and regulations. In the United States, projects that qualify as human subjects research are typically unethical unless they have been scrutinized by an Institutional Review Board (IRB), which acts to enforce the implementation of informed consent, to monitor and minimize risks in research, and to review procedures for ensuring privacy and confidentiality. IRB review does not generally include reflection on other key ethical issues. For example, is the broader community (beyond the research participants) adequately protected from harms that the study might generate (Johnson 2018)? Are the risks and benefits of research reasonably balanced and managed for members of the research team? How might the research be used in unexpected ways after publication by other actors? These larger issues may be viewed as falling outside the purview of the IRB, despite their importance.

Fourth, and finally, ethical reflection about a potential research project should include careful thought about how to maximize broader societal benefits, not merely about how to avoid harms (Kelman 1982). Could this project produce knowledge that matters to citizens, social movement leaders, and government officials? If so, it is an issue of ethics to reflect on whether and how special efforts could be made to communicate findings to such people outside of normal scholarly channels. Are participants willing to offer their time and effort to the project because they want their stories to be individually told and heard? Then it is worth considering how those individual narratives can be amplified, particularly if they are used in fragmented or statistical ways in the scholarly analysis.

Market-Testing

Once you have settled on a provisional topic, write it up and send it around to friends and colleagues. This serves as a form of market-testing. Note that unless there is an audience for what you are producing there is little point in producing it. Feedback will also help you to evaluate the various questions raised above – about feasibility, payoffs, and ethics.

Consider carefully responses from those who know a subject intimately, that is, experts and key informants. These are the people who are likely to review your work, so their opinion is especially valuable.

Consider also those who lie outside the subfield, for their opinions are less likely to be subject to whatever biases inhabit the subfield. Insofar as one aspires to reach outside a small circle of specialists, one must consider how non-specialists respond to one's work. Things that are taken for granted among specialists may need extra clarification, or justification, when presented to non-specialists.

In the arduous process of vetting a proposal, feedback and advice is welcome – from friends, family, advisors, experts in the field, or anyone who will speak to you. Solicit all the feedback you can. But make sure that, at the end of the day, you are comfortable with the choice you make. It should represent your considered judgment – for you will reap the rewards or suffer the consequences. There is no point in choosing a topic that someone else is excited about if you do not share that excitement.

The vetting of a potential project therefore involves a bit of introspection. Is this a topic that will hold your attention, and your excitement, over the long haul? Will you be happy becoming an expert on that topic? Is this your calling?

Going Public with Exploratory Work

Assuming you are convinced that your ideas offer some sort of contribution to the world of knowledge (along at least one of the dimensions reviewed in Chapter 3), when should you go public? When is a project complete enough to submit to the prying gaze – and possible criticism – of strangers?

When Linnaeas issued his *Critica Botanica*, in 1737, it was accompanied by an admonitory preface, intended to alert readers to a classificatory scheme – understood as a set of laws – that were new, provocative, and quite possibly wrong.

Before botanists can admit [such] laws, it is necessary that someone among them should take upon himself to offer proposals to be examined by other botanists, so that, if they are good they may be confirmed, if unsound they may be convicted of unsoundness and abandoned, while something better is put in their place. But, so long as botanists refuse to make this beginning, so long also will they remain in doubt and uncertainty, and false names will accumulate every day to burden Botany. Now as hitherto no one has thought fit to undertake this self-denying task, I have determined to make the attempt; for, if a citizen in a free commonwealth may speak his mind, it will be at least allowable for me to state my principles among botanists! I have not reached such an extreme hardihood as to believe that all my reasoning is so firmly based but that someone else may propound reasoning much more mature: still mine will be true until some other principles are shown to be truer. To you, my dearly-beloved botanists, I submit my rules, the rules which I have laid down for myself, and in accordance with which I intend to walk. If they seem to you worthy, let them be used by you also; if not, please propound something better! (quoted in Linsley, Usinger 1959: 40)

In the event, Linnaeas was (mostly) right, which is to say his principles of classification proved fruitful. But he might have been wrong. And at the time, as his preface makes clear, he was quite uncertain. Nor would it have been possible for him to fully verify this novel schema on his own, as this would have required knowledge of every corner of the natural world (beyond what an individual could undertake in their lifetime) and also into the future (to species not yet discovered).

Under the circumstances, there were only two options available: submitting a not yet fully formed and tested idea to the world or keeping it to himself. Thankfully, he chose the former course. But we may imagine there were countless others, with less spunk, who took the more conservative course. Darwin postponed publication of his theory of evolution for decades and would have waited longer were it not for the appearance of a competitor (Alfred Russel Wallace). It is difficult to say how much this may have slowed the progress of science – though, to be sure, the appearance of a mature work (*Origin of Species*), bolstered by corroborating evidence, may have eased the public reception of this controversial idea.

In principle, publication can take place at any time and may assume a variety of formats – working papers, blog posts, book chapters, as well as the conventional monograph. However, there is a general reluctance to place work in the public domain that is in an unfinished state. This may be understood as the product of several factors.

To begin with, top journals and presses in the social sciences are interested in publishing "definitive" studies; they do not see their task as nurturing work at an early stage of development. Since admittance to these venues determines the course of one's career, scholars are incentivized to postpone publication until they have formulated a mature theory, collected a wide range of data, and administered a great many tests. This incentive is enhanced by the fact that most journals will refuse even to review a paper that has been published in a preliminary form elsewhere (though the

definition of what is "published" varies). Consequently, work at an exploratory stage is likely to be suppressed or posted as a working paper in an
unofficial (often hard to locate) fashion.

In the natural sciences, by contrast, there is a virtual rush to publish. This is
motivated by the pragmatic concern that one may be scooped and an
appreciation of the fact that scientific progress can occur only if research is
made public. Speedy publication is assisted by the abbreviated format of most
articles (generally just a few pages in length) and the quick turnaround of the
review process at most journals. Some papers are published only in working
paper format on *arXiv* or an equivalent platform. Hardly anyone writes
book-length monographs.

There may be good reasons for divergent publication practices in social
science and natural science. However, because of the extraordinary length of
time it takes to bring a piece of research from intuition to publication in the
social sciences we believe that there ought to be more venues for research that
is still at an exploratory stage, aka "pre-studies" (Swedberg 2014a, 2019).

Publishing exploratory work has several salutary effects.

First, the researcher with a new idea has a formal venue for gaining
feedback. This is especially important for researchers who lack established
networks – perhaps because they are young, are at institutions that are off the
beaten track, or are working in an as yet obscure area where there is no defined
network.

Relatedly, going public early on in a project allows scholars who are at
work on similar or adjoining topics to find each other. If they wait until their
projects are completed, they will be unknown to each other until it is too late.
They may of course consult scholars who have already published in that area.
But their knowledge of the topic may be outdated and since they are probably
working on other things, they may be less motivated to engage.

Finally, publishing an idea allows the author to stake out a domain. This is
not simply a turf battle but also a matter of allocating research time and
money efficiently across the social sciences. If you have already become an
expert in a problem, there is less value-added from others joining the fray;
their efforts might be better spent elsewhere. So, the point is not to deter
other scholars from entering your domain but rather to make sure that they
are doing so in full awareness that they are not the first to do so. Knowing
who is doing what – and how far along they have come – will help them make
a rational decision and will serve the larger goal of efficiency in the outlay of
scientific time and resources. Here, as elsewhere, transparency should
improve coordination.

On the face of things, it is absurd that research reaches the light of day only once an author is truly finished with it (and oftentimes sick and tired of it). To encourage the timely publication of exploratory research we urge journals to offer space for short papers that are at an early stage of development. We also urge researchers to make use of working papers and other formats that do not involve formal peer review (or only minimal peer review).

Naturally, researchers may have concerns about losing control over their material. However, publishing a working paper or "exploratory paper" need not involve making the data public. Without that data, it is unlikely that the author will be scooped by a rival researcher. In any case, the author of the original (exploratory) paper will be able to establish their claim to authorship, for their work will have appeared prior to the paper that (allegedly) purloins their ideas. And a formal venue of publication will make this claim in a more authoritative fashion than a working paper or conference paper. Note that authors do not always feel obliged to cite works that are as yet unpublished and some journals will not allow citation of a paper that is not readily accessible to the public.

If an exploratory paper with an innovative idea is duly credited, as it should be, then the author will accrue citations. And citation counts seem to be gaining traction over publication counts as a measure of academic impact and achievement (Gerring, Karcher, Apfeld 2020).

Thus, on balance, we believe that scholars have more to gain from making their preliminary research public than from keeping it secret. And it seems clear that the progress of social science (at large) is enhanced when scholars place their ideas in the public domain as quickly as possible.

What to Reveal about the Exploratory Process

In this book, we have focused attention on an aspect of research normally hidden from view. Typically, a published article or book begins with a theory, proceeds to a hypothesis, and thence to the research design and the findings. However, this rarely conforms to the actual chronology of a project, which is considerably messier, as discussed in Chapter 1.

Now, we want to consider an adjacent question: Should this mess be revealed to the public in the finished product (the published article or book)?

In anthropology, it has become de rigueur to report a great deal of information on the author's relationship to their research site and on the development of their ideas more generally. Typically, the foreword or introductory chapter of a book includes a personal narrative revealing how the author established contact with their study subjects, what relationship they maintained with them, and how their own personal baggage became a part of what they studied. By bringing this sort of introspection into view the reader (not to mention, the author) has an opportunity to take note of possible biases and prejudices. And the process of understanding is properly framed as an interactive process, in which the author is not an objective bystander. In this fashion, the myth of complete scientific objectivity is dispelled.

For anthropologists, the process of self-revelation enhances the truth-value of the ethnography, or at the very least makes it more honest. Would the same hold true for disciplines like economics, political science, and sociology? If so, should we also adopt a norm of self-disclosure? What would this look like, in practice?

We can gain a glimpse of this scenario by examining those rare cases where authors do relate something about the story of a project, typically in the acknowledgments or introduction that accompanies a book-length monograph. Here, one may distinguish three meta-narratives.

The first narrative follows a Popperian format. The author had a theory about who committed a crime (the butler) and then went to test that theory. Gratifyingly, the theory was verified. It was the butler.

A second narrative begins with the Popperian setup but introduces a dramatic plot twist. After laying out their theoretical hunch – the perpetrator was the nephew of the deceased – the author reveals that their argument was disproven. What they thought initially turned out not to be true at all. It was the butler, after all.

A third narrative emphasizes the inductive quality of research. The author went ambling into the bush, oblivious of Theory, and eventually encountered phenomena that intrigued them (a crime). They tried to make sense of that phenomena and, after many twists and turns, developed their theory. It was the butler.

Note that the answer is the same, but these three meta-narratives offer three very different stories about how the author arrived at the solution. Curiously, they all seem to be serving the same rhetorical task. They are all striving (implicitly) to convince us that the findings contained in their study are true. The butler did it.

In the first narrative, this meta-claim rests on the idea that the theory was conceived prior to testing. Accordingly, there was no ex post adjustment of the theory ("post hoc theorizing") or of the tests ("fishing" or "curve-fitting").

In the second narrative, the author is also attempting to establish that they are not cooking the books. Far from it – they tried (so to speak) to force their theory on the data but the data refused to confess, even after harsh interrogation. Accordingly, the counter-theory – which the author initially discounted – must be true. If the author was willing to abandon their preconceptions, so should the reader. This narrative is reminiscent of testimony given by ex-adherents of a religion, organization, or ideology. If they no longer have faith, it can't possibly be true. Apostates know best.

In the third narrative, the author portrays their barefoot empiricism as a signal that their commitment is to the truth, in all its complexity, rather than to some prior theory. Instead of following the talisman of Grand Theory they are listening closely to the pulse of reality, remaining sensitive to its nuances, and not trying to force a particular framework.

All three of these stylized narratives can be read as attempts to establish the author's bona fides – an implicit recognition that authors cannot always be trusted. Unfortunately, there is usually no way to verify the author's version of events, which may be concocted, selectively reported, or simply misremembered. Nor is it clear what we should draw from the narrative, if true. Should we be more inclined to believe the truth of a study whose author followed paths 1, 2, or 3? We are not sure whether any of these three narratives enhances, or detracts from, the likely truth-value of the author's research.

Of course, narratives about the research process may be useful *for other purposes*. It presumably (so long as it is truthful) sheds light on the topic of this book, exploratory research, and as such may move forward our understanding of this process and the overall productivity of social science. It may also provide specific tips for researchers working on a particular topic, elucidating blind curves, dead-ends, and roads not traveled. This could prove extremely useful. It may, finally, serve the purpose that anthropologists envision – shedding light on the researcher's preconceptions and allowing readers to better judge the stated findings (if the author's personal narrative is truthful).

Thus, we encourage researchers to include a short exposition of how they came upon their topic and how that topic developed into a finished piece of research. But we do not view this information as so important that it should be regarded as a requirement of publication (on par with data transparency and replicability).

Toward Appraisal

The juncture at which theory exploration segues into theory testing is rarely clear-cut. Any method of exploration is also, in some degree, a method of testing, and vice versa. Moreover, the act of exploration has no precise start-date or completion-date. A line of exploratory research, if successful, gradually matures into finished research. And finished research generates exploratory research. A fertile research program is a continuous process of questions and findings, which in turn generate new questions.

Nonetheless, it is useful – and for some purposes essential – to distinguish these two phases of research. Once a key hypothesis has been identified it should be subjected to more formal, and probably more stringent, tests than were employed in its discovery. Ideally, these tests are out-of-sample, that is, the data used to test the thesis is different from the data used to develop the thesis.

For example, one might conduct a preliminary experiment or survey on a small sample, or a convenience sample, while the main test is conducted on a larger sample gathered randomly from a known population. If the research is qualitative and conducted "in the field," the preliminary work might be brief and scattershot, while the main study involves a much longer stay and more systematic data collection (with a specific hypothesis in mind).

There is also a shift in psychology. At the beginning, the researcher struggles to identify a topic. Here, the concern is "What can I possibly say about this subject?" The canny researcher does their best to nurture new ideas, to foster their growth and development, giving them every benefit of the doubt.

Once a project has been identified, the researcher must start to think with a second, more skeptical part of the brain. "Is this theory really true? What objections might be raised? In what ways might it be limited in scope, or even trivial? Can it be adequately tested?" Intoxicating new ideas are subjected to sober second thoughts.

Richard Swedberg (2012: 6) borrows an evocative analogy from law. "The context of discovery is where you have to figure out who the murderer is [or might be], while the context of justification is where you have to prove your case in court." Following this analogy, one might say that there is little harm in identifying suspects who did not commit the crime; but there is great harm if they are wrongfully convicted. In this respect, the emphasis of research shifts subtly but importantly from avoiding Type 2 errors (failing to reject a false null hypothesis) to avoiding Type 1 errors (incorrectly rejecting a true null hypothesis).

Given that the virtues of exploration are quite different from the virtues of appraisal it is not surprising that researchers often lean one way or the other in their practices and predilections. Some researchers are known primarily as idea generators ("theorists" or "case study researchers") and others as idea testers (often wearing a "methodology" hat).

For most researchers, however, these roles intermingle. Typically, the person who comes up with an idea must also test it. In this fashion we inhabit both roles in a sequential fashion. First, we are the hopeful inventor, looking for ways to innovate. Then, we are the skeptical judge, looking for problems and errors.

This transition is not easy, but it is essential. At the point when you have committed to a project you must also *de*-commit, which is to say, start thinking about why you might have been wrong. At this stage, Claudia Goldin (1998: 111) advises, "Be your own worst enemy."

The point of this psychological reversal is to overcome the tendency to collect, analyze, and interpret evidence in a manner prejudicial to one's own theory. Our faculty survey offers some grist for this mill, as discussed in Chapter 2. We saw in Figure 2.7 that nearly all research begins with a hunch and that most of these hunches are subsequently confirmed – a clue that social scientists might, on occasion, tilt the playing field in favor of their initial hypothesis.

To be clear, there is nothing wrong with having a hunch about what you are going to find before you invest in a lengthy – and perhaps expensive – study. Indeed, that is precisely what we advise (above). And one would hope that these hunches are right more often than they are wrong. Nor is there anything wrong with changing one's theory or research design.

However, there *is* a problem if these changes are opportunistic, that is, if they ignore contrary evidence and highlight supportive evidence, or if they carve up the universe in an arbitrary fashion so as to "define in" those empirical data points that confirm the theory and "define out" those data points that contradict it (scope gerrymandering).

This highlights the importance of distinguishing, and cleanly separating (as much as possible) the two core phases of research – (1) the phase when ideas are germinated and (2) the phase when they are tested. It also highlights the importance of reporting the results of (2) even when they run contrary to the author's hunch.

One technique for tying the researcher's hands is to pre-register the main hypothesis(es) along with a detailed pre-analysis plan (PAP) on a site such as the Open Science Foundation registry. Any deviations from the PAP should be explained in the completed report (e.g., a journal submission). If readers are unsure, they may consult the pre-registered document (which is publicly available, perhaps in an anonymized format) to see how closely the completed work follows the stated plan.

We don't mean to suggest that the PAP should always be followed. Sometimes this is impossible, as unforeseen problems in data collection or analysis may require a different approach than initially envisioned. Sometimes it is undesirable, as the research site may reveal new and exciting directions for investigation. The point is, pre-registration allows the reader to distinguish between what is confirmatory and what is exploratory, which is essential to judging the credibility of the findings.

We also want to acknowledge that not all research is suitable for pre-registration. Arguably, pre-registration makes sense only in settings where (a) the evidence on which the hypothesis will be tested is unavailable to the author at the time the study is pre-registered and (b) where a highly specific research design can be laid out, a priori (the PAP).

These are complicated issues, and this is not the place to explore them in any detail.[3] Suffice to say that pre-registration is helpful in distinguishing exploratory and confirmatory research *in some situations*. In other situations, achieving this goal will be harder and will likely depend upon the researcher's honesty and integrity, as no external enforcement mechanism is available.

Whatever the situation, it is essential to distinguish – and wherever possible, to separate – the tasks of exploration and appraisal. Having taken the reader through the exploratory stage, we reach the terminus of this book. Bon voyage!

---

[3] See Elman, Gerring, Mahoney (2020), and especially Jacobs (2020), who lays out an agenda for how this might apply to qualitative research.

Appendix A
Surveys and Interviews

Data Sources

We constructed two surveys, the first focused on graduate students (pre-PhD or very recently completed PhD) and the second focused on practitioners (post-PhD) in political science. In addition, we conducted interviews with a small number of political scientists whose work has been especially influential.

Invitations to participate in the two surveys were sent out by email and the surveys were administered online through a Qualtrics platform. Survey respondents were granted confidentiality unless they allow themselves to be identified. All surveys and interviews were completed in 2019.

The two surveys are similar in content, including a mix of closed- and open-ended questions. The main difference is that the graduate student survey focuses on dissertation work while the practitioner survey focuses on a (randomly chosen) published work. Complete questionnaires are included below. Survey data (anonymized, where requested) is posted on Dataverse. Interviews are posted on John Gerring's homepage, where they can be streamed.

Study group characteristics from these three samples are summarized in Table A.1. Most of the contrasts are commonsensical. With respect to age, practitioners are older than students and interviewees are older than practitioners. Likewise, for year of PhD. Interviewees are most likely to hail from the United States and PhD students least likely. Practitioner and interviewee samples are tilted heavily toward men, while the graduate student sample is evenly divided between men and women (with a small number of transgender or other). Subfield distributions and general methodological approaches are fairly similar across the three samples. However, our graduate student respondents are more likely than our other samples to employ qualitative data in their research.

Table A.1 Study group characteristics

		PhD students	Practitioners	Interviewees
General (non-exclusive)	Respondents (*N*)	84	556	12(15)
	Response rate (%)		27	45
	Missingness (%)	13	13	83
	Open-ended questions answered (%)	45	17	75
	Identity revealed (%)	11	15	50
Cohort (mean)	Age	31	53	62
	Year of PhD (anticipated)	(2021)	1998	1987
Country of origin (%)	European	36	33	17
	American	23	52	83
	Other	31	15	0
Gender (%)	Female	49	22	33
	Male	49	78	67
	Trans or other	2		0
Employer (%)	Research institute		5	0
	Policy institute		<1	0
	University		89	100
	Government		<1	0
	Private sector		<1	0
	Unemployed		0	0
	Retired		4	0
	Other		1	0
University position (%)	Non tenure track		1	0
	Research		4	0
	Assistant professor		8	0
	Associate professor		23	17
	Full professor		64	83
Teaching (%)	Teach graduate students		85	92
Subfields (%, non-exclusive)	American	7	27	42
	Comparative	48	60	67
	International relations	39	30	33
	Public policy	37	25	8
	Political theory	13	6	17
	Public Law	4	4	8
	Methodology	14	19	17
Approaches (%, non-exclusive)	Historical, archival	50	58	92

Continued

Table A.1 Continued

		PhD students	Practitioners	Interviewees
	Ethnography	27	14	17
	Focus groups	14	12	17
	Surveys	39	64	58
	Experiments	15	35	42
	Expert coding	32	31	25
Methods (%, non-exclusive)	Qualitative	81	59	75
	Quantitative	53	82	75

Numbers rounded to nearest integer. Response options are exclusive except where noted. Empty cells indicate that the question was not asked or is inapplicable. Of the fifteen interviewees, twelve took the standardized survey; results reflect their responses.

In the following sections we review the logistics of these data-gathering instruments and discuss concerns about bias and representativeness. Readers should be aware that we lean more heavily on the practitioner survey than on the graduate student survey or the interviews. This is because the practitioner survey is much larger and because it draws on a systematic (random) sample. Figures and tables found below, and in the book, draw on this survey, unless otherwise noted.

Graduate Student Survey

The graduate student survey targets those working toward (or having very recently completed) a doctorate in political science, including adjacent fields such as international relations and public policy. Our sampling frame consists of students attending summer schools in Berlin (sponsored by Humboldt University and WZB), Essex (sponsored by the European Consortium for Political Research), and Syracuse (sponsored by the Institute for Qualitative and Multimethod Research) during the summer of 2019.

The curriculum at these schools stretches across the various methodological divisions of contemporary political science and enlists students from PhD programs throughout Europe and North America along with a sprinkling of students from other regions of the world. In this diffuse sense our sample may be regarded as representative, even though it is by no means a random sample.

Practitioner Survey

A second survey focuses on practitioners, defined as those with a PhD in political science. The sampling frame is constructed with the *Publish or Perish* software developed by Harzing (2007), which allows us to conduct Google Scholar (GS) searches focused on (self-declared) political scientists with curated GS profiles. We choose to focus on those who were active between 1999 and 2019 so that memories about projects are relatively fresh. In this fashion, we generate a database composed of all publications found in the curated profiles of these political scientists, a total of 162,000 books and articles (including chapters in edited volumes).

We then sample publications randomly from this database with the following caveats. We discard works with more than three authors, anticipating that in this situation it may be difficult for the respondent to reconstruct the genesis of the study. We also discard works that are primarily methodological or theoretical, anticipating that creativity in these venues may operate somewhat differently. (Many of the questions on our survey assume an empirical focus and would not be answerable if the work is methodological or theoretical.)

Through this iterated process we select 2,080 publications randomly from our database of 162,000. An author from each of these studies was invited (by email) to fill out a short survey on Qualtrics. We prioritize the first author of each study, selecting the second or third if the preceding authors had already been issued an invitation (by virtue of their contribution to another publication). Respondents were granted confidentiality, though they could also choose to identify themselves publicly. 556 accepted our invitation and completed the survey, a response-rate of 27 percent. All surveys were completed in 2019.

It should be acknowledged that not every political scientist has a GS profile, and those that do are probably more engaged and better published than those who do not. Unfortunately, without a curated GS profile that specifies a scholarly field it is difficult to distinguish work in political science from work in other fields. In any case, our sampling frame is probably representative of highly engaged, well-trained scholars – arguably, the relevant population for a project whose goal is to shed light on best practices among those who aim high. (It is not clear what we might learn from scholars who are disengaged, as their lack of productivity may be owing to motivation rather than strategy.)

Interviews

In addition to these standardized surveys, we conduct interviews with a subset of practicing political scientists (active between 1999 and 2019) whose work has been especially influential. Since this is a much smaller sample participants are selected in a purposeful (non-random) fashion in order to assure that the resulting study group is reasonably diverse along multiple parameters – age, gender, race, location, doctoral institution, subfield, substantive focus, and methodology. (As previously, we exclude scholars whose contributions are primarily methodological or theoretical.)

This could have been accomplished through stratified sampling; however, this would have required gathering information on all of these dimensions for the entire sampling frame, a laborious process. In any case, the foundation of our evidence stems from the surveys; interviews are intended to add color and detail.

With this approach we selected thirty-three names, of whom sixteen agreed to participate: Barbara Geddes (UCLA), Don Green (Columbia University), Emilie Hafner-Burton(UCSD), Bryan Jones (University of Texas at Austin), Keith Krehbiel (Stanford School of Business), Margaret Levi (Center for Advanced Study in the Behavioral Sciences, Stanford University), Amy Mazur (Washington State University), Simeon Nichter (UCSD), Pippa Norris (Kennedy School of Government), Ben Page (Northwestern University), Will Reno (Northwestern University), Maggie Roberts (UCSD), Howard Rosenthal (NYU), Idean Salehyan (University of North Texas), Beth Simmons (University of Pennsylvania), and Rogers Smith (University of Pennsylvania). With a few exceptions, noted above, all are members of political science departments.

All consented to make their remarks public, though a few decided to redact small portions of the interview (understood as "off the record"). Conversations, recorded using Zencastr software, were wide-ranging and averaged about 42 minutes in length. These interviews can be streamed from John Gerring's website. (In some cases, there have been minor redactions.)

Social Desirability Bias

Before moving on, we must discuss the possibility of systematic measurement error. Our goal is to recover the processes by which researchers get ideas for research. To do so, we must encourage respondents to give an unvarnished view of this process, which may not always conform to methodological precepts about how research *should* be conducted.

To mitigate social desirability bias, we take several steps. First, as noted, we offer confidentiality to all survey respondents. (Only 15% volunteer to make their identity public.)

Second, we encourage respondents to answer truthfully, and assure them that we are not judging their actions. A prefatory note reads as follows:

> In answering the following questions, we ask you to be frank and not to worry about whether you "did it wrong." In our view, there are no wrong ways to get a research idea. Conversations with other people, inductive surprises from data, personal values or aspects of personal life history – all of these sometimes play a role alongside deductive theorizing or literature reviews. We hope this survey can teach us about the real story of your research process, not a sanitized version that conforms to an idealized view of the process.

We indicate the same idea (verbally) to our interviewees.

Third, all surveys focus on a particular study – the dissertation (for graduate students) or the randomly chosen publication (for practitioners). Likewise, most of the questions posed to interviewees focus on a particular study. In this fashion, we aim to focus the attention of respondents, avoiding the prospect of overly processed responses which might be susceptible to social desirability bias. Our thinking is that if one asks general questions about "how you conduct research" one is more likely to get answers that reflect how the respondent believes they *should* be conducting research. If one asks about a specific piece of research the answer is more likely to be truthful to the facts of the case.

Generalizability

Assuming the responses we received from our surveys and interviews are true, on average (i.e., they are not systematically biased), to what extent are they generalizable?

We have pointed out that respondents to both our surveys are likely to overrepresent graduate students and practitioners who are well-trained and ambitious. Arguably, the questions we ask are more understandable and meaningful among those who share a high level of training and ambition. But it should also be borne in mind that our respondents are not a cross-section of the discipline of political science.

A more serious limitation is that we have drawn all our informants from a single discipline. By reason of familiarity and access, we focus on the discipline of political science. We cannot say for sure whether patterns found among members of this tribe persist across other tribes. Surely, a few things are different, given the varying substantive and methodological focuses of these diverse disciplines.

Conveniently, political science occupies a centrist position in the contemporary social sciences, being somewhat less positivist (inclined toward the natural sciences) than economics and psychology, and somewhat more positivistic than sociology. It also lies in some kind of middle or mixed position with respect to a variety of other dimensions – quantitative-qualitative, macro-micro, present-historical, and so forth. If there is an "average" social science, it is probably political science.

Insofar as this positioning affects the conduct of exploratory research, we may expect political scientists to reflect the experiences of the social sciences, broadly considered. We shall adopt this tentative assumption, pending further investigation.

Pre-PhD Questionnaire

Introduction

1. Dear ___ ,

This survey focuses on how graduate students identify topics for dissertation (doctoral) research. Our hope is that it generates insights into this crucial stage of an academic career, offering suggestions that other students can benefit from. We would be grateful for your participation.

Eligible respondents should be working toward, or have recently completed, a doctorate in political science, international relations, or public policy.

The survey is voluntary and may be exited at any time. It takes approximately 10–15 minutes to complete.

The survey is confidential, which means that your identity will not be shared publicly – unless you consent. If, at the end of the survey, you feel comfortable making your identity public you may choose to do so. To be clear, this survey is confidential UNLESS you explicitly allow your identity to be revealed.

2. In answering the following questions, we ask you to be frank and not to worry about whether you "did it wrong." In our view, there are no wrong ways to get a research idea. Conversations with other people, inductive surprises from data, personal values or aspects of personal life history – all of these sometimes play a role alongside deductive theorizing or literature reviews. We hope this survey can teach us about the real story of your research process, not a sanitized version that conforms to an idealized view of the process. We also realize that some of the questions that follow may be difficult to answer in a precise fashion. For questions like that, please give the answer that feels most appropriate.

3. Are you currently working toward a doctoral degree (or equivalent) in political science, international relations, or public policy?

   a. Yes
   b. No

4. Have you recently completed a doctoral degree (or equivalent) in political science, international relations, or public policy?

   a. Yes
   b. No

   If you answered No to questions 3 *and* 4, please exit the survey.

The Dissertation

We are now going to ask a series of questions about work for your dissertation. If your dissertation consists of separate articles, you may answer the following questions with respect to that article which you feel is most important – the centerpiece of your dissertation. If the work is collaborative, please speak to the experience of the group, as best as you can ("You" = "Y'all").

5. At what stage of the dissertation are you, right now?

   a. Looking for a topic
   b. Have a preliminary topic but not finalized
   c. Have a topic which is well-developed and am working to carry it out
   d. Have completed, or substantially completed, the dissertation

6. How easy was/is it to find a topic for your dissertation?

   a. Extremely difficult – harder than any other part of graduate school
   b. Difficult – harder than most other parts of graduate school

c. Somewhat difficult – harder than a few other parts of graduate school
d. Somewhat easy – easier than a few other parts of graduate school
e. Easy – easier than almost all other parts of graduate school
f. Extremely easy – easier than any other part of graduate school

7. For those who have a topic (even if only provisional) . . . . . . When (in what calendar year) did you find it?

   a. [insert calendar year]

8. *For those who have a topic (even if only provisional)* . . . . . . Did you consider other topics before settling on this one?

   a. No
   b. One other topic
   c. Several other topics
   d. Many other topics

9. If you answered any response other than "No" in the previous question, describe briefly why you abandoned other topics before arriving at your current topic.

   [text]

10. For those who have a topic (even if only provisional) . . . . . . How happy are you with it?

    a. Very unhappy
    b. Somewhat unhappy
    c. Neither happy nor unhappy
    d. Somewhat happy
    e. Very happy

11. *For those who have a topic (even if only provisional)* . . . . . . What, in your view, is most innovative or special about it? (Choose all that pertain)

    a. A new method or research design, i.e., one that has not been applied to this question
    b. A new finding that goes beyond previous research
    c. A new finding that contradicts previous research
    d. A new topic (previously unexplored)
    e. A topic that is especially relevant to the concerns of citizens or policymakers
    f. There is nothing especially innovative

12. We'd like to know about the various formal and informal activities that you engaged in prior to finding a topic. (If you have not yet found a topic then this pertains to what you are doing now, as you look for a topic.) Specifically, how much time did/do you spend on each of the following activities? (The next question asks about which activity was most crucial to finding your topic. So in this question please limit yourself to activities that you happened to be engaging in – regardless of whether they were helpful or not.) (Choose all that pertain)
    No time at all/A little time/A moderate amount of time/A great deal of time

    a. Reading broadly across related literatures
    b. Careful reading and critical thought about a single key publication
    c. Reading news stories and following current events
    d. Conversing with friends outside academia
    e. Conversing with faculty advisors or mentors
    f. Conversing with graduate students
    g. Attending a panel at conferences or workshops
    h. Conversing with fellow attendees at conferences or workshops
    i. Conducting archival work
    j. Conducting field research
    k. Engaged in research on other topics
    l. Traveling (for fun or personal reasons)
    m. Playing with existing data (exploratory data analysis, scatterplots, simple statistical models, etc.)
    n. Reading about funding opportunities
    o. Other *[text]*

13. *For those who have a topic (even if only provisional)* . . . . . . To the best of your recollection, which of the following was most critical to identifying the topic for this project? (Choose all that pertain)

    a. Reading broadly across related literatures
    b. Careful reading and critical thought about a single key publication
    c. Reading news stories or following current events
    d. Conversing with friends outside academia
    e. Conversing with faculty advisors or mentors
    f. Conversing with graduate students
    g. Attending a conference or workshop
    h. Conducting archival work
    i. Conducting field research

    j. Engaging in research on other topics

    k. Traveling (for fun or personal reasons)

    l. Playing with existing data (exploratory data analysis, scatterplots, simple statistical models, etc.)

    m. Available funding

    n. Other *[text]*

14. *For those who have a topic (even if only provisional)* ...... Which of the following served as your point of entrée to this topic? Where did you begin? (Choose all that pertain)

    a. A seminal work

    b. A general topic

    c. A key concept

    d. A general theory

    e. A specific hypothesis

    f. A compelling anomaly

    g. An event of special interest

    h. A promising (extant) dataset

    i. A research site or archive of special interest

    j. A method of analysis

    k. One or more final paper(s) written for a substantive or theory-driven course

    l. One or more final paper(s) written for a methods course

    m. A previous study of someone else's

15. How important were/are your personal experiences (your life, outside of academe) to the development of your dissertation topic? (Answer whether you have a topic yet or are still in search of one.)
Not at all important/Not very important/Somewhat important/Very important

16. Do you see your dissertation project as inspired by (or likely to be inspired by) any of the following personal characteristics? (Choose all that pertain)

    a. Your sex

    b. Your sexual identity

    c. Your race

    d. Your ethnicity

    e. Your natal country

    f. Your natal language

g. Your family or family heritage

h. No (none)

17. How important was/is the prospect of addressing a problem in society or politics (i.e., something that could, through your research, be better understood or ameliorated) to the development of your dissertation project?
    Not at all important/Not very important/Somewhat important/Very important

18. How important was/is the promotion of social or political justice to the development of your dissertation project?
    Not at all important/Not very important/Somewhat important/Very important

19. How important was/is intellectual puzzle-solving to the development of your dissertation project?
    Not at all important/Not very important/Somewhat important/Very important

20. *For those who have a topic (even if only provisional) ......* Was there a "lightbulb" moment (a particular point in time when the idea for your dissertation project came together)?
    Y/N

21. *For those who have completed, or are nearing completion, of their dissertation ......* Between the time the prospectus was written and approved (or the equivalent project documents or proposals produced) and its completion, were there any major changes to the theory, hypothesis(es), or research design?
    Y/N

22. For the next series of questions, we will mention some common **sources of stress** in the dissertation process. For each, please reflect on your current situation (if you are working on developing your dissertation) or on that experience (if you recently completed it).
    Not a source of stress/A minor source of stress/A major source of stress/My most important source of stress

    a. ...... funding pressures?

    b. ...... managing your relationship with your advisor(s)?

    c. ...... finding a research topic?

    d. ...... choosing cases?

e. ...... selecting a research design?

f. ...... competition with other graduate students?

Personal Info

In this section, we ask some questions about yourself ......

23. In what year were you born?

    [year]

24. In what country were you born?

    [Dropdown menu]

25. What is your gender?

    a. Male
    b. Female
    c. Trans or other

26. When did you start your (first) MA or PhD program in political science (or IR)?

    [year]

27. In what year did you obtain, or do you anticipate obtaining, your PhD?

    [year]

28. From what university did you obtain, or do you anticipate obtaining, your PhD?

    [Dropdown menu]

29. In what subfields of political science do you currently work? (Choose all that pertain)

    a. American politics
    b. Comparative politics
    c. International relations
    d. Public policy
    e. Political theory
    f. Methodology

30. What approaches do you commonly employ in your work? (Choose all that pertain)

a. Historical and archival
b. Ethnography
c. Focus groups
d. Surveys
e. Experiments
f. Expert coding

31. What methods of analysis do you commonly employ in your work? (Choose all that pertain)

a. Qualitative
b. Quantitative

32. Having finished the survey, please consider whether you would be willing to be identified by name. (If you have further questions about this please contact us so we can address them. Our email addresses are at the end of the survey.)

a. I am willing to be identified.
b. I prefer that my identity remain confidential. [default]

33. If you are willing to be identified, please answer the following questions:
Name: [*text*]
Course of study: Dropdown menu: Political Science/International Relations/Public Policy/Sociology/Other [please list]
University: [*Dropdown menu*]

34. This ends the formal survey.
If you have time, there are several open-ended follow-up questions that we would like you to answer. Just hit the "next" option on your screen. Thank you!
John Gerring, Professor, Department of Government, UT Austin. jgerring@austin.utexas.edu
Jason Seawright, Professor, Department of Political Science, Northwestern University. j-seawright@northwestern.edu

Open-Ended Questions

35. Please describe the evolution of your dissertation project in your own words. Your description may be as long as you wish it to be. You may

touch upon the issues raised in the foregoing questions, or upon other issues. Please include as many details as you can.

[Open field]

36. What obstacles did you encounter in your search for a dissertation topic?

37. Are there ways in which the graduate educational experience – the curriculum or other aspects of the program – could be improved to make it easier to develop ideas for dissertation work?

    [Open field]

38. What advice would you give to advanced undergraduate or graduate students looking to identify a topic for a thesis, dissertation, article, or book?

    [Open field]

39. Is there anything you would like to add to your responses, or anything you would like to communicate to the PIs?

    [Open field]

40. Would you be willing to be identified by name for these open-ended answers (in this last part of the survey)?

    a. I am willing to be identified.
    b. I prefer that my identity remain confidential. [default]

Post-PhD Questionnaire

Introduction

1. Dear Dr.___,

   This survey focuses on the conduct of research in political science, specifically the origin and development of ideas that culminate in published work. Our hope is that it generates helpful tips for researchers – young and old – to improve their creativity and productivity. We would be grateful for your participation.

   Eligible respondents should have completed their doctorate in political science.

   The survey is voluntary and may be exited at any time. It takes approximately 5–10 minutes to complete.

The survey is confidential, which means that your identity will not be shared publicly – unless you consent. If, at the end of the survey, you feel comfortable making your identity public you may choose to do so. To be clear, this survey is confidential UNLESS you explicitly allow your identity to be revealed.

2. In answering the following questions, we ask you to be frank and not to worry about whether you "did it wrong." In our view, there are no wrong ways to get a research idea. Conversations with other people, inductive surprises from data, personal values or aspects of personal life history – all of these sometimes play a role alongside deductive theorizing or literature reviews. We hope this survey can teach us about the real story of your research process, not a sanitized version that conforms to an idealized view of the process. We also realize that some of the questions that follow may be difficult to answer in a precise fashion. For questions like that, please give the answer that feels most appropriate.

3. Are you the author or co-author of the following work?
   [Full reference]

   a. Yes
   b. No (if No, please exit the survey)

The Work

We are now going to ask a series of questions about this work. If it is part of a string of publications that are closely related you may consider them collectively. If the work is collaborative, please speak to the experience of the group, as best as you can ("You" = "Y'all").

1. What, in your view, is most innovative or special about this piece of research? (Choose all that pertain)

   a. A new method or research design, i.e., one that had not been applied to this question
   b. A new finding that went beyond previous research
   c. A new finding that contradicted previous research
   d. A new topic (previously unexplored)
   e. A topic that is especially relevant to the concerns of citizens or policymakers
   f. There is nothing especially innovative

2. Did this research grow out of your dissertation?

   a. It uses data analyzed in my dissertation
   b. It uses procedures developed in my dissertation
   c. It is part of a research trajectory that began with my dissertation
   d. It is not closely related to my dissertation

3. How long prior to this project's acceptance for publication was the initial idea for this project hatched?
   [years]

4. We'd like to know about the various formal and informal activities that took place *before* you started formal research activities on this project (i.e., before submission of an IRB proposal, pre-registration, the construction of a formal research design, first discussions with key informants, implementation of a key survey, experiment, or other data collection effort). Specifically, how much time did you spend on each of the following activities? (The next question asks about which activity was most crucial to finding your topic. So in this question please limit yourself to activities that you happened to be engaging in – regardless of whether they were helpful or not.)
   No time at all/A little time/A moderate amount of time/A great deal of time

   a. Reading broadly across related literatures
   b. Careful reading and critical thought about a single key publication
   c. Reading news stories and following current events
   d. Conversing with friends outside academia
   e. Conversing with colleagues
   f. Conversing with faculty advisors or mentors
   g. Conversing with students
   h. Attending conferences or workshops
   i. Conducting archival work
   j. Conducting field research
   k. Engaged in research on other topics
   l. Traveling (for fun or personal reasons)
   m. Playing with existing data (exploratory data analysis, scatterplots, simple statistical models, etc.)
   n. Reading about funding opportunities
   o. Other *[text]*

5. To the best of your recollection, which of the following was most critical to identifying the topic for this project? (Choose all that pertain)

   a. Reading broadly across related literatures
   b. Careful reading and critical thought about a single key publication
   c. Reading news stories or following current events
   d. Conversing with friends outside academia
   e. Conversing with colleagues
   f. Conversing with faculty advisors or mentors
   g. Conversing with students
   h. Attending a conference or workshop
   i. Conducting archival work
   j. Conducting field research
   k. Engaging in research on other topics
   l. Traveling (for fun or personal reasons)
   m. Playing with existing data (exploratory data analysis, scatterplots, simple statistical models, etc.)
   n. Available funding
   o. Other *[text]*

6. Which of the following served as your point of entrée to this topic? Where did you begin? (Choose all that pertain)

   a. A seminal work
   b. A general topic
   c. A key concept
   d. A general theory
   e. A specific hypothesis
   f. A compelling anomaly
   g. An event of special interest
   h. A promising (extant) dataset
   i. A research site or archive of special interest
   j. A method of analysis
   k. A previous study of your own
   l. A previous study of someone else's

7. How important were your personal experiences (your life, outside of academe) to the development of this project?
   Not at all important/Not very important/Somewhat important/Very important

8. Do you see this project as inspired by any of the following personal characteristics? (Choose all that pertain)

   a. Your sex (if not male)
   b. Your sexual identity (if not heterosexual)
   c. Your race (if not white)
   d. Your ethnicity
   e. Your natal country (if not US)
   f. Your natal language (if not English)
   g. Your family or family heritage
   h. No (none)

9. How important was the prospect of addressing a problem in society or politics (i.e., something that could, through your research, be better understood or ameliorated) to the development of this project?
   Not at all important/Not very important/Somewhat important/Very important

10. How important was the promotion of social or political justice to the development of this project?
    Not at all important/Not very important/Somewhat important/Very important

11. How important was intellectual puzzle-solving to the development of this project?
    Not at all important/Not very important/Somewhat important/Very important

12. Was there a "lightbulb" moment (a particular point in time when the idea for the project came together)?
    Y/N

13. Between the time the project was initially framed (e.g., the first project documents or proposals were produced) and its acceptance for publication, were there any major changes to the theory or hypothesis(es)?
    Y/N

14. Between the time the project was initially framed (e.g., the first project documents or proposals were produced) and its acceptance for publication, were there any major changes to the research design?
    Y/N

15. Between the time the project was initially framed (e.g., the first project documents or proposals were produced) and its acceptance for publication, were there any major changes to the analysis?
Y/N

16. Before the research was conducted, did you have a strong hunch about what you would find?

    a. No, I had no idea
    b. Yes, I had some idea
    c. Yes, I had a very strong idea

17. If you answered "Yes" to the previous question, was your hunch borne out?

    a. No, not at all. I was surprised by the findings
    b. Yes, to some extent
    c. Yes, very much so

File Drawer

18. In this section, we ask some questions about your recent "file drawer." This refers to ideas from the past ten years that consumed a fair bit of work on your part but were not published by a journal or a press and are unlikely ever to be published (though they may have been published as conference papers or working papers).

19. How many project ideas lie in your file drawer? (Estimate to the best of your abilities.)
[integer] (If you entered 0, please move on to the next section of the survey.)

20. Now, think back to the last instance – that is, the last time you had an idea for a project, invested time in it, and then gave up on it. Please insert a brief description (e.g., abstract) of that project.
[Open field]

21. What is the current status of the project? (Choose all that pertain)

    a. Unfinished
    b. Completed but not presented at a conference, submitted to a journal, or available online

  c. Presented at a conference but not currently available online as a conference/working paper

  d. Available online as a conference/working paper but not submitted to a journal or press

  e. Rejected by a journal or press

  f. Rejected by multiple journals or presses

22. How do you regard this project?

  a. Should have been published

  b. Probably does not deserve to be published

23. What obstacles did you encounter in this project? (Choose all that pertain)

  a. Anticipated data turned out to be unavailable

  b. Theory was insufficiently innovative

  c. Null hypothesis could not be disproved

  d. Findings were unsurprising

  e. We were scooped (other studies were subsequently published that made this one less innovative, or at least appear less innovative)

  f. Interest in the topic diminished

  g. Collaboration fell apart

  h. Funding was not secured

  i. Existing funding ran out

  j. I/we could not find time to complete the research in a timely manner

  k. The target publication venue(s) rejected the project

  l. Other (please explain)

24. Knowing what you know now, what would you have done differently?

  a. Nothing at all

  b. Avoided the project entirely

  c. Other (please explain)

Personal Info

25. In this section, we ask some questions about yourself . . ..

26. What is your year of birth?
[year]

27. In what country were you born?
   [Dropdown menu]

28. What is your gender?

   a. Male
   b. Female
   c. Trans or other

29. In what year did you obtain your PhD?
   [year]

30. From what university did you obtain your PhD?
   [Dropdown menu]

31. In what subfields of political science do you currently work? (Choose all that pertain)

   a. American politics
   b. Comparative politics
   c. International relations
   d. Public policy
   e. Political theory
   f. Methodology

32. What approaches do you commonly employ in your work? (Choose all that pertain)

   a. Historical and archival
   b. Ethnography
   c. Focus groups
   d. Surveys
   e. Experiments
   f. Expert coding

33. What methods of analysis do you commonly employ in your work? (Choose all that pertain)

   a. Qualitative
   b. Quantitative

34. What label best describes your current employer?

   a. Research institute
   b. Policy institute, non-profit

c. University
d. Government
e. Private sector
f. Unemployed
g. Retired
h. Other

35. If working for a university, how would you describe your position?

a. Non tenure track teaching
b. Research
c. Assistant professor without tenure
d. Associate professor with tenure
e. Full professor

36. If working for a university, what is the name of your university?
[Dropdown menu]

37. Do you regularly teach or supervise graduate students?
Y/N

38. Having finished the survey, please consider whether you would be willing to be identified by name. (If you have further questions about this please contact us so we can address them. Our email addresses are at the end of the survey.)

a. I am willing to be identified.
b. I prefer that my identity remain confidential. [default]

39. This ends the formal survey.
If you have time, there are several open-ended follow-up questions that we would like you to answer. Just hit the "next" option on your screen.
Thank you!
John Gerring, Professor, Department of Government, UT Austin. jgerring@austin.utexas.edu
Jason Seawright, Professor, Department of Political Science, Northwestern University. j-seawright@northwestern.ed

Open-Ended Questions

40. Please describe the evolution of this work (the study you identified at the outset of this survey) in your own words. Your description may be as long

Table A.2 Descriptive statistics

Name	Label	Obs	Mean	SD	Min	Max
Female	gender_num	509	0.22	0.42	0	1
Year	Year	555	2009	5.77	1989	2019
PhD in US	PhDinUSA	556	0.57	0.50	0	1
Hunches borne out	Ifyouansweredyestothepreviousque	453	1.30	0.55	0	2
Time spent: Field research	Conductingfieldresearch	513	3.05	1.19	1	4
Identifying topic: Reading broadly	critical_readbroad	510	0.77	0.42	0	1
Identifying topic: Other research	critical_otherresearch	510	0.18	0.38	0	1
Entrée: General	entree_general	510	0.44	0.50	0	1
Entrée: Hypothesis	entree_hypothesis	510	0.19	0.39	0	1
Entrée: Event	entree_event	510	0.15	0.36	0	1
Entrée: Data	entree_data	510	0.13	0.34	0	1
Entrée: Theory	entree_theory	510	0.17	0.38	0	1
Entrée: Concept	entree_concept	510	0.25	0.43	0	1
GS citations (log)	cites_num_ln	556	2.94	1.86	0	11
PhD year	Inwhatyeardidyouobtainyourphd	550	1998	12.41	1928	2020
University ranking (decile)	unidec_ext	556	4.81	4.31	1	11
GS citations total (1000s)	scholarcites_num_1000s	488	5.05	8.13	0.002	94
Subfield: American politics	subfield_ap	508	0.27	0.44	0	1
Subfield: Comparative politics	subfield_cp	508	0.60	0.49	0	1
Subfield: International relations	subfield_ir	508	0.30	0.46	0	1
Subfield: Theory	subfield_theory	508	0.06	0.24	0	1
Subfield: Public law	subfield_law	508	0.04	0.20	0	1
Subfield: Public policy	subfield_policy	508	0.25	0.43	0	1
Subfield: Methods	subfield_method	508	0.19	0.39	0	1
Method: Quantitative	method_quant	508	0.82	0.38	0	1
Method: Qualitative	method_qual	508	0.59	0.49	0	1
Book (0=article)	type_num	549	0.10	0.30	0	1
Authors (N)	Authorcount	553	2.21	0.65	1	3
Promotion of justice	howimportantwasthepromotionofsoc	513	2.39	1.05	1	4
Intellectual puzzle	Howimportantwasintellectualpuzzl	512	3.45	0.66	1	4
Time: Reading broadly	time_readingbroadly	512	3.26	0.75	1	4
Time: Funding opportunities	time_funding	510	3.18	0.93	1	4
Innovation index	publish_index	512	1.20	0.87	−1	4

Includes all variables employed in Tables 3.2–3.4.

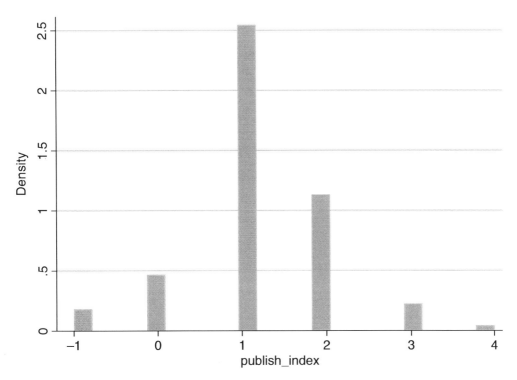

Figure A.1   Innovation index

Histogram of Innovation index. N=512. Mean=1.20. Standard deviation=0.87.

as you wish it to be. You may touch upon the issues raised in the foregoing questions, or upon other issues. Please include as many details as you can. *[Open field]*

41. What advice would you give to advanced undergraduate or graduate students looking to identify a topic for a thesis, dissertation, article, or book?
    [Open field]

42. Is there anything you would like to add to your responses, or anything you would like to communicate to the PIs?
    [Open field]

43. Would you be willing to be identified by name for these open-ended answers (in this last part of the survey)?

    a. I am willing to be identified.
    b. I prefer that my identity remain confidential. [default]

Descriptive Information

Cluster Analysis

Thus far, we have presented data from our surveys in a selective fashion, focusing on results that seem most important or counterintuitive. The figures presented above reveal some points of consensus but also a good deal of heterogeneity in approaches taken by political scientists as they look for topics and conduct exploratory research. There is more than one way to skin this cat.

One may wonder whether this heterogeneity clusters in recognizable patterns. Are there distinctive styles of exploratory research that might make sense of the broad array of questions and responses contained in our survey?

To answer this question, we approach questions posed about the research process on the faculty survey with a k-means cluster analysis (Wu 2012). A scree plot (not shown) reveals that the first two clusters provide much greater statistical power than the rest, although we also carried out more complex clustering with four and six means as a robustness check. The more complex cluster analyses maintained the key divisions found in the two-means analysis, simply splitting the two primary grounds into subordinate divisions. Hence, we focus here on the two main clusters.

Table A.3 reports the cluster means of each variable related to approaches that were central to starting the project: a scholar's reported entrée into the research, the activities that were critical to designing the research, where researchers allocated their time while looking for a topic, and whether personal traits were pivotal to finding the project. The variance across these means is also reported, providing a metric for how much overall separation each variable represents across the clusters.

The first variables (with the highest variance) are the most differentiating. They suggest that Cluster 1 is composed of scholars whose choice of topics is influenced by their personal experiences, concerns for social justice, policy significance, and current events. In developing topics, they are more likely to spend time in the archives, in the field, or with a data set – that is, in direct encounters with the data. They also appear to put more work into seeking funding and spend more time in discussions with colleagues, students, friends, and laypersons, and in conferences.

Table A.3 Cluster analysis

Variable	Cluster 1	Cluster 2	Variance	Variable	Cluster 1	Cluster 2	Variance
Personal experiences	3.07	2.19	0.39	*Personal*: Language	0.14	0.00	0.01
Time: Field research	2.62	1.73	0.39	*Entrée*: Event	0.27	0.13	0.01
Promotion of justice	3.03	2.23	0.32	*Entrée*: Concept	0.36	0.22	0.01
Time: Funding	2.25	1.69	0.16	*Critical*: News	0.45	0.32	0.01
Time: Archives	2.05	1.54	0.13	*Personal*: Family	0.17	0.04	0.01
Time: Students	2.21	1.72	0.12	*Entrée*: Own work	0.30	0.17	0.01
Time: Friends	2.07	1.64	0.09	*Critical*: Single work	0.28	0.15	0.01
Policy significance	3.51	3.09	0.09	*Entrée*: Seminal	0.59	0.47	0.01
Time: News	2.76	2.33	0.09	*Critical*: Other research	0.27	0.15	0.01
Time: Reading broadly	3.53	3.19	0.06	*Critical*: Leisure travel	0.11	0.00	0.01
Critical: Fieldwork	0.38	0.08	0.05	Changes to theory	0.41	0.30	0.01
Time: Fun	2.26	1.98	0.04	*Critical*: Conference	0.22	0.12	0.01
Critical: Laypersons	0.27	0.03	0.03	*Personal*: Gender	0.11	0.02	0.00
Time: Colleagues	3.12	2.90	0.02	Lightbulb moment	0.54	0.45	0.00
Critical: Reading broadly	0.94	0.72	0.02	*Critical*: Mentors	0.20	0.11	0.00
Time: Other topics	3.24	3.03	0.02	*Time*: Advisors	1.97	1.89	0.00
Changes to analysis	0.58	0.37	0.02	Intellectual puzzle	3.51	3.45	0.00
Time: Key work	2.63	2.41	0.02	*Critical*: Other	0.12	0.06	0.00
Time: Data	2.50	2.31	0.02	*Entrée*: Hypothesis	0.23	0.17	0.00
Critical: Archive	0.20	0.03	0.01	Hunch	0.98	1.04	0.00
Personal: Country	0.28	0.12	0.01	*Entrée*: Anomaly	0.20	0.14	0.00
Time: Conferences	2.62	2.46	0.01	*Personal*: Race	0.05	0.00	0.00
Critical: Students	0.19	0.03	0.01	*Entrée*: Data	0.17	0.12	0.00
Critical: Funding	0.16	0.01	0.01	*Entrée*: Theory	0.18	0.15	0.00
Entrée: Location	0.16	0.01	0.01	*Entrée*: Other work	0.15	0.12	0.00
Changes: Design	0.46	0.31	0.01	*Entrée*: Method	0.18	0.16	0.00
Personal: Ethnic	0.15	0.01	0.01	*Critical*: Data	0.16	0.16	0.00
Critical: Colleagues	0.51	0.37	0.01	*Entrée*: General	0.43	0.43	0.00

Results of cluster analysis. $N = 107$ (Cluster 1), 380 (Cluster 2). Variables listed in order of variance.

These traits seem consistent with an inductive approach to knowledge, while the second cluster ranks lower on each of these variables and is therefore more in synch with a deductive approach. On some attributes, one might say that Cluster 1 exhibits traits associated with the qualitative tradition of research (Goertz, Mahoney 2012). However, the fact that they also spend more time with large-N datasets suggests that "inductive" might be a better label for this group of scholars.

However one chooses to characterize Clusters 1 and 2, the contrasts noted in Table A.3 are rather underwhelming, especially when considered in light of all the traits across which the two groups register agreement, or near-agreement. Insofar as there are recognizable clusters, our analysis suggests that they represent differences of degree – not starkly opposed ("incommensurable") paradigms.

Innovation

Our faculty survey asks respondents what is "most innovative or special" about the chosen work, allowing multiple answers, as shown in Figure 2.9. Because our interest is in scientific innovation rather than contributions to public debates, we leave aside option *b* (a topic that is especially relevant to the concerns of citizens or policymakers). An index of innovativeness across the remaining categories is constructed by adding options (a), (c), (d), and (e) and subtracting option (f). The resulting index runs from -1 to +4. A histogram of this variable is shown in Figure A.1.

In Table A.4, we employ this index as an outcome in a series of regression tests to see what factors might predict scientific innovation. We find that two background factors predict greater (self-assessed) innovation. Those who obtained their PhD in the United States are more likely to rate their work as innovative along one or more parameters. This might be interpreted as a selection effect (admission to US institutions are perhaps more competitive than others), as a product of superior training, or as a product of learned norms (attending school in the United States may incline one to offer an optimistic view of one's own work).

We also find that work produced by women receives higher assessments than work produced by men. This would be expected if barriers to entry are higher for women than for men, meaning that only the most ambitious and intelligent women attain the ranks of university professors, a pattern of gendered selection for excellence we find in teaching within academia

Table A.4 Predictors of scientific innovation

	(1)	(2)	(3)	(4)	(5)	(6)	(7)	(8)	(9)
Female	0.173*	0.120	0.131	0.186**	0.197**	0.190**	0.203**	0.198**	0.154*
	(1.866)	(1.286)	(1.475)	(2.025)	(2.153)	(2.069)	(2.196)	(2.144)	(1.734)
PhD in USA	0.132*	0.167**	0.108	0.138*	0.130*	0.163**	0.128	0.135*	0.142*
	(1.659)	(2.106)	(1.411)	(1.760)	(1.655)	(2.062)	(1.625)	(1.712)	(1.884)
Time:									
Reading broadly		0.197***							0.120**
		(3.796)							(2.381)
Intellectual puzzle			0.385***						0.308***
			(6.681)						(5.277)
Critical:									
Other research				0.355***					0.265***
				(3.589)					(2.785)
Entrée:									
Theory					0.377***				0.238**
					(3.739)				(2.413)
Entrée:									
Concept						0.295***			0.200**
						(3.304)			(2.325)
Entrée:									
Hypothesis							0.275***		0.180*
							(2.786)		(1.909)
Entrée:									
Data								0.283**	0.274**
								(2.474)	(2.510)
Observations	507	505	505	504	504	504	504	504	497
R^2	0.0128	0.0403	0.0936	0.0370	0.0415	0.0357	0.0297	0.0266	0.165

Outcome: index of innovativeness, as explained in the text. Analysis: ordinary least squares, standard errors in parentheses. ***p<.01, **p<.05, *p<.10

(MacNell, Driscoll, Hunt 2015) and in other occupations, such as politics (Fulton 2012). It is also consistent with our findings for total citation counts, a seemingly objective measure of academic impact, discussed below.

Turning to processual factors, we find that time spent reading broadly in the literature (Model 2) is positively associated with innovation. We find that work directed at solving an intellectual puzzle is viewed as more innovative (Model 3). We find that when a topic is identified through research on other topics, the result is viewed as more innovative (Model 4). We find, finally, that the result is viewed as more innovative when entrée to the topic is provided by a general theory (Model 5), a concept of theoretical interest (Model 6), a key hypothesis (Model 7), or a promising extant data set (Model 8). All of these results are robust (though in most cases slightly diminished, as one would expect) in the full specification, including all of the foregoing variables (Model 9).

The patterns revealed in Table A.4 (leaving aside those centered on fixed characteristics of the respondents) seem to corroborate our overall view of research in political science. Work that is viewed as most innovative (by the authors) is motivated by engagement with the literature and with broad, theoretical concerns rather than by engagement with a particular research site, event, case, or a question of personal significance.

Impact

Having examined where ideas originate and what factors might contribute to scientific innovation, we turn to the question of impact. Every scholar seeks influence in their chosen field. Granted, long-term influence is difficult to measure. Likewise, it is important to bear in mind that science proceeds mostly by baby-steps, and it is not clear that progress would be faster if everyone aimed only for high-impact publications. Even so, and all things being equal, it is fair to say that high-impact publications are more important – for the author and for the field – than low-impact publications. With this understanding, it is reasonable to ask whether a given research strategy is more or less likely than some other strategy to culminate in high-impact work.

To measure impact, we rely on citations in Google Scholar (GS), an increasingly common metric (Gerring, Karcher, Apfeld 2020). The GS database includes published work along with some unpublished work (e.g., working papers). Books are referenced, though citations *within* books are not. This may tilt the playing field in favor of certain types of scholarship, for example, toward work that is quantitative, or work published in journals (Samuels 2013). To mitigate this potential bias, we include covariates measuring the type of work that is being evaluated – book/article, qualitative/quantitative, and so forth.

The outcome, GS citations, is right-skewed, as one might expect for an outcome that is bounded at zero. (Roughly 13% of the studies in our sample register no citations on GS, though it must be noted that some of these studies were just published and therefore had little opportunity to accrue citations.) On theoretical grounds, one may suppose that most factors that might contribute to variation on this outcome experience diminishing marginal returns. For both these reasons, it seems reasonable to transform the outcome by the natural logarithm. The distribution of this transformed variable is shown in Figure A.2.

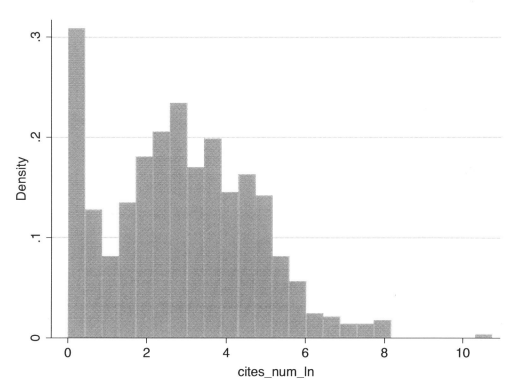

Figure A.2   Google Scholar citations
Histogram of Google Scholar citations (natural logarithm). *N*=556. Mean=2.94. Standard deviation=1.86.

Baseline Factors

We begin by exploring factors specific to the individual or the study that might affect its scholarly impact.[1] This includes the year of publication (earlier publications presumably have a greater opportunity to accrue citations), gender (which may reflect differences in motivation and training, or biases within the discipline), year PhD was granted (which may reflect changes in training, recruitment, and other cohort effects), location of PhD (classified as United States or other), university ranking (obtained by recoding the Shanghai Ranking Consultancy's Academic Ranking of World Universities into deciles), total GS citations across a scholar's career (a proxy for that individual's overall influence), the scholar's subfield (American, comparative, international relations, theory, public law, public policy, methods), the scholar's preferred methodology (quantitative and/or qualitative), the product itself (classified as an article or book), and the number of authors (up to 3).

For each predictor, we offer two specifications. The first is a minimal model including only year of publication. The second is a maximal model including all other covariates listed above. Results are shown in Table A.5. To conserve space, we report estimates only for the variable of theoretical interest in each test.

We find that year of publication is strongly and negatively correlated with citations, as anticipated. (Transforming this variable by a logarithm or a quadratic does not improve model fit.) This is true almost by construction since one cannot obtain fewer citations over time.

Studies with female authors obtain more citations than male authors in all specifications and estimates are fairly stable (though rarely surpassing standard thresholds of statistical significance). This seems to run counter to a spate of recent work suggesting that the publication process is biased against female authors (Teele, Thelen 2017). However, these two findings are not irreconcilable. It could be that a biased publication process imposes a higher barrier to publication for female authors, meaning that those articles and books that pass the barrier are, on average, superior to those produced by male authors, and hence receive more attention.

---

[1] This follows in a long tradition of work focusing on author characteristics (e.g., sex, country of origin, country of residence, employer, number of coauthors) or publication characteristics (e.g., publisher, year, field, method). See Breuer, Bowen (2014), Gingras (2016), Hamermesh (2018), Larivière et al. (2013), Lozano, Larivière, Gingras (2012), Malinak, Powers, Walter (2013).

Table A.5 Baseline predictors of impact

Predictor	Publication year		Female		PhD year		PhD in USA		University rank	
Model	(1)	(2)	(3)	(4)	(5)	(6)	(7)	(8)	(9)	(10)
Estimate	−0.136***	−0.148***	0.293	0.296	0.011*	0.021**	0.613***	0.439**	−0.057***	−0.032
	(−10.975)	(−9.828)	(1.640)	(1.537)	(1.765)	(2.534)	(4.260)	(2.066)	(−3.436)	(−1.440)
Publication year	✓		✓		✓		✓		✓	
All covariates		✓		✓		✓		✓		✓
Observations	555	440	508	440	549	440	555	440	555	440
R^2	0.179	0.292	0.203	0.292	0.184	0.292	0.205	0.292	0.196	0.292

Predictor	Total GS citations (1000s)		Subfield: American		Subfield: Comparative		Subfield: IR		Subfield: Theory	
Model	(11)	(12)	(13)	(14)	(15)	(16)	(17)	(18)	(19)	(20)
Estimate	0.021**	0.052***	0.074	−0.018	0.144	0.105	0.258	0.183	−0.279	0.117
	(2.232)	(3.891)	(0.443)	(−0.084)	(0.948)	(0.595)	(1.591)	(0.972)	(−0.914)	(0.335)
Publication year	✓		✓		✓		✓		✓	
All covariates		✓		✓		✓		✓		✓
Observations	487	440	507	440	507	440	507	440	507	440
R^2	0.205	0.292	0.202	0.292	0.203	0.292	0.206	0.292	0.203	0.292

Predictor	Subfield: Public law		Subfield: Policy		Subfield: Methods		Method: Quant		Method: Qual	
Model	(21)	(22)	(23)	(24)	(25)	(26)	(27)	(28)	(29)	(30)
Estimate	−0.345	−0.114	−0.510***	−0.225	−0.033	−0.235	0.348*	−0.083	−0.401***	−0.295*
	(−0.947)	(−0.297)	(−2.994)	(−1.198)	(−0.176)	(−1.157)	(1.800)	(−0.354)	(−2.677)	(−1.661)
Publication year	✓		✓		✓		✓		✓	
All covariates		✓		✓		✓		✓		✓

Continued

Table A.5 Continued

Predictor	Publication year		Female		PhD year		PhD in USA		University rank	
Observations	507	440	507	440	507	440	507	440	507	440
R^2	0.203	0.292	0.215	0.292	0.202	0.292	0.204	0.292	0.210	0.292

Predictor	Book		Co-authors (N)	
Model	(31)	(32)	(33)	(34)
Estimate	0.370	0.232	0.167	0.105
	(1.561)	(0.909)	(1.483)	(0.844)
Publication year	✓		✓	
All covariates		✓		✓
Observations	548	440	553	440
R^2	0.181	0.292	0.183	0.292

Outcome: Google Scholar citations (log). *Estimate*: for the predictor of theoretical interest, listed on the top row. Ordinary least squares analysis, t statistics in parentheses. *** $p<0.01$, ** $p<0.05$, * $p<0.1$

PhD year is associated with more citations, which may be an indication that younger scholars are obtaining superior training than their older colleagues or they are more motivated to conduct high-impact work.

Papers published by scholars with PhD's from American universities receive more citations than papers from scholars from non-US institutions, a robust finding across all specifications. This may be interpreted as a selection effect, a product of differences in curricula, or of the subsequent trajectory of graduates from these institutions (graduates from American universities may end up in positions where publications are more highly prized).

University rank is negatively correlated with GS cites (a lower rank corresponds to a higher number), as expected. However, it is a very weak predictor. Once PhD in USA is included in the model, university rank offers very little predictive value. This suggests that publications speak for themselves, and not just for the status of the author – or that the status of the author is independent of their university.

Total GS citations are associated with citations obtained by the chosen work, as expected. This may be interpreted as a reputation effect or simply a correlation (a publication chosen randomly from a scholar's corpus will, on average, receive as many citations as other published articles and books in that corpus).

Surprisingly, none of the subfield designations bear a robust relationship to GS citations. However, it should be cautioned that some of these categories are not well-populated (see Table A.1) and thus subject to stochastic error.

The use of quantitative methods is not consistently correlated with more citations, as shown in the flipped sign results between our minimal and maximal specifications (Models 27–28). However, the employment of qualitative methods is robustly correlated with a lower citation count.

We find that books receive marginally more citations than articles, and the number of coauthors is associated – very marginally – with an enhanced citation count. However, neither relationship is especially strong. (A project producing two or more articles would receive more citations on average than a project producing only a book.) It should also be noted that studies with more than three coauthors are discarded in this study (for reasons explained above) so we are not able to observe the full range of variation on this dimension.

Processual Factors

Our primary interest is in scholarly creativity, not the characteristics of authors or studies (as explored briefly above). In the present context, we want to understand why some ideas culminate in published work that carries considerable influence within a field, while others merely get published (attracting little subsequent notice, as registered by GS citations). Are some approaches to research more likely to generate impactful work than others?

To ascertain potential relationships between the *origins* of a study and its *impact* on the field, we regress GS citations (log) against various variables that seek to elicit what the researcher was doing and thinking about as they developed the germ of a new research project.

Since creativity may be regarded as downstream from fixed characteristics of the author and from *some* characteristics of the publication, we must consider the foregoing factors (explored in Table A.5) as potential confounders. Since causal order is often unclear, we offer two specifications for each hypothesis. The first includes only factors that we can be fairly certain are pre-treatment. The second includes additional factors that may or may not be pre-treatment.

In an idealized world of scientific inquiry, we might show results from *all* of these tests. However, this would overburden all but the most avid readers and would surpass the length limits of any journal. Accordingly, Table A.6 posts results for only those variables that appear to show a relationship with the outcome, that is, they predict variation in GS citations (using a fairly low threshold of statistical significance) in either one or both specifications. We shall regard them as prima facie causes (with further caveats to come).

The first factor is the researcher's motivation to promote social or political justice. This is negatively associated with GS citations, suggesting that politically motivated work may not be highly prized by the academy, or that in seeking to change the world other virtues that might make a study attractive to academics are left in abeyance.

The second factor concerns the author's motivation to solve an important intellectual puzzle. This feature is positively associated with GS citations. These two results resonate strongly with the patterns we observed above in scholars' descriptions of their own strategies for finding projects.

The remaining factors are answers to a question about the point of entrée, that is, what spurred the author's interest in a subject. Where entrée was stimulated by interest in a general topic, a specific hypothesis, or an extant data

Table A.6 Approaches as predictors of impact

	(1)	(2)	(3)	(4)	(5)	(6)	(7)	(8)	(9)	(10)	(11)	(12)	(13)	(14)
1. Justice	-0.164**	-0.170**											-0.107	-0.121
	(-2.266)	(-2.130)											(-1.456)	(-1.485)
2. Puzzle			0.297***	0.188									0.253**	0.155
			(2.612)	(1.526)									(2.212)	(1.257)
3. General topic					0.284*	0.304*							0.205	0.250
					(1.924)	(1.939)							(1.390)	(1.599)
4. Hypothesis							0.333*	0.330					0.239	0.273
							(1.754)	(1.634)					(1.263)	(1.354)
5. Event									-0.670***	-0.631***			-0.495**	-0.474**
									(-3.331)	(-2.907)			(-2.395)	(-2.135)
6. Dataset											0.285	0.461**	0.169	0.351
											(1.302)	(1.986)	(0.771)	(1.507)
Specification														
Minimal	✓		✓		✓		✓		✓		✓		✓	
Maximal		✓		✓		✓		✓		✓		✓		✓
Observations	511	441	510	441	509	439	509	439	509	439	509	439	506	437
R^2	0.225	0.290	0.227	0.288	0.222	0.288	0.221	0.286	0.233	0.296	0.219	0.288	0.250	0.314

Outcome: Google Scholar citations (log). *Minimal specification:* Year, Female, PhD year, PhD in USA. *Maximal specification:* Year, Female, PhD year, PhD in USA, Rank of university, Total GS citations (1000s), Subfields (AP, CP, IR, PP, PL, Th, Meth), Methods (Qual, Quant), Book, Authors. *Predictors of theoretical interest:* (1) How important was the promotion of social or political justice to the development of this project? (2) How important was intellectual puzzle-solving to the development of this project? Which of the following served as your point of entrée to this topic? (3) A general topic, (4) A specific topic, (5) An event of special interest, (6) A promising (extant) data set. Ordinary least squares analysis, t statistics in parentheses. *** $p<0.01$, ** $p<0.05$, * $p<0.1$

set we find a positive association with GS citations. By contrast, where entrée was stimulated by an event of special interest there is a negative association.

A caveat concerns the strength of the empirical relationships displayed in Table A.6, which are in only one case robust across all specifications. In light of problems of measurement and the instability of the empirical results we must regard these relationships with some skepticism.

Nonetheless, regarded collectively, they paint a portrait that is more convincing than any single hypothesis considered on its own. Specifically, we surmise that researchers who are motivated to contribute to an ongoing intellectual debate are more likely to make their mark – as judged by citation statistics – than researchers with other goals in mind such as promoting justice or explaining an event of intrinsic interest.

Methodological Considerations

Analyses offered in the preceding tables present several methodological concerns, which we shall now address.

First, it should be clarified that our attempt to explain innovation and impact are not founded on a coherent theory of scholarly creativity. This is a fairly novel field of inquiry; accordingly, there is no well-established theory, or set of existing hypotheses, that one might draw upon. By default, we have adopted an exploratory approach. Specifically, we have considered all of the questions on our survey as potential explanatory variables, so long as a plausible case can be made that a factor might be exogenous.

Our findings are therefore subject to the problem of stochastic variability ("fishing"), which may falsely identify some factors as robust even though they are the product of random variability across samples. We look forward to replicating this study with a small set of pre-registered hypotheses and a specific pre-analysis plan. Meanwhile, results should be regarded as preliminary, in common with virtually any initial study of a new topic.

Second, we must consider the possibility of recall bias and circularity between inputs and outputs. Bear in mind that Table A.4 (our analysis of innovation) treats some questions as outcomes and others as predictors even though they are all collected in the same survey instrument. Table A.6 (focused on impact) adopts an external measure of impact (citation counts); however, it is an outcome that is known to the author, and therefore may influence their answers to other questions.

When factual questions pertaining to the (static or historic) characteristics of the author (contained in the Personal Information section of our questionnaire) are considered on the right side of a regression model the assumption of exogeneity is fairly secure. But for other predictors, especially those related to the research process, one may wonder. A skeptical reading of Tables A.4–A.6 is that they show *associations* between answers but not causal relationships.

There are two ways to overcome this problem of hindsight bias. The first is to construct a panel analysis in which researchers are queried at regular intervals about their work as it progresses from a nascent idea to eventual publication – a period of several years, as discussed. Recruiting participants for such a study would be difficult and would probably result in a much smaller and less representative sample. Logistics such as identifying the "study" (highly ambiguous when research is at an exploratory stage) impose another obstacle.

Another approach exploits the possibility of experimental manipulation. Here, participants would be randomized into groups, each of which is assigned a different approach to exploratory research, for example, reading broadly on a subject, or replicating extant studies. At the end of the period of study, the resulting research proposals could be compared along various dimensions, perhaps by a panel of experts. This approach is probably workable only in small (and perhaps not entirely representative) settings such as summer schools and would be limited in duration. There are also questions about how one would define a realistic treatment, given that any real-world attempt to come up with a topic inevitably combines numerous approaches, a mélange of treatment. Although one might question the generalizability of the findings from an experimental study, we believe there is much we can learn.

We hope that studies of this sort – both panel and experimental – will be undertaken, someday. In the meanwhile, ex post recollections of past projects are all we have to draw upon. Results must be approached with caution. Even so, we see no reason to suppose that the particular patterns reported in previous regression tables are a product of recall bias.

References

Abbott, Andrew. 2004. *Methods of Discovery: Heuristics for the Social Sciences*. New York: W. W. Norton.

Acemoglu, Daron, James A. Robinson. 2005. *Economic Origins of Dictatorship and Democracy*. Cambridge: Cambridge University Press.

Acemoglu, Daron, James A. Robinson. 2012. *Why Nations Fail: Origins of Power, Poverty and Prosperity*. New York: Crown Publishers.

Acemoglu, Daron, Simon Johnson, James A. Robinson. 2003. "An African success story: Botswana." In Dani Rodrik (ed.), *In Search of Prosperity: Analytic Narratives on Economic Growth* (Princeton, NJ: Princeton University Press), 80–122.

Acemoglu, Daron, Simon Johnson, James A. Robinson. 2005. "Institutions as a fundamental cause of long-run growth." In Philippe Aghion, Steven N. Durlauf (eds.), *Handbook of Economic Growth*, Vol. 1A (Amsterdam: Elsevier), 385–472.

Adcock, Robert K. 2008. "The curious career of 'the comparative method': The case of Mill's methods." Paper presented at the Annual Meeting of the American Political Science Association, Boston, MA.

Agar, Michael. 1996. *The Professional Stranger: An Informal Introduction to Ethnography*. San Diego, CA: Academic Press.

Alesina, Alberto, Paola Giuliano, Nathan Nunn. 2013. "On the origins of gender roles: Women and the plough." *Quarterly Journal of Economics* 128, 2: 469–530.

Alesina, Alberto, Edward Glaeser, Bruce Sacerdote. 2001. "Why doesn't the US have a European-style welfare state?" *Brookings Papers on Economic Activity* 2: 187–277.

Alexander, Jeffrey C., Bernhard Giesen, Richard Münch, Neil J. Smelser (eds.) 1987. *The Micro-Macro Link*. Berkeley, CA: University of California Press.

Alford, Robert R., Roger Friedland. 1985. *The Powers of Theory: Capitalism, the State, and Democracy*. Cambridge: Cambridge University Press.

Allison, Paul D., John A. Stewart. 1974. "Productivity differences among scientists: Evidence for accumulative advantage." *American Sociological Review* 39, 4: 596–606.

Alperovitz, Gar. 1996. *The Decision to Use the Atomic Bomb*. New York: Vintage.

Alston, Lee J., Gary D. Libecap, Robert Schnieder. 1996. "The determinants and impact of property rights: Land titles on the Brazilian frontier." *Journal of Law Economics and Organization* 12: 25–61.

Alvarez, Mike, José Antonio Cheibub, Fernando Limongi, Adam Przeworski. 1996. "Classifying political regimes." *Studies in Comparative International Development* 31, 2: 3–36.

Alvesson, Mats, Dan Kärreman. 2011. *Qualitative Research and Theory Development: Mystery as Method*. London: Sage Publications.

Alvesson, Mats, Jörgen Sandberg. 2013. *Constructing Research Questions: Doing Interesting Research*. London: Sage Publications.

Amabile, Teresa M. 1982. *Creativity in Context: Update to the Social Psychology of Creativity*. New York: Springer.

Amenta, Edwin. 1991. "Making the most of a case study: Theories of the welfare state and the American experience." In Charles C. Ragin (ed.), *Issues and Alternatives in Comparative Social Research* (Leiden: E. J. Brill), 172–194.

Angrist, Joshua D. 1990. "Lifetime earnings and the Vietnam era draft lottery: Evidence from social security administrative records." *American Economic Review* 80, 3: 313–336.

Angrist, Joshua D., Stacey H. Chen. 2011. "Schooling and the Vietnam-era GI Bill: Evidence from the draft lottery." *American Economic Journal: Applied Economics* 3: 96–118.

Angrist, Joshua D., Alan B. Krueger. 2001. "Instrumental variables and the search for identification: From supply and demand to natural experiments." *Journal of Economic Perspectives* 15, 4: 69–85.

Angrist, Joshua D., Victor Lavy. 1999. "Using Maimonides' rule to estimate the effect of class size on scholastic achievement." *Quarterly Journal of Economics* 114, 2: 533–575.

Angrist, Joshua D., Jorn-Steffen Pischke. 2009. *Mostly Harmless Econometrics: An Empiricist's Companion*. Princeton, NJ: Princeton University Press.

Ansell, Ben W., David J. Samuels. 2014. *Inequality and Democratization*. Cambridge: Cambridge University Press.

Ansolabehere, Stephen, James M. Snyder Jr., Charles Stewart III. 2000. "Old voters, new voters, and the personal vote: Using redistricting to measure the incumbency advantage." *American Journal of Political Science* 1: 17–34.

Arieti, Silvano. 1980. *Creativity: The Magic Synthesis*. New York: Basic Books.

Arquilla, John. 2012. "Cyberwar is already upon us." *Foreign Policy* 192: 1–4.

Arrow, Kenneth J. 1994. "Methodological individualism and social knowledge." *American Economic Review (Papers and Proceedings)* 84, 2: 1–9.

Aymard, Maurice. 1982. "From feudalism to capitalism in Italy: The case that doesn't fit." *Review* 6: 131–208.

Azoulay, Pierre, Christian Fons-Rosen, Joshua S. Graff Zivin. 2019. "Does science advance one funeral at a time?" *American Economic Review* 109, 8: 2889–2920.

Backhouse, Roger E. 2007. "Lives in synopsis: The production and use of short biographies by historians of economics." *History of Political Economy* 39, 1: 51–75.

Baer, Michael A., Malcolm E. Jewell, Lee Sigelman (eds.) 2014. *Political Science in America: Oral Histories of a Discipline*. Lexington, KY: University Press of Kentucky.

Ball, Philip. 2012. *Curiosity: How Science Became Interested in Everything*. Chicago: University of Chicago Press.

Ballard, Michael J., Neil J. Mitchell. 1998. "The good, the better, and the best in political science." *PS: Political Science & Politics* 23: 826–828.

Ballas, Dimitris, Graham Clarke, Rachel S. Franklin, Andy Newing. 2017. *GIS and the Social Sciences: Theory and Applications*. London: Routledge.

Banks, Antoine J., Heather M. Hicks. 2016. "Fear and implicit racism: Whites' support for voter ID laws." *Political Psychology* 37, 5: 641–658.

Banks, Marcus. 2001. *Visual Methods in Social Research*. London: Sage.

Barsky, Robert F. 1998. *Noam Chomsky: A Life of Dissent*. Cambridge: MIT Press.

Baumol, William J. 2002. *The Free-Market Innovation Machine: Analyzing the Growth Miracle of Capitalism*. Princeton, NJ: Princeton University Press.

Bayer, Alan E., John C. Smart. 1991. "Career publication patterns and 'styles' in American academic science." *Journal of Higher Education* 62: 613–636.

Beard, Charles. 1913. *An Economic Interpretation of the Constitution of the United States*. New York: Free Press.

Becker, Gary S. 1960. "An economic analysis of fertility." In Robert M. Dinkel (ed.), *Demographic and Economic Change in Developed Countries* (Princeton, NJ: Princeton University Press), 209–240.

Becker, Gary S. 1976. *The Economic Approach to Human Behavior*. Chicago: University of Chicago Press.

Becker, Gary S., Kevin M. Murphy. 1988. "A theory of rational addiction." *Journal of Political Economy* 96, 4: 675–700.

Becker, Howard S. 1986. *Writing for Social Scientists: How to Start and Finish Your Thesis, Book, or Article*. Chicago: University of Chicago Press.

Becker, Howard S. 1998. *Tricks of the Trade: How to Think about Your Research while You're Doing It*. Chicago: University of Chicago Press.

Behrens, John T., Chong-ho Yu. 2003. "Exploratory data analysis." In Irving B. Weiner, Donald K. Freedheim, John A. Schinka, Wayne F. Velicer (eds.), *Handbook of Psychology 2nd ed.* (New York: Wiley), 33–64.

Benedict, Barbara. 2002. *Curiosity: A Cultural History of Early Modern Enquiry*. Chicago: Chicago University Press.

Bergan, Daniel E. 2009. "The draft lottery and attitudes towards the Vietnam war." *Public Opinion Quarterly* 73, 2: 379–384.

Berg-Schlosser, Dirk, Gisele De Meur. 1994. "Conditions of democracy in interwar Europe: A Boolean test of major hypotheses." *Comparative Politics* 26, 3: 253–279.

Berkun, Scott. 2010. *The Myths of Innovation*. Sebastopol, CA: O'Reilly Media.

Bertamini, Marco, Marcus R. Munafo. 2012. "Bite-size science and its undesired side effects." *Perspectives on Psychological Science* 7, 1: 67–71.

Bien Jacob, Jonathan Taylor, Robert Tibshirani. 2013. "A LASSO for hierarchical interactions." *Annals of Statistics* 41, 3: 1111–1141.

Birks, Melanie, Jane Mills. 2015. *Grounded Theory: A Practical Guide*. London: Sage.

Black, Max. 1962. *Models and Metaphors*. Ithaca, NY: Cornell University Press.

Blattman, Christopher. 2009. "From violence to voting: War and political participation in Uganda." *American Political Science Review* 103, 2: 231–247.

Blau, Peter M. 1964. *Exchange and Power in Social Life*. New York: Wiley.

Blaug, Mark. 1989. *Great Economists before Keynes: An Introduction to the Lives and Works of One Hundred Great Economists of the Past*. Cambridge: Cambridge University Press.

Bloxham, Donald, A. Dirk Moses (eds.) 2010. *The Oxford Handbook of Genocide Studies*. Oxford: Oxford University Press.

Blumstein, Alfred, Joel Wallman (eds.) 2006. *The Crime Drop in America*. Cambridge: Cambridge University Press.

Boden, Margaret. 2004. *The Creative Mind: Myths and Mechanisms*. London: Routledge.

Boix, Carles. 2003. *Democracy and Redistribution*. New York: Cambridge University Press.

Boix, Carles, Susan C. Stokes. 2003. "Endogenous democratization." *World Politics* 55, 4: 517–549.

Boix, Carles, Michael Miller, Sebastian Rosato. 2013. "A complete data set of political regimes, 1800–2007." *Comparative Political Studies* 46, 12: 1523–1554.

Bolles, Richard Nelson. 2009. *The 2009 What Color Is Your Parachute? A Practical Manual for Job-Hunters and Career-Changers*. Berkeley, CA: Random House.

Booth, Wayne C., Gregory G. Colomb, Joseph M. Williams, Joseph Bizup, William T. Fitzgerald. 2016. *The Craft of Research*. Chicago: University of Chicago Press.

Borgatti, Stephen P., Martin G. Everett, Jeffrey C. Johnson. 2018. *Analyzing Social Networks*. London: Sage.

Brady, Henry E. 2011. "The art of political science: Spatial diagrams as iconic and revelatory." *Perspectives on Politics* 9: 311–331.

Brady, Henry E., David Collier (eds.) 2004. *Rethinking Social Inquiry: Diverse Tools, Shared Standards*. Lanham, MD: Rowman & Littlefield.

Brady, Henry E., John E. McNulty. 2011. "Turning out to vote: The costs of finding and getting to the polling place." *American Political Science Review* 105, 1: 115–134.

Braumoeller, Bear F. 2019. *Only the Dead: The Persistence of War in the Modern Age*. New York: Oxford University Press.

Breiman, Leo. 1996. "Out-of-bag estimation." Manuscript. Statistics Department, University of California, Berkeley.

Breiman, Leo. 2001. "Random Forests." *Machine Learning* 45: 5–32.

Brennan, Jason. 2020. *Good Work If You Can Get It: How to Succeed in Academia*. Baltimore, MD: John Hopkins University Press.

Breuer, Peter T., Jonathan P. Bowen. 2014. "Empirical patterns in Google Scholar citation counts." *ArXiv:1401.1861 [Cs]*, April, 398–403. https://doi.org/10.1109/SOSE.2014.55.

Brickman, Philip, Dan Coates, Ronnie Janoff-Bulman. 1978. "Lottery winners and accident victims: Is happiness relative?" *Journal of Personality and Social Psychology* 36, 8: 917.

Briggs, John. 2000. *Fire in the Crucible: Understanding the Process of Creative Genius*. Grand Rapids: Phanes Press.

Brollo, Fernanda, Tommaso Nannicini, Roberto Perotti, Guido Tabellini. 2013. "The political resource curse." *American Economic Review* 103, 5: 1759–1796.

Brown, James Robert. 1991. *Laboratory of the Mind: Thought Experiments in the Natural Sciences*. London: Routledge.

Buchbinder Susan, Eric Vittinghoff. 1999. "HIV-infected long-term nonprogressors: Epidemiology, mechanisms of delayed progression, and clinical and research implications." *Microbes Infect* 1, 13: 1113–1120.

Buhaug, Halvard, Lars-Erik Cederman, Kristian S. Gleditsch. 2014. "Square pegs in round holes: Inequalities, grievances, and civil war." *International Studies Quarterly* 58, 2: 418–431.

Bunce, Valerie. 1981. *Do New Leaders Make a Difference? Executive Succession and Public Policy under Capitalism and Socialism*. Princeton, NJ: Princeton University Press.

Bunge, Mario. 1997. "Mechanism and explanation." *Philosophy of the Social Sciences* 27: 410–465.

Bunzl, Martin. 2004. "Counterfactual history: A user's guide." *American Historical Review* 109, 3: 845–858.

Burawoy, Michael. 1998. "The extended case method." *Sociological Theory* 16, 1: 4–33.

Burawoy, Michael. 2009. *The Extended Case Method: Four Countries, Four Decades, Four Great Transformations, and One Theoretical Tradition*. Berkeley, CA: University of California Press.

Burawoy, Michael, Joshua Gamson, Alice Burton. 1991. *Ethnography Unbound: Power and Resistance in the Modern Metropolis*. Berkeley, CA: University of California Press.

Burt, Ronald S. 2004. "Structural holes and good ideas." *American Journal of Sociology* 110, 2: 349–399.

Busby, Ethan C., Joshua R. Gubler, Kirk A. Hawkins. 2019. "Framing and blame attribution in populist rhetoric." *Journal of Politics* 81, 2: 616–630.

Buzan, Barry. 1995. "The level of analysis problem in international relations reconsidered." In Ken Booth, Steve Smith (eds.), *International Relations Theory Today* (Philadelphia, PA: Penn State University Press), 198–216.

Caldwell, John C. 1986. "Routes to low mortality in poor countries." *Population and Development Review* 12, 2: 171–220.

Campbell, Donald T. 1960. "Blind variation and selective retention in creative thought as in other knowledge processes." *Psychological Review* 67: 380–400.

Campbell, Donald T. 1975. "III. Degrees of freedom and the case study." *Comparative Political Studies* 8, 2: 178–193.

Campbell, John Paul, Richard L. Daft, Charles L. Hulin. 1982. *What to Study: Generating and Developing Research Questions.* Beverley Hills, CA: Sage.

Caplan, Bryan. 2018. *The Case against Education: Why the Education System Is a Waste of Time and Money.* Princeton, NJ: Princeton University Press.

Capoccia, Giovanni, R. Daniel Kelemen. 2007. "The study of critical junctures: Theory, narrative, and counterfactuals in historical institutionalism." *World Politics* 59, 3: 341–369.

Cartwright, Nancy. 1983. *How the Laws of Physics Lie.* Oxford: Clarendon Press.

Cartwright, Nancy. 2007. *Hunting Causes and Using Them: Approaches in Philosophy and Economics.* Cambridge: Cambridge University Press.

Cascio, Elizabeth U., Ethan G. Lewis. 2006. "Schooling and the armed forces qualifying test: Evidence from school-entry laws." *Journal of Human Resources* 41, 2: 294–318.

Cattaneo, Matias D., Nicolás Idrobo, Rocío Titiunik. 2019. *A Practical Introduction to Regression Discontinuity Designs: Foundations.* Cambridge: Cambridge University Press.

Caughey, Devin, Jasjeet S. Sekhon. 2011. "Elections and the regression discontinuity design: Lessons from close US House races, 1942–2008." *Political Analysis* 19, 4: 385–408.

Chamon, Marcos, Sergio Firpo, João M. P. de Mello, Renan Pieri. 2018. "Electoral rules, political competition and fiscal expenditures: Regression discontinuity evidence from Brazilian municipalities." *Journal of Development Studies* 55, 1: 1–20.

Chan, Winnie Wing-Yi. 2006. "A survey on multidimensional data visualization." Manuscript. Department of Computer Science and Engineering, Hong Kong University of Science and Technology.

Charmaz, Kathy. 2006. *Constructing Grounded Theory: A Practical Guide through Qualitative Analysis.* Thousand Oaks: Sage.

Chattopadhyay, Raghabendra, Esther Duflo. 2004. "Women as policy makers: Evidence from a randomized policy experiment in India." *Econometrica* 72, 5: 1409–1443.

Cheibub, José Antonio, Jennifer Gandhi, James Raymond Vreeland. 2010. "Democracy and dictatorship revisited." *Public choice* 143, 1–2: 67–101.

Chong, Alberto, Ana L. De La O, Dean Karlan, Leonard Wantchekon. 2015. "Does corruption information inspire the fight or quash the hope? A field experiment in Mexico on voter turnout, choice, and party identification." *Journal of Politics* 77, 1: 55–71.

Chong, Dennis, James N. Druckman. 2007. "Framing theory." *Annual Review of Political Science* 10: 103–126.

Christenson, Cornelia V. 1971. *Kinsey: A Biography.* Bloomington, IN: Indiana University Press.

Cirillo, Pasquale, Nassim Nicholas Taleb. 2016. "The decline of violent conflicts: What do the data really say?" *The Nobel Foundation, Causes of Peace, NYU Tandon Research Paper 2876315.*

Clarke, Kevin A., David M. Primo. 2012. *A Model Discipline: Political Science and the Logic of Representations.* Oxford: Oxford University Press.

Clement, John. 2008. *Creative Model Construction in Scientists and Students: The Role of Imagery, Analogy, and Mental Simulation.* Berlin: Springer Science & Business Media.

Cohen, Martin. 2008. *Wittgenstein's Beetle and Other Classic Thought Experiments.* New York: John Wiley & Sons.

Cohen, Morris R., Ernest Nagel. 1934. *An Introduction to Logic and Scientific Method.* New York: Harcourt, Brace and Company.

Coleman, James S. 1990. *Foundations of Social Theory.* Cambridge, MA: Harvard University Press.

Coleman, James S., Elihu Katz, Herbert Menzel. 1966. *Medical Innovation: A Diffusion Study.* New York: Bobbs-Merrill.

Collier, David. 1993. "The Comparative Method." In Ada W. Finifter (ed.), *Political Science: The State of the Discipline II* (Washington, DC: American Political Science Association), 105–119.

Collier, David. 1995. "Trajectory of a concept: 'Corporatism' in the study of Latin American politics." In Peter Smith (ed.), *Latin America in Comparative Perspective.* (Boulder, CO: Westview), 135–162.

Collier, David. 1999. "Data, fieldwork, and extracting new ideas at close range." *APSA-CP Newsletter of the Organized Section in Comparative Politics of the American Political Science Association* 10, 1–2: 4–6.

Collier, David, Steven Levitsky. 1997. "Democracy with adjectives: Conceptual innovation in comparative research." *World Politics* 49, 3: 430–451.

Collier, David, James Mahoney. 1996. "Insights and pitfalls: Selection bias in qualitative research." *World Politics* 49: 56–91.

Collier, David, John Gerring (eds.) 2009. *Concepts and Method in Social Science: The Tradition of Giovanni Sartori.* London: Routledge.

Collier, David, Jody LaPorte, Jason Seawright. 2012. "Putting typologies to work: Concept formation, measurement, and analytic rigor." *Political Research Quarterly* 65, 1: 217–232.

Collier, Ruth Berins. 1999. *Paths toward Democracy: The Working Class and Elites in Western Europe and Latin America.* Cambridge: Cambridge University Press.

Collier, Ruth Berins, David Collier. 1991. *Shaping the Political Arena: Critical Junctures, the Labor Movement, and Regime Dynamics in Latin America.* Princeton, NJ: Princeton University Press.

Collins, Randall. 1994. *Four Sociological Traditions.* New York: Oxford University Press.

Conley, Dalton, Jennifer Heerwig. 2012. "The long-term effects of military conscription on mortality: Estimates from the Vietnam-era draft lottery." *Demography* 49: 841–855.

Converse, Jean M. 2009. *Survey Research in the United States: Roots and Emergence 1890–1960.* London: Routledge.

Cook, Fay Lomax, Benjamin I. Page, Rachel L. Moskovitz. 2014. "Political engagement by wealthy Americans." *Political Science Quarterly* 129, 3: 381–398.

Coppedge, Michael. 2012. *Democratization and Research Methods.* Cambridge: Cambridge University Press.

Coppedge, Michael, John Gerring, David Altman, Michael Bernhard, Steven Fish, Allen Hicken, Matthew Kroenig, Staffan I. Lindberg, Kelly McMann, Pamela Paxton, Holli A. Semetko, Svend-Erik Skaaning, Jeffrey Staton, Jan Teorell. 2011. "Conceptualizing and measuring democracy: A new approach." *Perspectives on Politics* 9, 1: 247–267.

Coppedge, Michael, John Gerring, Adam Glynn, Staffan I. Lindberg, Daniel Pemstein, Svend-Erik Skaaning, Brigitte Seim, Jan Teorell. 2020. *Varieties of Democracy: Measuring a Century of Political Change.* Cambridge: Cambridge University Press.

Cordesman, Anthony H. 2017. *Trends in European Terrorism: 1970–2016.* Center for Strategic and International Studies.

Cornell, Svante E. 2002. "Autonomy as a source of conflict: Caucasian conflicts in theoretical perspective." *World Politics* 54: 245–276.

Cowley, Robert (ed.) 2000. *What If? The World's Foremost Historians Imagine What Might Have Been.* New York: Penguin.

Cowley, Robert (ed.) 2003. *More What If? Eminent Historians Imagine What Might Have Been.* London: Pan Macmillan.

Coyle, Diane. 2015. *GDP: A Brief but Affectionate History.* Princeton, NJ: Princeton University Press.

Cramer, Katherine J. 2016. *The Politics of Resentment: Rural Consciousness in Wisconsin and the Rise of Scott Walker.* Chicago: University of Chicago Press.

Csikszentmihalyi, Mihaly. 1997. *Flow and the Psychology of Discovery and Invention.* New York: Harper Perennial.

Cullen, Julie Berry, Brian A. Jacob, Steven Levitt. 2006. "The effect of school choice on participants: Evidence from randomized lotteries." *Econometrica* 74, 5: 1191–1230.

Curtiss, Susan. 1977. *Genie: A Psycholinguistic Study of a Modern-Day "Wild Child."* Boston, MA: Academic Press.

Cyr, Jennifer. 2019. *Focus Groups for the Social Science Researcher.* Cambridge: Cambridge University Press.

Daalder, Hans, Erik Allardt (eds.) 1997. *Comparative European Politics: The Story of a Profession.* London: Pinter.

Dacey, John S., Kathleen Lennon, Lisa B. Fiore. 1998. *Understanding Creativity: The Interplay of Biological, Psychological, and Social Factors.* San Francisco, CA: Jossey-Bass.

Dahl, Robert A. 1956. *A Preface to Democratic Theory.* Chicago: University of Chicago Press.

Dahl, Robert A. 1961. *Who Governs? Democracy and Power in an American City.* New Haven, CT: Yale University Press.

Dahl, Robert A. 1971. *Polyarchy: Participation and Opposition.* New Haven, CT: Yale University Press.

Dahl, Robert A. 1989. *Democracy and Its Critics.* New Haven, CT: Yale University Press.

Dahl, Robert A., Charles E. Lindblom. 1976. *Politics, Economics and Welfare: Planning and Politico-Economic Systems Resolved into Basic Social Processes*, 2nd ed. Chicago: University of Chicago Press.

Dahl, Robert A., Edward Tufte. 1973. *Size and Democracy.* Stanford, CA: Stanford University Press.

Dal Bó, Ernesto, Martín A. Rossi. 2011. "Term length and the effort of politicians." *The Review of Economic Studies* 78, 4: 1237–1263.

Daniels, Peter T., William Bright (eds.) 1996. *The World's Writing Systems.* Oxford: Oxford University Press.

Darwin, Charles. 1881. *The Formation of Vegetable Mould, through the Action of Worms, with Observations on Their Habits.* London: John Murray.

Darwin, Charles. 1942. *The Structure and Distribution of Coral Reefs.* London: Smith, Elder.

Davis, Joe C., Debra Morre Patterson. 2001. "Determinants of variations in journal publication rates of economists." *American Economist* 45, 1: 86–91.

Day, Kami, Michele Eodice. 2001. *(First person) 2: A Study of Co-authoring in the Academy.* Logan, UT: Utah State University Press.

Deaton, Angus. 2014. "Puzzles and paradoxes: A life in applied economics." In Michael Szenberg, Lall Ramrattan (eds.), *Eminent Economists II: Their Life and Work Philosophies* (Cambridge: Cambridge University Press), 84–101.

De Bono, Edward. 1992. *Serious Creativity: Using the Power of Lateral Thinking to Create New Ideas.* New York: Harper Collins.

De Chadarevian, Soraya, Nick Hopwood (eds.) 2004. *Models: The Third Dimension of Science*. Stanford, CA: Stanford University Press.

Deininger Klaus, Lyn Squire. 1998. "New ways of looking at old issues: Inequality and growth." *Journal of Development Economics* 57, 2: 259–287.

DeNicola, Daniel R. 2017. *Understanding Ignorance: The Surprising Impact of What We Don't Know*. Cambridge: MIT Press.

Denscombe, Martyn. 2012. *Research Proposals: A Practical Guide*. Maidenhead: McGraw-Hill Education.

Derthick, Martha. 1979. *Policymaking for Social Security*. Washington, DC: Brookings Institution Press.

Diamond, Ian, Margaret Newby, Sarah Varle. 1999. "Female education and fertility: Examining the links." In Caroline H. Bledsoe, John B. Casterline, Jennifer A. Johnson-Kuhn, John G. Haaga (eds.), *Critical Perspectives on Schooling and Fertility in the Developing World* (Washington, DC: National Academy Press), 23–48.

Diamond, Jared. 1992. *Guns, Germs, and Steel: The Fates of Human Societies*. New York: Norton.

Dion, Douglas. 1998. "Evidence and inference in the comparative case study." *Comparative Politics* 30, 2: 127–145.

Dixit, Avinash. 2014. "My philosophy of economics, life, and everything (not!)." In Michael Szenberg, Lall Ramrattan (eds.), *Eminent Economists II: Their Life and Work Philosophies* (Cambridge: Cambridge University Press), 118–128.

Dixit, Avinash K., Susan Skeath. 2015. *Games of Strategy: Fourth International Student Edition*. New York: W. W. Norton.

Dodge, Martin, Mary McDerby, Martin Turner (eds.) 2011. *Geographic Visualization: Concepts, Tools and Applications*. Chichester: John Wiley and Sons.

Doherty, Daniel, Alan S. Gerber, Donald P. Green. 2006. "Personal income and attitudes toward redistribution: A study of lottery winners." *Political Psychology* 27, 3: 441–458.

Donohue III, John J., Steven D. Levitt. 2001. "The impact of legalized abortion on crime." *The Quarterly Journal of Economics* 116, 2: 379–420.

Douglas, Mary. 1966. *Purity and Danger: An Analysis of Concepts of Pollution and Taboo*. London: Routledge & Kegan Paul.

Douglas, Mary, Aaron Wildavsky. 1982. *Risk and Culture: An Essay on the Selection of Technological and Environmental Dangers*. Berkeley, CA: University of California Press.

Douven, Igor. 2011. "Abduction" and "Supplement to abduction: Peirce on abduction." In Edward N. Zalta (ed.), *The Stanford Encyclopedia of Philosophy* (Spring 2011 Edition). http://plato.stanford.edu/archives/spr2011/entries/abduction/.

Downing, Brian M. 1992. *The Military Revolution and Political Change: Origins of Democracy and Autocracy in Early Modern Europe*. Princeton, NJ: Princeton University Press.

Dreze, Jean, Amartya Sen. 1989. *Hunger and Public Action*. Oxford: Clarendon Press.

Druckman, James N., Donald P. Green, James H. Kuklinski, Arthur Lupia (eds.) 2011. *Cambridge Handbook of Experimental Political Science*. Cambridge: Cambridge University Press.

Dubin, Robert. 1969. *Theory Building*. New York: Free Press.

Ductor, Lorenzo. 2015. "Does co-authorship lead to higher academic productivity?" *Oxford Bulletin of Economics and Statistics* 77, 3: 385–407.

Dunbar, Kevin. 2001. "What scientific thinking reveals about the nature of cognition." In Kevin Crowley, Christian D. Schunn, Takeshi Ocada (eds.), *Designing for Science: Implications from Everyday, Classroom, and Professional Settings* (Mahwah, NJ: Lawrence Erlbaum Associates), 115–140.

Dunleavy, Patrick. 2003. *Authoring a PhD: How to Plan, Draft, Write and Finish a Doctoral Thesis or Dissertation.* Basingstoke: Macmillan International Higher Education.

Dunning, Thad. 2008. *Crude Democracy: Natural Resource Wealth and Political Regimes.* Cambridge: Cambridge University Press.

Dunning, Thad. 2010. "Design-based inference: Beyond the pitfalls of regression analysis?" In Henry Brady, David Collier (eds.), *Rethinking Social Inquiry: Diverse Tools, Shared Standards* (Lanham, MD: Rowman & Littlefield), 273–311.

Dunning, Thad. 2012. *Natural Experiments in the Social Sciences: A Design-Based Approach.* Cambridge: Cambridge University Press.

Dyson, Tim. 2001. "A partial theory of world development: The neglected role of the demographic transition in the shaping of modern society." *International Journal of Population Geography* 7: 67–90.

Easterlin, Richard A. 1974. "Does economic growth improve the human lot? Some empirical evidence." In Paul A. David, Melvin W. Reder (eds.), *Nations and Households in Economic Growth* (New York: Academic Press), 89–125.

Easterly, William. 2006. *The White Man's Burden: Why the West's Efforts to Aid the Rest Have Done so Much Ill and so Little Good.* London: Penguin.

Easterly, William, Ross Levine. 2016. "The European origins of economic development." *Journal of Economic Growth* 21, 3: 225–257.

Eckstein, Harry. 1975. "Case studies and theory in political science." In Fred I. Greenstein, Nelson W. Polsby (eds.), *Handbook of Political Science, vol. 7 Political Science: Scope and Theory* (Reading, MA: Addison-Wesley), 79–138.

Eckstein, Harry, Ted Robert Gurr. 1975. *Patterns of Authority: A Structural Basis for Political Inquiry.* New York: Wiley.

Eidlin, Fred. 2011. "The method of problems versus the method of topics." *PS: Political Science & Politics* 44, 4: 758–761.

Einstein, Albert, L. Infeld. 1938. *The Evolution of Physics.* New York: Simon and Schuster.

Einstein, Albert. 1951. *Albert Einstein: Philosopher Scientist,* P. A. Schilpp (ed.), New York: Tudor.

Einstein, Albert. 1995. *Ideas and Opinions.* New York: Broadway Books.

Elman, Colin. 2005. "Explanatory typologies in qualitative studies of international politics." *International Organization* 59, 2: 293–326.

Elman, Colin, Miriam Elman. 2002. "How not to be Lakatos-intolerant: Appraising progress in IR research." *International Studies Quarterly* 46: 231–262.

Elman, Colin, John Gerring, James Mahoney (eds.) 2020. *The Production of Knowledge: Enhancing Progress in Social Science.* Cambridge: Cambridge University Press.

Elster, Jon. 1989. *Nuts and Bolts for the Social Sciences.* Cambridge: Cambridge University Press.

Elster, Jon. 1998. "A plea for mechanisms." In Peter Hedström, Richard Swedberg (eds.), *Social Mechanisms* (Cambridge: Cambridge University Press), 45–73.

Elster, Jon. 2015. *Explaining Social Behavior: More Nuts and Bolts for the Social Sciences,* 2nd ed. Cambridge: Cambridge University Press.

Emigh, Rebecca. 1997. "The power of negative thinking: The use of negative case methodology in the development of sociological theory." *Theory and Society* 26: 649–684.

Epstein, David. 2019. *Range: Why Generalists Triumph in a Specialized World.* New York: Riverhead Books.

Epstein, Leon D. 1964. "A comparative study of Canadian parties." *American Political Science Review* 58: 46–59.

Ericsson, Karl A., Ralf T. Krampe, Clemens Tesch-Römer. 1993. "The role of deliberate practice in the acquisition of expert performance." *Psychological Review* 100, 3: 363–406.

Erikson, Robert S., Laura Stoker. 2011. "Caught in the draft: The effects of Vietnam draft lottery status on political attitudes." *American Political Science Review* 105, 2: 221–237.

Evans, Peter B. 1995. *Embedded Autonomy: States and Industrial Transformation.* Princeton, NJ: Princeton University Press.

Fann, K. T. 1970. *Peirce's Theory of Abduction.* The Hague: Martinus Nijhoff.

Farr, James. 2004. "Social capital: A conceptual history." *Political Theory* 32, 1: 6–33.

Fauconnier, Gilles, Mark Turner. 2008. *The Way We Think: Conceptual Blending and the Mind's Hidden Complexities.* New York: Basic Books.

Fearon, James D., David D. Laitin. 2008. "Integrating qualitative and quantitative methods." In Janet M. Box-Steffensmeier, Henry E. Brady, David Collier (eds.), *The Oxford Handbook of Political Methodology* (Oxford: Oxford University Press), 756–777.

Fearon, James D., David D. Laitin. 2014. "Civil war non-onsets: The case of Japan." *Journal of Civilization Studies* 1, 1: 67–90.

Fearon, James D., David D. Laitin. 2015. "Random Narratives." Unpublished manuscript, Department of Political Science, Stanford University. web.stanford.edu/group/ethnic/Random%20Narratives/random%20narratives.htm.

Fender, Blakely F., Susan W. Taylor, Kimberly G. Burke. 2005. "Making the big leagues: Factors contributing to publication in elite economic journals." *Atlantic Economic Journal* 33: 93–103.

Fenno, Richard F., Jr. 1986. "Observation, context, and sequence in the study of politics." *American Political Science Review* 80, 1: 3–15.

Ferguson, Niall. 2008. *Virtual History: Alternatives and Counterfactuals.* New York: Basic Books.

Ferguson, R. Brian. 2013. "The prehistory of war and peace in Europe and the Near East." In Douglas P. Fry (ed.), *War, Peace, and Human Nature: The Convergence of Evolutionary and Cultural Views* (Oxford: Oxford University Press), 191–240.

Feyerabend, Paul. 1993 [1975]. *Against Method, 3rd ed.* London: Verso.

Fields, Gary. 2001. *Distribution and Development, A New Look at the Developing World.* Cambridge: MIT Press.

Findley, Michael G., Michael Denly, Kyosuke Kikuta. 2022. *External Validity for the Social Sciences.* Cambridge: Cambridge University Press.

Finlay, Linda, Brendan Gough (eds.) 2003. *Reflexivity: A Practical Guide for Researchers in Health and Social Sciences.* Oxford: Blackwell.

Fiorina, Morris P. 1977. *Congress: Keystone of the Washington Establishment.* New Haven, CT: Yale University Press.

Firebaugh, Glenn. 2008. *Seven Rules for Social Research.* Princeton, NJ: Princeton University Press.

Firestein, Stuart. 2012. *Ignorance: How It Drives Science.* New York: Oxford University Press.

Firestein, Stuart. 2015. *Failure: Why Science Is So Successful.* Oxford: Oxford University Press.

Fitzgerald, F. Scott. 2009. *The Crack-up.* New York: New Directions Publishing.

Fleck, Ludwik. 1935/1979. *The Genesis and Development of a Scientific Fact.* Chicago: University of Chicago Press.

Flyvbjerg, Bent. 2001. *Making Social Science Matter: Why Social Inquiry Fails and How It Can Succeed Again.* Cambridge: Cambridge University Press.

Fogel, Robert William. 1964. *Railroads and American Economic Growth.* Baltimore, MD: Johns Hopkins Press.

Fogel, Robert William. 1966. "The new economic history. Its findings and methods." *The Economic History Review* 19, 3: 642–656.

Ford, Cameron M., Dennis A. Gioia (eds.) 1995. *Creative Action in Organizations: Ivory Tower Visions and Real World Voices*. London: Sage.

Forrester, Andrew C., Benjamin Powell, Alex Nowrasteh, Michaelangelo Rastgrave. 2019. "Do immigrants import terrorism?" *Journal of Economic Behavior and Organization* 166: 529–543.

Forster, E. M. 1927. *Aspects of the Novel*. New York: Harcourt, Brace & World.

Foster, Jacob G., Andrey Rzhetsky, James A. Evans. 2015. "Tradition and innovation in scientists' research strategies." *American Sociological Review* 80, 5: 875–908.

Foucault, Michel. 1996. "The masked philosopher." In *Foucault Live: Interviews, 1966–1984*, 2nd ed. Sylvere Lotringer (ed.), Lysa Hochroth (trans.) (New York: Semiotext[e]), 302–307.

Fox, Mary Frank, Catherine A. Faver. 1984. "Independence and cooperation in research: The motivations and costs of collaboration." *The Journal of Higher Education* 55, 3: 347–359.

Franco, Annie, Neil Malhotra, Gabor Simonovits. 2014. "Publication bias in the social sciences: Unlocking the file drawer." *Science* 345, 6203: 1502–1505.

Frappier, Mélanie, Letitia Meynell, James Robert Brown (eds.) 2013. *Thought Experiments in Philosophy, Science, and the Arts*. London: Routledge.

Freedman, David A. 1991. "Statistical models and shoe leather." *Sociological Methodology* 21: 291–313.

Friedman, Milton. 1953. *Essays in Positive Economics*. Chicago: University of Chicago Press.

Friedrich, Carl J. 2001. "Corruption concepts in historical perspective." In Arnold J. Heidenheimer, Michael Johnston (eds.), *Political Corruption: Concepts & Contexts* (New York: Routledge), 15–23.

Fujii, Lee Ann. 2018. *Interviewing in Social Science Research: A Relational Approach*. New York: Routledge.

Fulton, Sarah A. 2012. "Running backwards and in high heels: The gendered quality gap and incumbent electoral success." *Political Research Quarterly* 65, 2: 303–314.

Gadamer, Hans-Georg. 1975. *Truth and Method*. Garrett Barden and John Cumming (trans.). New York: Seabury Press.

Galbraith, John Kenneth. 2009. *The Great Crash 1929*. Boston, MA: Houghton Mifflin Harcourt.

Galenson, David W. 2006. *Old Masters and Young Geniuses*. Princeton, NJ: Princeton University Press.

Galileo. 1974. *Two New Sciences*, trans. from the *Discorsi* by S. Drake. Madison, WI: University of Wisconsin Press.

Gallego, Aina. 2010. "Understanding unequal turnout: Education and voting in comparative perspective." *Electoral Studies* 29, 2: 239–248.

Gans-Morse, Jordan, Sebastian Mazzuca, Simeon Nichter. 2014. "Varieties of clientelism: Machine politics during elections." *American Journal of Political Science* 58, 2: 415–432.

Gardner, Howard. 2011. *Creating Minds: An Anatomy of Creativity Seen through the Lives of Freud, Einstein, Picasso, Stravinsky, Eliot, Graham, and Gandhi*. New York: Basic Civitas Books.

Garfinkel, Alan. 1981. *Forms of Explanation: Rethinking the Questions in Social Theory*. New Haven, CT: Yale University Press.

Gastil, Raymond Duncan. 1990. "The comparative survey of freedom: Experiences and suggestions." *Studies in Comparative International Development* 25, 1: 25–50.

Geddes, Barbara. 1990. "How the cases you choose affect the answers you get: Selection bias in comparative politics." *Political Analysis* 2: 131–150.

Geddes, Barbara. 1999. "What do we know about democratization after twenty years?" *Annual Review of Political Science* 2: 115–144.

Geddes, Barbara. 2003. *Paradigms and Sand Castles: Theory Building and Research Design in Comparative Politics*. Ann Arbor, MI: University of Michigan Press.

Geddes, Barbara, Joseph Wright, Erica Frantz. 2014. "Autocratic breakdown and regime transitions: A new data set." *Perspectives on Politics* 12, 2: 313–331.

Geer, John Gray. 1996. *From Tea Leaves to Opinion Polls: A Theory of Democratic Leadership*. New York: Columbia University Press.

Geertz, Clifford. 1963. *Peddlers and Princes: Social Change and Economic Modernization in Two Indonesian Towns*. Chicago: University of Chicago Press.

Geertz, Clifford. 1973. "Notes on the Balinese cockfight." In *The Interpretation of Cultures*. New York: Basic Books.

Geertz, Clifford. 1974. "'From the native's point of view': On the nature of anthropological understanding." *Bulletin of the American Academy of Arts and Sciences* 28, 1: 26–45.

Gelman, Andrew. 2003. "A Bayesian formulation of exploratory data analysis and goodness-of-fit testing." *International Statistical Review* 71, 2: 369–382.

Génaux, Maryvonne. 2004. "Social sciences and the evolving concept of corruption." *Crime, Law and Social Change* 42, 1: 13–24.

Gendler, Tamar Szabo. 2000. *Thought Experiment: On the Powers and Limits of Imaginary Cases*. New York: Garland.

George, Alexander L., Andrew Bennett. 2005. *Case Studies and Theory Development*. Cambridge: MIT Press.

George, Alexander L., Richard Smoke. 1974. *Deterrence in American Foreign Policy: Theory and Practice*. New York: Columbia University Press.

Gerard, Philip. 2017. *The Art of Creative Research*. Chicago: University of Chicago Press.

Gerber, Alan S., Donald P. Green. 2012. *Field Experiments: Design, Analysis, and Interpretation*. New York: W. W. Norton.

Gerring, John. 2008. "The mechanismic worldview: Thinking inside the box." *British Journal of Political Science* 38, 1: 161–179.

Gerring, John. 2010. "Causal mechanisms: Yes, but . . . " *Comparative Political Studies* 43, 11: 1499–1526.

Gerring, John. 2012a. "Mere description." *British Journal of Political Science* 42, 4: 721–746.

Gerring, John. 2012b. *Social Science Methodology: A Unified Framework*. Cambridge: Cambridge University Press.

Gerring, John. 2017. *Case Study Research: Principles and Practices, 2nd ed.* Cambridge University Press.

Gerring, John. 2020. "*Coordinating reappraisals.*" In Colin Elman, John Gerring, James Mahoney (eds.), *The Production of Knowledge: Enhancing Progress in Social Science* (Cambridge: Cambridge University Press), 334–353.

Gerring, John, Dino Christenson. 2017. *Applied Social Science Methodology: An Introductory Guide*. Cambridge: Cambridge University Press.

Gerring, John, Rose McDermott. 2007. "An experimental template for case-study research." *American Journal of Political Science* 51, 3: 688–701.

Gerring, John, Wouter Veenendaal. 2020. *Population and Politics: The Impact of Scale*. Cambridge: Cambridge University Press.

Gerring, John, Joshua Yesnowitz. 2006. "A normative turn in political science?" *Polity* 38, 1: 101–133.

Gerring, John, Sebastian Karcher, Brendan Apfeld. 2020. "Impact Metrics." In Colin Elman, John Gerring, James Mahoney (eds.), *The Production of Knowledge: Enhancing Progress in Social Science* (Cambridge: Cambridge University Press), 371–400.

Gerring, John, Jason Seawright, Kyle Shen. 2020. "Where do research ideas come from? Finding topics in political science research." Unpublished manuscript, Department of Government, University of Texas at Austin.

Gerring, John, Erzen Oncel, Kevin Morrison, Daniel Pemstein. 2019. "Who rules the world? A portrait of the global leadership class." *Perspectives on Politics* 17, 4: 1079–1097.

Gerring, John, Tore Wig, Andreas Tollefsen, Brendan Apfeld. 2018. "Harbors and Democracy." Varieties of Democracy Working Paper.

Gerring, John, Brendan Apfeld, Tore Wig, Andreas Tollefsen. 2022. *The Deep Roots of Modern Democracy.* Cambridge: Cambridge University Press.

Gerring, John, Daniel Ziblatt, Johan Van Gorp, Julian Arevalo. 2011. "An institutional theory of direct and indirect rule." *World Politics* 63, 3: 377–433.

Gertner, Jon. 2012. *The Idea Factory: Bell Labs and the Great Age of American Innovation.* New York: Penguin.

Ghiselin, Brewster (ed.) 1985. *The Creative Process: Reflections on the Invention in the Arts and Sciences.* Berkeley, CA: University of California Press.

Gholson, Barry, William R. Shadish, Robert A. Neimeyer, Arthur C. Houts (eds.) 1989. *Psychology of Science: Contributions to Metascience.* Cambridge: Cambridge University Press.

Giere, Ronald N. 1990. *Explaining Science: A Cognitive Approach.* Chicago: University of Chicago Press.

Gingras, Yves. 2016. *Bibliometrics and Research Evaluation: Uses and Abuses.* Cambridge, MA: MIT Press.

Gisselquist, Rachel M. 2014. "Paired comparison and theory development: Considerations for case selection." *PS: Political Science & Politics* 47, 2: 477–484.

Gladwell, Malcolm. 2008. *Outliers: The Story of Success.* New York: Hachette UK.

Gladwin, Christina H. 1989. *Ethnographic Decision Tree Modeling.* Newbury Park: Sage Publications.

Glaser, Barney, Anselm Strauss. 1967. *The Discovery of Grounded Theory: Strategies for Qualitative Research.* Chicago: Aldine Publishing Company.

Glǎveanu, Vlad Petre (ed.) 2019. *The Creativity Reader.* New York: Oxford University Press.

Gleditsch, Nils Petter, Håvard Hegre. 1997. "Peace and democracy: Three levels of analysis." *Journal of Conflict Resolution* 41, 2: 283–310.

Glynn, Adam N., Nahomi Ichino. 2015. "Using qualitative information to improve causal inference." *American Journal of Political Science* 59: 1055–1071.

Goemans, Henk E., Kristian Skrede Gleditsch, Giacomo Chiozza. 2009. "Introducing Archigos: A dataset of political leaders." *Journal of Peace research* 46, 2: 269–283.

Goertz, Gary. 2012. *Social Science Concepts: A User's Guide.* Princeton, NJ: Princeton University Press.

Goertz, Gary, James Mahoney. 2012. *A Tale of Two Cultures: Qualitative and Quantitative Research in the Social Sciences.* Princeton, NJ: Princeton University Press.

Goffman, Erving. 1959. *The Presentation of Self in Everyday Life.* New York: Anchor Books.

Goldin, Claudia. 1998. "The economist as detective." In Michael Szenberg (ed.), *Passion and Craft: Economists at Work* (Ann Arbor, MI: University of Michigan Press), 98–112.

Goldstone, Jack A. 1991. *Revolution and Rebellion in the Early Modern World.* Berkeley, CA: University of California Press.

Gooding, David C. 1990. *Experiment and the Making of Meaning: Human Agency in Scientific Observation and Experiment.* Berlin: Springer.

Gordon, David M. 1998. "Politics and precision: Pursuing economics outside the mainstream." In Michael Szenberg (ed.), *Passion and Craft: Economists at Work* (Ann Arbor, MI: University of Michigan Press), 113–132.

Gray, Paul S., John B. Williamson, David A. Karp, John R. Dalphin. 2007. *The Research Imagination: An Introduction to Qualitative and Quantitative Methods*. Cambridge: Cambridge University Press.

Green, Donald P., Alan S. Gerber. 2002. "The downstream benefits of experimentation." *Political Analysis* 10, 4: 394–402.

Green, Donald P., Shang E. Ha, John G. Bullock. 2010. "Enough already about 'black box' experiments: Studying mediation is more difficult than most scholars suppose." *The Annals of the American Academy of Political and Social Science* 628: 200–208.

Griffin, Larry J. 1995. "How is sociology informed by history?" *Social Forces* 73, 4: 1245–1254.

Grønhaug, Kjell, Geir Kaufmann (eds.) 1988. *Innovation: A Cross-Disciplinary Perspective*. Oxford: Oxford University Press.

Gross, Matthias, Linsey McGoey (eds.) 2015. *Routledge International Handbook of Ignorance Studies*. Abingdon: Routledge.

Gross, Neil. 2013. *Why Are Professors Liberal and Why Do Conservatives Care?* Cambridge, MA: Harvard University Press.

Grosul, Maya, Gregory J. Feist. 2014. "The creative person in science." *Psychology of Aesthetics, Creativity, and the Arts* 8, 1: 30–43.

Gruber, Howard E. 1974. *Darwin on Man: A Psychological Study of Scientific Creativity*. New York: E. P. Dutton.

Gruber, Howard E. 1989. "The evolving systems approach to creative work." In Doris B. Wallace and Howard E. Gruber (eds.), *Creative People at Work: Twelve Cognitive Case Studies* (Oxford: Oxford University Press), 3–24.

Gruber, Howard E., Katja Bödeker (eds.) 2005. *Creativity, Psychology and the History of Science*. Berlin: Springer.

Gutzkow, Joshua, Michèle Lamont, Grégoire Mallard. 2004. "What is originality in the humanities and the social sciences?" *American Sociological Review* 69: 190–212.

Hadenius, Axel, Jan Teorell. 2007. "Pathways from authoritarianism." *Journal of Democracy* 18, 1: 143–157.

Hage, Jerald. 1972. *Techniques and Problems of Theory Construction in Sociology*. New York: John Wiley & Sons.

Haggard, Stephan, Robert Kaufman. 2012. "Inequality and regime change: Democratic transitions and the stability of democratic rule." *American Political Science Review* 106: 1–22.

Hamermesh, Daniel S. 2018. "Citations in economics: measurement, uses and impacts." *Journal of Economic Literature* 56, 1: 115–156.

Hammond, Phillip (ed.) 1967. *Sociologists at Work*. New York: Doubleday & Company.

Haney, C., C. Banks, P. Zimbardo. 1973. "Interpersonal dynamics in a simulated prison." *International Journal of Criminology and Penology* 1: 69–97.

Hanson, Norwood Russell. 1958. *Patterns of Discovery*. Cambridge: Cambridge University Press.

Harcourt, Geoffrey Colin. 2016. *Post-Keynesian Essays in Biography: Portraits of Twentieth-Century Political Economists*. Berlin: Springer.

Harding, David J., Cybelle Fox, Jal D. Mehta. 2002. "Studying rare events through qualitative case studies: Lessons from a study of rampage school shootings." *Sociological Methods and Research* 11, 31: 174–217.

Harris, Marvin. 1974. *Cows, Pigs, Wars, and Witches: The Riddles of Culture*. New York: Vintage.

Hartwig, Frederick, Brian E. Dearing. 1979. *Exploratory Data Analysis*. Thousand Oaks: Sage.

Harzing, Anne-Wil. 2007. *Publish or Perish*. Melbourne: Tarma Software Research.

Hawthorn, Geoffrey. 1991. *Plausible Worlds: Possibility and Understanding in History and the Human Sciences*. Cambridge: Cambridge University Press.

Haynes, Barton F., Giuseppe Pantaleo, Anthony S. Fauci. 1996. "Toward an understanding of the correlates of protective immunity to HIV infection." *Science* 271: 324–328.

Healy, Kieran. 2017. "Fuck nuance." *Sociological Theory* 35, 2: 118–127.

Heclo, Hugh. 1974. *Modern Social Policies in Britain and Sweden: From Relief to Income Maintenance.* New Haven, CT: Yale University Press.

Hedström, Peter. 2005. *Dissecting the Social: On the Principles of Analytical Sociology.* Cambridge: Cambridge University Press.

Hedström, Peter, Richard Swedberg (eds.) 1998. *Social Mechanisms: An Analytical Approach to Social Theory.* Cambridge: Cambridge University Press.

Heemskerk, Marieke. 2002. "Livelihood decision making and environmental degradation: Small-scale gold mining in the Suriname Amazon." *Society and Natural Resources* 15: 327–344.

Heidenheimer, Arnold J., Michael Johnston (eds.) 2001. *Political Corruption: Concepts & Contexts.* London: Routledge.

Heilbroner, Robert L. 2011. *The Worldly Philosophers: The Lives, Times and Ideas of the Great Economic Thinkers.* New York: Simon and Schuster.

Hempel, Carl G., Paul Oppenheim. 1948. "Studies in the logic of explanation." *Philosophy of Science* 15, 2: 135–175.

Hempel, Sandra. 2007. *The Strange Case of the Broad Street Pump: John Snow and the Mystery of Cholera.* Berkeley, CA: University of California Press.

Hesli, Vicki L., Jae Mook Lee. 2011. "Why do some of our colleagues publish more than others?" *PS: Political Science & Politics* 44: 393–408.

Hesli, Vicki L., Jacqueline DeLaat, Jeremy Youde, Jeanette Mendez, Sang-shin Lee. 2006. "Success in graduate school and after: Survey results from the Midwest region." *PS: Political Science & Politics* 39, 2: 317–325.

Hesse, Mary. 1966. *Models and Analogies in Science.* Notre Dame: University of Notre Dame Press.

Hidalgo, F. Daniel, Simeon Nichter. 2016. "Voter buying: Shaping the electorate through clientelism." *American Journal of Political Science* 60, 2: 436–455.

Hill, Kim Quaile. 2020. "Research creativity and productivity in political science: A research agenda for understanding alternative career paths and attitudes toward professional work in the profession." *PS: Political Science & Politics* 53, 1: 79–83.

Hirschman, Albert O. 1967. *Development Projects Observed.* Washington, DC: Brookings Institution.

Hodgson, Geoffrey M. 2007. "Meanings of methodological individualism." *Journal of Economic Methodology* 14, 2: 211–226.

Hofstadter, Richard. 1963. *Anti-intellectualism in American Life.* New York: Vintage.

Holland, Paul W. 1986. "Statistics and causal inference." *Journal of the American Statistical Association* 81, 396: 945–960.

Holmes, Frederic Lawrence. 2004. *Investigative Pathways.* New Haven, CT: Yale University Press.

Homans, George C. 1958. "Social behavior as exchange." *American Journal of Sociology* 65: 597–606.

Horowitz, Tamara, Gerald Massey (eds.) 1991. *Thought Experiments in Science and Philosophy.* Savage, MD: Rowman & Littlefield.

Howard, Christopher. 2017. *Thinking Like a Political Scientist: A Practical Guide to Research Methods.* Chicago: University of Chicago Press.

Howitt, Susan M., Anna N. Wilson. 2014. "Revisiting 'Is the scientific paper a fraud?'" *EMBO Reports* 15, 5: 481–484.

Hoy, David Couzens. 1982. *The Critical Circle: Literature, History, and Philosophical Hermeneutics.* Berkeley, CA: University of California Press.

Humphreys, Macartan. 2016. *Political Games.* New York: W. W. Norton.

Hutchison, Andrew John, Lynne Halley Johnston, Jeff David Breckon. 2010. "Using QSR-NVivo to facilitate the development of a grounded theory project: an account of a worked example." *International Journal of Social Research Methodology* 13, 4: 283–302.

Hyde, Susan D. 2007. "The observer effect in international politics: Evidence from a natural experiment." *World Politics* 60, 1: 37–63.

Ierodiakonou, Katerina, Sophie Roux (eds.) 2011. *Thought Experiments in Methodological and Historical Contexts.* Leiden: Brill.

Imai, Kosuke, Luke Keele, Dustin Tingley, Teppei Yamamoto. 2011. "Unpacking the black box of causality: Learning about causal mechanisms from experimental and observational studies." *American Political Science Review* 105, 4: 765–789.

Imbens, Guido W., Thomas Lemieux. 2008. "Regression discontinuity designs: A guide to practice." *Journal of Econometrics* 142, 2: 615–635.

Inglehart, Ronald, Christian Welzel. 2005. *Modernization, Cultural Change, and Democracy: The Human Development Sequence.* Cambridge: Cambridge University Press.

Irvine, William Braxton. 2015. *Aha! The Moments of Insight that Shape Our World.* New York: Oxford University Press.

Isaksen, Scott G., Mary C. Murdock, Roger L. Firestein, D. J. Treffinger (eds.) 1993. *Understanding and Recognizing Creativity: The Emergence of a Discipline.* Westport, CT: Praeger.

Iyer, Lakshmi. 2010. "Direct versus indirect colonial rule in India: Long-term consequences." *The Review of Economics and Statistics* 92, 4: 693–713.

Jackson, Michelle, David R. Cox. 2013. "The principles of experimental design and their application in sociology." *Annual Review of Sociology* 39: 27–49.

Jacobs, Alan. 2020. "Pre-registration and Results-Free Review in Observational and Qualitative Research." In Colin Elman, John Gerring, James Mahoney (eds.), *The Production of Knowledge: Enhancing Progress in Social Science* (Cambridge: Cambridge University Press), 221–264.

Jacobs, Struan. 2006. "Models of scientific community: Charles Sanders Peirce to Thomas Kuhn." *Interdisciplinary Science Reviews* 31, 2: 163–173.

James, Gareth, Daniela Witten, Trevor Hastie, Robert Tibshirani. 2013. *An Introduction to Statistical Learning with Applications in R.* New York: Springer.

Jefferson, Thomas. 1967. *The Jefferson Cyclopedia. Vol. 1.* John P. Foley (ed.), New York: Russell and Russell.

Jenicek, Milos. 2001. *Clinical Case Reporting in Evidence-Based Medicine*, 2nd ed. New York: Oxford University Press.

Jodha, N. S. 1995. "Studying common property resources: Biography of a research project." *Economic and Political Weekly* 30, 11: 556–559.

Johnson, Chalmers. 1983. *MITI and the Japanese Miracle: The Growth of Industrial Policy, 1925–1975.* Stanford, CA: Stanford University Press.

Johnson, Jeremy B. 2018. "Protecting the community: Lessons from the Montana Flyer Project." *PS: Political Science & Politics* 51, 3: 615–619.

Johnson, Steven. 2006. *The Ghost Map: The Story of London's Most Terrifying Epidemic and How It Changed Science, Cities, and the Modern World.* London: Penguin.

Johnson, Steven. 2010. *Where Good Ideas Come from: The Seven Patterns of Innovation.* London: Penguin UK.

John-Steiner, Vera. 2000. *Creative Collaboration*. New York: Oxford University Press.

Joyner, Randy L., William A. Rouse, Allan A. Glatthorn. 2018. *Writing the Winning Thesis or Dissertation: A Step-by-Step Guide*. Thousand Oaks: Corwin Press.

Kagel, John H., Alvin E. Roth (eds.) 2016. *The Handbook of Experimental Economics*. Princeton, NJ: Princeton University Press.

Kapiszewski, Diana. 2012. *High Courts and Economic Governance in Argentina and Brazil*. Cambridge: Cambridge University Press.

Kapiszewski, Diana, Lauren McLean, Benjamin Read. 2015. *Field Research in Political Science*. Cambridge: Cambridge University Press.

Kaplan, Abraham. 1964. *The Conduct of Inquiry: Methodology for Behavioral Science*. San Francisco: Chandler Publishing.

Kaufmann, Geir. 1988. "Problem solving and creativity." In Kjell Grønhaug, Geir Kaufmann (eds.), *Innovation: A Cross-Disciplinary Perspective*. (Oxford: Oxford University Press), 87–137.

Kaufman, James C., Ronald A. Beghetto. 2009. "Beyond big and little: The four c model of creativity." *Review of General Psychology* 13, 1: 1–12.

Kaufman, James C., Robert J. Sternberg (eds.) 2010. *The Cambridge Handbook of Creativity*. Cambridge: Cambridge University Press.

Kauffman, Stuart A. 2000. *Investigations*. Oxford: Oxford University Press.

Kazancigil, Ali. 1994. "The deviant case in comparative analysis: High stateness in comparative analysis." In Mattei Dogan, Ali Kazancigil (eds.), *Comparing Nations: Concepts, Strategies, Substance* (Cambridge: Blackwell), 213–238.

Kellstedt, Paul M., Guy D. Whitten. 2018. *The Fundamentals of Political Science Research*. Cambridge: Cambridge University Press.

Kelman, Herbert C. 1982. "Ethical issues in different social science methods." In Tom L. Beauchamp, Ruth R. Faden, R. Jay Wallace, Jr., LeRoy Walters (eds.), *Ethical Issues in Social Science Research* (Baltimore, MD: Johns Hopkins University Press), 40–98.

Kendall, M. G., A. Stuart. 1950. "The law of cubic proportion in election results." *British Journal of Sociology* 1: 183–197.

Kendall, Patricia L., Katherine M. Wolf. 1949/1955. "The analysis of deviant cases in communications research." In Paul F. Lazarsfeld, Frank N. Stanton (eds.), *Communications Research, 1948–1949* (New York: Harper and Brothers, 1949). Reprinted in Paul F. Lazarsfeld, Morris Rosenberg (eds.), *The Language of Social Research* (New York: Free Press, 1995), 167–170.

Keohane, Robert. 2009. "Political science as a vocation." *PS: Political Science & Politics* 42, 2: 359–363.

Key, V. O., Jr. 1949. *Southern Politics in State and Nation*. New York: Vintage.

Kim, Hannah June, Bernard Grofman. 2019. "The political science 400: With citation counts by cohort, gender, and subfield." *PS: Political Science & Politics* 52, 2: 296–311.

Kindleberger, Charles P. 1996. *World Economic Primacy 1500–1990*. Oxford: Oxford University Press.

King, Gary, Robert O. Keohane, Sidney Verba. 1994. *Designing Social Inquiry: Scientific Inference in Qualitative Research*. Princeton, NJ: Princeton University Press.

Kirk, Dudley. 1996. "Demographic transition theory." *Population Studies* 50, 3: 361–387.

Kirton, Michael J. (ed.) 1994. *Adapters and Innovators: Styles of Creativity and Problem Solving*, 2nd ed. London: Routledge.

Klein, Gary. 2013. *Seeing What Others Don't: The Remarkable Ways We Gain Insights*. New York: Public Affairs.

Klein, Lawrence R., Suleyman Ozmucur. 2003. "The estimation of China's growth rate." *Journal of Economic and Social Measurement* 28, 4: 187–202.

Knoke, David, Song Yang. 2019. *Social Network Analysis*. Thousand Oaks: Sage Publications.

Knutsen, Carl Henrik, Jørgen Møller, Svend-Erik Skaaning. 2016. "Going historical: Measuring democraticness before the age of mass democracy." *International Political Science Review* 37, 5: 679–689.

Koestler, Arthur. 1964. *The Act of Creation*. New York: Macmillan.

Kohli, Atul. 2004. *State-Directed Development: Political Power and Industrialization in the Global Periphery*. Cambridge: Cambridge University Press.

Kohn, Melvin L. 1993. "Doing social research under conditions of radical social change: The biography of an ongoing research project." *Social Psychology Quarterly* 56, 1: 4–20.

Kollman, Ken, Allen Hicken, Daniele Caramani, David Backer, David Lublin. 2018. *Constituency-Level Elections Archive*. Ann Arbor, MI: Center for Political Studies, University of Michigan.

Kregel, J. A. (ed.) 1988. *Recollections of Eminent Economists, Vol I*. Houndmills, Basingstoke: Macmillan.

Kregel, J. A. (ed.) 1989. *Recollections of Eminent Economists, Vol II*. Houndmills, Basingstoke: Macmillan.

Krieger, Susan. 1991. *Social Science and the Self: Personal Essays on an Art Form*. New Brunswick: Rutgers University Press.

Krugman, Paul. 1998. "How I work." In Michael Szenberg (ed.), *Passion and Craft: Economists at Work* (Ann Arbor, MI: University of Michigan Press), 143–154.

Kuhn, Thomas S. 1970[1962]. *The Structure of Scientific Revolutions*. Chicago: University of Chicago Press.

Kuznets, Simon. 1955. "Economic growth and income inequality." *American Economic Review* 45: 1–28.

Lakatos, Imre. 1978. *The Methodology of Scientific Research Programmes*. Cambridge: Cambridge University Press.

Lalonde, Robert J. 1986. "Evaluating the econometric evaluations of training programs with experimental data." *American Economic Review* 76, 4: 604–620.

Landes, William M. 1998. "The art of law and economics: An autobiographical essay." In Michael Szenberg (ed.), *Passion and Craft: Economists at Work* (Ann Arbor, MI: University of Michigan Press), 155–175.

Lange, Matthew. 2009. *Lineages of Despotism and Development*. Chicago: University of Chicago Press.

Langley, Pat, Herbert A. Simon, Gary L. Bradshaw, Jan M. Mytkow. 1987. *Scientific Discovery: Computational Explorations of the Creative Process*. Cambridge, MA: MIT Press.

Langton, Christopher G. 1992. "Life at the edge of chaos." *Proc. Workshop on Artificial Life* 10: 41–91.

Larivière, Vincent, Chaoqun Ni, Yves Gingras, Blaise Cronin, Cassidy R. Sugimoto. 2013. "Bibliometrics: Global gender disparities in science." *Nature News* 504, 7479: 211.

Larkin, Jill H., Herbert A. Simon. 1987. "Why a diagram is (sometimes) worth ten thousand words." *Cognitive Science* 11, 1: 65–100.

Laudan, Larry. 1977. *Progress and Its Problems: Toward a Theory of Scientific Growth*. Berkeley, CA: University of California Press.

Laudan, Larry. 1981. "Why was the logic of discovery abandoned?" In *Science and Hypothesis*. (Dordrecht: Springer), 181–191.

Lave, Charles, James March. 1975. *An Introduction to Models in the Social Sciences*. New York: Harper.

Lazarsfeld, Paul F., Allen H. Barton. 1951. "Qualitative measurement in the social sciences: Classification, typologies, and indices." In Daniel Lerner, Harold D. Lasswell (eds.), *The Policy Sciences* (Stanford, CA: Stanford University Press), 155–192.

Lebow, Richard Ned. 2010. *Forbidden Fruit: Counterfactuals and International Relations*. Princeton, NJ: Princeton University Press.

Lebow, Richard Ned, Peer Schouten, Hidemi Suganami (eds.) 2016. *The Return of the Theorists: Dialogues with Great Thinkers in International Relations*. Basingstoke: Palgrave Macmillan.

Lee, Sooho, Barry Bozeman. 2005. "The impact of research collaboration on scientific productivity." *Social Studies of Science* 35, 5: 673–702.

LeGates, Richard T. 2005. *Think Globally, Act Regionally: GIS and Data Visualization for Social Science and Public Policy Research*. Redlands, CA: Esri Press.

Lehrer, Jonah. 2012. *Imagine: How Creativity Works*. New York: Houghton Mifflin Harcourt.

Lei, Simon A. 2009. "Strategies for finding and selecting an ideal thesis or dissertation topic: A review of literature." *College Student Journal* 43, 4: 1324+.

Lemert, Charles (ed.) 2018. *Social Theory: The Multicultural, Global, and Classic Readings*. New York: Routledge

Lemkin, Raphael. 1944. *Axis Rule in Occupied Europe*. Washington, DC: Carnegie.

Levi, Margaret. 1988. *Of Rule and Revenue*. Berkeley, CA: University of California Press.

Levi, Margaret. 1999. "Producing an analytic narrative." In John R. Bowen, Roger Petersen (eds.), *Critical Comparisons in Politics and Culture* (Cambridge: Cambridge University Press), 152–172.

Levin, Sharon G., Paula E. Stephan. 1991. "Research productivity over the life cycle: Evidence for academic scientists." *American Economic Review* 82, 1: 114–131.

Levitsky, Steven, Lucan A. Way. 2010. *Competitive Authoritarianism: Hybrid Regimes after the Cold War*. New York: Cambridge University Press.

Levitsky, Steven, Daniel Ziblatt. 2018. *How Democracies Die*. New York: Broadway Books.

Levitt, Steven D., Stephen J. Dubner. 2005. *Freakonomics: A Rogue Economist Explores the Hidden Side of Everything*. New York: William Morrow.

Levitt, Steven D., Stephen J. Dubner. 2009. *Superfreakonomics: Global Cooling, Patriotic Prostitutes and Why Suicide Bombers Should Buy Life Insurance*. New York: William Morrow.

Levitt, Steven D., Stephen J. Dubner. 2015. *Think Like a Freak: The Authors of Freakonomics Offer to Retrain Your Brain*. New York: William Morrow.

Lewis, Michael. 2016. *The Undoing Project: A Friendship That Changed the World*. London: Penguin UK.

Lichbach, Mark Irving, Alan S. Zuckerman (eds.) 1997. *Comparative Politics: Rationality, Culture, and Structure*. Cambridge: Cambridge University Press.

Lieberman, Evan S. 2003. *Race and Regionalism in the Politics of Taxation in Brazil and South Africa*. Cambridge: Cambridge University Press.

Lieberman, Evan S. 2016. "Can the biomedical research cycle be a model for political science?" *Perspectives on Politics* 14, 4: 1054–1066.

Lightman, Alan, Owen Gingerich. 1992. "When do anomalies begin?" *Science* 255, 5045: 690–695.

Lijphart, Arend. 1968. *The Politics of Accommodation: Pluralism and Democracy in the Netherlands*. Berkeley, CA: University of California Press.

Lijphart, Arend. 1971. "Comparative politics and the comparative method." *American Political Science Review* 65: 682–693.

Lijphart, Arend. 1975. "The comparable cases strategy in comparative research." *Comparative Political Studies* 8: 158–177.

Linsley, E. G., R. L. Usinger. 1959. "Linnaeus and the development of the international code of zoological nomenclature." *Systematic Zoology* 8: 39–47.

Linz, Juan J. 2000. *Totalitarian and Authoritarian Regimes*. Boulder, CO: Lynne Reinner.

Linz, Juan J., Alfred Stepan (eds.) 1978a. *The Breakdown of Democratic Regimes: Europe*. Baltimore, MD: Johns Hopkins University Press.

Linz, Juan J., Alfred Stepan (eds.) 1978b. *The Breakdown of Democratic Regimes: Latin America*. Baltimore, MD: Johns Hopkins University Press.

Lipset, Seymour Martin. 1959. "Some social requisites of democracy: Economic development and political legitimacy." *American Political Science Review* 53, 1: 69–105.

Lipset, Seymour Martin. 1964. *The Biography of a Research Project: Union Democracy*. New York: Basic Books.

Lipset, Seymour Martin. 1967. "The biography of a research project: Union democracy." In Phillip Hammond (ed.), *Sociologists at Work*. (New York: Doubleday & Company), 111–139.

Lipset, Seymour Martin, Martin A. Trow, James S. Coleman. 1956. *Union Democracy: The Internal Politics of the International Typographical Union*. New York: Free Press.

Little, Daniel. 1991. *Varieties of Social Explanation: An Introduction to the Philosophy of Social Science*. Oxford: Westview.

Little, Daniel. 1998. *Microfoundations, Method, and Causation*. New Brunswick, NJ: Transaction Publishing.

Locke, Edwin A. 2007. "The case for inductive theory building." *Journal of Management* 33, 6: 867–890.

Loehle, Craig. 1990. "A guide to increased creativity in research: inspiration or perspiration?" *Bioscience* 40, 2: 123–129.

Loehle, Craig. 2009. *Becoming a Successful Scientist: Strategic Thinking for Scientific Discovery*. Cambridge: Cambridge University Press.

Lozano, George A., Vincent Larivière, Yves Gingras. 2012. "The weakening relationship between the impact factor and papers' citations in the Digital Age." *Journal of the American Society for Information Science and Technology* 63, 11: 2140–2145.

Luebbert, Gregory M. 1991. *Liberalism, Fascism, or Social Democracy: Social Classes and the Political Origins of Regimes in Interwar Europe*. Berkeley, CA: University of California Press.

Luker, Kristin. 2008. *Salsa Dancing into the Social Sciences: Research in an Age of Info-glut*. Cambridge, MA: Harvard University Press.

Lynd, Robert Staughton. 1964[1939]. *Knowledge For What?: The Place of Social Science in American Culture*. New York: Grove Press.

MacDonald, Susan Peck. 1994. *Professional Academic Writing in the Humanities and Social Sciences*. Carbondale, IL: Southern Illinois University Press.

MacNell, Lillian, Adam Driscoll, Andrea N. Hunt. 2015. "What's in a name: Exposing gender bias in student ratings of teaching." *Innovative Higher Education* 40: 291–303.

Magnani, Lorenzo, Nancy Nersessian, Paul Thagard (eds.) 1999. *Model-Based Reasoning in Scientific Discovery*. Berlin: Springer Science & Business Media.

Mahdavi, Paasha. 2019. "Scraping public co-occurrences for statistical network analysis of political elites." *Political Science Research and Methods* 7, 2: 385–392.

Mahoney, James. 2000. "Path dependence in historical sociology." *History and Theory* 29, 4: 507–548.

Mahoney, James. 2001. "Beyond correlational analysis: Recent innovations in theory and method." *Sociological Forum* 16, 3: 575–593.

Mahoney, James. 2002. *The Legacies of Liberalism: Path Dependence and Political Regimes in Central America*. Baltimore, MD: Johns Hopkins University Press.

Mahoney, James, Dietrich Rueschemeyer (eds.) 2003. *Comparative Historical Analysis in the Social Sciences*. Cambridge: Cambridge University Press.

Mahoney, James, Rachel Sweet Vanderpoel. 2015. "Set diagrams and qualitative research." *Comparative Political Studies* 48, 1: 65–100.

Maliniak, Daniel, Ryan Powers, Barbara F. Walter. 2013. "The gender citation gap in International Relations." *International Organization* 67, 4: 889–922.

Mankiw, N. Gregory. 1998. "My rules of thumb." In Michael Szenberg (ed.), *Passion and Craft: Economists at Work* (Ann Arbor, MI: University of Michigan Press), 176–186.

Manski, Charles F. 1999. *Identification Problems in the Social Sciences.* Cambridge, MA: Harvard University Press.

Martin, Isaac William. 2008. *The Permanent Tax Revolt: How the Property Tax Transformed American Politics.* Stanford, CA: Stanford University Press.

Martin, John Levi. 2011. *The Explanation of Social Action.* New York: Oxford University Press.

Martin, John Levi. 2015. *Thinking through Theory.* New York: W. W. Norton.

Martin, John Levi. 2017. *Thinking through Methods: A Social Science Primer.* Chicago: University of Chicago Press.

Martindale, Colin. 1990. *The Clockwork Muse: The Predictability of Artistic Change.* New York: Basic Books.

Martinez, Wendy L., Angel R. Martinez, Jeffrey Solka. 2017. *Exploratory Data Analysis with MATLAB.* Boca Raton: Chapman and Hall/CRC.

Maske, Kellie L., Garey C. Durden, Patricia C. Gaynor. 2003. "Determinants of scholarly productivity among male and female economists." *Economic Inquiry* 41, 4: 555–564.

Matthes, Jorg. 2012. "Framing politics: An integrative approach." *American Behavioral Scientist* 56, 3: 247–259.

May, Rollo. 1994. *The Courage to Create.* New York: W. W. Norton.

Mayhew, David R. 2008. *Electoral Realignments: A Critique of an American Genre.* New Haven, CT: Yale University Press.

Mayhew, David R. 2015. "Robert A. Dahl: Questions, concepts, proving it." *Journal of Political Power* 8, 2: 175–187.

Mazur, Dennis J. 2007. *Evaluating the Science and Ethics of Research on Humans: A Guide for IRB Members.* Baltimore, MD: Johns Hopkins University Press.

McCauley, John F., Daniel N. Posner. 2015. "African borders as sources of natural experiments promise and pitfalls." *Political Science Research and Methods* 3, 2: 409–418.

McGuire, William J. 1973. "The yin and yang of progress in social psychology: Seven koan." *Journal of Personality and Social Psychology* 26, 3: 446.

McGuire, William J. 1997. "Creative hypothesis generating in psychology: Some useful heuristics." *Annual Review of Psychology* 48: 1–30.

McGuire, William J. 2004. "A perspectivist approach to theory construction." *Personality and Social Psychology Review* 8, 2: 173–182.

McHaffie, Patrick, Sungsoon Hwang, Cassie Follett. 2018. *GIS: An introduction to mapping technologies.* New York: CRC Press.

McLaughlin, Robert. 1982. "Invention and induction: Laudan, Simon and the logic of discovery." *Philosophy of Science* 49, 2: 198–211.

Mearsheimer, John J., Stephen Walt. 2013. "Leaving theory behind: Why simplistic hypothesis testing is bad for international relations." *European Journal of International Relations* 19, 3: 427–457.

Meckstroth, Theodore. 1975. "'Most different systems' and 'most similar systems': A study in the logic of comparative inquiry." *Comparative Political Studies* 8, 2: 133–177.

Medawar, Peter. 1963. "Is the scientific paper a fraud?" *Listener* 70: 377–378.

Meheus, Joke, Thomas Nickles (eds.) 2009. *Models of Discovery and Creativity.* Dordrecht: Springer.

Meissner, Shelbi Nahwilet. 2018. "How does the consideration of Indigenous identities in the US complicate conversations about tracking folk racial categories in epidemiologic research?" *Synthese* 198: 2439–2462.

Melin, Göran. 2000. "Pragmatism and self-organization: Research collaboration on the individual level." *Research Policy* 29, 1: 31–40.

Mertens, Donna M., Pauline E. Ginsberg (eds.) 2009. *The Handbook of Social Research Ethics*. Thousand Oaks: Sage.

Merton, Robert K. 1959. "Introduction: Notes on problem-finding in sociology." In Robert K. Merton, L. Broom, L. Cottrell (eds.), *Sociology Today* (New York: Basic Books), 9–34.

Merton, Robert K. 1963. "Resistance to the systematic study of multiple discoveries in science." *European Journal of Sociology* 4, 2: 237–282.

Merton, Robert K. 1967. *On Theoretical Sociology*. New York: Free Press.

Merton, Robert K. 1968. *Social Theory and Social Structure*. New York: Simon and Schuster.

Merton, Robert K., Elinor Barber. 2006. *The Travels and Adventures of Serendipity: A Study in Sociological Semantics and the Sociology of Science*. Princeton, NJ: Princeton University Press.

Miguel, Edward. 2004. "Tribe or nation: Nation-building and public goods in Kenya v. Tanzania." *World Politics* 56, 3: 327–362.

Mill, John Stuart. 1843/1872. *System of Logic*, 8th ed. London: Longmans, Green.

Mills, C. Wright. 1959. *The Sociological Imagination*. New York: Oxford University Press.

Molina, Oscar, Martin Rhodes. 2002. "Corporatism: The past, present, and future of a concept." *Annual Review of Political Science* 5, 1: 305–331.

Møller, Jørgen, Svend-Erik Skaaning. 2012. *Democracy and Democratization in Comparative Perspective: Conceptions, Conjunctures, Causes, and Consequences*. Abingdon: Routledge.

Monroe, Kristen Renwick. 1996. *The Heart of Altruism*. Princeton, NJ: Princeton University Press.

Monroe, Kristen Renwick. 2004. *The Hand of Compassion: Portraits of Moral Choice during the Holocaust*. Princeton, NJ: Princeton University Press.

Moore, Barrington, Jr. 1966. *Social Origins of Dictatorship and Democracy: Lord and Peasant in the Making of the Modern World*. Boston, MA: Beacon Press.

Morgan, Stephen L., Christopher Winship. 2015. *Counterfactuals and Causal Inference: Methods and Principles for Social Research, 2d ed.* Cambridge: Cambridge University Press.

Morgenthaler, Stephan. 2009. "Exploratory data analysis." *Wiley Interdisciplinary Reviews: Computational Statistics* 1, 1: 33–44.

Morrison, Margaret, Mary S. Morgan. 1999. "Models as mediating instruments." In Mary S. Morgan, Margaret Morrison (eds.), *Models as Mediators: Perspectives on Natural and Social Science* (Cambridge: Cambridge University Press), 10–37.

Morton, Rebecca B. 1999. *Methods and Models: A Guide to the Empirical Analysis of Formal Models in Political Science*. Cambridge: Cambridge University Press.

Most, Benjamin A. 1990. "Getting started on political research." *PS: Political Science & Politics* 23, 4: 592–596.

Mouzelis, Nicos P. 1995. *Sociological Theory: What Went Wrong? Diagnosis and Remedies*. London: Routledge.

Munck, Gerardo L., Richard Snyder (eds.) 2007. *Passion, Craft and Method in Comparative Politics*. Baltimore: Johns Hopkins University Press.

Murray, Penelope (ed.) 1989. *Genius: The History of an Idea*. Cambridge: Basil Blackwell.

Navarro, Vicente, Carme Borrell, Joan Benach, Carles Muntaner, Agueda Quiroga, Maica Rodríguez-Sanz, Nuria Verges, Jordi Guma, M. Isabel Pasarín. 2003. "The importance of the political and the social in explaining mortality differentials among the countries of the OECD, 1950–1998." *International Journal of Health Services* 33, 3: 419–494.

Nersessian, Nancy J. 2010. *Creating Scientific Concepts*. Cambridge, MA: MIT press.

Nichter, Simeon. 2008. "Vote buying or turnout buying? Machine politics and the secret ballot." *American Political Science Review* 102, 1: 19–31.

Nielsen, Richard A. 2017. *Deadly Clerics: Blocked Ambition and the Paths to Jihad*. Cambridge: Cambridge University Press.

Nisbett, Richard E. 1990. "The anticreativity letters: Advice from a senior tempter to a junior tempter." *American Psychologist* 45, 9: 1078.

Nisbett, Richard E., Timothy D. Wilson. 1977. "Telling more than we can know: Verbal reports on mental processes." *Psychology Review* 84, 3: 231–259.

North, Douglass C., Barry R. Weingast. 1989. "Constitutions and commitment: The evolution of institutions governing public choice in seventeenth-century England." *Journal of Economic History* 49: 803–832.

Notestein, Frank. 1945. "Population: The long view." In Theodore W. Schultz (ed.), *Food for the World* (Chicago: University of Chicago Press), 36–57.

Novick, Laura R. 2001. "Spatial diagrams: Key instruments in the toolbox for thought." *The Psychology of Learning and Motivation: Advances in Research and Theory* 40: 279–325.

NSF (National Science Foundation). 2016. Definition of Transformative Research. www.nsf.gov/about/transformative_research/definition.jsp

Nunn, Nathan. 2009. "The importance of history for economic development." *Annual Review of Economics* 1, 1: 65–92.

Ochse, R. A. 1990. *Before the Gates of Excellence: The Determinants of Creative Genius*. Cambridge: Cambridge University Press.

O'Donnell, Guillermo A. 1988. *Bureaucratic Authoritarianism: Argentina, 1966–1973, in Comparative Perspective*. Berkeley, CA: University of California Press.

O'Donnell, Guillermo A. 1998. "Horizontal accountability in new democracies." *Journal of Democracy* 9, 3: 112–126.

O'Donnell, Guillermo, Philippe C. Schmitter. 2013. *Transitions from Authoritarian Rule: Tentative Conclusions about Uncertain Democracies*. Baltimore, MD: Johns Hopkins University Press.

Ogburn, William F., Dorothy Thomas. 1922. "Are inventions inevitable? A note on social evolution." *Political Science Quarterly* 37, 1: 83–98.

Ogle, Richard. 2007. *Smart World: Breakthrough Creativity and the New Science of Ideas*. Cambridge, MA: Harvard Business School Press.

Okabe, Atsuyuki (ed.) 2016. *GIS-Based Studies in the Humanities and Social Sciences*. New York: CRC Press.

Oliver, Jack E. 1991. *The Incomplete Guide to the Art of Discovery*. New York: Columbia University Press.

Olsson, Ola. 2005. "Geography and institutions: plausible and implausible linkages." *Journal of Economics* 86, 1: 167–194.

Olsson, Ola. 2009. "On the Democratic Legacy of Colonialism." *Journal of Comparative Economics* 37, 4: 534–551.

O'Reilly, Karen. 2005. *Ethnographic Methods*. New York: Routledge.

Osborn, Alex. 2013. *Applied Imagination: Principles and Procedures of Creative Thinking*. Read Books.

Pachirat, Timothy. 2011. *Every Twelve Seconds: Industrialized Slaughter and the Politics of Sight*. New Haven, CT: Yale University Press.

Pampel, Fred. 2004. "Exploratory data analysis." In M. Lewis-Beck, A. Bryman, T. Futing Liao (eds.), *The SAGE Encyclopedia of Social Science Research Methods. Vol I*. (London: Sage), 359–360.

Panagopoulos, Costas, Sander van der Linden. 2016. "Conformity to implicit social pressure: The role of political identity." *Social Influence* 11: 177–184.

Parish, Austin J., Kevin W. Boyack, John P. A. Ioannidis. 2018. "Dynamics of co-authorship and productivity across different fields of scientific research." *PloS One* 13, 1.

Parsons, Craig. 2007. *How to Map Arguments in Political Science*. Oxford: Oxford University Press.

Parsons, Talcott, Edward Albert Shils. 1962. *Toward a General Theory of Action: Theoretical Foundations for the Social Sciences*. New York: Harper.

Patton, Michael Quinn. 2002. *Qualitative Evaluation and Research Methods*. Newbury Park, CA: Sage.

Paulus, Paul B., Bernard A. Nijstad (eds.) 2003. *Group Creativity: Innovation through Collaboration*. Oxford: Oxford University Press.

Pearce, Lisa D. 2002. "Integrating survey and ethnographic methods for systematic anomalous case analysis." *Sociological Methodology* 32: 103–132.

Pearl, Judea. 2000. *Causality: Models, Reasoning, and Inference*. Cambridge: Cambridge University Press.

Peirce, Charles S. 1929. "Guessing." *The Hound and Horn* 2, 3: 267–285.

Peirce, Charles S. 1934. *Collected Papers of Charles Sanders Peirce, Vol. 5*. Cambridge, MA: Belknap Press.

Peirce, Charles S. 1992. "Training in reasoning." in *Reasoning and the Logic of Things* (Cambridge, MA: Harvard University Press), 181–196.

Peters, Tom J., Robert H. Waterman. 1982. *In Search of Excellence: Lessons from America's Best-Run Companies*. New York: Harper & Row.

Philp, Mark. 1997. "Defining political corruption." *Political Studies* 45, 3: 436–462.

Pierson, Paul. 2011. *Politics in Time: History, Institutions, and Social Analysis*. Princeton, NJ: Princeton University Press.

Pincus, Steve. 2011. *1688: The First Modern Revolution*. New Haven, CT: Yale University Press.

Pinker, Steven. 2012. *The Better Angels of Our Nature: Why Violence Has Declined*. London: Penguin.

Planck, Max. 1968. *Scientific Autobiography and Other Papers*. New York: Philosophical Library.

Podolny, Joel M. 2003. "A picture is worth a thousand symbols: A sociologist's view of the economic pursuit of truth." *American Economic Review* 93, 2: 169–174.

Polanyi, Michael. 1966. *The Tacit Dimension*. Chicago: University of Chicago Press.

Poole, Keith T., Howard Rosenthal. 2000. *Congress: A Political-Economic History of Roll Call Voting*. New York: Oxford University Press.

Poole, Steven. 2016. *Rethink: The Surprising History of New Ideas*. New York: Simon and Schuster.

Popper, Karl. 1968[1934]. *The Logic of Scientific Discovery*. New York: Harper & Row.

Popper, Karl. 2014. *The Two Fundamental Problems of the Theory of Knowledge*. Abingdon: Routledge.

Porter, Michael. 1990. *The Competitive Advantage of Nations*. New York: Free Press.

Posner, Daniel N. 2005. *Institutions and Ethnic Politics in Africa*. Cambridge: Cambridge University Press.

Powdthavee, Nattavudh, Andrew J. Oswald. 2014. "Does money make people right-wing and inegalitarian? A longitudinal study of lottery winners." IZA Discussion Paper No. 7934. https://ssrn.com/abstract=2396429

Przeworski, Adam. 1985. *Capitalism and Social Democracy*. Cambridge: Cambridge University Press.

Przeworski, Adam, Fernando Limongi. 1997. "Modernization: Theories and facts." *World Politics* 49: 155–183.

Przeworski, Adam, John Sprague. 1986. *Paper Stones: A History of Electoral Socialism*. Chicago: University of Chicago Press.

Przeworski, Adam, Henry Teune. 1970. *The Logic of Comparative Social Inquiry*. New York: John Wiley.

Putnam, Robert D. 1988. "Diplomacy and domestic politics: The logic of two-level games." *International Organization* 42, 3: 427–460.

Putnam, Robert D., with Robert Leonardi, Raffaella Y. Nanetti. 1993. *Making Democracy Work: Civic Traditions in Modern Italy*. Princeton, NJ: Princeton University Press.

Raaflaub, Kurt A., Josiah Ober, Robert W. Wallace. 2007. *Origins of Democracy in Ancient Greece*. Berkeley, CA: University of California Press.

Ragin, Charles C. 1987. *The Comparative Method: Moving beyond Qualitative and Quantitative Strategies*. Berkeley, CA: University of California Press.

Ragin, Charles C. 1992. "'Casing' and the process of social inquiry." In Charles C. Ragin, Howard S. Becker (eds.), *What Is a Case? Exploring the Foundations of Social Inquiry*. (Cambridge: Cambridge University Press), 217–226.

Raub, Werner, Vincent Buskens, Marcel A. L. M. van Assen. 2011. "Micro-macro links and microfoundations in sociology." *The Journal of Mathematical Sociology* 35, 1–3: 1–25.

Ray, James Lee. 1995. *Democracy and International Conflict: An Evaluation of the Democratic Peace Proposition*. Columbia, SC: University of South Carolina Press.

Reichenbach, Hans. 1938. *Experience and Prediction: An Analysis of the Foundations and the Structure of Knowledge*. Chicago: University of Chicago Press.

Reichenbach, Hans. 1951. *The Rise of Scientific Philosophy*. Berkeley, CA: University of California Press.

Reilly, Benjamin. 2001. "Democracy, ethnic fragmentation, and internal conflict: Confused theories, faulty data, and the 'crucial case' of Papua New Guinea." *International Security* 25, 3: 162–185.

Rendgen, Sandra. 2018. *The Minard System: The Complete Statistical Graphics of Charles-Joseph Minard*. San Francisco: Chronicle Books.

Reyes, Jessica Wolpaw. 2007. "Environmental policy as social policy? The impact of childhood lead exposure on crime." *The BE Journal of Economic Analysis and Policy* 7, 1: 1–43.

Rihoux, Benoit, Gisele De Meur. 2009. "Crisp-Set Qualitative Comparative Analysis (csQCA)." In Benoit Rihoux, Charles C. Ragin (eds.), *Configurational Comparative Methods: Qualitative Comparative Analysis (QCA) and Related Techniques*. (Thousand Oaks: Sage), 33–68.

Roberts, Andrew (ed.) 2004. *What Might Have Been?: Leading Historians on Twelve 'What Ifs' of History*. London: Weidenfeld & Nicolson.

Roberts, Carol M. 2010. *The Dissertation Journey: A Practical and Comprehensive Guide to Planning, Writing, and Defending Your Dissertation*. Thousand Oaks: Corwin Press.

Roberts, Kenneth M. 2014. *Changing Course in Latin America*. Cambridge: Cambridge University Press.

Robinson, Richard. 1954. *Definition*. Oxford: Clarendon Press.

Roemer, John (ed.) 1986. *Analytical Marxism*. Cambridge: Cambridge University Press.

Rogowski, Ronald. 1995. "The role of theory and anomaly in social-scientific inference." *American Political Science Review* 89, 2: 467–470.

Romer, Christina D. 1990. "The great crash and the onset of the great depression." *The Quarterly Journal of Economics* 105, 3: 597–624.

Root-Bernstein, Robert. 1989. *Discovering: Inventing and Solving Problems at the Frontiers of Scientific Knowledge*. Cambridge: Harvard University Press.

Root-Bernstein, Robert S., Michele M. Root-Bernstein. 1999. *Sparks of Genius: The Thirteen Thinking Tools of the World's Most Creative People*. Boston: Houghton Mifflin.

Rosenbaum, Paul R., Jeffrey H. Silber. 2001. "Matching and thick description in an observational study of mortality after surgery." *Biostatistics* 2, 2: 217–232.

Ross, Michael L. 2001. "Does oil hinder democracy?" *World Politics* 53, 3: 325–361.

Ross, Michael L. 2013. *The Oil Curse: How Petroleum Wealth Shapes the Development of Nations*. Princeton: Princeton University Press.

Rostow, Walt W. 1956. "The take-off into self-sustained growth." *The Economic Journal* 66, 261: 25–48.

Rothenberg, Albert. 1976. "The process of Janusian thinking." In Albert Rothenberg, Carl R. Hausman (eds.), *The Creativity Question* (Durham: Duke University Press), 311–326.

Rothenberg, Albert, Bette Greenberg. 1976. *The Index of Scientific Writings on Creativity: General, 1566–1974*. Hamden, CT: Archon Books.

Rothenberg, Albert, Carl R. Hausman (eds.) 1976. *The Creativity Question*. Durham: Duke University Press.

Rothman, David J. 1971. *The Discovery of the Asylum: Social Order and Disorder in the New Republic*. Boston: Little, Brown.

Rubin, Donald B. 2008. "For objective causal inference, design trumps analysis." *The Annals of Applied Statistics* 2, 3: 808–840.

Rueschemeyer, Dietrich. 2009. *Usable Theory: Analytic Tools for Social Research*. Princeton: Princeton University Press.

Rueschemeyer, Dietrich, Evelyne Huber Stephens, John D. Stephens. 1992. *Capitalist Development and Democracy*. Chicago: University of Chicago Press.

Runciman, Walter Garrison. 1989. *A Treatise on Social Theory*. Cambridge: Cambridge University Press.

Runco, Mark A. (ed.) 1992. *Problem Finding, Problem Solving, and Creativity*. Westport, CT: Greenwood Publishing Group.

Runco, Mark A. 2014. *Creativity: Theories and Themes: Research, Development, and Practice*. Cambridge, MA: Elsevier.

Rustow, Dankwart. 1970. "Transitions to democracy: Toward a dynamic model." *Comparative Politics* 2, 3: 337–363.

Sadler-Smith, Eugene. 2015. "Wallas' four-stage model of the creative process: More than meets the eye?" *Creativity Research Journal* 27, 4: 342–352.

Sagan, Scott. 1993. *The Limits of Safety: Organizations, Accidents, and Nuclear Weapons*. Princeton: Princeton University Press.

Sahlins, Marshall. 1958. *Social Stratification in Polynesia*. Seattle: University of Washington Press.

Samuels, David. 2013. "Book citations count." *PS: Political Science & Politics* 46, 4: 785–790.

Samuelson, Paul A., William A. Barnett (eds.) 2009. *Inside the Economist's Mind: Conversations with Eminent Economists*. New York: John Wiley & Sons.

Sandberg, Jörgen, Mats Alvesson. 2011. "Ways of constructing research questions: gap-spotting or problematization?" *Organization* 18, 1: 23–44.

Sanders, Kristin E. G., Samuel Osburn, Ken A. Paller, Mark Beeman. 2019. "Targeted memory reactivation during sleep improves next-day problem solving." *Psychological Science* 30, 11: 1616–1624.

Sartori, Giovanni. 1970. "Concept misformation in comparative politics." *American Political Science Review* 64, 4: 1033–1046.

Sartori, Giovanni. 1975. "The tower of babble." In Giovanni Sartori, Fred W. Riggs, Henry Teune (eds.), *Tower of Babel: On the Definition and Analysis of Concepts in the Social Sciences* (International Studies), 6: 7–38.

Sartori, Giovanni (ed.) 1984. *Social Science Concepts: A Systematic Analysis*. Beverley Hills: Sage.

Sawyer, R. Keith. 2011. *Explaining Creativity: The Science of Human Innovation*. Oxford: Oxford University Press.

Schaffer, Frederic C. 2015. *Elucidating Social Science Concepts: An Interpretivist Guide*. London: Routledge.

Schattschneider, E. E. 1960. *The Semi-Sovereign People: A Realist's View of Democracy in America*. New York: Holt, Rinehart, and Winston.

Schedler, Andreas. 1999. "Conceptualizing accountability." In Andreas Schedler, Larry Jay Diamond, Marc F. Plattner (eds.), *The Self-Restraining State: Power and Accountability in New Democracies* (Colorado: Lynne Rienner Publishers), 13–28.

Schelling, Thomas C. 1971. "Dynamic models of segregation." *Journal of Mathematical Sociology* 1: 143–186.

Schelling, Thomas C. 1978. *Micromotives and Macrobehavior.* New York: W. W. Norton.

Scheper-Hughes, Nancy. 1992. *Death without Weeping: The Violence of Everyday Life in Brazil.* Berkeley, CA: University of California Press.

Schickore, Jutta, Friedrich Steinle (eds.) 2006. *Revisiting Discovery and Justification: Historical and Philosophical Perspectives on the Context Distinction.* Dordrecht: Springer.

Schmalensee, Richard. 1998. "Ways I have worked." In Michael Szenberg (ed.), *Passion and Craft: Economists at Work* (Ann Arbor, MI: University of Michigan Press), 243–255.

Schmitter, Philippe C. 1974. "Still the century of corporatism?" *Review of Politics* 36, 1: 85–131.

Schneider, Carsten Q., Ingo Rohlfing. 2016. "Case studies nested in fuzzy-set QCA on sufficiency: formalizing case selection and causal inference." *Sociological Methods and Research* 45, 3: 526–568.

Schultz, Kathryn. 2010. *Being Wrong: Adventures in the Margin of Error.* London: Granta Books.

Seawright, Jason. 2010. "Regression-based inference: A case study in failed causal assessment." In Henry Brady, David Collier (eds.), *Rethinking Social Inquiry: Diverse Tools, Shared Standards* (Lanham, MD: Rowman and Littlefield), 247–271.

Seawright, Jason. 2012. *Party-System Collapse: The Roots of Crisis in Peru and Venezuela.* Stanford, CA: Stanford University Press.

Seawright, Jason. 2016a. *Multi-Method Social Science: Combining Qualitative and Quantitative Tools.* Cambridge: Cambridge University Press.

Seawright, Jason. 2016b. "The case for selecting cases that are deviant or extreme on the independent variable." *Sociological Methods and Research* 45, 3: 493–525.

Seawright, Jason. 2018. "Roots in society: Attachment between citizens and party systems in Latin America." In Scott Mainwaring (ed.), *Party Systems in Latin America: Institutionalization, Decay, and Collapse* (Cambridge: Cambridge University Press), 380–407.

Seawright, Jason. 2019. "Statistical analysis of democratization: A constructive critique." *Democratization* 26, 1: 21–39.

Seawright, Jason, John Gerring. 2008. "Case-selection techniques in case study research: A menu of qualitative and quantitative options." *Political Research Quarterly* 61, 2: 294–308.

Sekhon, Jasjeet S. 2004. "Quality meets quantity: case studies, conditional probability and counterfactuals." *Perspectives in Politics* 2, 2: 281–293.

Shadish, William R., Thomas D. Cook, Donald T. Campbell. 2002. *Experimental and Quasi-experimental Designs for Generalized Causal Inference.* Boston, MA: Houghton Mifflin.

Shandra, John M., Jenna Nobles, Bruce London, and John B. Williamson. 2004. "Dependency, democracy, and infant mortality: a quantitative, cross-national analysis of less developed countries." *Social Science and Medicine* 59, 2: 321–333.

Shapiro, Ian. 2005. *The Flight from Reality in the Human Sciences.* Princeton, NJ: Princeton University Press.

Shapiro, Ian, Rogers M. Smith, Tarek E. Masoud (eds.) 2004. *Problems and Methods in the Study of Politics.* Cambridge: Cambridge University Press.

Shavinina, Larisa (ed.) 2003. *International Handbook on Innovation.* New York: Elsevier Science.

Shenk, Joshua Wolf. 2014. *Powers of Two: Finding the Essence of Innovation in Creative Pairs.* Boston, MA: Houghton Mifflin Harcourt.

Shepherd, Dean A., Roy Suddaby. 2017. "Theory building: A review and integration." *Journal of Management* 43, 1: 59–86.

Shively, W. Phillips. 2016. *The Craft of Political Research.* New York: Routledge.

Shoemaker, Pamela J., James William Tankard Jr., Dominic L. Lasorsa. 2004. *How to Build Social Science Theories*. Thousand Oaks: Sage.

Shugart, Matthew S., Rein Taagepera. 2017. *Votes from Seats: Logical Models of Electoral Systems*. Cambridge: Cambridge University Press.

Simon, Herbert A. 1996. *Models of My Life*. Cambridge, MA: MIT press.

Simonton, Dean Keith. 1995. "Creativity as heroic: Risk, success, failure, and acclaim." In Cameron M. Ford, Dennis A. Gioia (eds.), *Creative Action in Organizations: Ivory Tower Visions and Real World Voices* (London: Sage), 88–93.

Simonton, Dean Keith. 2004. *Creativity in Science: Chance, Logic, Genius, and Zeitgeist*. Cambridge: Cambridge University Press.

Simonton, Dean Keith (ed.) 2014. *The Wiley Handbook of Genius*. Chichester: Wiley Blackwell.

Singel, W. 2015. "Morton v. Mancari: Indian Status." Tribal Law Lecture, Michigan State University, East Lansing, MI (September 30).

Singer, Joel David. 1961. "The level-of-analysis problem in international relations." *World Politics* 14, 1: 77–92.

Singer, Joel David, Melvin Small. 1972. *The Wages of War, 1816-1965: A Statistical Handbook*. New York: John Wiley & Sons.

Singh, Prerna. 2015. *How Solidarity Works for Welfare Subnationalism and Social Development in India*. Cambridge: Cambridge University Press.

Single, Peg Boyle. 2009. *Demystifying Dissertation Writing: A Streamlined Process from Choice of Topic to Final Text*. Sterling: Stylus Publishing.

Sio, U. N., T. C. Ormerod. 2009. "Does incubation enhance problem solving? A meta-analytic review." *Psychological Bulletin* 135: 94–120.

Sio, U. N., P. Monaghan, T. Ormerod. 2013. "Sleep on it, but only if it is difficult: Effects of sleep on problem solving." *Memory and Cognition* 41: 159–166.

Skocpol, Theda. 1973. "A critical review of Barrington Moore's *Social Origins of Dictatorship and Democracy*." *Politics and Society* 4: 1–34.

Skocpol, Theda. 1979. *States and Social Revolutions: A Comparative Analysis of France, Russia, and China*. Cambridge: Cambridge University Press.

Skocpol, Theda. 1995. *Protecting Soldiers and Mothers*. Cambridge, MA: Harvard University Press.

Slater, Dan, Erica Simmons. 2010. "Informative regress: Critical antecedents in comparative politics." *Comparative Political Studies* 43, 7: 886–917.

Slater, Dan, Daniel Ziblatt. 2013. "The enduring indispensability of the controlled comparison." *Comparative Political Studies* 46, 10: 1301–1327.

Smith, Amy Erica. 2017. "Democratic talk in church: Religion and political socialization in the context of urban inequality." *World Development* 99: 441–451.

Smith, Ken G., Michael A. Hitt (eds.) 2005. *Great Minds in Management: The Process of Theory Development*. Oxford: Oxford University Press.

Smith, Rogers M. 2002. "Should we make political science more of a science or more about politics?" *PS: Political Science & Politics* 35, 2: 199–201.

Smith, Rogers M. 2003. "Reconnecting political theory to empirical inquiry, or a return to the cave?" In Edward D. Mansfield, Richard Sisson (eds.), *The Evolution of Political Knowledge: Theory and Inquiry in American Politics* (Columbus, OH: Ohio State University Press), 60–88.

Sniderman, Paul M., Edward G. Carmines. 1997. *Reaching Beyond Race*. Cambridge, MA: Harvard University Press.

Snijders, Tom A. B. 2011. *Multilevel Analysis*. Berlin: Springer.

Snow, John. 1855. *On the Mode of Communication of Cholera, 2nd ed.* London: Churchill.

Snyder, Richard. 2005. "Creative hypothesis generating in comparative research." Qualitative Methods: Newsletter of the American Political Science Association Organized Section on Qualitative Methods (Fall): 2–5.

Snyder, Richard. 2007. "The human dimension of comparative research." In Gerardo L. Munck, Richard Snyder (eds.), *Passion, Craft and Method in Comparative Politics* (Baltimore: Johns Hopkins University Press), 1–32.

Sombart, Werner. 1906/1976. *Why Is There No Socialism in the United States? White Plains.* New York: International Arts and Sciences.

Sorensen, Roy A. 1992. *Thought Experiments.* Oxford: Oxford University Press.

Sovey, Allison J., Donald P. Green. 2011. "Instrumental variables estimation in political science: A readers' guide." *American Journal of Political Science* 55, 1: 188–200.

Spiegler, Peter. 2015. *Behind the Model: A Constructive Critique of Economic Modeling.* Cambridge: Cambridge University Press.

Star, Susan Leigh, Elihu M. Gerson. 1987. "The management and dynamics of anomalies in scientific work." *Sociological Quarterly* 28, 2: 147–169.

Stasavage, David. 2016. "Representation and consent why they arose in Europe and not elsewhere." *Annual Review of Political Science* 19: 145–162.

Stebbins, Robert. 2001. *Exploratory Research in the Social Sciences. Qualitative Research Methods Series 48.* London: Sage Publications.

Stein, Morris I. 1974. *Stimulating Creativity: Individual Procedures.* Oxford: Academic Press.

Stekhoven, Daniel J., Peter Buhlmann. 2012. "MissForest: Non-parametric missing value imputation for mixed-type data." *Bioinformatics* 1, 1: 112–118.

Stevenson, Betsey, Justin Wolfers. 2008. *Economic Growth and Subjective Well-Being: Reassessing the Easterlin Paradox.* National Bureau of Economic Research, w14282.

Stinchcombe, Arthur L. 1968. *Constructing Social Theories.* New York: Harcourt, Brace.

Stokes, Susan C. 2001. *Mandates and Democracy: Neoliberalism by Surprise in Latin America.* Cambridge: Cambridge University Press.

Streb, Christoph. 2010. "Exploratory Case Study." In A. Mills, G. Durepos, E. Wiebe (eds.), *Encyclopedia of Case Study Research.* London: Sage. http://dx.doi.org.proxy.library.cornell.edu/10.4135/9781412957397.n139

Suhay, Elizabeth. 2015. "Explaining group influence: The role of identity and emotion in political conformity and polarization." *Political Behavior* 37: 221–251.

Swedberg, Richard. 2012. "Theorizing in sociology and social science: Turning to the context of discovery." *Theory and Society* 41, 1: 1–40.

Swedberg, Richard. 2014a. *The Art of Social Theory.* Princeton, NJ: Princeton University Press.

Swedberg, Richard (ed.) 2014b. *Theorizing in Social Science: The Context of Discovery.* Stanford, CA: Stanford University Press.

Swedberg, Richard. 2016. "Before theory comes theorizing or how to make social science more interesting." *British Journal of Sociology* 67, 1: 5–70.

Swedberg, Richard. 2019. "On the use of abstractions in sociology: the classics and beyond." *Journal of Classical Sociology* 20, 4: 257–280.

Swedberg, Richard. 2020. "Exploratory Research." In Colin Elman, John Gerring, James Mahoney (eds.), *The Production of Knowledge: Enhancing Progress in Social Science* (Cambridge: Cambridge University Press).

Szenberg, Michael (ed.) 1993. *Eminent Economists: Their Life Philosophies.* Cambridge: Cambridge University Press.

Szenberg, Michael (ed.) 1998. *Passion and Craft: Economists at Work*. Ann Arbor, MI: University of Michigan Press.

Szenberg, Michael, Lall Ramrattan (eds.) 2004. *Reflections of Eminent Economists*. Cheltenham: Edward Elgar.

Szenberg, Michael, Lall Ramrattan (eds.) 2014. *Eminent Economists II: Their Life and Work Philosophies*. Cambridge: Cambridge University Press.

Taagepera, Rein. 2008. *Making Social Sciences More Scientific: The Need for Predictive Models*. Oxford: Oxford University Press.

Tarrow, Sidney. 2010. "The strategy of paired comparison: Toward a theory of practice." *Comparative Political Studies* 43: 230–259.

Tavory, Iddo, Stefan Timmermans. 2014. *Abductive Analysis: Theorizing Qualitative Research*. Chicago: University of Chicago Press.

Taylor, Calvin W., Frank Ed Barron (eds.) 1963. *Scientific Creativity: Its Recognition and Development*. New York: John Wiley and Sons.

Teele, Dawn Langan, Kathleen Thelen. 2017. "Gender in the journals: Publication patterns in political science." *PS: Political Science & Politics* 50, 2: 433–447.

Teorell, Jan. 2010. *Determinants of Democratization: Explaining Regime Change in the World, 1972–2006*. Cambridge: Cambridge University Press.

Tetlock, Philip E., Aaron Belkin (eds.) 1996. *Counterfactual Thought Experiments in World Politics: Logical, Methodological, and Psychological Perspectives*. Princeton, NJ: Princeton University Press.

Tetlock, Philip E., Richard Ned Lebow, Geoffrey Parker. 2006. *Unmaking the West: "What-If" Scenarios that Rewrite World History*. Ann Arbor, MI: University of Michigan Press.

Thagard, Paul. 1992. *Conceptual Revolutions*. Princeton, NJ: Princeton University Press.

Thompson, Edward P. 1963. *The Making of the English Working Class*. New York: Vintage Books.

Tibshirani, Robert. 1996. "Regression shrinkage and selection via the LASSO." *Journal of the Royal Statistical Society: Series B (Methodological)* 58, 1: 267–288.

Tilly, Charles. 1964. *The Vendee*. Cambridge, MA: Harvard University Press.

Tilly, Charles. 1992. *Coercion, Capital, and European States, AD 990–1992*. Cambridge, MA: Blackwell.

Tilly, Charles, Sidney G. Tarrow. 2006. *Contentious Politics*. Oxford: Oxford University Press.

Timmermans, Stefan, Iddo Tavory. 2012. "Theory construction in qualitative research: From grounded theory to abductive analysis." *Sociological Theory* 30, 3: 167–186.

Tomz, Michael R., Jessica L. P. Weeks. 2013. "Public opinion and the democratic peace." *American Political Science Review* 107, 4: 849–865.

Tsai, Lily. 2007. *Accountability without Democracy: How Solidary Groups Provide Public Goods in Rural China*. Cambridge: Cambridge University Press.

Tufte, Edward R. 2001. *The Visual Display of Quantitative Information*. Cheshire, CT: Connecticut Graphics Press.

Tufte, Edward R. 2006. *Beautiful Evidence*. Cheshire, CT: Graphics Press.

Tufte, Edward R., Peter R. Graves-Morris. 1983. *The Visual Display of Quantitative Information*. Cheshire, CT: Graphics Press.

Tufte, Edward R., Nora Hillman Goeler, Richard Benson. 1990. *Envisioning Information*. Cheshire, CT: Graphics Press.

Tukey, John Wilder. 1977. *Exploratory Data Analysis*. Reading, MA: Addison-Wesley.

Udehn, L. 2001. *Methodological Individualism*. London: Routledge.

Useem, Bert. 1997. "Choosing a dissertation topic." *PS: Political Science & Politics* 30, 213–216.

Valenzuela, Ali A., Tyler T. Reny. 2021. "The evolution of experiments on racial priming." In James N. Druckman, Donald P. Green (eds.), *Advances in Experimental Political Science* (Cambridge: Cambridge University Press), 447–467.

Van Dijk, Jan, Andromachi Tseloni, Graham Farrell (eds.) 2012. *The International Crime Drop: New Directions in Research*. Berlin: Springer.

Van Evera, Stephen. 1997. *Guide to Methods for Students of Political Science*. Ithaca, NY: Cornell University Press.

Varian, Hal R. 2016. "How to build an economic model in your spare time." *The American Economist* 61, 1: 81–90.

Vaughan, Diane. 1996. *The Challenger Launch Decision: Risky Technology, Culture, and Deviance at NASA*. Chicago: University of Chicago Press.

Veenendaal, Wouter. 2015. *Politics and Democracy in Microstates*. London: Routledge.

Verba, Sidney, Kay Lehman Schlozman, Henry E. Brady. 1995. *Voice and Equality: Civic Voluntarism in American Politics*. Cambridge, MA: Harvard University Press.

Vinten-Johansen, Peter, Howard Brody, Nigel Paneth, Stephen Rachman, David Zuck, Michael Rip. 2003. *Cholera, Chloroform, and the Science of Medicine: A Life of John Snow*. Oxford: Oxford University Press.

Von Hippel, Eric. 2005. *Democratizing Innovation*. Cambridge, MA: MIT press.

Vosniadou, Stella, Andrew Ortony (eds.) 1989. *Similarity and Analogical Reasoning*. Cambridge: Cambridge University Press.

Walford, Gregory. 2001. "Site selection within comparative case study and ethnographic research." *Compare: A Journal of Comparative and International Education* 31, 2: 151–164.

Wallas, Graham. 1926. *The Art of Thought*. London: Jonathan Cape.

Walters, Ronald G. 1980. "Signs of the times: Clifford Geertz and historians." *Social Research* 47, 3: 537.

Waltz, Kenneth N. 1979. *Theory of International Politics*. Reading, MA: Addison-Wesley.

Ward, Matthew O., Georges Grinstein, Daniel Keim. 2015. *Interactive Data Visualization: Foundations, Techniques, and Applications*. Boca Raton: CRC Press.

Ward, Michael D., Kristian Skrede Gleditsch. 2018. *Spatial Regression Models*. Thousand Oaks: Sage Publications.

Ward, Thomas B., Steven M. Smith, Jyotsna Vaid (eds.) 1997. *Creative Thought: An Investigation of Conceptual Structures and Processes*. Washington, DC: American Psychological Association.

Watson, James D. 1969. *The Double Helix: A Personal Account of the Discovery of the Structure of DNA*. New York: Athenium.

Weart, Spencer R. 1998. *Never at War: Why Democracies Will Not Fight One Another*. New Haven, CT: Yale University Press.

Weber, Marianne. 1975. *Max Weber: A Biography*. New York: Wiley.

Weber, Max. 1946. *From Max Weber: Essays in Sociology*. New York: Oxford University Press.

Weber, Max. 1949. *Methodology of Social Sciences*. New York: Free Press.

Wedeen, Lisa. 1999. *Ambiguities of Domination: Politics, Rhetoric, and Symbols in Contemporary Syria*. Chicago: University of Chicago Press.

Weisberg, Robert W. 1993. *Creativity: Beyond the Myth of Genius*. New York: W. H. Freeman.

Weisberg, Robert W. 2006. *Creativity: Understanding Innovation in Problem Solving, Science, Invention, and the Arts*. New York: John Wiley & Sons.

Weisberg, Robert W., Lauretta M. Reeves. 2013. *Cognition: From Memory to Creativity*. New York: John Wiley & Sons.

Weiss, B. 2000. "Generalizing brains in a vat." *Analysis* 60: 112–123.

White, Patrick. 2009. *Developing Research Questions.* Basingstoke: Palgrave Macmillan.

White, Patrick. 2013. "Who's afraid of research questions? The neglect of research questions in the methods literature and a call for question-led methods teaching." *International Journal of Research and Method in Education* 36, 3: 213–227.

Wicker, Allan W. 1985. "Getting out of our conceptual ruts: Strategies for expanding conceptual frameworks." *American Psychologist* 40, 10: 1094.

Wildavsky, Aaron. 1964. *Politics of the Budgetary Process.* Boston, MA: Little, Brown.

Wildavsky, Aaron. 1969. "The two presidencies." *Trans-Action* 4: 230–243.

Wildavsky, Aaron. 1984. *The Nursing Father: Moses as a Political Leader.* Tuscaloosa, AL: University of Alabama Press.

Wildavsky, Aaron. 1987. "Choosing preferences by constructing institutions: A cultural theory of preference formation." *American Political Science Review* 81, 1: 3–21.

Wildavsky, Aaron. 1993. *Craftways: On the Organization of Scholarly Work, 2nd ed.* New Brunswick: Transaction.

Wilson, Edward O. 1999. *Consilience: The Unity of Knowledge.* New York: Vintage.

Wilson, Steven. 2022. *Social Media as Social Science Data.* Cambridge: Cambridge University Press.

Wood, Elisabeth Jean. 2000. *Forging Democracy from Below: Insurgent Transitions in South Africa and El Salvador.* Cambridge: Cambridge University Press.

Woodward, James. 2005. *Making Things Happen: A Theory of Causal Explanation.* Oxford: Oxford University Press.

Woolcock, Michael. 1998. "Social capital and economic development: Toward a theoretical synthesis and policy framework." *Theory and Society* 27, 2: 151–208.

Wooldridge, Jeffrey M. 2016. *Introductory Econometrics: A Modern Approach.* Toronto: Nelson Education.

Wright, Erik Olin. 1997. *Class Counts: Comparative Studies in Class Analysis.* Cambridge: Cambridge University Press.

Wu, Junjie. 2012. *Advances in K-Means Clustering: A Data Mining Thinking.* Berlin: Springer-Verlag.

Wuchty, Stefan, Benjamin F. Jones, Brian Uzzi. 2007. "The increasing dominance of teams in production of knowledge." *Science* 316, 5827: 1036–1039.

Yammarino, Francis J., Shelley D. Dionne, Jae Uk Chun, Fred Dansereau. 2005. "Leadership and levels of analysis: A state-of-the-science review." *The Leadership Quarterly* 16, 6: 879–919.

Yatchew, Adonis. 2003. *Semiparametric Regression for the Applied Econometrician.* Cambridge: Cambridge University Press.

Zahar, Elie. 1983. "Logic of discovery or psychology of invention?" *British Journal for the Philosophy of Science* 34, 3: 243–261.

Zetterberg, Hans L. 1954. *On Theory and Verification in Sociology.* Totowa, NJ: The Bedminster Press.

Ziblatt, Daniel. 2004. "Rethinking the origins of federalism: Puzzle, theory, and evidence from nineteenth-century Europe." *World Politics* 57: 70–98.

Ziblatt, Daniel. 2008. *Structuring the State: The Formation of Italy and Germany and the Puzzle of Federalism.* Cambridge: Cambridge University Press.

Zhao, Shanyang. 1996. "The beginning of the end or the end of the beginning? The theory construction movement revisited." *Sociological Forum* 11, 2: 305–318.

Zuckerman, Harriet. 1967. "Nobel laureates in science: Patterns of productivity, collaboration, and authorship." *American Sociological Review* 32, 3: 391–403.

Zweifel, Thomas D., Patricio Navia. 2000. "Democracy, dictatorship, and infant mortality." *Journal of Democracy* 11, 2: 99–114.

Index

Made in the USA
Las Vegas, NV
02 April 2025

20442887R00195